IN THE
TROUGH
OF THE SEA

IN THE
TROUGH
OF THE SEA

Selected American
Sea-Deliverance Narratives, 1610-1766

edited by
Donald P. Wharton

Contributions in American Studies, Number 44

Greenwood Press
Westport, Connecticut . London, England

Library of Congress Cataloging in Publication Data
Main entry under title:

In the trough of the sea.

(Contributions in American studies ; no. 44
ISSN 0084-9227)
  Bibliography: p.
  Includes index.
  1. Sea stories. 2. Shipwrecks. I. Wharton,
Donald P.
G525.I59   910'.453   78-22721
ISBN 0-313-20870-0

Library of Congress Catalog Card Number: 78-22721
ISBN: 0-313-20870-0
ISSN: 0084-9227

First published in 1979

Greenwood Press, Inc.
51 Riverside Avenue, Westport, Connecticut 06880

Printed in the United States of America

10 9 8 7 6 5 4 3 2 1

for

Donald C. Wharton, 1916-1967,
Incertas spes mea virtute sua aluit,
and
Strother B. Jackson, 1889-1970,
mariner

". . . when we lay a Shipp under the Sea, (that is, when we lay her broadside to the Sea) wee saie shee lies in the Trowgh of the Sea."
—Henry Manwayring, *Nomenclator Navalis,* 1625

"We say a ship doth *Labour* much when she doth rowle much any way; but if she will neither Try nor Hull, then *Spoone,* that is, put her right before the wind. This way, although shee will rowle more than the other, yet if she be weake, it will not straine her any thing so much in the *Trough* of the Sea, which is the distance betwixt two waves or Billowes. If none of this will doe well, then she is in danger to *founder,* if not sink." Captain John Smith, *A Sea Grammar,* 1627

"As the setting of the sea is always produced by the wind, it is evident that the waves, and consequently the trough or hollow space between them, will be at right angles with the direction of the wind. Hence a ships rolls heaviest when she lies in the trough of the sea."
William Falconer, *A Universal Dictionary of the Marine,* 1769

"Many great seas were shipp'd as she came to work thro' the trough of the sea. . . ." Henry Norwood, *A Voyage to Virginia,* 1649

". . . there appeared a Vessel in sight, but at so great a Distance that we could not see her when we lay in the Trough of the Sea."
William Walling, *The Wonderful Providence of God,* 1726

CONTENTS

ILLUSTRATIONS

PREFACE

In the Trough of the Sea makes available for the first time a selection of sea-deliverance narratives drawn entirely from the colonial period of American history. That the adventures of the often obscure men in these stories should be brought together here is appropriate for at least three reasons.

First, the narratives are in themselves rattling good tales, filled with instances of extraordinary heroism and endurance, of great courage and incredible hardship. These are powerful accounts of terrible storms in which ships founder or capsize or sailors are washed overboard; of men adrift in a small boat, delirious and suffering from exposure and thirst; of ships' companies cast ashore in unfamiliar lands among savage or hostile inhabitants; of abduction and piracy on the high seas; and even, in rare instances, of starving crews reduced to cannibalism to survive. Written by the participants themselves, these are exciting tales of adventure whose appeal is timeless.

Second, these narratives have considerable historical and antiquarian value. They are windows (one is tempted to say portholes) into the past, each providing valuable insight into the texture of the time in which it was written. For instance, the narratives of the Virginians, William Strachey and Henry Norwood, tell us much about the conditions of early settlement in that colony, and Anthony Thacher's relation of his shipwreck offers us important clues to life in early Massachusetts. Representation from other colonies is provided by Nathaniel Peirce of New Hampshire, Richard Steere of Connecticut, David Harrison of New York, William Walling of New Jersey, Joseph Bailey of Antigua, and one anonymous writer caught in a gale off the Atlantic coast of Florida who may have been the resident of any of several colonies. Philip Ashton (with the help of John Barnard) gives us a gripping account of the exploits of an infamous buccaneer of colonial waters, Captain Ned Low. Briton Hammon, a black man, adds to the already uncommon sufferings of his thirteen years away from home the special tragedy of a man enslaved.

Third, these sea-deliverance narratives together constitute an important subgenre in American literature. Some writers, like Richard Steere, Benjamin Bartholomew, and the anonymous author of *A Description of a Great Sea-Storm,* chose to adapt their narratives to verse, thus making, at least in Steere's case, a valuable contribution to early American poetry. Of course, most writers of the sea-deliverance, not literary men to begin with, but rather sea captains and sailors, chose to report their experiences in prose. We should not, however, dismiss the literary dimensions of these nonfiction narratives, for their authors, like the writers of fiction, confronted a task requiring nearly all the several skills of narration, including emphasis and selection, pace, tone, plot, verisimilitude, and relevancy of detail. The narratives that resulted from these efforts became, like the more familiar Indian-captivity narratives, important phenomena of popular culture in early America. For the Puritan audience, the sea-deliverance also had explicit theological value and was prized for the doctrinal lesson it might impart; countless seventeenth- and eighteenth-century sermons pointed to a shipwreck or rescue at sea as yet another instance of God's wonder-working providence in the New World. Both John Dean's and Philip Ashton's narratives first appeared with accompanying sermons, and Anthony Thacher's relation was first printed in Increase Mather's *Essay for the Recording of Illustrious Providences,* an explicitly didactic work. But there is also a tradition of realism in these narratives, and in the richness of detail and heightened expression there is an aesthetic sensibility that later figures prominently in the sea fiction of Cooper, Melville, London, and Crane.

In selecting the narratives for this edition I have sought first to include those that possessed both literary value and intrinsic interest. I also chose with an eye to achieving a chronological (and to a lesser extent, geographical) balance among the narratives. Given these principles, some things were inevitably omitted. For instance, *A Monumental Gratitude Attempted, In a Poetical Relation* (1727), the lugubrious efforts of John Hubbard and several other Yale undergraduates caught in a squall on Long Island Sound, failed of the first principle, while Thomas Purnell's *True and Faithful Account of the Loss of the Brigantine Tyrrell* (1766) was excluded because of my preference for David Harrison's narrative of the same date. Jonathan Dickinson's *God's Protecting Providence* (1699), although in other respects more than satisfactory, was simply too long and not conducive to shortening. (It has received skillful editing in book form by Charles M. Andrews [New Haven: Yale University Press, 1945].)

In adopting texts for these narratives I have in every instance gone to the first edition of the work to appear or to the earliest edition extant. In John Dean's case this means the first authoritative edition, for a second-hand account was printed in Boston with Cotton Mather's *Compassions Called for* a few months before Dean's Tookey and Popping edition was released in London in 1711. Another London edition—but without Jasper Dean's preface—was also printed earlier for distribution in Northern Ireland. Two other narratives—Anthony Thacher's and Benjamin Bartholomew's—have been edited from manuscript. Bartholomew's is here printed for the first time.

Later editions of the sea-deliverances have sometimes been shortened or changed. Harrison's narrative of the famine aboard the *Peggy*, for example, appeared early in the nineteenth century in a version that eliminated 50 percent of the original. This truncated version served as the basis for several reprintings in the nineteenth century and for one as late as 1974. The full text of Harrison's narrative is now printed for the first time since 1766. John Dean's *Voyage of the Nottingham Galley*, perhaps the most famous of colonial narratives, has been reprinted frequently since 1711, including twice in the last decade, but always from the editions of 1727 or 1762. The later editions omit the important preface and postscript that Dean's brother added to the 1711 edition. It is to this edition that Dean's first mate, Christopher Langman, replies in his own version of the events before and after the *Nottingham Galley* ran aground on Boon Island. At the very least, Langman's account casts serious doubt on Dean's veracity. A special feature of the present edition is the inclusion of both versions, Langman's narrative not having appeared in print since its first publication in 1711.

The narratives of Joseph Bailey, Briton Hammon, Nathaniel Peirce, William Walling, and the anonymous *Description* are reprinted here for the first time since their original appearances in the seventeenth or eighteenth centuries. The manuscript version of Anthony Thacher's narrative has been edited recently by Everett Emerson in *Letters from New England* (Amherst: University of Massachusetts Press, 1976), but in a modernized text. The same is true of William Strachey's *True Reportory*, edited by Louis B. Wright, in *A Voyage to Virginia in 1609* (Charlottesville: University Press at Virginia, 1964). Richard Steere's poem and Philip Ashton's narrative have been well edited recently, the latter in a separate edition by Russel W. Knight (Salem, Mass.: Peabody Museum, 1976), the former in Harrison T. Meserole's *Seventeenth-Century American Poetry* (New York: New York University Press, 1968). None has appeared before in a collection of the present sort. In such company hopefully all may benefit.

In editing the sea-deliverances I have sought to preserve as much of the character of the original as possible, retaining original spelling, capitalization, punctuation, and usage. Only in a few instances has it been necessary to provide marks of punctuation or glosses where confusion might otherwise result. The distinction between roman and italic type has also been retained. However, the use of u and v, i and j, has been regularized, and u substituted for w when used as a vowel. Manuscript superscript "ye" has been expanded to "the," but the shorthand "Mr" has simply been regularized to "Mr." Printers' errors that require additional letters or words, or omissions of words from the text, have been corrected by supplying the missing material in brackets, but letters simply mispositioned, wrongly substituted, or broken have been silently emended. Paragraphing has been instituted in Anthony Thacher's narrative, and in Benjamin Bartholomew's poem the double-letter convention of Bartholomew's scribe, Mordecay Hunton, has been eliminated in favor of standard practice. On the other hand, double letters have been retained where, as in Thacher's case, they appear to be the work of the author and not the copyist.

All narratives included in this edition save one are printed in complete versions. From William Strachey's *True Reportory* I have selected those portions that constitute the sea-deliverance. For the most part the prefaces, sermons, and affidavits often attached to the narratives have been omitted. Only when such papers provide information not contained in the narrative proper, as, for example, in the Boon Island narratives, have they been retained.

Preparation of this edition has benefited from the kindness of many persons. To Samuel Hough and his gracious staff at the John Carter Brown Library of Brown University, where a portion of the research for this project was done, I am especially grateful. I am similarly indebted to the respective staffs of the Rare Books Department of the Library of Congress, the Folger Shakespeare Library, and the Library Company of Philadelphia for their generous and often timely assistance. The British Library, the Houghton Library of Harvard University, and the Massachusetts Historical Society kindly provided manuscripts and maps.

My friends and colleagues have at all times been extraordinarily generous and encouraging. Professors Harrison Meserole of Pennsylvania State University, Thomas Philbrick of the University of Pittsburgh, and Roger Stein of the State University of New York at Binghamton all graciously consented to read earlier versions of the manuscript. From their illuminating scholarship and criticism I have gained much, and whatever advance over previous versions has been made, I owe to them.

My students Donna Litzinger, Mary Jane Fogel, Shane Hogan, Pamela Lambert, Greg Myers, Rosemary Montecalvo, and especially John Mesner and Chuck Yackern were most helpful in many ways, and their enthusiasm and good humor were unflagging.

Much of the material support for the edition was provided by a grant from the Liberal Arts College Fund for Research of the Pennsylvania State University.

A NOTE ON COLONIAL VESSELS AND TERMS

The reader with no background in seamanship may well sympathize with the frustration of the anonymous author of *A Description of a Great Sea-Storm*, who complained that

> The Saylers speak such *Babel* words as these:
> *Hale in maine Bowlin, Mizen tack aboard;*
> A Language, like a Storm, to be abhorr'd.

It is hardly a new problem. The landsman has always been confused by the sailor's easy reference to the language of ships and the sea. In *A Monumental Memorial of Marine Mercy* we find Richard Steere apologizing to his audience for the necessity of such language in his narrative, explaining that "I could not Conveniently avoyd the use of some *Sea phrases* The Subject being a *Sea Deliverance*, tho they may seem improper and unintelligible to a *Land Capacity*."

The often bewildering array of nautical terms and phrases in this edition posed an immediate editorial problem. To gloss the edition in the usual way would have required a large and often repetitious set of explanatory notes for each narrative. To avoid this awkwardness, it was thought best to construct a separate glossary for what Steere called the "*Tarpolin* Tongue." Thus only nonmarine glosses will be found in the apparatus of individual narratives (where, because the sea-deliverances are likely to be read individually rather than continuously, I have not hesitated to repeat glosses to geographical or historical allusions that appear in more than one narrative). It should be noted that the glossary includes only those terms found in narratives, so it is in no sense a complete marine dictionary. Entries are spelled as they occur in the narratives (sometimes variously), and are defined according to the context in which they appear. Explanations have been drawn largely from Henry Manwayring's *Nomenclator Navalis* as finally printed in his *Seaman's Dictionary* (1644) and from William Falconer's *Universal Dictionary of the Marine* (1769).

Identification of colonial vessels by type is often made difficult by the practice, common in the period, of applying the same label to ships of varying rigs and sizes. Because in the seventeenth and eighteenth centuries a standard terminology was still evolving, the reader cannot always be sure that a given vessel identified by the colonial narrative as of such-and-such type is really quite what our modern system of classification calls for. For example, today the distinction between what is understood to be a *brig* (a two-masted vessel, square-rigged on both masts) and a *brigantine* (also a two-masted vessel, square-rigged on the foresail, fore-and-aft rigged on the main-mast but carrying a square main topsail) is well defined. In the colonial period, however, *brig* was simply a shortened form of *brigantine,* and the two were often used interchangeably. For instance, evidence from Joseph Bailey's narrative makes clear that his *Catharine and Alida* is a brigantine in the modern sense. On the other hand, Nathaniel Peirce's "brigantine," the *Portsmouth,* appears to be square-rigged on both masts.

Further confusion results when in Anthony Thacher's narrative he calls the vessel in which the company sailed from Ipswich both a "pinnace" and a "barque." (See William A. Baker, *Colonial Vessels: Some Seventeenth-Century Sailing Craft* [Barre, Mass.: Barre, 1962] for a discussion of the general problem.) All we really know about Thacher's vessel is that it was small and had two masts, no indication as to rig.

John Dean's *Nottingham Galley* is either a two- or three-masted vessel, presumably square-rigged, *galley* in this instance being used to distinguish the structure of the upper deck, running continuously throughout the vessel, uninterrupted by either forecastle or quarterdeck. The *ships* of William Strachey, Henry Norwood, and Benjamin Bartholomew all seem to fit the standard definition of that type—a three-masted, square-rigged vessel. So, too, does Richard Steere's *Adventure,* except that he calls it a *pink,* a term used to designate a vessel that possessed, in addition to a ship's rig, an unusually narrow stern.

David Harrison's *Peggy* was a sloop, as was the vessel on which Briton Hammon sailed from Plymouth. Philip Ashton's narrative embraces the greatest variety of vessels. Originally seized by Low's pirates while aboard a fishing shallop off Nova Scotia, Ashton was subsequently taken on board a brigantine, a schooner, a French banker, a pink, and a sloop.

Finally, William Walling's leaky craft appears to have been a small, single-masted sailboat with sprit mainsail and jib.

IN THE
TROUGH
OF THE SEA

INTRODUCTION

I

At sea in November 1639, on a voyage from New England to London, the Essexman and sometime resident of Maine, John Josselyn, observed that "about three of the clock in the afternoon, the Mariners observed the rising of a little black cloud in the *N. W.* which increasing apace, made them prepare against a coming storm; the wind in short time grew to boisterous, bringing after us a huge grown Sea; at 5 of the clock it was pitchie dark." Josselyn was so struck by the violent onset of the storm that he later recorded his impressions in lines of finely crafted verse:

> And the bitter storm augments; the wild winds wage
> War from all parts; and joyn with the Seas rage.
> The sad clouds sink in showers; you would have thought,
> That high-swoln-seas even unto Heaven had wrought;
> And Heaven to Seas descended: no star shown;
> Blind night in darkness, tempests, and her own
> Dread terrours lost; yet this dire lightning turns
> To more fear'd light; the Sea with lightning Burns.
> The Pilot knew not what to chuse or fly,
>   Art stood amaz'd in Ambiguity.

The storm lasted another forty-eight hours, the winds ending only during the night of the third day. Thereafter it remained calm for a week, in the course of which time Josselyn noted, "all the while we saw many dead bodies of men and women floating by us."[1]

The recording of incidents that, like this one, testified to the destructive and terrifying power of the ocean were common in colonial America, a consequence of her having been from the beginning a seafaring country. It is well to remember that the Atlantic was the first American frontier, and that during the first two centuries of the American consciousness, the ocean occupied a place at least as important as that of the western, terrestrial frontier.[2]

Economically the colonies were predetermined to sea trade, whether in coastal waters or on the ocean. The resources of the sea were vast and largely unexploited. As an avenue of commerce the sea seemed to promise riches, offering an arena in which an individual's fortitude and initiative might be pitted against great risks and dangers in the quest of great rewards. The pursuit of such trade influenced the character of those who lived along the Atlantic seaboard, a populous that was often turbulent and inventive, individualistic and adventuresome—a people sometimes heroic, sometimes, too, impatient and grasping.

Yet, even as the sea represented enormous economic opportunity for the colonists, that opportunity was controlled and to a degree fostered by Crown and Parliament, drawing the colonies closer to the empire. Politically and socially, the colonies' connecting link to Europe was the sea, the umbilical that nourished ancient traditions and institutions in a new world. Yet the link was a fragile one, and perhaps more than it connected men to their European homeland, it threw them upon their own resources, isolating them from the security and guidance of former practice. By its mere vastness alone—a voyage of six weeks was uncommonly swift—the ocean forced modification of European precedent and rule. Altogether, the sea in American colonial life was a force that profoundly affected the European heritage of the colonies, even as it offered them an amazingly rich source of experience and metaphor through which well-established ideas and aspirations might be expressed in dramatically new ways. The colonial sea-deliverance narrative is one example of the new possibility for expression that Americans discovered in their experience on the ocean. Indeed, before the American Revolution the number of separately printed sea-deliverances rivals that of Indian-captivity narratives. Nor is it any accident that in Increase Mather's 1684 *Essay for the Recording of Illustrious Providences*—a book that gathered together all sorts of curious and often sensational phenomena—the sea-deliverances occupy the important first chapter.

Ocean travel was a dangerous venture in the colonial period, and a man at sea faced far more constant peril than he was apt to find in the wilderness beyond the line of settlements. So great was the potential for death at sea that often a storm was, as William Strachey expressed it in 1610, a harrowing experience, utterly terrifying in its promise of destruction. "For surely," Strachey observed, "as death comes not so sodaine nor apparant, so he comes not so elvish and painfull (to men especially even then in health and prefect habitudes of body) as at Sea. . . . For indeede death is accompanied at no time, nor place with circumstances every way so uncapable of particularities of goodnesse and inward comforts, as at Sea."

Captain David Harrison, writing of the storms that crippled his sloop *Peggy* in 1765, recalled that "the weather was intolerably bad, the seas excessively heavy, and the continued peals of thunder joined to our incapacity of carrying any sail, unless for a few hours, threw a horror over our situation, which is not to be conceived by any but those who have unhappily experienced something like our circumstances."

Even such hardened characters as the pirates of Captain Ned Low's crew could be found to quail before the elemental force of the sea. In 1725 Philip Ashton remembered that

> such mighty Hectors as they were, in a clear Sky and a fair
> Gale, yet a fierce Wind and a boisterous Sea sunk their Spirits
> to a Cowardly dejection . . . and tho' they were so habituated
> to Cursing and Swearing, that the Dismal Prospect of Death,
> & this of so long Continuance, could not Correct the Language
> of the most of them, yet you might plainly see the inward
> Horror and Anguish of their Minds, visible in their Counte-
> nances, and like Men amazed, or starting out of Sleep in a
> fright, I could hear them every now and then, cry out, Oh!
> *I wish I were at Home.*

Of course, storms were not the only dangers the sea traveler was likely to face. The seventeenth and eighteenth centuries comprised the great age of pirates, and as Philip Ashton learned to his sorrow, even home waters were scarcely safe from buccaneers. Then, too, the several wars involving England, France, and Spain in the years 1690-1763 made the presence of rival navies and privateers in colonial waters a constant danger. Such circumstances explain the special care ships in this time took to avoid each other. A strange sail on the horizon was likely to mean trouble, not succor, and the usual reaction in such cases was to pile on sail and get away as quickly as possible. Confrontations between fighting ships, when they did occur, were invariably bloody. Briton Hammon reports with seeming detachment on such a battle in 1759 when aboard the English man 'o war *Hercules.* "We sail'd on a Cruize," Hammon reports, "and met with a French 84 Gun Ship, and had a very smart Engagment, in which about 70 of our Hands were Kill'd and Wounded, the Captain lost his Leg in the Engagement, and I was Wounded in the Head by a small Shot."

A ship that escaped sinking by the elements or destruction at the hands of an enemy or pirate was liable to still other dangers. Vessels that weathered storms might well be disabled and, thus slowed, run out of provisions. Faced with starvation, sailors and passengers were likely to resort to any means necessary to stay alive. Harrison reports that in such circumstances the ship's cat was divided and "The head fell to my share, and, in all my days, I never feasted on any thing which appeared so delicious to my appetite,—the piercing sharpness of necessity had entirely conquered my aversion to such food."

Henry Norwood, in describing the reduced state of the *Virginia Merchant* in 1649, observed that "The infinite number of rats that all the voyage had been our plague, we now were glad to make our prey to feed on; and as they were insnared and taken, a well grown rat was sold for sixteen shillings as a market rate. Nay, before the voyage did end (as I was credibly inform'd) a woman great with child offered twenty shillings for a rat, which the proprietor refusing, the woman died."

In each of these instances famine ultimately drove the survivors to cannibalism, as it did the men of the *Nottingham Galley* in 1710. Their commander, John Dean, described the plight of his crew stranded on a desolate rock off the coast of Maine this way: "This, of all I had met with, was the most greivous and shocking to me, to see my self and Company, who came thither laded with Provisions but three Weeks before, now reduc'd to such a deplorable Circumstance, as to have two of us absolutely starv'd to Death, other two we knew not what was become of, and the Rest of us at the last Extreamity and (tho' still living, yet) requiring to eat the Dead for Support."

Ships that were driven ashore might, like the *Nottingham Galley,* face the prospect of starvation. They might also have to confront the native inhabitants. The experience of colonial vessels meeting with Indians varied considerably. To Henry Norwood the Indians were "angels of light" who fed, sheltered, and ultimately escorted the marooned passengers of the *Virginia Merchant* to Jamestown. William Strachey, on the other hand, accused the Indians of murdering the crew of the long boat sent from Bermuda and at Jamestown observed that "the *Indian* killed as fast without, if our men stirred but beyond the bounds of their Block-house, as Famine and Pestilence did within." To Briton Hammon, the Indians were "barbarous and inhuman Savages" who slaughtered his shipmates and threatened to roast him alive.

The men who lived to write of their deliverance from the manifold perils of the sea were prompted by a variety of motives. Some, like the Virginians Strachey and Norwood, wrote at least partly with an eye to promoting the New World to an England eager for information. Others, like Dean, Christopher Langman, and Harrison, felt the need to justify their conduct and judgment, and in these narratives there is more than a little self-interest at work. For some, the desire to see their experience recorded drove them to special exertions. When finally too weak to continue his daily journal, David Harrison scrawled on his cabin wall with chalk, and Joseph Bailey, determined that his story should not go untold, began, while still on shipboard, to carve vital information on a barrel stave with his pocket knife. Several writers were ravaged by their experience and, haunted by the personal anguish they had suffered, were driven to recreate the circumstances of their suffering. For example, feelings of personal recrimination play a major role in the narratives of Anthony Thacher (1635) and William Walling (1726). For Thacher, who was helpless to prevent the loss of his children, the remorse was excruciating: "Then it Came into my minde how I had accationed the death of my Children, who had accasioned them out of their native land, who might have Left them there, yea and might have sent some of them backe againe and cost me nothing, These and many such thoughts do presse downe my heavy heart very much."

Walling, whose desire to return home quickly contrived to send him out in a leaky boat with a stranger, later agonized over the effects of his impatience: "I tho't my self the Author, not only of my own, but another Man's Misfortune also because I hindred *Gardner* from going back when it was in his Power. I repented very much that I did not let him take his own Course, as being more us'd to the Water than I, and consequently

saw the Danger we were in sooner. In short it is impossible to describe
the Horrour & anguish of my Mind."

   This variety of motives was also to be found among those who read
the sea-deliverance. Some readers were attracted to those same compul-
sions that moved the authors. Others were drawn to the sensational aspects
of many of the narratives. A morbid interest in disaster and catastrophe
was hardly less keen in colonial times than in our own. But more important
than any of these motives—what is really essential for a proper understanding of all the narratives—is the concept of Providence that united
both author and audience in a common perception of the sea-deliverance
experience.

II

   For the writers of the sea-deliverance and for the men and women who
read them, the concept of Providence defined God's relationship to the
world. It meant not only that God was active in the world, but that the
world is constantly preserved by Him, is quite literally upheld in being
by the Divine Will. Because, in this view, the dependence of humanity
and nature is absolute, no occurrence is accidental in the sense that a
modern reader might understand the term. Rather, all things, including
events, have their origin in God, who either intervenes directly in the
world or operates through natural or "second" causes. Thus the observation in St. Matthew that there is Providence in the fall of a sparrow would
have been understood literally in the period in which these narratives
were written. To be sure, the rise of Deism in the eighteenth century
vitiated the dynamism of the concept of Providence (the Deists tended
to limit the world's dependence on God to His original act of creation).
Nevertheless, it is a characteristic of all these narratives to perceive both
deliverance and catastrophe as manifestations of the Divine Will. Belief
in Providence was widespread, not exclusively a Puritan conviction. In the
narratives of Strachey and Norwood, for example, both of whom express
considerable dislike of Puritanism, the concept of Providence is accepted
without question. Yet it is equally true of the Puritans—authors and audience together—that the doctrine of Providence reinforced their sense of
themselves as a people especially called to a historic mission.

Because those things that were thought to be acts of Providence invited, indeed demanded, interpretation, the literature of early America is replete with efforts to understand God's intention in all sorts of phenomena. Uncommon occurrences in particular brought renewed efforts to discern God's message for His people, and so we find that earthquakes, crop failures, Indian raids, storms, epidemics, and political upheavals consistently occupy the interpretative faculties of colonial Americans.

For the seventeenth- and early eighteenth-century audience, particularly the Puritan audience of colonial America, the doctrine of Providence allowed a way of ordering experience, of making sense out of it. This shared frame of reference united both author and audience in a common understanding of the narrative's ultimate purpose: the outward reality of the sea-deliverance experience is, in the telling, made to conform to the spiritual reality of the Christian life. The terrifying and disorienting experience of a storm, a shipwreck, or capture by pirates is brought under control by a creative act of the literary imagination. By telling the story the author (and by extension, the audience who hears or reads it) not only masters the material artistically, he also comprehends the experience spiritually. Thus that which is to purely human eyes terrifying and mysterious is by the doctrine of Providence made comforting and comprehensible. The terrors of the ocean are, by an act of faith and imagination, transformed to the Lord's Wonders in the Great Deep.[3]

The writers of the narratives before us regularly identify the hand of God in specific occurrences. Norwood, for instance, credits his ship's escape from a waterspout to an act of Providence. When Philip Ashton is threatened with murder by one of his pirate captors, Providence intervenes to save his life. As Ashton tells it, the pirate quartermaster "clapt his Pistol to my Head, and snap'd it; but it miss'd Fire; this enraged him the more; and he repeated the snapping of his Pistol at my Head three times, and it as often miss'd Fire; upon which he held it over-board, and snap'd it the fourth time, and then it went off very readily. (Thus did GOD mercifully quench the violence of the Fire, that was meant to destroy me!)" Nathaniel Peirce, writing in 1752, also identifies the hand of Providence in his narrow escape from a raging sea. Describing the incident in the third person, Peirce explains how "one large Sea in particular, wash'd the Master from the main chains of the Wreck to Leeward, but by a kind Providence, he happen'd to fall on the Main-mast, where the

Sea left him; by the help of which and the Barricado, he got again on the Windward Side, and was securing himself to the main Chains when the Squall abated, and the Vessel righted on her Bottom as before."

All this dependence on Providence to which the writers of sea-deliverances exhorted their audiences did not, it is important to note, relieve the participants of the responsibility for human effort, nor did it reduce them to passivity or despair. On the contrary, those who endured the experience were often energized by their recognition of providential design. Inimitable expression of this typical attitude is provided by John Dean, who, when his ship ran aground on Boon Island, "call'd down all Hands to the Cabin, where we continu'd a few Minutes earnestly supplicating Mercy; but knowing Prayers without Endeavours are vain, I order'd all up again, to cut the Masts by the board." The master of the *Nottingham Galley* was not alone in recognizing that piety was not a substitute for seamanship. In 1660 the captain of the ship *Exchange,* when his crew (including the poet Benjamin Bartholomew) implored him to lead them in prayer as the vessel appeared certain of sinking, replied:

> to pray I would agree
> Yet for our lives Let all means used be:
> Therfore I think tis beast to hoyse foreyarde.

William Walling, although terrified by the prospect of being blown out to sea in a leaky boat, nevertheless resisted the temptation to despair, and "thinking my self oblig'd to make the best of all Means for our Preservation, I went to Pumping, and encouraged my companion to mind the helm." Nathaniel Peirce, whose narrative is testimony to his own considerable courage, put the whole matter most eloquently in declaring, "But what will not a Man attempt to save Life? and no Man knows what Hardship he can bear, 'till he is bro't to the Test."

Whatever their other qualities, the seamen who shipped in these colonial vessels appear to have been a mixed lot. Most vessels recruited their crews from home ports, but a colonial ship's company might include strangers and men of foreign lands as well. Peirce's crew, which was in many ways typical, had in addition to its six New Hampshiremen two crewmen from the north of England and a Dutchman. John Dean's *Nottingham Galley* included a Swede (although Dean's mate, Christopher Langman, who contradicts Dean in practically every particular, informs us that the sailor in question was a Dutchman). Black men were also frequently numbered among colonial crews. Briton Hammon, of course, authored one of our narratives. A black man named Langford sailed with Peirce, and Anthony Suga, a black, was a member of Joseph Bailey's crew. Another black man was the servant of Philip Ashton's companion on Roatan, and there was, finally, the unfortunate black slave included in the cargo of Harrison's *Peggy*.

Not all these sailors were prayerful types, to be sure. Harrison, on the subject of his crew, complained of the "continual excess to which they drank—and the continual course of execration and blasphemy, which was occasioned by that excess." According to Henry Norwood, one of the *Virginia Merchant*'s long boats was lost "by the seamens neglect, who had all tasted so liberally of new wine, by the commodiousness of the vintage, that they lay up and down dead drunk in all quarters, in a sad pickle." The crewmen who accompanied William Strachey on the *Sea Venture* in 1610 turned out to be a mutinous lot, and one of them, when ordered to his post, bluntly told the watch commander that the governor had no authority over him or anyone else, and—as Strachey delicately related the incident—*"therefore let the Governour* (said hee) *Kisse, &c."* Nathaniel Peirce may have expressed the opinion of many when he contemplated the spiritual condition of the majority of sailors in this wise: "They past this Night in great Distress, and horrible Apprehensions of every Moments being their last, and their State fixt to all Eternity. And having so sudden a Call, what must be the Consternation of such miserable unthinking Wretches as the generality of Seamen Are?" Of course, out-and-out pirates such as those who kidnapped Philip Ashton were bound to be hardbitten sorts, and we should hardly be surprised to hear young Ashton describe them as "a vile Crew of Miscreants, to whom it was a sport to do Mischief; where prodigious Drinking, monstrous Cursing and Swearing, hideous Blasphemies, and open defiance of Heaven, and contempt of Hell it self, was the constant Employment, unless when Sleep something abated the Noise and Revellings."

However unthinking the sailors may have been in the absence of a crisis, the sea-deliverance was apt to make them reflective and talkative afterwards. Moreover, there was in the doctrine of Providence a con-comitant demand for witness. Those who were the beneficiaries of the sea-deliverance felt impelled to declare publicly the special mercies of God. "Dangers and Deliverances are to be carefully recorded as remembered," declared the Englishman James Janeway in the sermon accompanying his *Legacy to His Friends,* a collection of sea-deliverances first published in 1674: "O, what sweet Musick doth it make in God's Ears, that you thankfully record Sea-Mercies, and *Sea-Deliverances;* this is the Musick of the Waters; that makes Melody in God's Ears."[4] The same rationale underlay Increase Mather's collection of sea-deliverance in his *Essay for the Recording of Illustrious Providences* published ten years later in Boston. Joseph Bailey, in the preface to his narrative, similarly declared, "IT's not with a View or Design to move any One's Pity or Compassion towards the Unfortunate and Distress'd; neither is it out of vain Ostentation that my Name may be recorded, that moves me to write the following Narrative; but it is, as I conceive, My bounden Duty towards the Supreme Being, to declare his wonderful Acts of Providence, and tender Mercies towards the most undeserving of Mankind." In 1717 Thomas Prince, newly arrived in Boston after a tempestuous ocean crossing, declared, "How can we Praise the Lord for those His wondrous Works Unless we either behold them or hear of them? It is Our Business and Duty therefore who have seen them to declare and publish them; and Yours to hear and join in admiring them and in offering Him His Dues and Tributes of Praise and Glory."[5] Benjamin Bartholomew expressed much the same thought in his poem of 1660:

> Twase God alone that in our state did Move
> What for to render doth it us Behove:
> O let us tel abrod his wondrous acts
> Lets Glorifie his Name for all his facts
> Who bringeth loe and raiseth up againe
> God surly doth not these great things in vaine
> He is expecting from us som Great thing
> And lookes more prayes we to his name should bring.

At the conclusion of his narrative, Briton Hammon explains his need to preserve the record of Providence in his deliverance by assuring the reader that "tho I have omitted a great many Things, yet what is wrote may suffice to convince the Reader, that I have been most grievously afflicted, and yet thro' the Divine Goodness, as miraculously preserved, and delivered out of many Dangers; of which I desire to retain a *grateful Remembrance,* as long as I live in the world."

III

The often surprising verisimilitude of the narratives is a direct result of the writers' desire to effect a change in the hearts of their readers. Behind the Defoelike realism and wealth of detail that often characterizes the narratives, behind the attention paid to matters of pace and tone, and behind even the attempts at plot and characterization lies the writer's recognition that to challenge the moral complacency of his audience he must recreate all the drama and terror of his own experience. The most explicit comment on this matter is found in Richard Steere's *Monumental Memorial of Marine Mercy.* Although Steere is quick to admit the artist's limitations in attempting to recapture the reality of his experience—"Every *Quill* is silent to relate / What being known must needs be wonder'd at"— he nevertheless accepts the challenge to make the reader see in the writer's contrivance what no one could apprehend in a simple recitation of the facts:

> I take the boldness to present your *Eye*
> With Safty's *Prospect* in Extremity,
> Which tho not Cloath'd with Academick Skill
> Or lofty Raptures of a Poet's Quill;
> But wrapt in *raggs,* through which your eyes may see
> The *Naked* Truth in plain simplicitee.

The distinction Steere insists upon is that art is superior to mere description; that although art's function is to reveal truth rather than embellish it, to do justice to the truth one must organize and shape one's narrative. Otherwise the effect of the experience is diluted by distractions and irrelevancies.

In Steere's New England the sea voyage was a familiar metaphor for spiritual pilgrimage, both as it was manifested in individual lives and in the development of the community. Puritan historians from John Winthrop to William Hubbard, William Bradford to Cotton Mather, spoke of the world as a vast ocean fraught with dangers for the small band of pilgrims whose journey to the New World was seen as an expression of divine mis-

sion.[6] In Steere's poem, the dramatic voyage is contrived to enlarge the
reader's understanding of human dependence on Providence. The narrative structure conveniently parallels the spiritual passage: the ocean crossing reveals the participants' (and readers') progress from ignorance to
truth, from indifference to understanding. From this perspective, then,
the several physical crises that confront the passengers and crew of the
Adventure are fortunate indeed, for they bring to all a better understanding of the blessings of Providence. A voyage without such peril might well
induce complacency, a condition of acute spiritual danger:

> Had we continu'd *thus* upon the Deep
> We had bin Charm'd into a drowsie sleep
> Of calme Security, nor had we known
> The Excellence of *PRESERVATION:*
> We had been Dumb and silent to Express
> Affectedly the Voy'ges good success.

The phrase "Express Affectedly" is an essential one for understanding
the motive of this and other narratives. The writer's intention is not only
to recount the events, but to do so in a way that will move and improve
the audience, making clear that the successful ocean crossing implies a
spiritual as well as a temporal progress. Steere's method involves more
than a simple appeal to the emotions. The "affections" to which he makes
reference are the affections of the will, the third part of the faculties of
the soul (memory, understanding, and will) as it was then understood.
According to the method of Puritan meditation advocated by Richard
Baxter in his *Saints Everlasting Rest* (1653), the affections of the will
were aroused after the subject of the meditation, the doctrine, is supplied
by the memory and then analyzed by the understanding. Baxter further
described the action of the affections as progressing from love and desire
through hope, courage, and finally to joy. None of the colonial sea-
deliverances employ the extensive logical analysis Baxter recommended,
but it is true that writers like Steere did intend their narratives should
be read so as to engage and unify the faculties of the reader, fixing his
attention upon the operation of divine Providence. This, then, is "the
Voy'ges good success" of *A Monumental Memorial of Marine Mercy,*
which concludes, appropriately, in joy, with a hymn of praise and thanksgiving: "O who can tast thy Good, and not Thanksgiving Raise."

The emotional appeal of the colonial sea-deliverance is thus the opposite of sensationalism, for far from indulging in the narratives' often violent and terrifying emotions for their own sake, Steere and the others use the sea-deliverance experience to involve the whole personality of the reader, to integrate rather than separate the intellectual and emotional responses of the audience.

The hold that this essentially seventeenth-century theory exercised upon the aesthetic of the sea-deliverance tradition lasted well into the latter half of the eighteenth century, despite the changes in epistemology wrought by John Locke's *Essay Concerning Human Understanding* (1690). In the post-Lockean era men argued (as Jonathan Edwards did in America) that the mind knows only its own ideas of things and apprehends these only through the senses, and thus the pattern or form of a thing that one understands is to some degree a function of perception—and not, as Baxter would have it, the other way around. Applied to the aesthetics of the colonial sea-deliverances, Locke's (and Edwards's) theory would enlarge the importance of the mode of presentation at the expense of the verifiable external reality of the experience. To assert that this happens in the narratives is to suggest that the sea-deliverances experiment with narrative point-of-view in ways that would later be adopted by writers of sea fiction,[7] a development that is quite unlikely except at the end of the colonial period. Locke was so little understood in America (as Edwards's own experience was to show) it is doubtful that the authors of the sea-deliverances appreciated the epistemological revolution that was taking place. Only in Captain David Harrison's narrative is there any evidence that the narrator's relationship to his subject differs at all from that found in the earlier Providential deliverances.

Thus the sea-deliverance was not merely an adventure or the occasion for uncommon suffering. It was an experience charged with meaning for both the individual who endured it and for the audience called upon to bear witness through the medium of the narrative. In Anthony Thacher's narrative for example, we find the author struggling to balance the agony of his personal loss against what he knows to be the goodness of an all-wise Providence. This tension between the harrowed heart and the theologically conditioned intellect was a characteristic of Puritan life and literature (one thinks of Anne Bradstreet's elegies on her grandchildren as an example of this often incompletely resolved dilemma). Nathaniel Peirce, writing more than one hundred years after Thacher, could, with

an urgency his audience immediately understood, advise his crew "to
endeavour to secure their eternal Happiness in the next [world], by looking unto Jesus Christ their merciful Redeemer for sincere Repentance of
all their Sins, and Salvation thro' his Blood, and to let that take up all
their Thoughts, as they had nothing before their Eyes, but Death, and
an Eternity of Joy or Misery." In addition, the narrative often contained
an object lesson for the audience that vicariously experienced the demand
for repentance and for submission to the Divine Will. On his distressed
ship in 1749, Joseph Bailey prays not only that God will deliver them,
but that he will also "give us a due Sense of all the Mercies he had be-
stowed upon us; and that he would give us Grace to make a right Improve-
ment thereof; that we might amend our Lives, and live to shew forth his
wonderful Acts of Providence, and loving Kindness to us the sinful
Children of Men."

The narrative was also the record of an individual's spiritual trial and
call to faithfulness, for if the sea-deliverance provided both narrator and
Puritan audience a shared sense of theology and perception, it also gave
them a common sense of community and purpose. That the narrative had
a function beyond the exemplum was plain for all to see. To the Puritans,
the special Providence of the sea-deliverance gave evidence of God's particular concern for the people of New England. However much Puritans
sought to avoid the "allegorizing" they found so objectionable in the
medieval fathers, they consistently looked to nature for evidence of God's
revealed will—evidence that might complement the revelation in Scripture.
Both Scripture and nature were searched for analogues confirming New
England's special "errand into the wilderness." For the audience, then,
a special individual Providence, including the sea-deliverance, may be
said to have possessed an authority not unlike that of Scripture. However
because the Puritans mistrusted this kind of evidence (even if of God's
favor), they often made a conscious effort to establish analogues between
a biblical type (Job, Daniel, Jeremiah) or event and the characteristic(s)
of the special Providence. For example, in his sermon, *God's Ability to
Save His People Out of All Their Dangers,* which accompanied *Ashton's
Memorial,* John Barnard develops the comparison between Ashton's trial
and deliverance and the witness of Shadrach, Meschach, and Abednego
in the fiery furnace. What Barnard's audience could not miss was not only
the parallel, the alikeness of the two experiences, but more importantly,

the unifying principle connecting scriptual type and providential event. In this way the sea-deliverance gave the audience a renewed sense of participation in the unfolding drama of God's Will working in history.

So with or without an accompanying sermon, the sea-deliverance not only provided the Puritan reader an exemplum, it also reinforced his sense of historical uniqueness and special favor. The trial of Ashton or Thacher or Peirce was also the trial (and triumph) of a chosen people. The sea-deliverance was an artifice by which construction a tribal people like the Puritans might respond to external dangers that threatened the physical and psychological well-being of the community. By an act of imagination the external threat was controlled and made expressive of the highest aspirations and most deeply held convictions of a people. Language conquered the sea.

In America the traditional use of the sea as a metaphor for experience became inextricably linked with this sense of uniqueness and mission. Of this fusion the sea-deliverance narrative is the most fully developed form in a larger pattern of sea-experiences. For immigrants in the colonial period (and of a later time as well), the trans-Atlantic crossing was the fundamental experience, the trial by which one began a new life. The Atlantic offered a rich source of metaphor around which the ocean traveler might organize and express the inner personal and group meaning of the crossing. William Bradford, in a famous passage, could speak of the ocean voyage—across "the vast and furious ocean"—as uniting the Pilgrims in praise and thanksgiving for their deliverance, and Edward Johnson in his *Wonder-Working Providence of Sions Savior in New England* identified the common purpose of the Puritans in their having been chosen by the Lord for special work: "his People, who are pickt out by his providence to passe this Westerne Ocean for this honourable service." The successful crossing as a sign of providential protection, of spiritual—later patriotic—fitness did not end with the demise of Puritanism in America. Rather it remained, in altered form, in the national consciousness as a metaphor for the manifest destiny of a nation. The ocean crossing, which for the Puritans might be seen as a metaphor for the soul's pilgrimage to the City of God or a trial of faith for a people especially chosen to do the Lord's work in the wilderness, became later the rite of passage for Crevecoeur's American, the new man forsaking Europe and the past. This American—and succeeding generations of immigrants—is separated from

the Old World literally by a trial by water through which passage he is
made worthy of regeneration in the New.

IV

As the record of an individual's trial of faith and as an illustration of
Providence acting in support of the community, the colonial sea-deliverance bears immediate comparison with the Indian-captivity narrative.
Both are products of an American frontier experience. Both tended to
give heroic and communal meaning to individual suffering and adventure.
Both, as genre, were to experience a growing secularization following
several decades in which the religious framework guided and shaped the
aesthetic considerations of the writer. Both narratives are important,
finally, not so much for what they tell us about the Indians or the sea,
but for what they reveal about the culture that produced it. As the
colonial period drew to a close, the cultural needs that produced the
providential captivity narrative of a Mary Rowlandson or the sea-deliverance of a Philip Ashton diminished in the face of demands for the sensationalism of a Peter Williamson (1757) or David Harrison (1766). Like
the Indian captivity, the sea-deliverance is both an index to cultural values
and an influence in American literature.

A more intriguing and perhaps equally significant aspect of the comparison between the Indian captivity and sea-deliverance is the ritualistic
and archetypal possibilities already explored in the captivity narratives
by Richard VanDerBeets. At the core of the Indian captivity, VanDerBeets
sees a series of ritualistic practices, chief among them cannibalism and
scalping. The latter does not figure in any of the sea-deliverances, but
cannibalism does occur in three of the present narratives (Norwood,
Dean-Langman, and Harrison) and is threatened in a fourth (Hammon).
The presence of this barbarism in the narratives is evidently part of their
appeal. Why? Some of it, certainly, is pure sensationalism—the shocking
transgression against human dignity and convention. But this is not all.
Surely VanDerBeets is right in ascribing the appeal of cannibalism to its
power to evoke ritualistic and metaphorical meanings deeply held in
common by the human consciousness, regardless of time and space. Yet
the consuming of human flesh that occurs as a part of the ritual or stylization of the Indian captivity (or sea-deliverance) operates as part of a larger

mythologic pattern. Arguing from Joseph Campbell's *Hero with a Thousand Faces*, VanDerBeets sees the controlling myth of all the captivity narratives as

> that of the Hero embarked upon the archetypal journey
> of initiation. The quest, or ancient ritual of initiation, is
> a variation of the fundamental Death-Rebirth archetype and
> traditionally involves the separation of the Hero from his
> culture, his undertaking a long journey, and his undergoing
> a series of excruciating ordeals in passing from ignorance to
> knowledge. In the monomyth, this consists of three stages
> or phases: separation, transformation, and enlightened
> return.[8]

This archetypal design that VanDerBeets has identified in the Indian captivity also informs the sea-deliverances. In fact, the tripart plot of separation, transformation, and enlightened return is particularly well expressed in the providential deliverances of the colonial era, composed as they are by a familiar pattern of voyage (or abduction), storm-shipwreck, and deliverance. Using VanDerBeets's description of the myth (substituting the sea-deliverance for Indian captivity), one finds that the hero must leave his community and enter an area of unknown dangers (in the present case, the sea). He may undertake the journey voluntarily (for example, Thacher, Norwood, Steere, and Bailey) or be taken away forcibly by some malevolent agent (Ashton). In the second stage the hero must endure a series of trials—storms, shipwreck, starvation—and at the moment of greatest peril is transformed by the ordeal. Having successfully passed the test, he returns to his community with increased understanding and insight. This mythical configuration may be used to explain further the continuing popularity of the genre. The sea-deliverance in all ages is an expression of one of the most fundamental of all archetypal patterns: the passage of the hero through separation, transformation, and return. The significance of the deliverance is not merely historical, not only literary, but something more, touching as it does on fundamental truths of human experience—truths for which man's imagination has continually, through a plethora of forms, sought expression. It is not too much to say that the sea-deliverances, far from being a mere collection of random tales, are, as a group, an expression of very complex feelings and ideas, a fitting medium for man's most profound art.

V

The middle decades of the eighteenth century brought an increasingly secular spirit to the sea-deliverance, and the neoclassic sublime gradually replaced Providence as the controlling aesthetic in the narratives. This in turn gave way in the nineteenth century to the romantic and symbolic conception of the sea found in the work of writers such as Cooper and Melville. To follow these changes all the way is beyond the province of the present work; but we can observe the alteration in the providential aesthetic that was taking place even as the colonial period was drawing to a close. This shift in the sea-deliverance is most easily seen in its changing relationship to the sermon. We have noted how *Ashton's Memorial* was used to complement Barnard's *God's Ability to Save His People Out of All Their Dangers.* In the decline of the providential sea-deliverance two things occur: the sea-deliverance loses the typological dimension, and the sermon takes on a dramatic context that in earlier times was usually left to the narrative. To observe this we need only contrast Harrison's 1766 narrative—which in addition to stylistic differences from earlier narratives has also lost its typological content—and a sermon written in 1769 by the Reverend William Whitwell, John Barnard's successor in the pulpit at Marblehead.

Harrison's acknowledgement of Providence, as opposed to, say, Bailey's (1749) or Peirce's (1756), is merely formal, even perfunctory. The God of Captain Harrison is not the Puritan Jehovah who catechizes men by storm in His Wonders of the Deep. He is, rather, "the great disposer of all things" whose "Divine goodness" must be acknowledged. Even the motive differs. Harrison writes not out of the sense of obligation that impelled earlier writers, but only to avoid what might otherwise be interpreted as a "want of gratitude." The change is signaled most of all by Harrison's address to the casual reader—an idea a Puritan writer would have found insupportable:

> The solemnity of this sentiment will not, I hope, terrify
> a reader of elegance from the perusal of the following
> pages.—Those who read for mere amusement, will
> probably find something to entertain them, unless they
> are too refined to put up in real distress with those cir-

cumstances which would possibly yield them most satisfaction in a work of mere imagination,—while those who
are actuated by a more serious turn, will possibly exclaim
in the exalted language of the Psalmist, "How wonderful
are the works of the Lord, how great in wisdom all."

This designation of the split in the readership of the sea-deliverance marks
a subtle yet fundamental change in the nature of the genre. The shift away
from a providential interpretation of the deliverance has aesthetic consequences as well as theological ones. More and more in the later eighteenth
century the sea-deliverances depict violence, terror, and sensation not as
providential wonders to be heeded by the spiritually unready, but as warn-
ings of the antisocial character of nature, the dangers to human welfare
posed by disordered forces outside the restraining influence of reason and
society. In the hands of a Poe or Melville the sea as the symbol of such
forces is made far more romantic and attractive (even if more terrifying),
but for eighteenth-century writers like Captain Harrison the metaphorical
possibilities were defined by a different aesthetic. The lesson of the *Peggy*'s
voyage has less to do with Providence than with the dangers of a break-
down in the social order, in a disorder abetted by the antisocial influences of the sea—Philip Freneau's "Dread Neptune's wild, unsocial sea."

The shift away from the providential framework of the sea-deliverance
was not without influence in another genre. Ministers who could no longer
depend on a belief in Providence to control the aesthetic of the lay writer
of sea-deliverances responded by adapting a portion of the narrative's
dramatic context to their sermons. To illustrate the point with a single
example: On December 17, 1769, William Whitwell addressed his congregation on the occasion of a series of maritime disasters that had befallen Salem in recent weeks. A generation earlier, from the same pulpit,
John Barnard, secure in the knowledge that his audience would understand and respond to the typology of the sea-deliverance, preached not
on Philip Ashton among the pirates, but of the three Hebrews in the
fiery furnace. For Whitwell, on the other hand, the difference was not
the absence of a story like Ashton's, but the weakening of the aesthetic
that had formerly made the connection possible. So the new pastor of
Marblehead brought the sea-deliverance into his sermon, partitioning the

narrative and adapting its drama for purely theological purposes. In the
middle of his sermon, Whitwell, like Thacher, Steere, Ashton, Bailey
and others, took his audience into the depths:

> The sky, which looked serene and fair, gathers blackness:
> The winds, which were moderate, rise and blow with vio-
> lence: The sea, which was as smooth as glass, tosses its waves
> mountains high: The night comes on: The storm increases:
> The winds rage: The rain beats upon you, and the sea is
> ready to swallow you up: "you reel to and fro, and stagger
> like a drunken man;" "are at your wit's end," and "your
> souls melt within you because of trouble." Oh! who can
> describe how great that trouble is? your hearts can paint
> it in more lively colours than I am capable of.[9]

Thus the work of Harrison (1766) and Whitwell (1769) together form a
convenient point at which to mark the decline of the colonial sea-deliverance. Similar narratives continue, of course, but deprived of the aesthetic
consequences of the doctrine of Providence. The end of the providential
sea-deliverance also meant the loss of a rich source of spiritual allegory
for the Puritan sermon.

Yet this change in the colonial sea-deliverance as a genre did not bring
an end to its influence. The popularity of secular narratives of shipwreck
and maritime disaster continued unabated. Collections such as R. Thomas's
Remarkable Shipwrecks and Archiband Duncan's *Mariners Chronicle*
were widely read, and the continued appeal of the sea-deliverance as
entertainment had important literary consequences.

There is, first, the sea-deliverance as source material for later works.
Such influence is demonstrable in *The Narrative of Arthur Gorden Pym*,
Poe having read Harrison's *Voyage of the Peggy* (probably in the bowd-
lerized version that appeared in Thomas's *Remarkable Shipwrecks*). But
more significant for American literature, especially American fiction, is
the tradition of realistic treatment of the sea established by the colonial
sea-deliverances. The need of the writers of sea-deliverances to compel
belief in the Lord's Wonders of the Deep led them to a treatment of
nautical materials that were rich in realistic detail. Consider, for example,
the following passage from Joseph Bailey's narrative:

On Sunday the 24th of *December,* the Sea hove our
Boat out of her Chocks, and we had like to have lost her,
but secur'd her again. The badness of the Weather drowned
most of our Stock upon Deck; and the Weather continued
with very little Alteration, still veering around once in 24
Hours, till Wednesday the 27th of *December.* Towards noon
reft our Fore-sail, and settled our Fore-Yard, but the bad
weather coming on, oblig'd us to hand and scud a Hull before
Night. A terrible hard Gale ensu'd that wash'd our Deck of
every thing that was moveable, Lumber, Coops, and Water-
Casks; and for some Time the People were up to their
Necks in Water at the Pump. Night came on and the Weather
increas'd; and about 8 Clock in the Evening a Sea poopt
us, and drove in our two Larboard Lights in the Cabbin,
which almost fill'd it and the Steerage, putting out all our
Lights below, and spoil'd our Tinder; but by the Help of a
Pistol with Powder I got light again. I found the Sea had
carry'd away one dead Light, so that to supply the deficency, was obliged to put my Bed into one of the Windows,
and secur'd it in the best Manner I was capable. I then set
the Boys to bailing the Water out of the Steerage with
Buckets as fast as they could, and call's for the Broad-Ax
and plac'd it at the Cabbin-Door, so that I might readily
find it in Case she Broached too, to have cut away her
Main-Mast.

What is remarkable here is the succession of concrete images combining
to create an idelible scene of violent action and drama. More than a
hundred years earlier Anthony Thacher used a similar technique to create an equally compelling picture of peril and tragedy:

Wee were by the violence of the waves and fury of the
windes by the Lords permission Lifted up upon a rocke
betweene to hie rockes, yet all was but one Rocke, but
ragged, with the strocke where of the water came into
the Pinace. So as we were presently up to the midles in
watter as wete, the Watters Came furiously and violently

over us and against us, but by reasen of the Rockes preportion Could not Lift us off, but beate her all to peeces: Now
Looke with mee upon our distresses, and Consider of my
misery; who beheld the Shippe broken, the watter in her and
violently overwhelming us: my goods and provisions Swiming in the Seas, my Freends almost drowned and mine owne
poore Children So ultimely (if I may so terme it without
offence) before mine eyes halfe drowned and ready to be
Swollowed up and dashed to peeces against the rockes by
the merciless waves, and my Selfe ready to accompany them.

In their literary use of the sea, including the habit of realism, these
colonial narratives are a part of the tradition that also produced the
great American sea novels of Cooper and Melville. One need not fall into
the trap of viewing the narratives as the necessary but bungling ante-
cedents of some inevitably progressive development in American fiction.
The sea-deliverances can and should be read on their own terms. But
what is important from the view of literary history is the long-standing
narrative tradition of the sea. Over the years this tradition was to take
many forms. The providential sea-deliverance was one, the sensational
and sentimental narratives of the later eighteenth century another,
the romantic fiction of the nineteenth century yet a third. There is continuity in the tradition, but the existence of such continuity is not an
invitation to read backwards from later works, imposing standards of
form and method that have no relevance to an earlier period.

In English literature there existed from the sixteenth century on (in
addition to the nonfiction narrative) healthy traditions of fictionalized
travel and fabulous voyages. Out of a meeting of these two came the
sea novels of Defoe and Smollett in the eighteenth century. However,
in America in the late eighteenth century native writers turned away
from sea for literary material; when they did use it, it was often for
satire or sentiment.[10] In addition, a lingering American prejudice against
the novel delayed its New World development until the very end of the
century, and it is not until William Williams's *Mr. Penrose,* written in the
1770s but not published until 1815, and the appearance of the anonymous *History of Constantius and Pulchera* in 1794 and the much superior
Algerine Captive by Royall Tyler in 1797 that we find serious, or at
least extended, use of the sea in American prose fiction. There are of

course references to the sea in some colonial and early national poetry—
in Josselyn, Steere, John Saffin, Philip Freneau—as there are in a few
early dramas such as William Dunlap's *Yankee Chronology* (1812).

But the greatness of the sea tradition in American literature did not
"rise" in the nineteenth century, springing full-blown from eighteenth-
century roots. American literary associations with the sea began, as we
have seen, much earlier—in the Puritan histories and sermon literature
and especially in the sea-deliverance narratives in prose and verse. Thus
between the period of exploration and the Revolution, the literary tradition of the sea in America is largely vested in the nonfiction deliverance
narrative. At its earliest—as in Strachey's *True Reportory*—the style of
the narrative exhibits a decidedly Elizabethan quality; toward the end of
our period we see—briefly in Ashton, often in Harrison—evidence of the
sentimentality pervasive in eighteenth-century British and American
literature. But irrespective of "period style," these narratives frequently
exhibit impressive qualities of realism, power, and compelling drama—
qualities that make them a worthy part of the tradition that also witnessed the greatest of American literary use of the sea: the novels of
Cooper, Melville, and London, of Stephen Crane's "Open Boat," of
Whitman's "Sea-Drift" poems.

When these later writers turned to the sea they were making use not
of a new source in American literature but a very old one indeed. It is
certainly true that the War of 1812 served to focus America's attention
on the importance of sea power. But by that time there already existed,
in addition to a renewed sense of the economic and political tradition
derived from the sea, a literary tradition. However much the war galva-
nized America's sense of herself as a growing naval power, her citizens
were already long used to reading about the sea, were conditioned by a
long-standing literary tradition that treated the sea allegorically and
metaphorically. The rich symbolic uses of the sea found in Poe, Cooper,
Melville, Whitman, and others have their roots in the habit of mind that
produced the special Providences of the colonial sea-deliverances. Then
the nautical experiences of sea-deliverance authors provided analogies
to corroborate the scriptual foundations of their faith. Transferred
through the neoclassic perception of the sublime, this Puritan tendency
to spiritualize nature became in the nineteenth century the neoplatonism
of Emerson, the romantic symbolism of Melville. In works such as Poe's
Pym, Cooper's *Sea Lions,* Dana's *Two Years Before the Mast,* or Melville's

Moby Dick the familiar territory of the colonial sea-deliverance is again explored, and Providence once again looms large in the work, not because it is there, of course, but precisely because it is not. Roger Stein, in his masterful study of the relation of seventeenth-century seascape to nineteenth-century literature, has put the matter succinctly:

> Yet despite the boldness of the American romantic voyage, in Ishmael's tortured readings of the harpoon, the line, and the tryworks, the failed typologist is continually present; in the Cooper hero's attempt to master the art of sailing on perilous seas, the colonial image of order constantly breaks through; in Pym's final journey into the whiteness or Whiteman's exclamation, "Are they not all the seas of God?", the search for a lost coherence, a lost cosmology is clearly evident.[11]

The writers of the colonial sea-deliverance, far from being an isolated group, are merely the first generation of those American authors who have again and again gone down to the sea.

NOTES

1. John Josselyn, *An Account of Two Voyages* (London, 1674), pp. 30-32.

2. Thomas Philbrick, *James Fenimore Cooper and the Development of American Sea Fiction* (Cambridge: Harvard University Press, 1961), pp. 1-3.

3. Roger B. Stein, "Seascape and the American Imagination: The Puritan Seventeenth Century," *Early American Literature* 7 (1972): 21-25.

4. James Janeway, "The Seaman's Preacher; or, Sea-Dangers and Deliverances Improv'd," *Mr. James Janeway's Legacy to His Friends* (London, 1674), p. 9.

5. Thomas Prince, *God brings to the Desired Haven. A Thanksgiving-Sermon* (Boston, 1717), p. 1.

6. Cecelia Tichi, "Spiritual Biography and the 'Lords Remembrancers,' " *William and Mary Quarterly* 28 (1971): 74-81.

7. See, for example, Roger Stein's exploration of this idea in "Pulled Out of the Bay: American Fiction in the Eighteenth Century," *Studies in American Fiction* 2 (1974): 22-26.

8. Richard VanDerBeets, "The Indian Captivity Narrative as Ritual," *American Literature* 43 (1972): 553.

9. William Whitwell, *A Discourse, Occasioned By The Loss of a Number of Vessels, With Their Mariners Belonging to the Town of Marblehead* (Salem, 1770), pp. 8-9.

10. Philbrick, *Cooper and American Sea Fiction*, pp. 3-15.

11. Stein, "Seascape and the American Imagination," p. 34.

William Strachey

A true reportory of the wracke, and redemption of Sir Thomas Gates Knight;[1] upon, and from the Ilands of the Bermudas: his comming to Virginia, and the estate of that Colonie then, and after, under the government of the Lord La Warre,[2] July 15, 1610

"Now would I give a thousand furlongs of sea for an acre of barren ground—long heath, brown furze, anything. The wills above be done, but I would fain die a dry death."
—from *The Tempest* (I, i.)

The words are Shakespeare's, but the inspiration may well have come from the Bard's reading of a manuscript by one William Strachey, Esquire, a gentleman adventurer who had on June 2, 1609, sailed aboard the *Sea Venture,* the flagship of a fleet of seven ships, two pinnaces, and six hundred passengers bound for Jamestown in the new colony of Virginia.

Before the ships reached Virginia, a storm scattered the fleet, and on July 28 the *Sea Venture* was driven ashore on the Bermuda archipelago. The ship carried the governor, Sir Thomas Gates, and the admiral of the fleet, Sir George Somers, as well as Strachey and one hundred and fifty men, women, and children. The ship's longboat was dispatched to Virginia, and although the castaways watched the horizon anxiously for some sign of her successful mission, neither boat nor crew were ever seen again. The survivors then began to build two pinnaces from the timbers of the *Sea Venture* and from native cedar, a project that somehow went forward despite mutiny and despair among the passengers and crew.

Important as Strachey's narrative is to the history of early Virginia, it is of even greater value as a literary document. A conscious stylist, Strachey carefully organized and structured his *True Reportory,* skillfully orchestrating its rhythms and assembling an array of graphic details and colorful images. The storm scene in particular is, as Shakespeare discovered, compelling. Dramatic in rhetoric, image, and rhythm, Strachey's description is a powerful sample of Renaissance prose at its very best.

The *True Reportory* was taken to England in 1610 by Sir Thomas Gates, who returned to London after the arrival of the new governor, Lord La Warre. From the Council of Virginia, to whom the *Reportory* was delivered, the manuscript passed to the attention of Shakespeare and afterwards to Samuel Purchas, who later printed it in his collection of voyages.

Much speculation has been directed at the identity of the "Excellent Lady" to whom the narrative is addressed. It seems sufficient to say that although she could have been one of the wives of members of the Council of Virginia, it is in character for an Elizabethan gentleman such as Strachey to have adopted this form of address as a literary convention.

In 1611 Strachey returned to England where he began the composition of his *History of Travel into Virginia Britannia.* He died in London in 1621.

The *True Reportory* was first published by Samuel Purchas in 1625 in his *Hakluytus Posthumus; or Purchas His Pilgrimes.* It has been edited in modern dress by Louis B. Wright in *A Voyage to Virginia in 1609* (Charlottesville: University Press at Virginia, 1964). For more information on Strachey see S. G. Culliford, *William Strachey, 1572-1621* (Charlottesville: University Press at Virginia, 1965), and Howard Mumford Jones, *The Literature of Virginia in the Seventeenth Century,* 2nd ed. (Charlottesville: University Press at Virginia, 1968).

TEXT: Original issue of *Purchas His Pilgrimes* in the
Folger Shakespeare Library. Those portions of the narrative
that contain Strachey's lengthy description of the Burmudas,
the governance of Jamestown, and the government of Lord
La Warre have been omitted.

EXcellent Lady, know that upon Friday late in the evening, we brake
ground out of the Sound of *Plymouth,* our whole Fleet then consisting
of seven good Ships, and two Pinnaces, all which from the said second
of June, unto the twenty three of July, kept in friendly consort together, not a whole watch at any time, loosing the sight each of other.
Our course when we came about the height of betweene 26. and 27.
degrees, we declined to the Northward, and according to our Governours instructions altered the trade and ordinary way used heretofore
by *Dominico,* and *Mevis,* [3] in the West *Indies,* and found the winde to
this course indeede as friendly, as in the judgement of all Sea-men, it is
upon a more direct line, and by Sir *George Summers* our Admirall had
bin likewise in former time sailed, being a Gentleman of approved
assurednesse, and ready knowledge in Sea-faring actions, having often
carried command, and chiefe charge in many Ships Royall of her Majesties, and in sundry Voyages made many defeats and attempts in the time
of the *Spaniards* quarrelling with us, upon the *Ilands* and *Indies,* &c.
We had followed this course so long, as now we were within seven or
eight dayes at the most, by Cap. *Newports* reckoning of making Cape
Henry upon the coast of *Virginia:* When on S. *James* his day, July 24.
being Monday (preparing for no lesse all the blacke night before) the
cloudes gathering thicke upon us, and the windes singing, and whistling
most unusually, which made us to cast off our Pinnace towing the same
untill then asterne, a dreadfull storme and hideous began to blow from
out the North-east, which swelling, and roaring as it were by fits, some
houres with more violence then others, at length did beate all light from
heaven; which like an hell of darkenesse turned blacke upon us, so much
the more fuller of horror, as in such cases horror and feare use to over-
runne the troubled, and overmastered sences of all, which (taken up with
amazement) the eares lay so sensible to the terrible cries, and murmurs
of the windes, and distraction of our Company, as who was most armed,
and best prepared, was not a little shaken. For surely (Noble Lady) as

death comes not so sodaine nor apparant, so he comes not so elvish and painful (to men especially even then in health and perfect habitudes of body) as at Sea; who comes at no time so welcome, but our frailty (so weake is the hold of hope in miserable demonstrations of danger) it makes guilty of many contrary changes, and conflicts: For indeede death is accompanied at no time, nor place with circumstances every way so uncapable of particularities of goodnesse and inward comforts, as at Sea. For it is most true, there ariseth commonly no such unmercifull tempest, compound of so many contrary and divers Nations, but that it worketh upon the whole frame of the body, and most loathsomely affecteth all the powers thereof: and the manner of the sicknesse it laies upon the body, being so unsufferable, gives not the minde any free and quiet time, to use her judgment and Empire: which made the Poet say:

Hostium uxores,[4] puerique caecos
Sentiant motus orientis Haedi, &
AEquoris nigri fremitum, & trementes
    Verbere ripas.

For foure and twenty houres the storme in a restlesse tumult, had blowne so exceedingly, as we could not apprehend in our imaginations any possibility of greater violence, yet did wee still finde it, not onely more terrible, but more constant, fury added to fury, and one storme urging a second more outragious then the former; whether it so wrought upon our feares, or indeede met with new forces: Sometimes strikes in our Ship amongst women, and passengers, not used to such hurly and discomforts, made us looke one upon the other with troubled hearts, and panting bosomes: our clamours dround in the windes, and the windes in thunder. Prayers might well be in the heart and lips, but drowned in the outcries of the Officers: nothing heard that could give comfort, nothing seene that might incourage hope. It is impossible for me, had I the voyce of *Stentor,*[5] and expression of as many tongues, as his throate of voyces, to expresse the outcries and miseries, not languishing, but wasting his spirits, and art constant to his owne principles, but not prevailing. Our sailes wound up lay without their use, and if at any time wee bore but a Hollocke, or halfe forecourse, to guide her before the Sea, six and sometimes eight men were not inough to hold the whipstaffe in the steerage, and the tiller below in the Gunner roome, by which may be

imagined the strength of the storme: In which, the Sea swelled above the
Clouds, and gave battell unto Heaven. It could not be said to raine, the
waters like whole Rivers did flood in the ayre. And this I did still observe,
that whereas upon the Land, when a storme hath powred it selfe forth
once in drifts of raine, the winde as beaten downe, and vanquished therewith, not long after indureth: here the glut of water (as if throatling in
the winde ere while) was no sooner a little emptied and qualified, but
instantly the windes (as having gotten their mouthes now free, and at
liberty) spake more loud, and grew more loud, and grew more tumultuous,
and malignant. What shall I say? Windes and Seas were as mad, as fury and
rage could make them; for mine owne part, I had bin in some stormes before, as well upon the coast of *Barbary* and *Algeere,* in the *Levant,* and
once more distressfull in the *Adriatique* gulfe, in a bottome of Candy,[6]
so as I may well say. *Ego quid*[7] *sit ater Adrae novi sinus, & quid albus
Peccet Iapex.* Yet all that I had ever suffered gathered together, might
not hold comparison with this: there was not a moment in which the
sodaine splitting, or instant over-setting of the Shippe was not expected.

   Howbeit this was not all; It pleased God to bring a greater affliction
yet upon us; for in the beginning of the storme we had received likewise
a mighty leake. And the Ship in every joynt almost, having spued out her
Okam, before we were aware (a casualty more desperate then any other
that a Voyage by Sea draweth with it) was growne five foote suddenly
deepe with water above her ballast, and we almost drowned within,
whilest we sat looking when to perish from above. This imparting no
lesse terrour then danger, ranne through the whole Ship with much fright
and amazement, startled and turned the bloud, and tooke downe the
braves of the most hardy Marriner of them all, insomuch as he that before
happily felt not the sorrow of others, now began to sorrow for himselfe,
when he saw such a pond of water so suddenly broken in, and which he
knew could not (without present avoiding) but instantly sinke him. So
as joyning (onely for his owne sake, not yet worth the saving) in the
publique safety; there might be seene Master, Masters Mate, Boateswaine,
Quarter Master, Coopers, Carpenters, and who not, with candels in their
hands, creeping along the ribs viewing the sides, searching every corner,
and listening in every place, if they could heare the water runne. Many
a weeping leake was this way found, and hastily stopt, and at length one
in the Gunner roome made up with I know not how many peeces of
Beefe: but all was to no purpose, the Leake (if it were but one) which

drunke in our greatest Seas, and tooke in our destruction fastest, could
not then be found, nor ever was, by any labour, counsell, or search. The
waters still increasing, and the Pumpes going, which at length choaked
with bringing up whole and continuall Bisket (and indeede all we had,
tenne thousand weight) it was conceived, as most likely, that the Leake
might be sprung in the Breadroome, whereupon the Carpenter went
downe, and ript up all the roome, but could not finde it so.

I am not able to give unto your Ladiship every mans thought in this
perplexity, to which we were now brought; but to me, this Leakage appeared as a wound given to men that were before dead. The Lord knoweth,
I had as little hope, as desire of life in the storme, & in this, it went beyond
my will; because beyond my reason, why we should labour to preserve
life; yet we did, either because so deare are a few lingring houres of life
in all mankinde, or that our *Christian* knowledges taught us, how much
we owed to the rites of Nature, as bound, not to be false to our selves,
or to neglect the meanes of our owne preservation; the most despairefull
things amongst men, being matters of no wonder nor moment with him,
who is the rich Fountaine and admirable Essence of all mercy.

Our Governour, upon the tuesday morning (at what time, by such who
had bin below in the hold, the Leake was first discovered) had caused the
whole Company, about one hundred and forty, besides women, to be
equally divided into three parts, and opening the Ship in three places
(under the forecastle, in the waste, and hard by the Bitacke) appointed
each man where to attend; and thereunto every man came duely upon
his watch, tooke the Bucket, or Pumpe for one houre, and rested another.
Then men might be seene to labour, I may well say, for life, and the
better sort, even our Governour, and Admirall themselves, not refusing
their turne, and to spell each the other, to give example to other. The
common sort stripped naked, as men in Gallies, the easier both to hold
out, and to shrinke from under the salt water, which continually leapt
in among them, kept their eyes waking, and their thoughts and hands
working, with tyred bodies, and wasted spirits, three dayes and foure
nights destitute of outward comfort, and desperate of any deliverance,
testifying how mutually willing they were, yet by labour to keepe each
other from drowning, albeit each one drowned whilest he laboured.

Once, so huge a Sea brake upon the poope and quarter, upon us, as it
covered our Shippe from stearne to stemme, like a garment or a vast
cloude, it filled her brimme full for a while within, from the hatches up

to the sparre decke. This source or confluence of water was so violent, as it rusht and carried the Helm-man from the Helme, and wrested the Whipstaffe out of his hand, which so flew from side to side, that when he would have ceased the same againe, it so tossed him from Star-boord to Lar-boord, as it was Gods mercy it had not split him: It so beat him from his hold, and so bruised him, as a fresh man hazarding in by chance fell faire with it, and by maine strength bearing somewhat up, made good his place, and with much clamour incouraged and called upon others; who gave her now up, rent in pieces and absolutely lost. Our Governour was at this time below at the Capstone, both by his speech and authoritie heartening every man unto his labour. It strooke him from the place where hee sate, and groveled him, and all us about him on our faces, beating together with our breaths all thoughts from our bosomes, else, then that wee were now sinking. For my part, I thought her alreadie in the bottome of the Sea; and I have heard him say, wading out of the floud thereof, all his ambition was but to climbe up above hatches to dye in *Aperto coelo,*[8] and in the company of his old friends. It so stun'd the ship in her full pace, that shee stirred no more, then if shee had beene caught in a net, or then, as if the fabulous *Remora*[9] had stucke to her fore-castle. Yet without bearing one inch of saile, even then shee was making her way nine or ten leagues in a watch. One thing, it is not without his wonder (whether it were the feare of death in so great a storme, or that it pleased God to be gracious unto us) there was not a passenger, gentleman, or other, after hee beganne to stirre and labour, but was able to relieve his fellow, and make good his course: And it is most true, such as in all their life times had never done houres worke before (their mindes now helping their bodies) were able twice fortie eight hours together to toile with the best.

During all this time, the heavens look'd so blacke upon us, that it was not possible the elevation of the Pole[10] might be observed: nor a Starre by night, not Sunne beame by day was to be seene. Onely upon the thursday night Sir *George Summers* being upon the watch, had an apparition of a little round light, like a faint Starre, trembling, and streaming along with a sparkeling blaze, halfe the height upon the Maine Mast, and shooting sometimes from Shroud to Shroud, tempting to settle as it were upon any of the foure Shrouds: and for three or foure houres together, or rather more, halfe the night it kept with us; running sometimes along the Maine-yard to the very end, and then returning. At which, Sir *George*

Summers called divers about him, and shewed them the same, who observed it with much wonder, and carefulnesse: but upon a sodaine, towards the morning watch, they lost the sight of it, and knew not what way it made. The superstitious Sea-men make many constructions of this Sea-fire, which neverthelesse is usuall in stormes: the same (it may be) which the *Graecians* were wont in the *Mediterranean* to call *Castor* and *Pollux*,[11] of which, if one onely appeared without the other, they tooke it for an evill signe of great tempest. The *Italians,* and such, who lye open to the *Adriatique* and *Tyrrene* Sea, call it (a *sacred Body*) *Corpo sancto:* the *Spaniards* call it *Saint Elmo,*[12] and have an authentique and miraculous Legend for it. Be it what it will, we laid other foundations of safety or ruine, then in the rising or falling of it, could it have served us now miraculously to have taken our height by, it might have strucken amazement, and a reverence in our devotions, according to the due of a miracle. But it did not light us any whit the more to our knowne way, who ran now (as doe hoodwinked men) at all adventures, sometimes North, and North-east, then North and by West, and in an instant againe varying two or three points, and sometimes halfe the compasse. East and by South we steered away as much as we could to beare upright, which was no small carefulnesse nor paine to doe, albeit we much unrigged our Ship, threw over-boord much luggage, many a Trunke and Chest (in which I suffered no meane losse) and staved many a Butt of Beere, Hogsheads of Oyle, Syder, Wine, and Vinegar, and heaved away all our Ordnance on the Starboord side, and had now purposed to have cut downe the Maine Mast, the more to lighten her, for we were much spent, and our men so weary, as their strengths together failed them, with their hearts, having travailed now from Tuesday till Friday morning, day and night, without either sleepe or foode; for the leakage taking up all the hold, wee could neither come by Beere nor fresh water; fire we could keepe none in the Cooke-roome to dresse any meate, and carefulnesse, griefe, and our turne at the Pumpe or Bucket, were sufficient to hold sleepe from our eyes.

And surely Madam, it is most true, there was not any houre (a matter of admiration) all these dayes, in which we freed not twelve hundred Barricos[13] of water, the least whereof contained six gallons, and some eight, besides three deepe Pumpes continually going, two beneath at the Capstone, and the other above in the halfe Decke, and at each Pumpe foure thousand stroakes at the least in a watch; so as I may well say, every foure houres, we quitted one hundred tunnes of water: and from

tuesday noone till friday noone, we bailed and pumped two thousand
tunne, and yet doe what we could, when our Ship held least in her,
(after tuesday night second watch) shee bore ten foote deepe, at which
stay our extreame working kept her one eight glasses,[14] forbearance
whereof had instantly sunke us, and it being now Friday, the fourth
morning, it wanted little, but that there had bin a generall determination, to have shut up hatches, and commending our sinfull soules to God,
committed the Shippe to the mercy of the Sea: surely, that night we must
have done it, and that night had we then perished: but see the goodnesse
and sweet introduction of better hope, by our mercifull God given unto us.
Sir *George Summers,* when no man dreamed of such happinesse, had discovered and cried Land. Indeed the morning now three quarters spent,
had wonne a little cleerenesse from the dayes before, and it being better
surveyed, the very trees were seene to move with the winde upon the
shoare side: whereupon our Governour commanded the Helme-man to
beare up, the Boateswaine sounding at the first, found it thirteene fathome,
& when we stood a little in seven fatham; and presently heaving his lead
the third time, had ground at foure fathome, and by this, we had got her
within a mile under the South-east point of the land, where we had somewhat smooth water. But having no hope to save her by comming to an
anker in the same, we were inforced to runne her ashoare, as neere the
land as we could, which brought us within three quarters of a mile of
shoare, and by the mercy of God unto us, making out our Boates, we had
ere night brought all our men, women, and children, about the number
of one hundred and fifty, safe into the Iland.

We found it to be the dangerous and dreaded Iland, or rather Ilands of
the *Bermuda:* whereof let mee give your Ladyship a briefe description,
before I proceed to my narration. And that the rather, because they be
so terrible to all that ever touched on them, and such tempests, thunders,
and other fearefull objects are seene and heard about them, that they be
called commonly, *The Devils Ilands,* and are feared and avoyded of all
sea travellers alive, above any other place in the world. Yet it pleased our
mercifull God, to make even this hideous and hated place, both the place
of our safetie, and meanes of our deliverance. . . .

SO soone as wee were a little setled after our landing, with all the con-
veniencie wee might, and as the place, and our many wants would give us
leave, wee made up our long Boate (as your Ladyship hath heard) in fashion
of a Pinnace, fitting her with a little Deck, made of the Hatches of our

ruin'd ship, so close that no water could goe in her, gave her Sayles and
Oares, and intreating with our Masters Mate *Henry Ravens* (who was supposed a sufficient Pilot) wee found him easily wonne to make over therewith, as a Barke of *Aviso*[15] for *Virginia,* which being in the height of
thirtie seven degrees, five degrees from the Iland which we were, might
bee some one hundred and fortie leagues from us, or thereabouts (reckoning to every degree that lies North-east, and Westerly twentie eight
English leagues) who the twentie eight of August being Munday, with sixe
Saylers, and our Cape Merchant *Thomas Whittingham* departed from us
out of *Gates* his Bay: but to our much wonder returned againe upon the
Wednesday night after, having attempted to have got cleere of the Iland,
from the North North-east to the South-west, but could not as little water
as shee drew, which might not bee above twentie inches for shoales and
breaches, so as he was faine to go out from *Summers* Creeks, and the same
way we came in on the South South-east of the Ilands, and from thence
wee made to Sea the Friday after the first of September, promising if hee
lived and arrived safe there, to returne unto us the next new Moone with
the Pinnace belonging to the Colony there: according unto which instructions were directed unto the new Leiftenant Governour, and Councell
for our Governour here, for which the Ilands were appointed carefully
to be watched, and fires prepared as Beacons to have directed and wafted
him in, but two Moones were wasted upon the Promontory before mentioned, and gave many a long and wished looke round about the Horizon,
from the North-east to the South-West, but in vaine, discovering nothing
all the while, which way soever we turned our eye, but ayre and sea.

You may please, excellent Lady, to know the reason which moved our
Governour to dispatch this long Boat, was the care which hee tooke for
the estate of the Colony in this his inforced absence: for by a long practised experience, foreseeing and fearing what innovation and tumult
might happily arise, amongst the younger and ambitious sprits of the new
companies to arrive in *Virginia,* now coming with him along in this same
Fleet, hee framed his letters to the Colony, and by a particular Commission confirmed Captaine *Peter Win* his Lieutenant Governour, with an
Assistance of sixe Counsellours, writing withall to divers and such Gentlemen of qualitie and knowledge of vertue, and to such lovers of goodnesse
in this cause whom hee knew, intreating them by giving examples in themselves of duty and obedience, to assist likewise the said Lieutenant Governour, against such as should attempt the innovating of the person (now

named by him) or forme of government, which in some Articles hee did
likewise prescribe unto them: and had faire hopes all should goe well, if
these his letters might arrive there, untill such time as either some Ship
there (which hee fairely beleeved) might bee moved presently to adventure
for him: or that it should please the right honourable, the Lordes, and the
rest of his Majesties Councell in *England,* to addresse thither the right
honourable the *Lord Lawar* (one of more eminencie and worthinesse) as
the project was before his comming forth, whilest by their honourable
favours, a charitable consideration in like manner might bee taken of
our estates to redeeme us from hence. For which purpose likewise our
Governour directed a particular letter to the Councell in *England,* and
sent it to the foresaid Captaine *Peter Winne* (his now to bee chosen
Lieutenant Governour) by him to bee dispatched (which is the first)
from thence into *England.*

In his absence Sir *George Summers* coasted the Ilands, and drew the
former plat of them, and daily fished, and hunted for our whole company,
untill the seven and twentieth of November, when then well perceiving
that we were not likely to heare from *Virginia,* and conceiving how the
Pinnace which *Richard Frubbusher* was a building would not be of burthen
sufficient to transport all our men from thence into *Virginia* (especially
considering the season of the yeare, wherein we were likely to put off)
he consulted with our Governour, that if hee might have two Carpenters
(for we had foure, such as they were) and twenty men, over with him into
the maine Iland, he would quickly frame up another little Barke, to second
ours, for the better fitting and conveiance of our people. Our Governour,
with many thankes (as the cause required) cherishing this so carefull and
religious consideration in him (and whose experience likewise was somewhat in these affaires) granted him all things sutable to his desire, and to
the furthering of the worke: who therefore had made ready for him all
such tooles and instruments, as our owne use required not: and for him,
were drawne forth twenty of the ablest and stoutest of the company,
and the best of our men, to hew and square timber, when himselfe then,
with daily paines and labour, wrought upon a small Vessell, which was
soone ready as ours: at which wee leave him a while busied, and returne
to our selves. In the meane space did one *Frubbusher,* borne at *Graves
end,* and at his comming forth now dwelling at *Lime* House (a painefull
and well experienced Shipwright, and skilfull workman) labour the building of a little Pinnace: for the furtherance of which, the Governour dis-

pensed with no travaile of his body, nor forbare any care or study of minde, perswading (as much and more) an ill qualified parcell of people, by his owne performance, then by authority, thereby to hold them at their worke, namely to fell, carry, and sawe Cedar, fit for the Carpenters purpose (for what was so meane, whereto he would not himselfe set his hand, being therefore up earely and downe late?) yet neverthelesse were they hardly drawne to it, as the Tortoise to the inchantment, as the Proverbe is, but his owne presence and hand being set to every meane labour, and imployed so readily to every office, made our people at length more diligent, and willing to be called thereunto, where, they should see him before they came. In which, we may observe how much example prevailes above precepts, and how readier men are to be led by eyes, then eares.

And sure it was happy for us, who had now runne this fortune, and were fallen into the bottome of this misery, that we both had our Governour with us, and one so solicitous and carefull, whose both example (as I said) and authority, could lay shame, and command upon our people: else, I am perswaded, we had most of us finished our dayes there, so willing were the major part of the common sort (especially when they found such a plenty of victuals) to settle a foundation of ever inhabiting there; as well appeared by many practises of theirs (and perhaps of some of the better sort) Loe, what are our affections and passions, if not rightly squared? how irreligious, and irregular they expresse us? not perhaps so ill as we would be, but yet as wee are; some dangerous and secret discontents nourished amonst us, had like to have bin the parents of bloudy issues and mischiefes; they began first in the Sea-men, who in time had fastened unto them (by false baits) many of our land-men likewise, and some of whom (for opinion of their Religion) was carried an extraordinary and good respect. The Angles wherewith chiefly they thus hooked in these disquieted Pooles, were, how that *in Virginia, nothing but wretchednesse and labour must be expected, with many wants, and a churlish intreaty, there being neither that Fish, Flesh, nor Fowle, which here (without wasting on the one part, or watching on theirs, or any threatning, and are of authority) at ease, and pleasure might be injoyed: and since both in the one, and the other place, they were (for the time) to loose the fruition both of their friends and Countrey, as good, and better were it for them, to repose and seate them where they should have the least outward wants the while.* This, thus preached, and published each to

other, though by such who never had bin more onward towards *Virginia,*
then (before this Voyage) a Sculler could happily rowe him (and what
hath a more adamantive power to draw unto it the consent and attraction
of the idle, untoward, and wretched number of the many, then liberty,
and fulnesse of sensuality?) begat such a murmur, and such a discontent,
and disunion of hearts and hands from this labour, and forwarding the
meanes of redeeming us from hence, as each one wrought with his Mate
how to divorse him from the same.

And first (and it was the first of September) a conspiracy was discovered, of which six were found principals, who had promised each
unto the other, not to set their hands to any travaile or endeavour which
might expedite or forward this Pinnace: and each of these had severally
(according to appointment) sought his opportunity to draw the Smith,
and one of our Carpenters, *Nicholas Bennit,* who made much profession
of Scripture, a mutinous and dissembling Imposter; the Captaine, and one
of the chiefe perswaders of others, who afterwards brake from the society
of the Colony, and like outlawes retired into the Woods, to make a settlement and habitation there, on their party, with whom they purposed to
leave our Quarter, and possesse another Iland by themselves: but this
happily found out, they were condemned to the same punishment which
they would have chosen (but without Smith or Carpenter) and to an Iland
farre by it selfe, they were carried, and there left. Their names were *John
Want,* the chiefe of them, an *Essex* man of *Newport* by *Saffronwalden,*
both seditious, and a sectary[16] in points of Religion, in his owne prayers
much devout and frequent, but hardly drawne to the publique, insomuch
as being suspected by our Minister for a *Brownist,*[17] he was often compelled to the common Liturgie and forme of Prayer.[18] The rest of the
confederates were *Christopher Carter, Francis Pearepoint, William Brian,
William Martin, Richard Knowles:* but soone they missed comfort (who
were farre removed from our store) besides, the society of their acquaintance had wrought in some of them, if not a loathsomenesse of their offence,
yet a sorrow that their complement was not more full, and therefore a
wearinesse of their being thus untimely prescribed; insomuch, as many
humble petitions were sent unto our Governor, fraught full of their seeming sorrow and repentance, and earnest vowes to redeeme the former trespasse, with example of dueties in them all, to the common cause, and
generall businesse; upon which our Governour (not easie to admit any
accusation, and hard to remit an offence, but at all times sorry in the

punishment of him, in whom may appeare either shame or contrition) was easily content to reacknowledge them againe.

Yet could not this be any warning to others, who more subtilly began to shake the foundation of our quiet safety, and therein did one *Stephen Hopkins* commence the first act or overture: A fellow who had much knowledge in the Scriptures, and could reason well therein, whom our Minister therefore chose to be his Clarke,[19] to reade the Psalmes, and Chapters upon Sondayes, at the assembly of the Congregation under him: who in January the twenty foure, brake with one *Samuel Sharpe* and *Humfrey Reede* (who presently discovered it to the Governour) and alleaged substantiall arguments, both civill and divine (the Scripture falsly quoted) that it was no breach of honesty, conscience, nor Religion, to decline from the obedience of the Governour, or refuse to goe any further, led by his authority (except it so pleased themselves) since the authority ceased when the wracke was committed, and with it, they were all then freed from the government of any man; and for a matter of Conscience, it was not unknowne to the meanest, how much we were therein bound each one to provide for himselfe, and his owne family: for which were two apparant reasons to stay them even in this place; first, abundance by Gods providence of all manner of good foode: next, some hope in reasonable time, when they might grow weary of the place, to build a small Barke, with the skill and helpe of the aforesaid *Nicholas Bennit,* whom they insinuated to them, albeit hee was now absent from his quarter, and working in the maine Iland with Sir *George Summers* upon his Pinnace, to be of the conspiracy, that so might get cleere from hence at their owne pleasures: when in *Virginia,* the first would be assuredly wanting, and they might well feare to be detained in that Countrie by the authority of the Commander thereof, and their whole life to serve the turnes of the Adventurers, with their travailes and labours. This being thus laid, and by such a one, who had gotten an opinion (as I before remembred) of Religion; when it was declared by those two accusers, not knowing what further ground it had or complices, it pleased the Governour to let this his factious offence to have a publique affrant, and contestation by these two witnesses before the whole Company, who at the toling of a Bell, assemble before a Corps du guard, where the Prisoner was brought forth in manacles, and both accused, and suffered to make at large, to every particular, his answere; which was onely full of sorrow and teares, pleading simplicity, and deniall. But hee being onely found, at theis time,

both the Captaine, and the follower of this Mutinie, and generally held
worthy to satisfie the punishment of his offence, with the sacrifice of
his life, our Governour passed the sentence of a Martiall Court upon him,
such as belongs to Mutinie and Rebellion. But so penitent hee was, and
made so much moane, alleadging the ruine of his Wife and Children in
this his trespasse, as it wrought in the hearts of all the better sort of the
Company, who therefore with humble intreaties, and earnest supplica-
tions, went unto our Governor, whom they besought (as likewise did
Captaine *Newport,* and my selfe) and never left him untill we had got
his pardon.

In these dangers and divellish disquiets (whilest the almighty God
wrought for us, and sent us miraculously delivered from the calamities
of the Sea, all blessings upon the shoare, to content and binde us to grate-
fulnesse) thus inraged amongst our selves, to the destruction each of
other, into what a mischiefe and misery had wee bin given up, had wee
not had a Governour with his authority, to have suppressed the same?
Yet was there a worse practise, faction, and conjuration a foote, deadly
and bloudy, in which the life of our governour, with many others were
threatned, and could not but miscarry in his fall. But such is ever the
will of God (who in the execution of his judgements, breaketh the fire-
brands upon the head of him, who first kindleth them) there were, who
conceived that our Governour indeede neither durst, nor had authority
to put in execution, or passe the act of Justice upon any one, how
treacherous or impious so ever; their owne opinions as much deceiving
them for the unlawfulnesse of any act, which they would execute: daring
to justifie among themselves, that if they should be apprehended, before
the performance, they should happily suffer as Martyrs. They persevered
therefore not onely to draw unto them such a number, and associates as
they could worke in, to the abandoning of our Governour, and to the
inhabiting of this Iland. They had now purposed to have made a surprise
of the Store-house, and to have forced from thence, what was therein
either of Meale, Cloath, Cables, Armes, Sailes, Oares, or what else it
pleased God that we had recovered from the wracke, and was to serve
our generall necessity and use, either for the reliefe of us, while wee staied
here, or for the carrying of us from this place againe, when our Pinnace
should have bin furnished.

But as all giddy and lawlesse attempts, have alwayes something of
imperfection, and that as well by the property of the action, which

holdeth of disobedience and rebellion (both full of feare) as through the ignorance of the devisers themselves; so in this (besides those defects) there were some of the association, who not strong inough fortified in their owne conceits, brake from the plot it self, and (before the time was ripe for the execution thereof) discovered the whole order, and every Agent, and Actor thereof, who neverthelesse were not suddenly apprehended, by reason the confederates were divided and seperated in place, some with us, and the chiefe with Sir *George Summers* in his Iland (and indeede all his whole company) but good watch passed upon them, every man from thenceforth commanded to weare his weapon, without which before, we freely walked from quarter to quarter, and conversed among our selves, and every man advised to stand upon his guard, his owne life not being in safety, whilest his next neighbour was not be be trusted. The Centinels, and nightwarders doubled, the passages of both the quarters were carefully observed, by which meanes nothing was further attempted; untill a Gentleman amongst them, one *Henry Paine,* the thirteenth of March, full of mischiefe, and every houre preparing something or other, stealing Swords, Adises, Axes, Hatchets, Sawes, Augers, Planes, Mallets, &c. to make good his owne bad end, his watch night comming about, and being called by the Captaine of the same, to be upon the guard, did not onely give his said Commander evill language, but strucke at him, doubled his blowes, and when hee was not suffered to close with him, went off the Guard, scoffing at the double diligence and attendance of the Watch, appointed by the Governour for much purpose, as he said: upon which, the Watch telling him, if the Governour should understand of this his insolency, it might turne him to much blame, and happily be as much as his life were worth. The said *Paine* replyed with a setled and bitter violence, and in such unreverent tearmes, as I should offend the modest eare too much to expresse it in his owne phrase; but the contents were, how *that the Governour had no authoritie of that qualitie, to justifie upon any one (how meane soever in the Colonie) an action of that nature, and therefore let the Governour* (said hee) *kisse, &c.* Which words, being with the omitted additions, brought the next day unto every common and publique discourse, at length they were delivered over to the Governour, who examining well the fact (the transgression so much the more exemplary and odious, as being in a dangerous time, in a Confederate, and the successe of the same wishtly listened after, with a doubtfull conceit, what might be the issue of so notorious a boldnesse and impudency) calling the said *Paine* before him, and the whole Company, where (being soone convinced both by the witnesse, of the Commander, and many which were upon the watch with him) our Governour, who had now the eyes of the whole Colony fixed upon him, condemned him to be instantly hanged; and the ladder being ready, after he had made many confessions, hee earnestly desired, being a Gentleman, that hee might be shot to death, and towards the evening he had his desire, the Sunne and his life setting together.

But for the other which were with Sir *George,* upon the Sunday following (the Barke beeing now in good forwardnesse) and readie to lanch in short time, from that place (as we supposed) to meet ours at a pond of fresh water, where they were both to bee mored, untill such time as being fully tackled, the wind should serve faire, for our putting to Sea together, being the eighteenth of March, hearing of *Paynes* death, and fearing hee had appeached them, and discovered the attempt (who poore Gentleman therein, in so bad a cause, was too secret and constant to his owne faith ingaged unto them, and as little needed, as urged thereunto, though somewhat was voluntarily delivered by him) by a mutuall consent forsooke their labour, and Sir *George Summers,* and like Out-lawes betooke them to the wild Woods: whether meere rage, and greedinesse after some little Pearle (as it was thought) wherewith they conceived they should for ever inrich themselves, and saw how to obtaine the same easily in this place, or whether, the desire for ever to inhabite heere, or what other secret else moved them thereunto, true it is, they sent an audacious and formall Petition to our Governour, subscribed with all their names and Seales: not only intreating him, that they might stay heere, but (with great art) importuned him, that he would performe other conditions with them, and not wave, nor evade from some of his owne promises, as namely to furnish each of them with two Sutes of Apparell, contribute Meale rateably for one whole yeere, so much among them, as they had weekly now, which was one pound and an halfe a weeke (for such had beene our proportion for nine moneths). Our Governour answered this their Peition, writing to Sir *George Summers* to this effect.

That true it was, at their first arrivall upon this Iland, when it was feared how our meanes would not extend to the making of a Vessell, capeable and large enough, to transport all our Countrimen at once, indeed out of his Christian consideration (mourning for such his Contrimen, who comming under his command, he foresaw that for a while, he

*was like enough to leave here behind, compelled by tyrannie of necessitie)
his purpose was not yet to forsake them so, as given up like Savages: but
to leave them all things fitting to defend them from want and wretchednesse, as much at least as lay in his power, to spare from the present use
(and perhaps necessitie of others, whose fortunes should be to be transported with him) for one whole yeere or more (if so long by any casualtie,
the ships which he would send unto them might be staied before their
arrivall, so many hazards accompanying the Sea) but withall intreated
Sir* George *to remember unto his Company (if by any meanes he could
learne where they were) how he had vowed unto him, that if either his
owne meanes, his authoritie in* Virginia, *or love with his friends in*
England, *could dispatch for them sooner, how farre it was from him,
to let them remayne abandoned, and neglected without their redemption
so long: and then proceeded, requesting Sir* George Summers *againe, to
signifie unto them, since now our owne Pinnasse did arise to that burthen,
and that it would sufficiently transport them all, beside the necessitie of
any other Barke: and yet, that since his Barke was now readie too, that
those consultations, howsoever charitable and most passionate in themselves, might determine, as taken away thereby, and therefore, that he
should now bee pleased to advise them well, how unanswerable this grant
or consent of his should be: first, to his Majestie for so many of his subjects, next to the Adventurers, and lastly, what an imputation and infamy
it might be, to both their owne proper reputations, and honours, having
each of them authoritie in their places, to compell the adversant and
irregular multitude, at any time, to what should bee obedient and honest,
which if they should not execute, the blame would not lye upon the
people (at all times wavering and insolent) but upon themselves so weake
and unworthy in their command. And moreover intreated him by any
secret practice to apprehend them, since that the obstinate, and precipitate
many, were no more in such a condition and state to bee favoured, then
the murmuring and mutinie of such Rebellious and turbulent Humorists,
who had not conscience nor knowledge, to draw in the yoke of goodnesse, and in the businesse for which they were sent out of* England:
*for which likewise, at the expence and charge of the Adventurers, they
were to him committed, and that the meanest in the whole Fleet stood
the Company in no lesse than twentie pounds, for his owne personall
Transportation, and things necessary to accompany him. And therefore
lovingly conjured Sir* George, *by the worthinesse of his (heretofore) well*

*mayntayned reputation, and by the powers of his owne judgement, and
by the verture of that ancient love and friendship, which had these many
yeeres beene setled betweene them, to doe his best, to give this revolted
Company (if he could send unto them) the consideration of these particulars, and so worke with them (if he might) that by faire meanes (the
Mutinie reconciled) they would at length survey their owne errours,
which hee would bee as readie, upon their rendring and comming into
pardon, as he did now pittie them; assuring them in generall and particular, that whatsoever they had sinisterly committed, or practised
hitherto against the Lawes of dutie and honestie, should not in any sort
be imputed against them.*

In which good Office Sir *George Summers* did so nobly worke, and
heartily labour, as hee brought most of them in, and indeed all, but
Christopher Carter, and *Robert Waters,* who (by no meanes) would any
more come amongst Sire *Georges* men, hearing that Sir *George* had commanded his men indeed (since they would not be intreated by faire
meanes) to surprize them (if they could) by any device or force. From
which time they grew so cautelous and wary, for their owne ill, as at our
comming away, wee were faine to leave them behind. That *Waters* was
a Sayler, who at his first landing upon the Iland (as after you shall heare)
killed another fellow Sayler of his, the bodie of the murthered and
Murtherer so dwelling, as prescribed now together.

During out time of abode upon these Ilands, wee had daily every
Sunday two Sermons preached by our Minister, besides every Morning
and Evening at the ringing of a Bell, wee repayred all to publique Prayer,
at what time the names of our whole Company were called by Bill, and
such as were wanting, were duly punished.

The contents (for the most part) of all our Preachers Sermons, were
especially of Thankefulnesse and Unitie, &c.

It pleased God also to give us opportunitie, to performe all the other
Offices, and Rites of our Christian Profession in this Iland: as Marriage,
for the sixe and twentieth of November, we had one of Sir *George Summers*
his men, his Cooke, named *Thomas Powell,* who married a Maid Servant
of one Mistris *Horton,* whose name was *Elizabeth Persons:* and upon
Christmasse Eve, as also once before, the first of October; our Minister
preached a godly Sermon, which being ended, he celebrated a Communion,
at the partaking whereof our Governour was, and the greatest part of our
Company: and the eleventh of February, wee had the childe of one *John*

Ro[l]fe christened a Daughter, to which Captaine *Newport* and my selfe
were Witnesses, and the aforesaid Mistris *Horton* and we named it *Bermuda,*
as also the five and twentieth of March, the wife of one *Edward Eason,*
being delivered the weeke before of a Boy, had him then christened, to
which Captaine *Newport* and my selfe, and Master *James Swift* were God-
fathers, and were named it *Bermudas.*

Likewise, we buried five of our company, *Jeffery Briars, Richard Lewis,
William Hitchman,* and my God-daughter, *Bermuda Rolfe,* and one untimely *Edward Samuell* a Sayler, being vilanously killed by the foresaid
Robert Waters, (Sayler likewise) with a shovell, who strake him therewith
under the lift of the Eare, for which he was apprehended, and appointed
to be hanged the next day, (the fact being done in the twilight) but being
bound fast to a Tree all night, with many Ropes, and a Guard of five or
six to attend him, his fellow Saylers (watching the advantage of the
Centinels sleeping) in despight and disdaine that Justice should bee shewed
upon a Sayler, and that one of their crue should be an example to others,
not taking into consideration, the unmanlinesse of the murther, nor the
horror of the sinne, they cut his bands, and conveyed him into the Woods,
where they fed him nightly, and closely, who afterward by the mediation
of Sir *George Summers,* upon many conditions, had his tryall respited
by our Governour.

Wee had brought our Pinnasse so forward by this time, as the eight
and twentieth of August we having laid her Keele. The sixe and twentieth
of February, we now began to calke: old Cables we had preserved unto
us, which affoorded Ocam enough: and one barrell of Pitch, and another
of Tarre, we likewise saved, which served our use some little way upon the
Bilg, wee breamed her otherwise with Lime made of Wilke-shels, and an
hard white stone which we burned in a Kill, slaked with fresh water, and
tempered with Tortoyses Oyle. The thirtieth of March being Frieday,
we towed her out in the morning Spring-tyde, from the Wharfe where she
was built, boying her with foure Caske in her runne only: which opened
into the North-west, and into which when the Breeze stood North and by
West with any stiffe gale, and upon the Spring-tydes, the Sea would increase with that violence, especially twice it did so, as at the first time
(before our Governour had caused a solid Causey of an hundred load of
stone to bee brought from the Hils and Neighbour Rockes, and round
about her ribs from stemme to stemme, where it made a pointed Baulke,
and thereby brake the violence of the Flowe and Billowe) it indangered

her overthrow and ruine, beeing greene as it were upon the Stockes. With
much difficultie, diligence, and labour, we saved her at the first, all her
Bases, Shores, and Piles, which under-set her, being almost carried from
her, which was the second of January, when her knees were not set to,
nor one joynt firme: We launched her unrigged, to carrie her to a little
round Iland, lying West North-West, and close aboord to the backe side of
our Iland, both neerer the Ponds and Wels of some fresh water, as also
from thence to make our way to the Sea the better: the Channell being
there sufficient and deepe enough to leade her forth, when her Masts,
Sayles, and all her Trimme should bee about her. Shee was fortie foot by
the Keele, and nineteene foot broad at the Beame, six foote floore, her
Rake forward was fourteene foot, her Rake aft from the top of her Post
(which was twelve foot long) was three foot, shee was eight foot deepe
under the Beame, betweene her Deckes she was foure foot and an halfe,
with a rising of halfe a foot more under the fore Castle, of purpose to
scowre the Decke with small shot, if at any time wee should bee borded
by the Enemie. Shee had a fall of eighteene inches aft, to make her
sterage and her great Cabbin the more large: her sterage was five foote
long, and sixe foote high, with a close Gallerie right aft, with a window
on each side, and two right aft. The most part of her timber was Cedar,
which we found to be bad for shipping, for that it is wonderous false inward, and besides it is so spault or brickle, that it will make no good
plankes, her Beames were all Oke of our ruine ship, and some plankes in
her Bow of Oke, and all the rest as is aforesaid. When shee began to
swimme (upon her launching) our Governour called her The Deliverance,
and shee might be some eighty tunnes of burthen.

Before we quited our old quarter, and dislodged to the fresh water
with our Pinnasse, our Governour set up in Sire *George Summers* Garden
a faire *Muemosynon* in figure of a Crosse, made of some of the timber
of our ruined shippe, which was scrued in with strong and great trunnels[20]
to a mightie Cedar, which grew in the middest of the said Garden, and
whose top and upper brances he caused to be lopped, that the violence
of the winde and weather might have the lesse power over her.

In the middest of the Crosse, our Governour fastened the Picture of
his Majestie in a piece of Silver of twelve pence, and on each side of the
Crosse, hee set an Inscription graven in Copper, in the *Latine* and *English*
to this purpose.

In memory of our great Deliverance, both from a mightie storme and leake: wee have set up this to the honour of God. It is the spoyle of an English *ship (of three hundred tunne) called the* Sea Venture, *bound with seven ships more (from which the storme divided us) to* Virginia, *or* Nova Britania, *in* America. *In it were two Knights, Sir* Thomas Gates *Knight, Governour of the* English *Forces and Colonie there: and Sir* George Summers *Knight, Admirall of the Seas. Her Captaine was* Christopher Newport, *Passengers and Mariners shee had beside (which came all safe to Land) one hundred and fiftie. We were forced to runne her ashore (by reason of her leake) under a Point that bore South-east from the Northerne Point of the Iland, which wee discovered first the eight and twentieth of July 1609.*

About the last of Aprill, Sir *George Summers* launched his Pinnasse, and brought her from his building Bay, in the Mayne Iland, into the Channell where ours did ride, and shee was by the Keele nine and twentie foot: at the Beame fifteene foot and an halfe: at the Loofe fourteene, at the Trausam nine, and she was eight foote deepe, and drew sixe foote water, and hee called her the *Patience*.

FRom this time we only awaited a favourable Westerly wind to carrie us forth, which longer then usuall now kept at the East, and South-east, the way which wee were to goe. The tenth of May early, Sir *George Summers* and Captaine *Newport* went off with their long Boates, and with two Canoaes boyed the Channell, which we were to leade it out in, and which was no broader from Shoales on the one side and Rockes on the other, then about three times the length of our Pinnasse. About ten of the clocke, that day being Thursday, we set sayle an easie gale, the wind at South, and by reason no more winde blew, we were faine to towe her with our long Boat, yet neither with the helpe of that, were we able to fit our Bowyes, but even when we came just upon them, we strucke a Rocke on the starboord side, over which the Bowye rid, and had it not beene a soft Rocke, by which meanes she bore it before her, crushed it to pieces, God knowes we might have beene like enough, to have returned anew, and dwelt there, after tenne monethes of carefulness and great labour a longer time: but God was more mercifull unto us. When shee strucke upon the Rocke, the Cock-swayne one *Walsingham* beeing in the Boat with a quicke spirit (when wee were all amazed, and our hearts failed) and so by Gods goodnesse we led it out at three fadome,

and three fadome and an halfe water. The wind served us easily all that
day and the next, when (God be ever praysed for it) to the no little joy
of us all, we got cleere of the Ilands. After which holding a Southerly
course, for seven dayes wee had the winde sometimes faire, and sometimes scarce and contrarie: in which time we lost Sir *George Summers*
twice, albeit we still spared him our mayne top-sayle, and sometimes
our fore course too.

The seventeenth of May we saw change of water, and had much Rubbish
swimme by our ship side, whereby wee knew wee were not farre from
Land. The eighteenth about midnight wee sounded, with the Dipsing
Lead, and found thirtie seven fadome. The nineteenth in the morning
we sounded, and had nineteene and an halfe fadome, stonie, and sandie
ground. The twentieth about midnight, we had a marvellous sweet smell
from the shoare (as from the Coast of *Spaine,* short of the Straits) strong
and pleasant, which did not a little glad us. In the morning by day breake
(so soone as one might well see from the fore-top) one of the Saylers
descryed Land about an houre after, I went up and might discover two
Hummockes[21] to the Southward, from which (Northward all along) lay
the Land, which wee were to Coast to *Cape Henrie.*[22] About seven of
the clocke we cast forth an Anchor, because the tyde (by reason of the
Freshet that set into the Bay) made a strong Ebbe there, and the winde
was but easie, so as not beeing able to stemme the Tyde, we purposed to
lye at an Anchor untill the next flood, but the wind comming South-west
a loome gale about eleven, we set sayle againe, and having got over the
Barre, bore in for the Cape.

This is the famous *Chesipiacke Bay,* which wee have called (in honour
of our young Prince) Cape *Henrie* over against which within the Bay,
lyeth another Head-land, which wee called in honour of our Princely
Duke of *Yorke* Cape Charles; and these lye North-east and by East, and
South-west and by West, and they may bee distant each from the other
in breadth seven leagues, betweene which the Sea runnes in as broad as
betweene *Queeneburrough* and *Lee.*[23] Indeed it is a goodly Bay and a
fairer, not easily to be found.

The one and twentieth, beeing Munday in the morning, wee came up
within two miles of *Point Comfort,*[24] when the Captaine of the Fort discharged a warning Peece at us, whereupon we came to an Anchor, and
sent off our long Boat to the Fort, to certifie who we were; by reason of
the shoales which lye on the South-side, this Fort easily commands the

mouth of the River, albeit it is as broad as betweene *Greenwich,* and the Ile of *Dogges.* [25]

True it is, such who talked with our men from the shoare, delivered how safely all our ships the last yeere (excepting only the Admirall, and the little Pinnasse in which one *Michael Philes* commanded of some twentie tunne, which we towed a sterne till the storme blew) arrived, and how our people (well increased) had therefore builded this Fort; only wee could not learne any thing of our long Boat, sent from the *Bermudas,* but what wee gathered by the *Indians* themselves, especially from *Powhatan,* [26] who would tell our men of such a Boat landed in one of his Rivers, and would describe the people, and make much scoffing sport thereat: by which wee have gathered, that it is most likely, how it arrived upon our Coast, and not meeting with our River were taken at some time or other, at some advantage by the Savages, and so cut off. When our Skiffe came up againe, the good newes of our ships, and mens arrivall the last yeere, did not a little glad our Governour: who went soone ashoare, and assoone (contrary to all our faire hopes) had new unexpected, uncomfortable, and heavie newes of a worse conditon of our people above at *James* Towne.

Upon *Point Comfort* our men did the last yeere (as you have heard) rayse a little Fortification, which since hath beene better perfected, and is likely to proove a strong Fort, and is now kept by Captaine *James Davies* with forty men, and hath to name *Algernoone* Fort, so called by Captaine *George Percy,* whom we found at our arrival President of the Colony, and at this time like-wise in the Fort. When we got into the Point, which was the one and twentieth of May, being Munday about noone; where riding before an *Indian* Towne called *Kecoughton,* [27] a mightie Storm of Thunder, Lightning, and Raine, gave us a shrewd and fearefull welcome.

From hence in two dayes (only by the helpe of Tydes, no winde stirring) wee plyed it sadly up the River, and the three and twentieth of May we cast Anchor before *James* Towne, where we landed, and our much grieved Governour first visiting the Church caused the Bell to be rung, at which (all such as were able to come forth of their houses) repayred to Church where our Minister Master *Bucke* made a zealous and sorrowfull Prayer; finding all things so contrary to our expectations, so full of misery and misgovernment. After Service our Governour caused mee to reade his Commission, and Captaine *Percie* (then President) delivered up unto him his Commission, the old Patent and the Councell Seale. Viewing the Fort, we found the Pallisadoes torne downe, the Ports open, the Gates from off the hinges, and emptie houses (which Owners death had taken from them) rent up and burnt, rather then the dwellers would step into the Woods a stones cast off from them, to fetch other fire-wood: and it is true, the *Indian* killed as fast without, if our men stirred but beyond the bounds of their Block-house, as Famine and Pestilence did within; with many more particularities of their sufferances (brought upon them by their owne disorders the last yeere) then I have heart to expresse. In this desolation and misery our Governour found the condition and state of the Colonie, and (which added more to his griefe) no hope how to amend it or save his owne Company, and those yet remayning alive, from falling into the like necessities. For we had brought from the *Bermudas* no greater store of provision (fearing no such accidents possible to befall the Colony here) then might well serve one hundred and fiftie for a Sea Voyage: and it was not possible, at this time of the yeere to amend it, by any helpe from the *Indian.* For besides that they (at their best) have little more, then from hand to mouth, it was now likewise but their Seed-time, and all their Corne scarce put into the ground: nor was there at the Fort, (as they whom we found related unto us) any meanes to take fish, neither sufficient Seine, nor other convenient Net, and yet if there had, there was not one eye of Sturgeon yet come into the River. All which considered, it pleased our Governour to make a Speech unto the Company, giving them to understand, that what provision he had, they should equally share with him, and if he should find it not possible, and easie to supply them with some thing from the Countrey, by the endevours of his able men, hee would make readie, and transport them all into their Native Countrey (accommodating them the best that he could) at which there was a generall acclamation, and shoute of joy on both sides, for even our owne men began to be disheartened and faint, when they saw this misery amongst the others, and no lesse threatned unto themselves. . . .

[S] uch as we found in the Fort, had wee staid but foure dayes, had doubtlesse ben the most part of them starved, for their best reliefe was onely Mushrums, and some hearbes, which sod together, made but a thin and unsavory broath, and swelled them much. The pitty hereof moved our Governour to draw forth such provision as he had brought, proportioning a measure equally to every one a like. But then our Governor began to examine how long this his store would hold out, and found it (husbanded to the best advantage) not possible to serve longer then sixteene dayes: after which, nothing was to be possible supposed out of the Countrey (as before remembred) nor remained there then any meanes to transport him elsewhere. Whereupon hee then entred into the consultation with Sir *George Summers,* and Captaine *Newport,* calling unto the same the Gentlemen and Counsell of the former Government, intreating both the one and the other to advise with him what was best to be done. The provision which they both had aboord himselfe and Sir *George Summers,* was examined, and delivered, how it, being rackt to the uttermost, extended not above, as I said, sixteene dayes, after two Cakes a day. The Gentlemen of the Town, who knew better of the Country, could not give him any hope, or wayes, how to improve it from the *Indian.* It soone then appeared most fit, by a generall approbation, that to preserve and save all from starving, there could be no readier course thought on, then to abandon the Country, and accommodating themselves the best that they might, in the present Pinnaces then in the road, namely in the *Discovery* and the *Virginia,* and in the two, brought from, and builded at the *Bermudas,* the *Deliverance,* and the *Patience,* with all speede convenient to make for the New found Land, where (being the fishing time) they might meete with many *English* Ships into which happily they might disperse most of the Company.

This Consultation taking effect, our Governor having caused to be carried aboord all the Armes, and all the best things in the store, which might to the Adventurers make some commodity upon the sale thereof at home, and burying our Ordnances before the Fort gate, which looked into the River. The seventh of June having appointed to every Pinnace likewise his complement and number, also delivered thereunto a proportionable rate of provision, hee commanded every man at the beating of the Drum to repaire aboord. And because hee would preserve the Towne (albeit now to be quitted) unburned, which some intemperate and malicious people threatned, his owne Company he caused to be left ashoare, and was himselfe the last of them, when about noone giving a farewell, with a peale of small shot, wee set saile, and that night, with the tide, fell downe to an Iland in the River, which our people have called *Hogge Iland;* and the morning tide brought us to another Iland, which we have called *Mulberry Iland;* where lying at an ancor, in the afternoone stemming the tide, we discovered a long Boate making toward us, from Point Comfort: much descant we made thereof, about an houre it came up; by which, to our no little joyes, we had intelligence of the honorable my Lord *La Warr* his arrival before *Algarnoone* Fort the sixt of June, at what time, true it is, his Lordship having understood of our Governours resolution to depart the Country, with all expedition caused his Skiffe to be manned, and in it dispatched his letters by Captain *Edward Bruster* (who commandeth his Lordships Company) to our Governour, which preventing us before the aforesaid *Mulberry Iland,* (the eight of June aforesaid) upon the receipt of his honours letters, our Governour bore up the helme, with the winde comming Easterly, and that night (the winde so favourable) relanded all his men at the Fort againe: before which (the tenth of June, being Sunday) his Lordship had likewise brought his Ships, and in the afternoone, came a shoare with Sir *Ferdinando Weinman,* and all his Lordships followers. . . .

NOTES

1. Thomas Gates. Gates (1596-1621) was the first lt. governor of the Virginia Company; governor of Virginia 1611-14.

2. Lord La Warre. Thomas West, third Baron De La Warre (1577-1618), first governor and captain-general of the Virginia Company. In Virginia 1610-11; died on the voyage to the colony in 1618.

3. *Dominico* and *Mevis* [Nevis]. Islands in the West Indies discovered by Columbus in 1493.

4. *Hostium uxores* . . . "May the wives and children of our foes be the ones to feel the blind onset of rising Auster [southwind] and the roaring of the darkling sea, and the shores quivering with the shock!" Horace, *Odes,* III, xxvii, 21-24, trans. by C. E. Bennett (Cambridge, Mass.: Harvard University Press, 1914). Strachey has substituted *Haedi* for *Austri* in the original.

5. *Stentor.* A Greek herald before Troy, who in Homer's *Iliad* had a voice as loud as fifty men.

6. Candy. A vessel from Candia, the island of Crete.

7. *Ego quid* . . . "Full well I know what Hadria's [Adriatic's] black gulf can be and what the sins of clear Iapyx [northwest wind]." *Odes,* trans. Bennett.

8. *Aperto coelo.* Open air.

9. *Remora.* Any of several fishes with a highly developed suctorial disk on the top of the head; in legend the Remora was said to guide ships through perilous seas.

10. Pole, The North Star.

11. *Castor* and *Pollux*. The twin sons of Leda and brothers to Helen of Troy and Clytemnestra. They were among the argonauts who accompanied Jason to Colchis to recover the Golden Fleece.

12. *Saint Elmo.* A phenomenon of electrical storms, the bluish light or "fire" that appeared on mastheads was called St. Elmo after St. Erasmus (d. 303), who according to legend was martyred aboard ship. Spanish and Italian sailors regarded the fire as a sign of the Saint's protection.

13. Barricos. Small casks or kegs.

14. One eight glasses. At the same level during each four-hour period (eight glasses).

15. Barke of *Aviso*. A messenger vessel.

16. Sectary. A nonconformist in religious matters.

17. *Brownist:* A follower of Robert Browne (1550?-?1633). One of the earliest of English Puritans to advocate complete separation from the Church of England. His followers were also frequently described as Separatists (as were the American Pilgrims at Plymouth).

18. Common Liturgie and forme of Prayer. The Book of Common Prayer.

19. Clarke. Clerk, or lector.

20. Trunnels. Large wooden pegs, also called treenails.

21. Hummockes. Low, rounded hills, or a clump of trees as seen from the sea.

22. *Cape Henrie.* Cape of Northeast coast of Princess Anne County, Virginia, at present-day Virginia Beach; the southern boundary of the entrance of Chesapeake Bay.

23. *Queeneburrough* and *Lee* [Leigh]. That is, across the Thames estuary between Queenborough on Sheppey Island, Kent, and Leigh, Essex, a distance of approximately ten miles.

24. *Point Comfort.* Southern point of the Virginia peninsula between the York and James Rivers, south of Hampton at the site of present-day Fort Monroe.

25. *Greenwich* and the Ile of *Dogges.* Across the Thames at a point six miles southeast of London Bridge, a distance of approximately one-half mile.

26. *Powhatan.* Powhatan (1550?-1618), American Indian chief of a federation of Algonquian tribes, the Confederacy of Powhatan, in eastern Virginia. The father of Pocahontas, Powhatan figures largely in Captain John Smith's captivity and rescue.

27. *Kecoughton.* The site of present-day Newport News, Virginia.

Anthony Thacher

Some part of a Letter of Mr Anthony Thachar Written in
New England and sent to his Brother Mr Peter Thachar in
Old England Consarning his grat Deliverance Out of the
deapes of the Sea

The hurricane that struck the coast of New England
on the night of August 14, 1635, was remembered for
decades afterwards as the worst storm in anyone's experience. Trees were uprooted by the hundreds, houses were
smashed and overturned, ships were driven ashore; even
the tide was reversed for a time. It was also remembered
for the tragedy that devastated the Thacher and Avery
families, colonists who had only recently arrived in Massachusetts from Wiltshire, England. The Thachers and
Averys were on their way from Newbury to Marblehead
when the hurricane overtook the vessel in which they were
sailing. The disaster quickly achieved prominence in New
England history and legend, and even today the physical
reminders remain as Thacher's Island and Avery's Rock.

Anthony Thacher later described the tragedy in a letter
to his brother Peter in Salisbury, Wiltshire. According to
Increase Mather, the letter was written "within a few dayes
after that eminent Providence hapned unto him, matters
were then fresh in his memory." Thacher, who had been a
tailor in England, thereafter settled in Marshfield, Massachusetts, and later in Yarmouth, where he died in 1668.

Thacher's letter is one of the most eloquent of the sea-

Anthony Thacher's narrative is from the manuscript in the British
Library, London, and is published with the permission of the British
Library Board.

deliverances, emotionally charged and marked at every turn
by the writer's inward struggle. In precise, methodical prose,
Thacher supplies detail after graphic detail, sparing nothing,
conveying the full depth of his anguish. In the recording of
his personal struggle to accept emotionally what he knew to
be an act of Providence, Thacher achieved a sustained eloquence
of expression reminiscent of Anne Bradstreet's elegies on her
grandchildren, poems in which a similar tension is evident.
To the Puritan audience, ever mindful of the conflict between
the theologically conditioned head and the emotionally
ravished heart, Thacher's narrative had special meaning. At
any time, his is a heartrending and affecting story.

The original letter Thacher wrote to his brother has now been
lost, but two versions of the narrative exist. In 1684 Increase
Mather included a version in his *Essay for the Recording of
Illustrious Providences.* A somewhat longer manuscript version
has recently been discovered in the British Library by Everett
Emerson, who provided a modernized text of it in his *Letters
from New England* (Amherst: University of Massachusetts
Press, 1976). Apparently both Mather's version and the manuscript copy (which is not in Thacher's hand) worked from the
original letter. Mather was a good editor, and his is the tauter
narrative, but the manuscript version has the advantage of
including more of the original. Mather's version was also edited
by Alexander Young for his *Chronicles of the First Planters
of the Colony of Massachusetts Bay* (Boston: Little, Brown,
1846).

TEXT: Sloane Manuscript 922 in the British Library,
London.

But now with the Leafe I must alter my matter and Subject and turne my
drowned pen with my Shaking hand to write other newes and to rowes
up my heavy heart and Sadded Spirits to indite the story of Such sad
newes as never before this happened in New England And been Lamented
both in the publik on the pulpitt and concourse of the people and in
private in the Closett and in the same places hath Gods Name bene mangni-
fied for his great mercy and wonderfull deliverance of mee out of the
bottom of the angry Sea.

The Story is thus First there was a League of pertianall frendship Solumly made betweene my Cozen Avary[1] and my Selfe, made in Mr Graves his Ship,[2] never to forsake each other to the death but to be partaker each of others misery or welfare as also of habitation in one place.

Now it pleased God immeadiatly on our arivall unto New England there was an offer made unto us, and my Cozen Avary was invited to Marblehed by the men of that place to be their pastore there being as yeet no Church there planted, but there a town appointed by the whole Country to be planted there, intended for the good of the whole contry to set up the trade of fishing. Now because that many there (the most being fishers) were something Loose and remise in their cariage and behaviour; my Cozen was unwilling to goe thither and so refusing it We went to Newberry to Mr Parker and others of his acquaintance intending there to sitt downe and plant. But being Solicited so often both by the men of the place and by the Magistrats and Counselled to it by Mr Cotten[3] and most of the Ministers in the patten,[4] alleaging what a benifet we might doe both to the people there and also unto the Country and Common weal to Settel there a plantation, at Length we empraced it: and there Consented to goe. The men of Marblehed forth with sent a penace for us and our goods And we ware at Ipswich on twsday the XII of Agust[5] 1635 imbarked our Selves and all and every one of our familys, with all our goods and Substance for Marblehed, we being in all twenty three Souls, to witt eleven in my Cozens family and seven in mine and one Master William Elliott and fore Mariners, Whence the next morning haveing recommended our Selves unto the Lord, With Cherefull & Contented hearts we hoysed Saile for Marblehed.

But the Lord Sudenly turned our Chearfulnes into mourning and sadd Lamentation, Thus on friday the foretenth of August 1635 in the evening about tenn of the Clocke our Sails being old and donn, Wee haveing a fine fresh gale of winde were Split. Our Sailers because it was somthing darke would not put on new Sails presently, but determined to Cast their sheet Anchor and so to ride at Anchor untill the next morning and then to put on. But before daylight it pleased God to send so mighty a Storme as the Like was never felt in New England sence the English Came there nor in the memory of any of the Indeans; it was [so] Furious that our Anchor Came home, Where upon our Mariners Let Slipp more cable, yea even to the utmost end there of and so made it fast onely about the bitte whence it slipt a way end for end. Then our Saillers knew not what to doe but

were driven as pleased the Storme and waves. My Cozen and wee perceiving our danger, Solemly recommended our Selves to God the Lord both of
earch and Seas, exspectting with every wave to be Swollowed up &
drenched in the deepes. And as my Cozen, his Wife and Children and maid
Sarvant, My wife and my tender babes Sate Comforting and Chearing on
the other in the Lord, against gastly death which every moment Stares
us in the face and satte tryomphingly on each others forehead, Wee were
by the violence of the waves and fury of the windes by the Lords permission Lifted up upon a rocke betweene to hie rockes, yet all was but one
Rocke, but ragged, with the strocke where of the watter came into the
Pinace. So as we were presently up to the midles in watter as wete, The
Watters Came furiously and violently over us and against us, but by reasen
of the Rockes preportion Could not Lift us off, but beate her all to peeces:
Now Looke with mee upon our distresses, and Consider of my misery; who
beheld the Shippe broken, the watter in her and violently overwhelming
us: my goods and provision Swiming in the Seas, my Freendes almost
drowned and mine owne poore Children So untimely (if I may so terme
it without offence) before mine eyes halfe drowned and ready to be
Swollowed up and dashed to peeces against the rockes by the mercilesse
waves, and my Selfe ready to accompany them.

But I must goe one to an ende of this woefull relation. In the same
roome with us sate he that went Master of the Pinnace, not knowing what
to doe, Our fore mast was Cutt downe, our maine mast broken in three
peeces, the forepart of our Pinnace beaten away, Our goods Swimming
about the Seaes: My Children bewailing mee as not Pittying themselvs
And my Selfe bemoneing them poore Soules Whom I had accationed to
such an ende in their tender yeers, when as they Could Scarse be Cencible
of death, And so Likewise my Cozen, his Wife & his Children and both of
us bewailing each other in Our Lord and onely Saviour Jesus Christ in
whome onely we had Comfort and Cherefulnes in so much that from the
gratest to the Lest of us, there was not one Screech or out cry made,
but all as silent Sheepe were contentedly resolved to dye together Lovingly
as since our acquaintance we had Lived together frendly.

Now as I was sitting in the Cabbin roome doore, Loe one of the Saylors
by a wave being washed out of the pinnace was gotten in again, and Comming into the Cabbin roome over my backe Cryed out, Oh we are all Cast
away, Lord have mercy on us, I have bin washed over bord in to the Sea
and am gotten in againe; his speeches made mee Looke forth, and Look-

ing toward the Sea and seeing how wee were, I turned my selfe toward
my Cozen and the rest and [said] these words, Oh Cozen it hath pleased
God heare to Cast us between too Rockes, and the Shore not farr of from
us, for I saw the topp of trees when I Looked forth. Where upon the said
Master of the pinnace Looking up at the Suttel hole of the halfe decke
went out of it but I never saw him afterward. Then he that had bin in the
Sea went out againe by mee and Leapt over bord toward the rocke whom
afterward also I Could never see.

Now none were Left in the barke that I knew or Saw, but my Cozen
and his wife & Children, My Selfe and mine and his maid Sarvant. I put
[on] my grat Coat, a wascot of Cotten bit had neithe[r] Sleaves nor
skirts, a thine paire of breches, a paire of bots without Stockens. My
Coate I putt of me and Laid it under my poore babes feete to raise it out
of the watter (a poore Suporter) but my Cozen thought I would have fled
from him And sayd unto mee, O Cozen Leave us not, Let us die together,
and reached forth his hand unto mee, then I Letting goe my Sonne
Peters hand tooke him by the hand and said to him, I purpose it not
Whither Shall I goe, I am Willing & ready here to die with you, And my
poore Children, God be mercifull to us, ading these words, the Lord is
able to helpe and to deliver us. Hee replied Saying true Cozen, but what
his Pleasure is wee know not. I feare we have bin to unthankfull for former
marcys. But hee hath promised to deliver us from Sinne and Condemna-
tion through the all Sufficent Satisfaction of Jesus Christ, this therefore
we may Chalenge of him. To which I replying said that is all the deliverance I now desier and expect: Which words I had no sooner Spoken but
by a mighty wave, I was with a peece of the Barke washed out upon part
of the Rock where the wave Left mee almost drowned but recovering
my feet. [I] Saw above me on the Rocke my daughter Mary, to whom
I was no sooner gotten, but my Cozen Avary and his Eldest Sonne Came
to us; being all foure of us washed out with one and the same wave, Wee
went all into a small hole on the tope of the Rock whence Wee Called
to those in the pinace to Come unto Us. Supposing we had bin in more
Safty then they were in, my Wife seeing us there was Crept in to the
Scuttel of the halfe decke to Come unto us but presently another wave
dashing the Pinñace all to peeces Carried away my wife in the Scuttele as
shee was with the grater part of the halfe decke to the Shore where shee
was Safely Cast; but her Leges were something brused and much timber
of the Vessel being there also Cast Shee was sometime before shee Could

geet away washed with the waves. All the rest that were in the barke were drowned in the mercyles Seas.

We foure by that wave were Cleane swept away from off the Rocke also into the Sea, the Lord in one enstant of time disposing of the Souls of Us to his good Pleasure and Will. His Wonderfull mercy to mee was thus: Standing on the rocke as before you heard with my eldest daughter my Cozen and his eldest Son Looking upon and talking unto them in the barke, When as we ware by that Crewel wave washed of the rocke as before you heard. God in his marcy Caused me to fall by the stroche of the wave flat on my face, for my face was toward the Sea insomuch that as I was sliding downe the Rocke into the Sea, the Lord directed my tooes into a Joint in the rockes side as also the topes of Some of my fingers with my right hand by meanes whereof the waves Leaving mee I remained so, haveing only my head above the water. One my Left hand I espied a bord or Planke of the pinnace, and as I was reaching but my Left hand to Lay hold on it, by another wave Coming one the tope of the rocke I was washed away from the rocke and by the violence of the waves was driven hither & thither in the Sea a great while and had many dashes against the Rockes; at Length past hope of Life and wearied both in body and Spirit, I even gave out to nature, and being ready to receive in the Watters of death, I Lefted up both my heart and hands to the God of heaven (for note I had my Sences remaining & perfect with me all the time I was under and in the water) who at that instant, Lifted my head Clean above the tope of watters that so I might breath without hindrance by the waters. I stood boult upright as if I stood upon my feete but I felt no bottom, nor had any footing for to stand upon but the waters. While I was thus above the waters I saw a peece of the mast as I supposed about three foot Longe which I Labored to cach into my armes, but Suddenly I was over welmed with water and driven to and froe againe and at Last I felt the ground with my right foote. Immediatly I was violently throwen groveling on my face. When presently I recovering my feete was in the water up to my brest, and through Gods great mercy had my face to the Shore and not to the Sea. I made hast to get out, but was throwen down on my hands with the waves, and so with Saftie Crep forth to the dry Shore, Where blessing God, I turned about to Looke for my Children and freends, but saw neither them nor any part of the pinnace where I Left them as I supposed. But I saw my wife about a but Length from mee geeting her Selfe forth from amongst the timber of the broken barke,

but before I could geet unto her shee was gotten to the Shore. When we
ware Come ech to other we went up into the Land, and sat us downe
under a Ceder tree Which the winde had thrown down where wee Sate
about an hower even dead with Could, for I was glad to put of my bretchs
they being rent all to peeces in the rockes.

But now the storme was broken up, and the winde was Calme, but the
Sea remained rough and fearfull to us. My Legges was much brused and
Loe was my heart and other hurt had I none, neither had I taken in much
water.

But my hart would not Suffer me to sit still any Longer, but I would
goe to see if any more was gotten to the Land in Safty, especially hoping
to have met with Some of mine owe poore Children, but I could fine
none, neither dead nor yet Living. You Condole with mee, my further
miseryes, Who now began to Consider of my Losses. Now Called to my
remembrance the time and manner how and when I Last saw and Left
my Children and freends. One was severed from me Sitting on the Rocke
at my feete, the other three in the Pinnace. My Little babe (ah poore
Peter) Sitting in hiss Sister Ediths arms Who to the utmost of her power
Sheltered him out of the waters, My poore William standing Close unto
her. All three of them Looking rufully on mee on the Rocke, there very
Countinance Calling unto mee to helpe them, Whom I Could not goe
unto, neither Could they Come unto mee, neither Could the mercilesse
waves aforde mee Space or time to use any meanes attall either to helpe
them or my Selfe.

Oh I yeet See their Cheekes poore Silent Lambs pleading pity and
helpe at my hands. Then on the other side to Consider the Losse of my
deare freends with the spoile and Losse of all our goods and provisuins,
my Selfe Cast upon an unknowen Land in a wilderness, I know not where,
and how to gett there we did not know. Then it Came into my minde
how I had accationed the death of my Children, who had accasioned
them out of their native Land, Who might have Left them there yea and
might have sent Some of them backe againe and Cost me nothing. These
and many such thoughts doe presse downe my heavy heart very much
but I Leave this till I see your face, before which time I feere I shall never
attaine Comfort. Now haveing no frende to whom I Can freely impart
my Selfe, Mr Cotton is now my Chifest frend to whom I have free welcome & accesse as also Mr Mavericke, Mr Warde, Mr Ward, Mr Hocker,
Mr Weles, Mr Warhad and Mr Parker also, Mr Noyes,[6] who use me frendly.

This is Gods goodnes to me, as also to sett the eyes of all the Country on mee especially of the Magistrates who much favour and Comfort mee.

But I let this Passe, and will proceed on in the Relation of Gods goodnesse unto mee. While I was in that desolate Island on which I was Cast, I and my Wife were almost naked both of us and wett and Could even unto death. When goeing downe to the Shore as before I Said, I found Cast one the Shore a Snapsacke in which I had a Steele and a flint & a powder horne, goeing further I found a drowned goate, then I found a hatt and my Sonne Willes Coat, both which I put on. My wife found on of her owne petticots which see putt on. I found also tow Cheeses and some butter driven ashore.

Thus the Lord sent us some Clothes to putt one & food to Sustaine our new Lives which he had given Lately unto us, and meanes also to make fire, for in my horne I had some gunpowder, which to my owne and other mens admiration was drie. So taking a peece of my wives neckclot which I dried in the Sunne I struck fire and so dried and warmed our wett bodies. And then Skined the goate, and haveing found a small brass pott wee boyled some of it. Our drinke was brakish water. Bread wee had none, there wee remained untill the Monday following where about three a Clocke in the Afternoone in a boat that Came that way we went off that desolate Island which I named after my own Name Thachers Woe. And the Rocke I named Avary his fall,[7] to the ende their fall and Losse and mine owne might be had in perpetuall remembrance. In the Island Lieth beuried the body of my Cozens eldest daughter whom I found dead on the Shore. On the Tuesday following in the afternoone, We arived att Marblehead Where I am now remaining in helth and good respect though very poore, and thus you have hard such relation as never before happened in New England, and as much bewailed as it was strang. What I shall doe or what Corse I shall take I know not; the Lord in his mercy derect me that I may so Lead the new Life which he hath given mee as may be most to his owne glory.

Praise God, and pray to God for mee.

NOTES

1. Avary. Rev. John Avery, formerly minister in Wiltshire, England.

2. Mr Graves his ship. The *James,* on which the Thachers and Averys sailed from Southampton in April 1635 and arrived in Boston on June 3.

3. Mr Cotton. Rev. John Cotton (1584-1652), teacher of Boston's First Church, the leading Puritan divine of early New England.

4. patten. Patent. The charter of Massachusetts Bay.

5. XII of August. Increase Mather's edition has this the eleventh, which seems correct as Thacher later refers to the following Friday as the fourteenth.

6. Mr Mavericke . . . Mr Noyes. John Maverick of Dorchester, Nathaniel Ward of Ipswich, Thomas Hook of Cambridge (and later Connecticut), Thomas Welde of Roxbury, John Warham of Dorchester, and Thomas Parker and James Noyes of Newbury. All were ministers. "Mr. Warde" has not been identified.

7. Thachers Woe; Avary his fall. Today called Thacher's Island and Avery's Rock, about two miles east of the southeast point of Cape Ann.

Henry Norwood

A Voyage to Virginia

A staunch royalist and loyal subject of King Charles I, Henry Norwood had battled Cromwell and the Puritans while a major in His Majesty's army during the English Civil War of 1642-48. Such then was his dismay at the execution of the king on January 30, 1649, that he, along with many others, determined to emigrate to Virginia. There the governor, Norwood's relative Sir William Berkeley, maintained a colony whose sympathies were decidedly royalist.

Perhaps none of our narratives is so embued with the spirit and personality of the man as is this one. The cavalier is on every page: courtly, brave, vigorously masculine, and disarmingly frank about his own short-comings. Even his apparent selfishness is more a reflection of his own bluff conviction in the propriety of the prerogatives of his rank and station. A physically imposing man, Norwood was a natural leader, quick to take charge of things, yet equally quick to admire courage and skill in others. Not only did his strong leadership help preserve the abandoned party of the unfortunate *Virginia Merchant,* but his natural tact and diplomacy stood him in good stead in his relations with the Indians of Virginia.

In 1650 Norwood was named Treasurer of Virginia by the exiled Charles II. Then from 1655 to 1659 he was imprisoned for his part in a royalist uprising in Worcestershire. After the Restoration he exercised his treasurership for twelve years, although apparently he did not return to Virginia again during his lifetime. He did, however, participate in the capture of New York from the Dutch in 1664. Later, using his quitrents from Virginia, Norwood purchased the ancestral estate and settled down to the life of a country gentleman in Gloucestershire, where among his other duties he wrote *A Voyage to Virginia.*

The manuscript of Norwood's *Voyage* has not been discovered, and the text was not printed until 1732 when it appeared in the second edition of Awnsham Churchill's *Collection of Voyages and Travels.* The narrative also appeared in Churchill's third edition (1744-46), and as number ten of volume III of Peter Force's *Tracts* (1836-46). An abbreviated version was published in the *Virginia Historical Register and Literary Advertiser* 2 (1849): 121-37, and Francis C. Rosenberger reprinted the narrative without notes in his *Virginia Reader: A Treasury of Writings from the First Voyages to the Present* (New York, Dutton: 1948; rpt. New York: Octagon, 1972).

Further information on Norwood is available in Fairfax Harrison, "Henry Norwood (1615-1689), Treasurer of Virginia," *Virginia Magazine of History and Biography* 33 (1925): 1-10; Howard Mumford Jones, *The Literature of Virginia in the Seventeenth Century,* 2nd ed. (Charlottesville: University Press of Virginia, 1968); and Leota Harris Hirsch, "Henry Norwood and His Voyage to Virginia," in *Essays in Early Virginia Literature,* ed. J. A. Leo Lemay (New York: Burt Franklin, 1977).

TEXT: Original issue of Churchill's second edition in the Folger Shakespeare Library.

THE month of *August Anno* 1649, being the time I engag'd to meet my two comrades, Major *Francis Morrison,* and Major *Richard Fox,* at *London,* in order to a full accomplishment of our purpose to seek our for-

tunes in *Virginia,* (pursuant to our agreement the year before in *Holland*)
all parties very punctually appear'd at the time and place assign'd, and
were all still in the same mind, fully bent to put in practice what we had
so solemnly agreed upon, our inclinations that way being nothing abated,
but were rather quicken'd, by the new changes that we saw in the state
of things, and that very much for the worse: For if our spirits were somewhat depress'd in contemplation of a barbarous restraint upon the person
of our king in the *Isle of Wight;* to what horrors and despair must our
minds be reduc'd at the bloody and bitter stroke of his assassination, at
his palace of *Whitehall?*[1]

This unparallel'd butchery made the rebels cast away the scabbards of
their swords with both their hand, in full resolution never to let them
meet again, either by submission or capitulation; so that the sad prospect
of affairs in this juncture, gave such a damp to all the royal party who
had resolv'd to persevere in the principle which engag'd them in the war,
that a very considerable number of nobility, clergy, and gentry, so cir-
cumstanc'd, did fly from their native country, as from a place infected
with the plague, and did betake themselves to travel any where to shun
so hot a contagion, there being no point on the compass that would not
suit with some of our tempers and circumstances, for transportation
into foreign lands.

Of the number who chose to steer their course for *America,* such of
them as inclin'd to try their fortunes at *Surinam,*[2] *Barbadoes,*[3] *Antigua,*[4]
and the *Leeward Islands,*[5] were to be men of the first rate, who wanted
not money or credit to balance the expence necessary to the carrying on
the sugar works: And this consideration alone was enough to determine
our choice for *Virginia,* had we wanted other arguments to engage us in
the voyage. The honour I had of being nearly related to Sir *William
Barkeley*[6] the governor, was no small incitation to encourage me with a
little stock to this adventure: Major *Morrison* had the king's commission
to be captain of the fort; and Mr. *Fox* was to share in our good or bad
success: But my best cargaroon[7] was his majesty's gracious letter in my
favour, which took effect beyond my expectation, because it recommended
me (above whatever I had or could deserve) to the governor's particular
care.

To proceed then, without any further *exordium,* to the subject of this
narrative: It fell out to be about the first day of *September,* Anno 1649,
that we grew acquainted on the *Royal-Exchange*[8] with Capt. *John Locker,*

A New Map of Virginia, Maryland, Pensilvania and New Yarsey by Robert Morden, from Richard Blome, *The Present State of His Majesties Isles and Terrories in America* (London, 1687). Courtesy of the Folger Shakespeare Library, Washington, D.C.

whose bills upon the posts made us know he was master of a good ship, (untruly so call'd) *The Virginia Merchant,* burden three hundred tons, of force thirty guns, or more: We were not long in treaty with the captain, but agreed with him for ourselves and servants at six pounds a head, to be transported into *James River;* our goods to be paid for at the current price.

About the fifteenth day, we were order'd to meet the ship at *Gravesend,*[9] where the captain was to clear with his merchants, and we to make our several payments; which when we had perform'd, we staid not for the ship, but took post for the *Downs,*[10] where, with some impatience, we expected her coming there. About the sixteenth *ditto,* we could see the whole fleet under sail, with a south-west wind; which having brought them to that road, kept them there at anchor, until our money was almost spent at *Deal.*[11]

September 23. the wind veered to the east, and we were summoned by signs and guns to repair on board. We had a fresh large gale three days, which cleared us of the channel, and put us out of soundings. With this propitious beginning we pursued our course for about twenty days, desiring to make the western islands; at which time the cooper began to complain, that our water-cask was almost empty, alledging, that there was not enough in hold, for our great family (about three hundred and thirty souls) to serve a month.

Our early want of water gave the master an alarm, and an occasion to consult with his officers for a remedy to so important an evil as that might be, if not timely helped. We were now, by all accounts, very near the western islands: *Fyall*[12] was that we were likely first to see, and our captain resolved to touch there to supply this defect, as the most commodious port for our purpose; and this was good news to the passengers, who are always glad at sight of land.

The day-break of *October* 14th, shewed us the peek of that island, the highest and most conspicuous land of any I have heard the seamen mention for land-marks, except that of *Teneriff.*[13] We stood directly for the harbour, which is also a good road, land-lock'd by the peek, which stands easterly about a mile distant from the town.

Assoon as we had saluted the castle, and return'd thanks for being civilly answer'd, captain *John Tatam,* our countryman, did the same from aboard his goodly ship the *John.* He was newly return'd from *Brasil,* in the kingdom of *Portugal*'s service, and now bound for *Lisbon,* with a rich freight, and some lady of great note, who with her family took passage with him.

The *English* merchants from the town came soon on board our ship, and gave us a very civil welcome. Of them, one Mr. *Andrews* invited me, with my two comrades, to refresh ourselves with fruit and meat such as the island produced. Our captain dined with us at his house, and so did captain *Tatam*, who in like courteous manner engaged us all to dine on board his ship the next day. We visited the peach-trees for our desert, of which I took at least a double share, and did not fail to visit and re-visit them in the dead of night, to satisfy a ravenous appetite nature has too prodigally given me for that species.

The next morning we surveyed the island, and thought the castle well fortified, especially on the sea-barr'd parts. The governor very civilly de-clared, he had lately received command from his majesty the king of *Portugal,* to treat all ships that belong'd and were faithful to the king of *Great Britain,* with more than common courtesy, as he, for his part, did in all we could desire.

A little before the time of dinner captain *Tatam* had sent his boats to bring us on board his ship; and it was well for us he did so, our ship's long-boat having been staved in pieces the night before, by the seamens neglect, who had all tasted so liberally of new wine, by the commodious-ness of the vintage, that they lay up and down dead drunk in all quarters, in a sad pickle.

The loss of our long-boat, as it was likely to make our watering tedious, and chargeable to the owners, so did it expose us to the hazard of many inconveniencies and perils in the whole course of our voyage, wherein frequent occasions occur that render that boat necessary to preserve the whole fabrick and lives of the ship and company; but to this breach no other reparation was applicable, but by recourse to that great stock of patience we were to be furnish'd withal for our support in the mighty straights we must encounter before we come to safe port.

Our captain disabled hereby to take the best course for our dispatch, made choice of the next best way to effect it, by the island boats; and having order'd his officers to use all diligence, and greater care than be-fore, he led the van into *Tatam*'s boat, which brought us safe on board the *John*.

At our arrival we were welcomed with a whole tyre of guns, and with a very kind aspect in the captain. He gave us excellent wines to drink before dinner, and at our meat as good of other sorts for concoction.

There was a handsome plenty of fish and fowl, several ways cooked, to
relish the Portuguese's and the English palates; and, which made our
entertainment more complete, he had prevailed with that great lady,
with her pretty son of about twelve years old (tho' contrary to the custom
even of the meaner sort at land) to sit at the table with us. She was taller
than the ordinary stature of that nation, finely shap'd, and had a very
clear skin; her eyes and hair vying for the blackness and beauty of the
jet; her modesty served, without any other art, to put a tincture of red
upon her face; for when she saw herself environed with a company of
strange faces, that had or might have had beards upon them, her blushes
raised in her face a delicate complexion of red and white.

The captain was our interpreter to tell her how much we esteemed
our selves honoured with her presence, which (for her better justification)
she was in a manner forced to grant us, the ship affording her no other
place fit for her retreat whilst we were there. Her young son sat by her,
on whom all our eyes were fix'd; and our minds united with one opinion,
that the air and lineaments of his face, full of sweetness, made him so
like our king when he was of that age, that, every one whispering his
thoughts to his neighbour, we all broke out at length in an open admiration of so great resemblance.

The healths of the two kings were passing about with thundering peals
of cannon; the youth was permitted by his mother to kiss the cup, and
drink a small portion to that of our king; and she was in so pleasant an
humour at this honour done to her son, that, to close our feast, she
ordered the table to be covered anew, and a handsome banquet placed
upon it, which we must partake of before we parted. To conclude this
rare treat, she repeated the health of our king in a sort of choice rich
wine that they make in *Brasil,* and drank the proportion she would take,
without the allay of water, which till then she drank with little or no
wine.

The approaching night made us take leave sooner than our inclinations
would have led us ashore, the merchants having told us, there was no safe
walking the streets in the night, for fear the *Pycaroes* (a sort of land-
pyrates) should snatch away our hats and looser garments, as they use
to treat strangers.

When we had paid our thanks to the captain, we desired his best language to make our compliments to the lady and her son, which she returned
with her wishes for our happy voyage.

Whilst we were caress'd in this manner on shipboard, the seamen on shore continued in their debauchery, with very little advance of our dispatch; the getting water was so tedious in itself for lack of our boat, and so full of delays by drunken contests of ours with the islanders, and with themselves, that, after some days stay upon the island, when our captain resolved to sail away, he found the ship in worse condition for liquors, than when we came on shore; for if we got a new supply of water, the proportion was hardly enough to balance the expence of beer that was spent in the time we got it.

Some days before we parted, we saw the *John* under sail, bound for *Lisbon;* where the captain no sooner arrived and discharged his ship, but he listed himself as a man of war in a squadron of ships then there, under command of the prince Rupert: which I mention for his honour, because I have heard the prince acknowledge in his favour, that he did his duty very well when there was like to be an occasion of trying his valour.

It was about the 22d of *October* that we took leave of our landlord and *Fyal.* We had store of black pigs for fresh meat, and I carry'd peaches without number. We parted with an easterly wind a topsail gale, which soon brought us into a trade-wind that favoured us at fifty or sixty leagues in twenty-four hours, till we came to the height of *Bermudas.* In that latitude it is the general observation of seamen, that the seas are rough, and the weather stormy. It was my fortune to have a curiosity to look out, when the officer on the watch shewed me a more than ordinary agitation of the sea in one particular place above the rest; which was the effect of what they call a spout, a raging in the bowels of the sea (like a violent birth) striving to break out, and at last springs up like a mine at land, with weight and force enough to have hoisted our ship out of her proper element, into the air (had the helm been for it) and to have made her do the supersalt; but God's providence secured us from that danger.

The sight of the island was welcome to all: the mariners learned thereby our true distance from cape *Hatteras;*[14] and passengers were relieved with hopes to be soon at shore from a hungry pester'd ship and company.

The gale continued fair till *November* 8: then we observed the water changed; and heaving the lead, we had thirty-five fathom of water, which was joyful news; our want of all things necessary for human life, made it so.

Towards break of day, weary of my lodging, I visited mate *Putts* on the watch, and would have treated him with brandy, but he refused that offer, unless I could also give him tobacco, which I had not. He said, it was near break of day, and he would look out to see what change there was in the water. No sooner were his feet upon the deck, but with stamps and noise he calls up the seamen, crying out, *All hands aloft! Breaches, breaches on both sides! All hands aloft!*

The seamen were soon on deck with this dismal alarm, and saw the cause thereof; but instead of applying their hands for their presevation (through a general despondency) they fell on their knees, commending their souls as at the last gasp. The captain came out at the noise to rectify what was amiss; but seeing how the case stood, his courage failed. Mate *Putts* (a stout seaman) took heart again, and cryed out, Is there no good fellow that will stand to the helm, and loose a sail? But of all the ship's crew there were but two foremast men that would be perswaded to obey commands, namely, *Thomas Reasin* and *John Smith,* men of innate courage, who, for their good resolution on that and divers other occasions in the various traverses of this voyage, deserve to have their names kept in lasting remembrance.

One of them got up and loosed the fore top-sail, to put the ship (if possible) in steerage way, and under command; the other stood to the helm, and he shifted it in a nick of time; for the ship was at the point of dashing on the starboard breach: and although, in the rest of the voyage, she was wont to be blamed for the ill quality of not feeling the helm, she did, in this important instance, redeem her credit, and fell round off for our rescue from that danger. But the sense of this escape lasted but a moment; for no sooner was she fallen from that breach, but another on the larboard-bow was ready to receive her. The ship's crew, by this time (reproached by the courage of *Reasin* and *Smith*) were all at work; and the helm shifting opportunely, she fell off again as before. The light of the day (which now broke forth) did discover our condition to be altogether as perillous as possible; for we now saw our selves surrounded with breaches; scarce any water like a channel appeared for a way to shun them. In this sad condition the ship struck ground, and raised such a war of water and sand together, which fell on the main-chains, that now all hopes of safety were laid aside; but the ship being still afloat, and the seamen all of them now under command, nothing was omitted for our preservation that was in their power.

Tom Reasin, seeing the ship go a-head in the likeliest water for a channel, and ordering the helm accordingly, heaved the lead; and after a little further advance into that new channel, wholly against his hopes, he had a good deal of water more than the ship drew, which soon mended upon

us, the next cast of the lead affording eighteen or twenty foot. We stood
to this channel, and the light of the morning enabling the quarter masters
to con the ship, we were by this miraculous mercy of God, soon clear of
the breaches at cape *Hatteras,* and got out to sea.

No sooner was the ship freed of this danger, and gotten a little into
the offing, but the seamen (like so many spirits) surveyed each other, as
if they doubted the reality of the thing, and shook hands like strangers,
or men risen from the other world, and did scarce believe they were,
what they seemed to be, men of flesh and blood. As they recovered
force, they made what sail they could to stand to sea-ward.

The gale came fresh at north-west, and this fresh gale did soon grow
up to a violent storm, which increased to so great a rigour, separating us
from the land at the rate of eight leagues a watch, merely with our fore-
courses, insomuch that the master thought it necessary to stop that
career; and, in order thereunto, he did advise with his officers to bring
the ship about, to furl all sails, and to try with the mizzen.

The mountainous towring north-west seas that this storm made, were
so unruly, that the seamen knew not how to work the ship about. We
were already at a great distance from land, and something must be done
to hinder our running off at that excessive rate. The first thing they did,
was to lower the main-yard, to give some ease to that mast, by laying it
on the ship's waste. Our great difficulty was, how to deal so with the
fore-sails, that the ship might work about with safety, or at least with
as little hazard as possible. All hands were too little to hale the sheet
close, in order to bring the ship about. Many great seas were shipp'd as
she came to work thro' the trough of the sea: amongst the rest one
chanc'd to break upon the poop (where we were quartered) and that with
so sad a weight, that we guessed a tun of water (at the least) did enter the
tarpaulin, and set us all on float who were in the round-house. The noise
it made by discharging itself in that manner, was like the report of a great
gun, and did put us all into a horrible fright, which we could not soon
shake off. This shock being past, the ship about, and our fore-sail handled,
we now lay trying with our mizzen.

I cannot forget the prodigious number of porpoises that did that evening
appear about the ship, to the astonishment of the oldest seamen in her.
They seemed to cover the surface of the sea as far as our eyes could discern; insomuch that a musket bullet, shot at random, could hardly fail to
do execution on some of them. This the seamen would look upon as of

bad portent, predicting ill weather; but in our case, who were in present possession of a storm, they appeared too late to gain the credit of fore-telling what should come upon us in that kind.

The seas thus enraged, and all in foam, the gale still increasing upon us, the officers on the watch made frequent visits to the round-house, to prepare the captain for some evil encounter which this mighty tempest must bring forth: and their fears proved reasonable; for, about the hours of ten or eleven, our new disasters did begin with a crash from aloft. All hands were summon'd up with loud cries, that the fore-topmast was come by the board, not alone, but in conjunction with the fore-mast head broken short off, just under the cap.

This was a sore business, and put all to their wits end to recover to any competent condition; what could be done was done to prevent further mischiefs; but the whole trim and rigging of a ship depending much upon stays and tackle fixed to that mast, we had reason to expect greater ruins to follow, than what had already befallen us. Mate *Putts* was then on the watch, and did not want his apprehension of what did soon ensue, which in all likelihood was to end in our utter perdition; for about the hours of twelve or one at night, we heard and felt a mighty sea break on our fore-ship, which made such an inundation on the deck where the mate was walking, that he retired back with all diligence up to his knees in water, with short ejaculations of prayers in his mouth, supposing the ship was foundering, and at the last gasp. This looked like a stroke of death in every seaman's opinion: the ship stood stock still, with her head under water, seeming to bore her way into the sea. My two comrades and my-self lay on our platform, sharing liberally in the general consternation. We took a short leave of each other, men, women, and children. All as-saulted with the fresh terror of death, made a most dolorous outcry throughout the ship, whilst mate *Putts* perceiving the deck almost freed of water, called out aloud for hands to pump. This we thought a lightning before death, but gave me occasion (as having the best sea legs) to look out and learn the subject of this astonishing alarm, which proved to arise from no less cause than the loss of our forecastle, with six guns, and our anchors (all but one that was fastened to a cable) together with our two cooks, whereof one was recovered by a strange providence.

This great gap, made by want of our forecastle, did open a passage into the hold for other seas that should break there before a remedy was found out to carry them off, and this made our danger almost insuperable; but it

fell out propitiously, that there were divers land-carpenter passengers, who
were very helpful in this distress; and, in a little time, a slight platform
of deal was tack'd to the timbers, to carry off any ordinary sea in the
present straight we were in; every moment of this growing tempest cutting
out new work to employ all hands to labour.

The bowsprit, too top-heavy in itself, having lost all stays and rigging
that should keep it steady, sway'd to and fro with such bangs on the
bows, that at no less rate than the cutting it close off, could the ship
subsist.

All things were in miserable disorder, and it was evident our danger
increas'd upon us: the stays of all the masts were gone, the shrouds that
remained were loose and useless, and it was easy to fortel, our main-top-
mast would soon come by the board. *Tom Reasin* (who was always ready
to expose himself) with an ax in his hand, ran up with speed to prevent
that evil, hoping thereby to ease the main-mast, and preserve it; but the
danger of his person, in the enterprize, was so manifest, that he was called
down amain; and no sooner was his foot upon the deck, but what was
feared came to pass with a witness, both main and topmast all came down
together, and, in one shock, fell all to the windward clear into the sea,
without hurt to any man's person.

Our main-mast thus fallen to the broadside, was like to incommode
us more in the sea, than in her proper station; for the shrouds and rigging
not losing the hold they had of the ship, every surge did so check the
mast (whose but-end lay charg'd to fall perpendicular on the ship's side)
that it became a ram to batter and force the plank, and was doing the
last execution upon us, if not prevented in time by edge-tools, which
freed the ship from that unexpected assault and battery.

Abandon'd in this manner to the fury of the raging sea, tossed up and
down without any rigging to keep the ship steady, our seamen frequently
fell overboard, without any one regarding the loss of another, every man
expecting the same fate, tho' in a different manner. The ceilings of this
hulk (for it was no better) were for the same cause so uneasy, that, in
many tumbles, the deck would touch the sea, and there stand still as if
she would never make another. Our mizzen mast only remained, by which
we hoped to bring the ship about in proper season, which now lay stemming to the east.

In this posture did we pass the tenth and eleventh days of *November;*
the twelfth in the morning we saw an *English* merchant, who shewed his

ensign, but would not speak with us, tho' the storm was abated, and the season more fit for communication. We imagined the reason was, because he would not be compelled to be civil to us: he thought our condition desperate, and we had more guns than he could resist, which might enable us to take what he would not sell or give. He shot a gun to leeward, stood his course, and turn'd his poop upon us.

Before we attempted to bring the ship about, it was necessary to refresh the seamen, who were almost worn out with toil and want of rest, having had no leisure of eating set meals for many days. The passengers, overcharged with excessive fears, had no appetite to eat; and (which was worst of all) both seamen and passengers were in a deplorable state as to the remaining victuals, all like to fall under extreme want; for the storm, by taking away the forecastle, having thrown much water into the hold, our stock of bread (the staff of life) was greatly damnified; and there remained no way to dress our meat, now that the cook-room was gone: the incessant tumbling of the ship (as has been observ'd) made all such cookery wholly impracticable. The only expedient to make fire betwixt decks, was, by sawing a cask in the middle, and filling it with ballast, which made a hearth, to parch pease, and broil salt beef; nor could this be done but with great attendance, which was many times frustrated by being thrown topsy-turvy in spite of all circumspection, to the great defeat of empty stomachs.

The seas were much appeas'd the seventeenth day, and divers *English* ships saw, and were seen by us, but would not speak with us; only one, who kept the pump always going, for having tasted too liberally of the storm, he was so kind as to accost us. He lay by till our wherry (the only surviving boat that was left us) made him a visit. The master shewed our men his leaks, and proposed, that ours would spare him hands to pump in lieu of any thing he could spare for our relief. He promised however to keep us company, and give us a tow to help to weather the cape, if occasion offered; but that was only a copy of his countenance; for in the night we lost each other, and we never heard more of him, tho' he was bound to our port.

The weather now invited us to get the ship about with our mizzen; and having done so, the next consideration was, how to make sail. The fore mast, all this while (as much as was of it) stood its ground: and as it was without dispute, that a yard must in the first place be fixed to it, so was it a matter of no small difficulty how to advance to the top of that great slippery stump, since he that would attempt it, could take no hold himself, nor receive any help for his rise, by other hands. This was a case that put all the ship's crew to a nonplus; but *Tom Reasin* (a constant friend at need, that would not be baffled by any difficulty) shewed by his countenance, he had a mind to try his skill to bring us out of this un-happy crisis. To encourage him the more, all passengers did promise and subscribe to reward his service, in *Virginia,* by tobacco, when God should enable us so to ḍo. The proportions being set down, many were the more generous because they never thought to see the place of payment, but expected to anticipate that by the payment of a greater debt to nature, which was like to be exacted every hour by an arrest of the merciless sea, which made small shew of taking bail for our appearance in *Virginia.*

The manner of *Tom Reasin's* ascent to this important work, was thus. Among the scatter'd parcels of the ship's stores he had the luck to find about half a dozen iron spikes fit for his purpose. His first onset was to drive one of them into the mast, almost to the head, as high as he could reach; which being done, he took a rope of about ten foot long and hav-ing threaded the same in a block or pulley, so as to divide it in the middle, he made both ends meet in a knot upon the spike, on both sides of the mast; so that the block falling on the contrary side, became a stirrup to mount upon for driving another spike in the same manner and thus from step to step, observing the best advantage of striking with his hammer in the smoothest sea, he got aloft, drove cleats for shrouds, to rest upon, and was soon in a posture of receiving help from his comrades, who got a yard and sails (with other accommodation) such as could be had, and thus we were enabled, in few hours time, to make some sail for our port.

The main-yard, that in the storm had been lowered to the wast to lie out of harm's way, was now preferred to the place of a main mast, and was accordingly fitted and accoutred, and grafted into the stump of what was left in the storm, some eight or ten foot from the deck. It was a hard matter to find out rigging answerable to that new-fashioned mast and yard; top-gallant sails and yards were most agreeable to this equipage, and was the best part of our remaining stores. The seas grew every moment smoother, and the weather more comfortable; so that for a while we began to shake off the visage of utter despair, as hoping ere long to see our selves in some capacity to fetch the cape. We discovered another ship bound to *Virginia,* who as frankly promised to stand by us, the wind at N. N. W. We did what could be done by a ship so mangled, to get the

weather-gage of the cape *Henry*,[15] conceiving ourselves to the southward
of cape *Hatteras:* but by taking an observation on a sun-shine day, we
found our selves carried by a current we knew not of, to the windward,
much beyond all our dead reckonings and allowances for sailing, insomuch
that when we thought we had been to the southward of the cape, we
found ourselves considerably shot to the north of *Achomat*,[16] and that
in the opinion of mate *Putts*, who was as our north star.

We passed this night with greater alacrity than we had done any other
since we had left *Fyall;* for mate *Putts*, our trusty pilot, did confidently
affirm, that, if the gale stood, there would be no question of our dining
the next day within the capes. This was seasonable news, our water being long since spent, our meat spoiled (or useless) no kind of victuals remaining to sustain life, but a bisket cake a day for a man; at which allowance there was not a quantity to hold out many days. In the dark time
of the night, in tacking about, we lost our new comrade, and with much
impatience we expected the approaching day; the wind N. W.

The morning appeared foggy, as the wind veered to the east, and that
did cover and conceal the land from our clearer sight; howbeit we concluded by mate *Putt*'s computation, we were well to the northward of
the capes. Many times he would mount the mizzen top for discovery,
as the weather seemed to clear up, and would espy and point at certain
hum-works[17] of trees that used to be his several land-marks in most of
the twenty-two voyages he had made to that plantation. Under this confidence he made more sail, the day-light confirming him in what he thought
was right.

All the forenoon we lost the sight of land and marks by trees, by reason
of the dark fogs and mists that were not yet dispelled; but assoon as the
sun, with a north-west gale, had cleared all the coast (which was about
the hours of two or three o'clock) mate *Putts* perceived his error from
the deck, and was convinced, that the hum-works of trees he had seen
and relied on for sure land-marks, had counter points to the south cape,
which had misguided him; and that it was the opening of the bay which
made the land at distance out of sight.

This fatal disappointment (which was now past human help) might
have met an easy remedy, had our sails and rigging been in any tolerable
condition to keep the windward gage (for we had both the capes in our
sight); but under our circumstances it was vain to endeavour such a thing;
all our equipage, from stem to stern, being no better than that of a west-

ern barge, and we could not lie within eleven or twelve points of the wind.

Defeated thus of lively hopes we had the night before entertain'd to sleep in warm beds with our friends in *Virginia*, it was a heavy spectacle to see our selves running at a round rate from it, notwithstanding all that could be done to the contrary. Nothing was now to be heard but sighs and groans thro' all that wretched family, which must be soon reduced to so short allowance, as would just keep life and soul together. Half a bisket cake a day to each (of which five whole ones made a pound) was all we had to trust to. Of liquors there remained none to quench thirst: *Malaga* sack[18] was given plentifully to every one, which served rather to inflame and increase thirst, than to extinguish it.

The gale blew fresh (as it uses to do) towards night, and made a western sea that carry'd us off at a great rate. Mate *Putts,* extremely abash'd to see his confidence so miserably deluded, grew sad and contemplative, even to the moving compassion in those whom his unhappy mistake had reduc'd to this misery. We cherish'd him the best we could, and would not have him so profoundly sad, for what was rather his misfortune than his fault.

The wind continued many days and nights to send us out into the ocean, insomuch that until we thought our selves at least an hundred leagues from the capes, the north-west gale gave us no truce to consider what was best to do. All little helps were used by top-gallant sails, and masts placed where they could be fixed, to keep the windward gage; but, for lack of borolins and other tackle to keep them stiff to draw, every great head-sea would check them in the wind, and rend and tear them in pieces; so that it was an ordinary exercise with us to lie tumbling in the sea a watch or two together, driving to leeward, whilst the broken sails were in hand to be repaired.

It would be too great a trial of the reader's patience to be entertain'd with every circumstance of our sufferings in the remaining part of this voyage, which continued in great extremity for at least forty days from the time we left the land, our miseries increasing every hour: I shall therefore omit the greatest number of our ill encounters, which were frequently repeated on us, and remember only what has in my thoughts been most remarkable, and have made the deepest impression in my memory.

To give us a little breathing, about the nineteenth day the wind shifted to the east, but so little to our avail (the gale so gentle, and the seas made against us like a strong current) that, with the sail we were able to make, we could hardly reckon the ship shortened the way, but that she rather lost ground. In less than two watches the gale faced about; and if we saved our own by the change, it was all we could pretend unto.

Our mortal enemy, the north-west gale, began afresh to send us out to sea, and to raise our terrors to a higher pitch. One of our pumps grew so unfix'd, that it could not be repair'd; the other was kept in perpetual motion; no man was excus'd to take his turn that had strength to perform it. Amongst the manifold perils that threatened every hour to be our last, we were in mortal apprehension, that the guns which were all aloft, would shew us a slippery trick, and some of them break loose, the tackle that held them being grown very rotten: and it was another providence they held so long, considering how immoderately the ship rolled, especially when the sails were mending that should keep them steady, which was very near a third part of our time, whilst we plied to the windward with a contrary gale.

To prevent this danger which must befal when any one gun should get loose, mate *Putts* found an expedient by a more than ordinary smooth water; and by placing timber on the hatch-way, to supply the place of shrouds, he got them safe in hold; which tended much to our good, not only in removing the present danger, but by making the ship (as seamen say) more wholesome, by haveing so great weight removed from her upper works into her centre, where ballast was much wanted.

But the intolerable want of all provisions both of meat and drink, jostled the sense of this happiness soon out of our minds. And to aggravate our misery yet the more, it was now our interest to pray that the contrary gale might stand; for whilst the westerly wind held, we had rain water to drink whereas at east the wind blew dry.

In this miserable posture of ship and provision, we reckoned our selves driven to the east, in less than a week's time, at least two hundred leagues, which we despaired ever to recover without a miracle of divine mercy. The storm continued so fresh against us, that it confounded the most knowing of our ship's company in advising what course to take. Some reckoned the ship had made her way most southerly, and therefore counselled we should put ourselves in quest of the *Bermudas* islands, as to the nearest land we could hope to make: but that motion had great opposition in regard of the winter season, which would daily produce insuperable difficulties, and give greater puzzle in the discovery of it, than our circumstances would admit. Others would say, The furthest way about, in our case, would prove the nearest way home; and judged it best to take advantage of the westerly winds, and impetuous seas made to our hands, to attempt returning back to the western islands, as a thing more likely to succeed (tho' at a great distance) than thus to strive against the stream without any hopeful prospect of gaining the capes. But that motion met with a more general aversion, because the run was so long, that tho' the gale had been in our own power to continue it, we could not have subsisted. Backwards we could not go, nor forwards we could not go in the course we desired: it followed then of consequence, that we must take the middle way; and it was resolved, that, without further persisting in endeavouring to gain our port by a close hale, we should raise our tackle, and sail tardy for the first *American* land we could fetch, tho' we ran to the leeward as far as the coast of *New England*.

Whilst this determination was agreed and put in practice, the famine grew sharp upon us. Women and children made dismal cries and grievous complaints. The infinite number of rats that all the voyage had been our plague, we now were glad to make our prey to feed on; and as they were insnared and taken, a well grown rat was sold for sixteen shillings as a market rate. Nay, before the voyage did end (as I was credibly inform'd) a woman great with child offered twenty shillings for a rat, which the proprietor refusing, the woman died.

Many sorrowful days and nights we spun out in this manner, till the blessed feast of *Christmas* came upon us, which we began with a very melancholy solemnity; and yet, to make some distinction of times, the scrapings of the meal-tubs were all amassed together to compose a pudding. *Malaga* sack, sea water, with fruit and spice, all well fryed in oyl, were the ingredients of this regale, which raised some envy in the spectators; but allowing some privilege to the captain's mess, we met no obstruction, but did peaceably enjoy our *Christmas* pudding.

My greatest impatience was of thirst, and my dreams were all of cellars, and taps running down my throat, which made my waking much the worse by that tantalizing fancy. Some relief I found very real by the captain's favour in allowing me a share of some butts of small claret he had concealed in a private cellar for a dead lift. It wanted a mixture of water for qualifying it to quench thirst; however, it was a present remedy, and a great refreshment to me.

I cannot forget another instance of the captain's kindness to me, of a like obligation. He singled me out one day to go with him into the hold to seek fresh water in the bottoms of the empty casks. With much ado we got a quantity to satisfy our longing, tho' for the thickness thereof it was not palatable. We were now each of us astride on a butt of *Malaga,* which gave the captain occasion to taste of their contents. We tasted and tasted it again; and tho' the total we drank was not considerable, yet it had an effect on our heads that made us suspend (tho' we could not forget) our wants of water. The operation this little debauch had upon the captain, was very different from what it wrought on me, who felt myself refresh'd as with a cordial; but the poor captain fell to contemplate (as it better became him) our sad condition; and being troubled in mind for having brought so many wretched souls into misery, by a false confidence he gave them of his having a good ship, which he now thought would prove their ruin; and being conscious, that their loss would lie all at his door, it was no easy matter to appease his troubled thoughts. He made me a particular compliment for having engaged me and my friends in the same bottom, and upon that burst into tears. I comforted him the best I could, and told him, We must all submit to the hand of God, and rely on his goodness, hoping, that the same providence which had hitherto so miraculously preserved us, would still be continued in our favour till we were in safety. We retired obscurely to our friends, who had been wondering at our absence.

The Westerly wind continued to shorten our way to the shore, tho' very distant from our port; but this did not at all incline us to change our resolution of sailing large for the first land; it did rather animate and support us in our present disasters of hunger and thirst, toil and fatigue. The hopes of touching land was food and raiment to us.

In this wearisome expectation we pass'd our time for eight or nine days and nights, and then we saw the water change colour, and had soundings. We approach'd the shore the night of *January* 3d, with little sail; and, as the morning of the fourth day gave us light, we saw the land; but in what latitude we could not tell, for that the officers, whose duty it was to keep the reckoning of the ship, had for many days past totally omitted that part; nor had we seen the sun a great while, to take observations, which (tho' a lame excuse) was all they had to say for that omission. But in truth it was evident, that the desperate estate of the ship, and hourly jeopardy of life did make them careless of keeping either log or

journal; the thoughts of another account they feared to be at hand, did
make them neglect that of the ship as inconsiderable.

About the hours of three or four in the afternoon of the twelfth eve,
we were shot in fair to the shore. The evening was clear and calm, the
water smooth; the land we saw nearest was some six or seven *English*
miles distant from us, our soundings twenty-five fathoms in good ground
for anchor-hold.

These invitations were all attractive to encourage the generality (especially the passengers) to execute what we had resolved on for the shore;
but one old officer who was husband for the ship's stores whilst there
were any, would not consent on any terms to trust the only anchor that
was left us for preservation, out of his sight at sea. His arguments to back
his opinion were plausible; as, *first,* The hazard of losing that only anchor
by any sudden storm, bringing with it a necessity to cut or slip, on which
every life depended. *2dly,* The shortness of the cable, very unfit for anchorage in the ocean: And *3dly,* The weakness of the ship's crew, many
dead and fallen over board, and the passengers weakened by hunger,
dying every day on the decks, or at the pump, which with great difficulty
was kept going, but must not rest.

Against the old man's reasonings was urged the very small remains of
bisket, at our short allowance, which would hardly hold a week; the assurance of our loss by famine if we should be forced to sea again by a north-
west storm, and the great possibility of finding a harbour to save our
ship, with our lives and goods, in some creek on the coast. These last reasons prevailed upon the majority against all negatives; and when the anchor
was let loose, mate *Putts* was ordered to make the first discovery of what
we might expect from the nearest land. He took with him twelve sickly
passengers, who fancied the shore would cure them; and he carri'd major
Morrison on shore with him in pursuit of such adventures as are next in
coarse to be related; for according to the intelligence that could be got
from land, we were to take our measures at sea, either to proceed on in
our voyage in that sad condition that has been in some proportion set
forth, or to land ourselves, and unload the ship, and try our fortunes
amongst the *Indians.*

In four or five hours time we could discover the boat returning with
mate *Putts* alone for a fetter, which we look'd upon as a signal of happy
success. When he came on board his mouth was full of good tidings, as

namely, That he discovered a creek that would harbour our ship, and that there was a depth of water on the bar, sufficient for her draught when she was light. That there was excellent fresh water, (a taste whereof major *Morrison* had sent me in a bottle.) That the shore swarm'd with fowl, and that major *Morrison* stayed behind in expectation of the whole ship's company to follow.

I opened mine ears wide to the motion, and promoted the design of our landing there with all the rhetorick and interest I had. The captain was no less forward for it, hoping thereby to save the lives of the passengers that remained: and that he might not wholly rely on mate *Putt*'s judgment in a matter wherein he was most concern'd, he embark'd with me in the wherry, with a kinsman of his, and some others; and the seamen were glad of my help to put the boat to shore, my hands having been very well season'd at the pump, by taking my turn for many weeks at the rate of three hours in twenty four. My passionate desires to be on shore at the fountain head to drink without stint, did not a little quicken me, insomuch that the six or seven miles I rowed on this occasion, were no more than the breadth of the *Thames* at *London,* at another time, would have been toilsome to me.

In our passage to the shore, the darkness of the evening made us glad to see the fires of our friends at land, which were not only our beacons to direct us to the company, but were also a comfortable relief to our chill bodies when we came near them, the weather being very cold (as it ever is) the wind northwest on that coast.

Assoon as I had set my foot on land, and had rendred thanks to almighty God for opening this door of deliverance to us, after so many rescues even from the jaws of death at sea, major *Morrison* was pleased to oblige me beyond all requital, in conducting me to the running stream of water, where, without any limitation of short allowance, I might drink my fill. I was glad of so great liberty, and made use of it accordingly, by prostrating myself on my belly, and setting my mouth against the stream, that it might run into my thirsty stomach without stop. The rest of the company were at liberty to use their own methods to quench their thirst; but this I thought the greatest pleasure I ever enjoyed on earth.

After this sweet refreshment, the captain, myself, and his kinsman crossed the creek in our wherry, invited thither by the cackling of wild-fowl. The captain had a gun charged, and the moon shining bright in his favour, he killed one duck of the flock that flew over us, which was roasted on a stick out of hand by the seamen, whilst we walk'd on the shore of the creek for further discovery.

In passing a small gullet we trod on an oyster bank that did happily furnish us with a good addition to our duck. When the cooks had done their parts, we were not long about ours, but fell on without using the ceremony of calling the rest of our company, which would have been no entertainment to so many, the proverb telling us, *The fewer the better chear.* The bones, head, legs, and inwards were agreed to be the cook's fees; so we gave God thanks, and return'd to our friends, without making boast of our good fortunes.

Fortifi'd with this repast, we inform'd our selves of the depth of water at the bar of the creek, in which the captain seem'd satisfi'd, and made shews in all his deportment, of his resolution to discharge the ship there in order to our safety. Towards break of day he ask'd me in my ear, If I would go back with him on board the ship? I told him, No, because it would be labour lost, in case he would persist in his resolution to do what he pretended, which he ratifi'd again by protestations, and so went off with his kinsman, who had a large coarse cloth gown I borrow'd of him to shelter me from the sharpest cold I ever felt, That which had some-times been a paradox to me, was by this experience made demonstrable, (*viz.*) That the land on the continent is much colder than that of islands tho' in the same latitude; and the reason is evident to any who shall con-sider the many accidents on the continent that cool the air by winds that come from the land; as in those parts of *America,* the mighty towring mountains to the northwest, covered all the year with snow, which does refrigerate the air even in the heat of summer; whereas winds coming from the sea are generally warm; and this hath proved a fatal truth to the in-habitants of *Virginia,* who, in the southeast winds, have gone to bed in sultry heat and sweat, without any covering, and have awaked in the night stiff and benumb'd with cold, without the use of their limbs, occa-sion'd by a shifting of the wind in the night from sea to land.

No sooner had the captain cleared himself of the shore but the day-break made me see my error in not closing with his motion in my ear. The first object we saw at sea was the ship under sail, standing for the capes with what canvass could be made to serve the turn. It was a very heavy prospect to us who remained (we knew not where) on shore, to see our selves thus abandon'd by the ship, and more, to be forsaken by

the boat, so contrary to our mutual agreement. Many hours of hard
labour and toil were spent before the boat could fetch the ship: and the
seamen (whose act it was to set sail without the captain's order, as we
were told after) car'd not for the boat whilst the wind was large to carry
them to the capes. But mate *Putts,* who was more sober and better natur'd,
discovering the boat from the mizzen-top, lay by till she came with the
captain on board.

In this amazement and confusion of mind that no words can express,
did our miserable distress'd party condole with each other our being so
cruelly abandon'd and left to the last despairs of human help, or indeed
of ever seeing more the face of man. We entered into a sad consultation
what course to take; and having, in the first place, by united prayers, implored the protection of Almighty God, and recommended our miserable
estate to the same providence, which in so many instances of mercy, had
been propitious to us at sea; the whole party desired me to be as it were
the father of this distressed family, to advise and conduct them in all
things I thought might most tend to our preservation. This way of government we agreed must necessarily reside in one, to avoid disputes, and
variety of contradictory humours, which would render our deliverance
the more impracticable; and it was thought most reasonable to be placed
in me, for the health and strength it had pleased God to preserve unto
me above my fellows, more than for any other qualification.

At the time I quitted the ship my servant *Thomas Harman,* a *Dutchman,* did, at parting, advertise me (for I left him on board to look to my
goods), that, in the bundle I ordered to be carri'd with me on shore, I
should find about thirty bisket cakes, which he, by unparallel'd frugality,
had saved out of his own belly in the great dearth and scarcity we lived
in. The thoughts of these biskets entring upon me at the time I was pressed
to accept this charge, I thought myself obliged in a christian equity, to let
every one partake of what I had; and so dividing the bread into nineteen
parts (which was our number) perhaps I added the fraction to my own
share.

It was, to the best of my remembrance, upon the fifth day of *January*
that we entred into this method of life, or rather into an orderly way
unto our graves, since nothing but the image of death was represented to
us: but that we might use our utmost endeavours to extract all the good
we could out of those evil symptoms that did every way seem to con-
found us, I made a muster of the most able bodies for arms and labour;

and, in the first place, I put a fowling-piece into every man's hand that
could tell how to use it. Amongst the rest, a young gentleman, Mr. *Francis
Cary* by name, was very helpful to me in the fatigue and active part of
this undertaking. He was strong and healthy, and was very ready for any
employment I could put upon him. He came recommended to me by Sir
Edward Thurlan, his genius leading him rather to a planter's life abroad,
than to any course his friends could propose to him in *England;* and this
rough entrance was like to let him know the worst at first.

All our woodmen and fowlers had powder and shot given them, and
some geese were killed for supper. Evening came on apace, and our resolution being taken to stay one night more in these quarters, I sent my
cousin *Cary* to head the creek, and make what discovery he could as he
passed along the shore, whether of *Indians* or any other living creatures
that were likely to relieve our wants, or end our days. To prepare like
men for the latter, we resolved to die fighting, if that should be the case;
or if, on the contrary, the *Indians* should accost us in a mein of amity,
then to meet them with all imaginable courtesy, and please them with
such trivial presents as they love to deal in, and so engage them into a
friendship with us.

My cousin *Cary* was not absent much above an hour, when we saw
him return in a contrary point to that he sallied out upon. His face was
clouded with ill news he had to tell us, namely, that we were now re-
siding on an island without any inhabitant, and that he had seen its whole
extent, surrounded (as he believed) with water deeper than his head; that
he had not seen any native, or any thing in human shape, in all his round,
nor any other creature besides the fowls of the air, which he would, but
could not, bring unto us.

This dismal success of so unexpected a nature, did startle us more than
any single misfortune that had befallen us, and was like to plunge us into
utter despair. We beheld each other as miserable wretches sentenc'd to a
lingering death, no man knowing what to propose for prolonging life any
longer than he was able to fast. My cousin *Cary* was gone from us without notice, and we had reason (for what followed) to believe he was
under the conduct of an angel; for we soon saw him return with a chearful look, his hands carrying somewhat we could not distinguish by any
name at a distance; but by nearer approach we were able to descry they
were a parcel of oysters, which, in crossing the island, as he stept over a
small current of water, he trode upon to his hurt; but laying hands on

what he felt with his feet, and pulling it with all his force, he found himself possessed of this booty of oysters, which grew in clusters, and were contiguous to a large bank of the same species, that was our staple subsistence whilst we remained there.

Whilst this very cold season continued, great flights of fowl frequented the island, geese, ducks, curlieus, and some of every sort we killed and roasted on sticks, eating all but the feathers. It was the only perquisite belonging to my place of preference to the rest, that the right of carving was annexed to it, wherein, if I was partial to my own interest, it was in cutting the wing as large and full of meat as possible; whereas the rest was measured out as it were with scale and compass.

But as the wind veered to the southward, we had greater warmth and fewer fowl, for they would then be gone to colder climates. In their absence we were confined to the oyster bank, and a sort of weed some four inches long, as thick as houseleek, and the only green (except pines) that the island afforded. It was very insipid on the palate; but being boiled with a little pepper (of which one had brought a pound on shore) and helped with five or six oysters, it became a regale for every one in turn.

In quartering our family we did observe the decency of distinguishing sexes: we made a small hut for the poor weak women to be by themselves; our cabbin for men was of the same fashion, but much more spacious, as our numbers were. One morning, in walking on the shore by the sea side, with a long gun in my hand loaden with small shot, I fired at a great flight of small birds called *Oxeyes*,[19] and made great slaughter among them, which gave refreshment to all our company.

But this harvest had a short end; and as the weather by its warmth, chased the fowl to the north, our hunger grew sharper upon us. And in fine, all the strength that remained unto us was employed in a heartless struggling to spin out life a little longer; for we still deemed our selves doom'd to die by famine, from whose sharpest and most immediate darts tho' we seemed to be rescued for a small time, by meeting these contingent helps on shore, yet still we apprehended (and that on too great probability) they only served to reprieve us for a little longer day of execution, with all the dreadful circumstances of a lingering death.

For the south-west winds that had carri'd away the fowl, brought store of rain; which meeting with a spring-tide, our chief magazine, the oyster bank, was overflown; and as they became more accessible, our bodies also decayed so sensibly, that we could hardly pull them out of their muddy beds they grew on. And from this time forward we rarely saw fowl; they now grew shy and kept aloof when they saw us contriving against their lives.

Add to this, our guns most of them unfix'd and out of order, and our powder much decayed, insomuch that nothing did now remain to prolong life, but what is counted rather sauce to whet, than substance to satisfy the appetite; I mean the oysters, which were not easily gotten by our crazy bodies after the quantity was spent that lay most commodious to be reach'd, and which had fed us for the first six days we had been on the island. And thus we wish'd every day to be the last of our lives (if God had so pleased) so hopeless and desperate was our condition, all expectation of human succour being vanished and gone.

Of the three weak women before mentioned, one had the envied happiness to die about this time; and it was my advice to the survivors, who were following her apace, to endeavour their own preservation by converting her dead carcase into food, as they did to good effect. The same counsel was embrac'd by those of our sex: the living fed upon the dead; four of our company having the happiness to end their miserable lives on *Sunday* night the—day of *January*. Their chief distemper, 'tis true, was hunger; but it pleased God to hasten their *exit* by an immoderate access of cold, caused by a most terrible storm of hail and snow at northwest, on the *Sunday* aforesaid, which did not only dispatch those four to their long homes, but did sorely threaten all that remained alive, to perish by the same fate.

Great was the toil that lay on my hands (as the strongest to labour) to get fuel together sufficient for our preservation. In the first place I divested myself of my great gown, which I spread at large, and extended against the wind in nature of screen, having first shifted our quarters to the most calm commodious place that could be found to keep us, as much as possible, from the inclemency of that prodigious storm.

Under the shelter of this traverse I took as many of my comrades as could be comprehended in so small a space; whereas those who could not partake of that accommodation, and were enabled to make provision for themselves, were forced to suffer for it. And it was remarkable, that notwithstanding all the provision that could possibly be made against the sharpness of this cold, either by a well-burning fire consisting of two or three loads of wood, or shelter of this great gown to the windward, we could not be warm. That side of our wearing cloaths was singed and

burnt which lay towards the flames, whilst the other side that was from
the fire, became frozen and congeal'd. Those who lay to the leeward of
the flame, could not stay long to enjoy the warmth so necessary to life,
but were forced to quit and be gone to avoid suffocation by the smoke
and flame.

When the day appeared, and the sun got up to dissipate the clouds,
with downcast looks and dejected, the survivors of us entred into a final
deliberation of what remained to be done on our parts (besides our prayers to Almighty God) to spin out a little longer time of life, and wait a
further providence from heaven for our better relief. There were still
some hands that retained vigour, tho' not in proportion to those difficulties we were to encounter, which humanly did seem insuperable. The
unhappy circumstance of our being coop'd up in an island, was that which
took from us all probable hopes of escaping this terrible death that did
threaten us every hour. Major *Morrison,* on whose counsel I had reason
to rely most, was extremely decayed in his strength, his legs not being
able to support him. It was a wonderful mercy that mine remained in
competent strength, for our common good, which I resolved, by God's
help, to employ for that end to the last gasp.

In this last resolution we had to make, I could not think on any thing
worthy my proposal, but by an attempt to cross the creek, and swim to
the main (which was not above an hundred yards over) and being there
to coast along the woods to the south-west (which was the bearing of
Virginia) until I should meet *Indians,* who would either relieve or destroy
us. I fancied the former would be our lot when they should see our conditions, and that no hurt was intended to them; or if they should prove
inhuman, and of a bloody nature, and would not give us quarter, why
even in that case it would be worth this labour of mine to procure a
sudden period to all our miseries.

I open'd my thoughts to this purpose to the company, who were sadly
surprized at the motion; but being fully convinc'd in their judgment,
that this was the only course that could be depended on (humanly speaking) for our relief, they all agreed it must be done.

To fortify me for this expedition, it was necessary that some provision
should be made for a daily support to me in this my peregrination. Our
choice was small; our only friend the oyster bank was all we had to rely
on; which being well stew'd in their own liquor, and put up into bottles,
I made no doubt, by God's blessing, but that two of them well filled,

would suffice to prolong my life in moderate strength, until I had obtain'd
my end. To accomplish this design, my cousin *Cary* laboured hard for
oysters, hoping to make one in the adventure.

About the ninth day of our being in the island, I fell to my oyster-
cookery, and made a good progress that very day; when in the heat of my
labour my cousin *Cary* brought me word, That he had just in that instant
seen *Indians* walking on the main, I suspended my cookery out of hand,
and hastened with all possible speed to be an eye-witness of that happy
intelligence; but with all the haste I could make I could see no such thing,
but judg'd it a chimera that proceeded from some operations of my cousin's
fancy, who was more than ordinary of a sanguine nature, which made him
see (as it were by inchantment) things that were not, having many times
been deluded (as I judg'd) by the same deception.

Defeated in this manner of my hopes to see *Indians* without the pains
of seeking them, I returned to my work, and continued at it till one
bottle was full, and myself tired: wherefore, that I might be a little re-
created, I took a gun in my hand; and hearing the noise of geese on our
shore, I approach'd them privately, and had the good hap to be the death
of one. This goose, now in my possession without witnesses, I resolved
to eat alone (deducting the head, bones, guts, &c. which were the cook's
fees) hoping thereby to be much the better enabled to swim the creek,
and perform the work I had upon my hand. I hung my goose upon the
twist of a tree in a shrubby part of the wood, whilst I went to call aside
our cook with his broach, and a coal of fire to begin the roast. But when
we came to the place of execution, my goose was gone all but the head,
the body stollen by wolves, which the *Indians* told us after, do abound
greatly in that island.

The loss of this goose, which my empty stomach look'd for with no
small hopes of satisfaction, did vex me heartily. I wished I could have
taken the thief of my goose to have serv'd him in the same kind, and to
have taken my revenge in the law of retaliation. But that which troubled
me more, was an apprehension that came into my mind, that this loss
had been the effect of divine justice on me, for designing to deal unequally
with the rest of my fellow-sufferers; which I thought, at first blush,
looked like a breach of trust: but then again when I consider'd the equity
of the thing, that I did it merely to enable myself to attain their preservation, and which otherwise I could not have done, I found I could absolve
myself from any guilt of that kind. Whatever I suffered in this disappoint-

ment, the cook lost not all his fees; the head and neck remained for him on the tree.

Being thus over-reach'd by the wolf, it was time to return to my cookery, in order to [prepare] my sally out of the island; for I had little confidence in the notice frequently brought me of more and more *Indians* seen on the other side, since my own eyes could never bear witness of their being there.

The next morning, being the ninth or tenth of our being there, I fell to work afresh, hoping to be ready to begin my journey that day; and being very busy, intelligence was brought, that a canoe was seen to lie on the broken ground to the south of our island, which was not discovered till now, since our being there: but this I thought might be a mistake cast in the same mould of many others that had deceived those discoverers, who fanci'd all things real according to their own wishes. But when it was told me, That *Indians* had been at the poor womens cabbin in the night, and had given them shell-fish to eat, that was a demonstration of reality beyond all suspicion. I went immediately to be inform'd from themselves, and they both avowed it for truth, shewing the shells (the like whereof I ne'er had seen) and this I took for proof of what they said.

The further account these women gave of the *Indians,* was, that they pointed to the south-east with their hands, which they knew not how to interpret, but did imagine by their several gestures, they would be with them again to-morrow. Their pointing to the south-east was like to be the time they would come, meaning nine o'clock to be their hour, where the sun will be at that time. Had the women understood their language, they could not have learned the time of the day by any other computation than pointing at the sun. It is all the clock they have for the day, as the coming and going of the *Cabuncks* (the geese) is their almanack or prognostick for the winter and summer seasons.

This news gave us all new life, almost working miracles amongst us, by making those who desponded, and totally yielded themselves up to the weight of despair, and lay down with an intent never more to rise again, to take up their beds and walk. This friendly charitable visit of the *Indians* did also put a stop to my preparations to seek them, who had so humanely prevented me, by their seeking ways to preserve and save our lives.

Instead of those preparations for my march which had cost me so much pains, I passed my time now in contriving the fittest posture our present condition would allow us to put on when these angels of light should appear again with the glad tidings of our relief; and the result was, that every able man should have his gun lying by his side, laden with shot, and as fit for use as possible, but not to be handled unless the *Indians* came to us like enemies (which was very unlikely, the premises considered) and then to sell our lives at as dear a rate as we could; but if they came in an amicable posture, then would we meet them unarm'd, chearfully, which the *Indians* like, and hate to see a melancholy face.

In these joyful hopes of unexpected deliverance by these *Indians,* did we pass the interval of their absence. Every eye look'd sharply out when the sun was at south-east, to peep through the avenues of the wood to discover the approaches of our new friends. When the sun came to the South we thought our selves forgotten by them, and began to doubt the worst, as losing gamesters, at play for their last estate, suspect some stab-cast[20] to defeat the hopes of the fairest game. We feared some miscarriage, either from their inconstancy by change of their mind, or that some un-look'd-for misfortune, that our evil fates reserved for us, had interposed for our ruin.

Scouts were sent out to the right and left hands, without discovery of any body all the forenoon: and then, considering our case admitted no delay, I began to resume my former resolution of swiming to them that would not come to us. But how wholesome soever this counsel might seem in itself, it was most difficult to be put in practice, in regard of the cold time.

The northerly wind that in these climates does blow very cold in the heat of summer, does much more distemper the air in the winter season (as our poor comrades felt that *Sunday* night to their cost) and did send so cold a gale upon the surface of the water in the creek I was to pass, that, in the general opinion of all the concern'd, it was not a thing to be attempted; and that if I did, I must surely perish in the act. I was easily perswaded to forbear an action so dangerous, and the rather, because I verily believed the *Indians* would bring us off, if our patience would hold out.

About the hours of two or three o'clock it pleased God to change the face of our condition for the best; for whilst I was busy at the fire in preparations to wait on them, the *Indians,* who had placed themselves behind a very great tree, discovered their faces with most chearful smiles, without any kind of arms, or appearance of evil design; the whole number of them (perhaps twenty or thirty in all) consisting of men, women and children; all that could speak accosting us with joyful countenances, shaking hands with every one they met. The words *Ny Top,* often repeated by them, made us believe they bore a friendly signification, as they were soon interpreted to signify my friend.

After many salutations and *Ny Tops* interchanged, the night approaching, we fell to parley with each other; but perform'd it in signs more confounded and unintelligible than any other conversation I ever met withal; as hard to be interpreted as if they had express'd their thoughts in the *Hebrew* and *Chaldean*[21] tongues.

They did me the honour to make all applications to me, as being of largest dimensions, equip'd in a camlet[22] coat glittering with galoon[23] lace of gold and silver, it being generally true, that where knowledge informs not, the habit qualifies.

The ears of *Indian* corn they gave us for present sustenance, needed no other interpreter to let them know how much more acceptable it was to us than the sight of dead and living corpses, which raised great compassion in them, especially in the women, who are observed to be of a soft tender nature.

One of them made me a present of the leg of a swan, which I eat as privately as it was given me, and thought it so much the more excellent, by how much it was larger than the greatest limb of any fowl I ever saw.

The *Indians* stayed with us about two hours, and parted not without a new appointment to see us again the next day: and the hour we were to expect them by their pointing to the sun, was to be at two o'clock in the afternoon. I made the chief of them presents of ribbon and other slight trade, which they lov'd, designing, by mutual endearment, to let them see, it would gratify their interest as well as their charity, to treat as well. *Ha-na Haw* was their parting word, which is farewel, pointing again at the place where the sun would be at our next meeting. We took leave in their own words *Ha-na Haw.*

The going away of the *Indians,* and leaving us behind, was a separation hard to be born by our hungry company, who nevertheless had received a competent quantity of corn and bread to keep us till they returned to do better things for our relief; we did not fail to give glory to God for our approaching deliverance, and the joy we conceiv'd in our minds in the sense of so great a mercy, kept us awake all the night, and was a cordial to the sick and weak to recover their health and strength.

The delay of the *Indians* coming next day, beyond their set time, we thought an age of tedious years: At two o'clock we had no news of them, but by attending their own time with a little patience, we might see a considerable number of them, men, women and children, all about our huts, with recruits of bread and corn to stop every mouth. Many of them desir'd beads and little truck they use to deal in, as exchange for what they gave us; and we as freely gave them what we had brought on shore; but to such of us as gave them nothing, the *Indians* failed not however to give them bread for nothing.

One old man of their company, who seem'd, by the preference they gave him, to be the most considerable of the party, apply'd himself to me by gestures and signs, to learn something (if possible) of our country, and occasion of the sad posture he saw us in, to the end that he might inform his master, the king of *Kickotank*,[24] (on whose territories we stood) and dispose him to succour us, as we had need.

I made return to him in many vain words, and in as many insignificant signs as himself had made to me, and neither of us one jot the wiser. The several nonplus's we both were at in striving to be better understood, afforded so little of edification to either party, that our time was almost spent in vain. It came at last into my head, that I had long since read Mr. *Smith*'s travels[25] thro' those parts of *America,* and that the word *Werowance* (word frequently pronounced by the old man) was in *English* the king. That word, spoken by me, with strong emphasis, together with the motions of my body, speaking my desire of going to him, was very pleasing to the old man, who thereupon embrac'd me with more than common kindness, and by all demonstrations of satisfaction, did shew that he understood my meaning. This one word was all the *Indian* I could speak, which (like a little armour well placed) contributed to the saving of our lives.

In order to what was next to be done, he took me by the hand and led me to the sea side, where I embarked with himself and one more *Indian* in a canoe, that had brought him there, which the third man rowed over to that broken ground, where, not long before, we made discovery of a canoe ready for our transport, at such time as they thought fit to fetch us off; and the reason of their taking me with them was to help launce this weighty embarkation, which was very heavy for its proportion, as being made of the body of an oak or pine, some twenty-two foot in length, hollowed like a pig-trough, which is the true description of a canoe. The manner of its being put into motion is very particular; the labourers with long booms place their feet on the starboard and larboard sides of the boat, and with this fickle footing do they heave it forward.

I cannot omit a passage of one major *Stephens,* who had been an officer in the late civil war, under Sir *William Waller,* [26] and was now one of our fellow-sufferers. He could not be persuaded by any means to give his vote for prosecuting the way we were in for our relief, but differ'd as much in judgment with us, in this our design of going to the king of this country, as he had done in *England,* by engaging against his natural sovereign; he cry'd out these rogues would draw us into their power, and take away our lives, advising, rather than to put our trust in this king, we should put ourselves into one of these canoes, and taking advantage of the calm time, we should try to get the north cape.

His fears and objections were so unreasonable, that they were not worth an answer, and his project of going thus by sea was so ridiculous, that it did exceed all chimera's of knight-errantry, and his apprehending the king would ensnare us, we all esteemed vain, as nothing could be more childish: We had been in the king's power (though we knew it not) ever since we set foot on that ground, so that had his mind been that way bent, he need use no other stratagem to end our lives, than to have forborn the sending us relief; every one dissented to the main project, and I did unfeignedly profess, for my own part, that I would much rather expose my life to the honour of a king (tho' never so mean) than to the billows of the sea, in such a bottom; which would be to tempt God to destroy us, and punish our presumption by his justice, at the same time that he was saving us by a miracle of his mercy.

I should not have remembred this passage of major *Stephens,* had he only shew'd his antipathy in this single instance, but because he repeated the rancor of his mind, in two other very small occasions, which will follow, 'tis just that the malignity of so ill an humour should suffer some reprimand.

The canoes being fitted to take us in and waft us to the main, I made a fair muster of the remnant we had to carry off, and found we wanted six of the number we brought on shore, (*viz.*) four men and two women: five of those six we knew were dead, but missing one of our living women, we made the *Indians* understand the same, who as readily made us know that she was in their thoughts, and should be cared for assoon as we were settled in our quarters.

In passing the creek that was to lead us to an honest fisherman's house
we entred a branch of it to the southward, that was the road-way to it.
The tide was going out, and the water very shoal, which gave occasion
to any one that had a knife, to treat himself with oysters all the way. At
the head of that branch we were able in a short time to discover that
heaven of happiness where our most courteous host did, with a chearful
countenance, receive and entertain us. Several fires were kindled out of
hand, our arms and powder were laid up in safety, and divers earthen
pipkins were put to boil with such varieties as the season would afford.
Every body had something or other to defend and save them from the cold;
and my obligation to him, by a peculiar care that he had of me, exceeded
all the rest. I had one intire side of the fire, with a large platform to repose
on, to my self; furrs and deer skins to cover my body, and support my
head, with a priority of respect and friendly usage, which, to my great
trouble, I was not able to deserve at his hands, by any requital then in
my power to return.

Our kind entertainment in the house of this poor fisherman, had so
many circumstances of hearty compassion and tenderness in every part of
it, that as it ought to be a perpetual motive to engage all of us who enjoyed
the benefit of it, to a daily acknowledgment of the Almighty's goodness
for conducting us in this manner by his immediate hand, out of our afflictions, so may it ever be look'd upon as a just reproach to christians who,
on all our sea-coasts, are so far from affording succour to those, who by
shipwreck and misfortunes of the sea do fall into their power, that they
treat with all inhuman savage barbarity those unhappy souls whom God
hath thus afflicted, seizing on their goods as their proper perquisites,
which the waves of the sea (by divine providence) would cast upon the
shoar for the true proprieters; and many times dispatching them out of
the world to silence complaints, and to prevent all after-reckonings. And
the better to intitle themselves to what they get in this way of rapine,
they wickedly call such devilish acquests by the sacred name of God's
good, prophaning and blaspheming at the same time that holy name, as
they violate all the laws of hospitality and human society: whereas, on
the contrary, our charitable host, influenced only by natural law, without
the least shew of coveting any thing we had, or prospect of requital in the
future, did not only treat in this manner our persons, but did also, with
as much honesty, secure for us our small stores of guns, powder, &c. as if
he had read and understood the duty of the gospel, or had given his only

child as a hostage to secure his dealing justly with us; so that I can never sufficiently applaud the humanity of this *Indian,* nor express the high contentment that I enjoyed in this poor man's cottage, which was made of nothing but mat and reeds, and bark of trees fix'd to poles. It had a loveliness and symmetry in the air of it, so pleasing to the eye, and refreshing to the mind, that neither the splendor of the *Escurial,* nor the glorious appearance of *Versailles* were able to stand in competition with it. We had a boiled swan for supper, which gave plentiful repasts to all our upper mess.

Our bodies thus refresh'd with meat and sleep, comforted with fires, and secured from all the changes and inclemencies of that sharp piercing cold season, we thought the morning (tho' clad in sunshine) did come too fast upon us. Breakfast was liberally provided and set before us, our arms faithfully delivered up to my order for carriage; and thus in readiness to set forward, we put our selves in a posture to proceed to the place where the king resided. The woman left behind at the island, had been well look'd to, and was now brought off to the care of her comrade that came with us; neither of them in a condition to take a journey, but they were carefully attended and nourished in this poor man's house, till such time as boats came to fetch them to *Virginia,* where they did soon arrive in perfect health, and lived (one or both of them) to be well married, and to bear children, and to subsist in as plentiful a condition as they could wish.

In beginning our journey thro' the woods, we had not advanced half a mile till we heard a great noise of mens voices, directed to meet and stop our further passage. These were several *Indians* sent by the king to order us back to our quarters. Major *Stephens* (not cured of his jealous humour by the experience of what he felt the night before) took this alarm in a very bad sense, and as much different from the rest of the company as in his former fit. He was again deluded with a strong fancy, that these violent motions in the *Indians* who approached us, were the effect of some sudden change in their counsels to our detriment, and that nothing less than our perdition could be the consequence thereof, which he feared would immediately be put in practice by the clamorous men that made such haste to meet us, and (as he would apprehend) to kill and destroy us.

This passion of major *Stephens,* cast in the same mould with that other he discovered in the island, had not (as we all thought and told him) whereon to raise the least foundation of terror to affright a child; for besides the earnest we had received of their good intentions the night before, these men who came so fast upon us, were all unarm'd; nor was it likely, that king would now possibly imbrew his hands in our blood, and provoke he knew not how powerful a nation to destroy him, after such kind caresses, and voluntary expressions of a temper very contrary to such cruelty. In fine, we saw no cause in all the carriage of the *Indians* on which I could ground any fear, and therefore I long'd with all impatience to see this king, and to enjoy the plenty of his table, as we quickly did.

When these *Indians* came up to us, this doubt was soon cleared. The good-natur'd king being inform'd of our bodily weakness, and inability to walk thro' the woods to his house, on foot (which might be about four miles distant from our setting out) had a real tenderness for us, and sent canoes to carry us to the place nearest his house, by the favour of another branch of the same creek; and to the end we might take no vain steps (as we were going to do) and exhaust our strength to no purpose, these *Indians* made this noise to stop us.

We entred the canoes that were mann'd, and lay ready to receive us. We had a pleasant passage in the shallow water, eat oysters all the way: for altho' the breakfast we had newly made, might well excuse a longer abstinence than we were like to be put to, our arrear to our stomachs was so great, that all we swallowed as soon concocted, and our appetite still fresh and craving more.

Having pass'd this new course for some three *English* miles in another branch of the creek, our landing place was contriv'd to be near the house of the queen then in waiting. She was a very plain lady to see to, not young, nor yet ill-favour'd. Her complexion was of a sad white: but the measures of beauty in those parts where they are exposed to the scorching sun from their infancy, are not taken from red and white, but from colours that will better lie upon their tawny skins, as hereafter will be seen.

The beauty of this queen's mind (which is more permanent than that of colour) was conspicuous in her charity and generosity to us poor starved weather-beaten creatures, who were the object of it. A mat was spread without the house, upon the ground, furnish'd with *Pone, Homini,* oysters, and other things. The queen made us sit down and eat, with gestures that shewed more of courtesy than majesty, but did speak as hearty welcome as could in silence be expected: and these were the graces that, in our opinion, transcended all other beauties in the world, and did abundantly supply all defects of outward appearance in the person and garb of

the queen. The southerly wind made the season tolerable; but that lasted
but little, the north-west gale coming violently on us again.

When this collation of the queen was at an end, we took leave of her
majesty with all the shews of gratitude that silence knew how to utter.
We were now within half an hour's walk of the king's mansion, which we
soon discovered by the smoak, and saw it was made of the same stuff with
the other houses from which we had newly parted, namely, of mat and
reed. Locust ports sunk in the ground at corners and partitions, was the
strength of the whole fabrick. The roof was tied fast to the body with a
sort of strong rushes that grow there, which supply'd the place of nails
and pins, mortises and tenants.

The breadth of this palace was about eighteen or twenty foot, the
length about twenty yards. The only furniture was several platforms for
lodging, each about two yards long and more, plac'd on both sides of the
house, distant from each other about five foot; the space in the middle
was the chimney, which had a hole in the roof over it, to receive as much
of the smoak as would naturally repair to it; the rest we shared amongst
us, which was the greatest part; and the sitters divided to each side, as our
soldiers do in their *corps de guarde*.

Fourteen great fires, thus situated, were burning all at once. The king's
apartment had a distinction from the rest; it was twice as long, and the
bank he sat on was adorn'd with deer skins finely dress'd, and the best
furrs of otter and beaver that the country did produce.

The fire assign'd to us was suitable to our number, to which we were
conducted, without intermixture of any *Indian* but such as came to do
us offices of friendship. There we were permitted to take our rest until
the king pleased to enter into communication with us. Previous to which
he sent his daughter, a well-favour'd young girl of about ten or twelve
years old, with a great wooden bowl full of homini (which is the corn of
that country, beat and boiled to a mash). She did in a most obliging
manner give me the first taste of it, which I would have handed to my
next neighbour after I had eaten, but the young princess interposed her
hand, and taking the bowl out of mine, delivered it to the same party I
aimed to give it, and so to all the rest in order. Instead of a spoon there
was a well-shap'd muscle-shell that accompanied the bowl.

The linen of that country grows ready made on the branches of oak
trees (or pine) the *English* call it *moss*. It is like the threads of unwhited
cotton-yarn ravelled, and hangs in parcels on the lower boughs, divine

provi[de]nce having so ordered it for the conveniency and sustenance of the deer, which is all the food they can get in times of snow. It is very soft, sweet and cleanly, and fit for the purpose of wiping clean the hands, and doing the duty of napkins.

About three hours after this meal was ended, the king sent to have me come to him. He called me *Ny a Mutt,* which is to say, My brother, and compelled me to sit down on the same bank with himself, which I had reason to look upon as a mighty favour. After I had sat there about half an hour, and had taken notice of many earnest discourses and repartees betwixt the king and his *crotemen* (so the *Indians* call the king's council) I could plainly discover, that the debate they held was concerning our adventure and coming there. To make it more clear, the king address'd himself to me with many gestures of his body, his arms display'd in various postures, to explain what he had in his mind to utter for my better under-standing. By all which motions I was not edifi'd in the least, nor could imagine what return to make by voice or sign, to satisfy the king's de-mands in any thing that related to the present straits of our condition. In fine, I admir'd their patient sufferance of my dulness to comprehend what they meant, and shew'd myself to be troubled at it; which being perceived by the king, he turn'd all into mirth and jollity, and never left till he made me laugh with him, tho' I knew not why.

I took that occasion to present the king with a sword and long shoulder-belt, which he received very kindly; and to witness his gracious acceptance, he threw off his *Mach coat* (or upper covering of skin) stood upright on his bank, and, with my aid, did accoutre his naked body with his new harness, which had no other apparel to adorn it, besides a few skins about his loyns to cover his nakedness. In this dress he seemed to be much de-lighted; but to me he appear'd a figure of such extraordinary shape, with sword and belt to set it off, that he needed now no other art to stir me up to laughter and mirth, than the sight of his own proper person.

Having made this short acquaintance with the king, I took leave, and returned to my comrades. In passing the spaces betwixt fire and fire, one space amongst the rest was blinded with a traverse of mat; and by the noise I heard from thence, like the beating of hemp, I took it to be some kind of elaboratory. To satisfy a curiosity I had to be more particularly inform'd, I edg'd close to the mat; and, by standing on tiptoe for a full discovery, I saw a sight that gave me no small trouble. The same specifical queen (whose courtesy for our kind usage the other day, can never be

enough applauded) was now employed in the hard servile labour of beating corn for the king's dinner, which raised the noise that made me thus
inquisitive. I wish'd myself in her place for her ease: but the queens of
that country do esteem it a privilege to serve their husbands in all kind
of cookery, which they would be as loth to lose, as any christian queen
would be to take it from them.

Several *Indians* of the first rank followed me to our quarters, and used
their best endeavours to sift something from us that might give them
light into knowing what we were. They sought many ways to make their
thoughts intelligible to us, but still we parted without knowing what to
fix upon, or how to steer our course in advance of our way to *Virginia*.

In this doubtful condition we thought it reasonable to fall upon a
speedy resolution what was next to be done on our parts, in order to the
accomplishment of our voyage by land, which we hop'd (by the divine
aid) we might be able to effect after a little more refreshment by the plenty
of victuals allowed us by the king, who was no less indulgent and careful
to feed and caress us, than if we had been his children.

Towards morning we were treated with a new regale brought to us by
the same fair hand again. It was a sort of spoon-meat, in colour and taste
not unlike to almond-milk temper'd and mix'd with boiled rice. The
ground still was *Indian* corn boiled to a pap, which they call *Homini*, but
the ingredient which performed the milky part, was nothing but dry
pokickery[27] nuts, beaten shells and all to powder, and they are like our
walnuts, but thicker shell'd, and the kernel sweeter; but being beaten in
a mortar, and put into a tray, hollow'd in the middle to make place for
fair water, no sooner is the water poured into the powder, but it rises
again white and creamish; and after a little ferment it does partake so
much of the delicate taste of the kernel of that nut, that it becomes a
rarity to a miracle.

Major *Morrison,* who had been almost at death's door, found himself
abundantly refreshed and comforted with this delicacy; he wished the
bowl had been a fathom deep, and would say, when his stomach called
on him for fresh supplies, that if this princess royal would give him his
fill of that food, he should soon recover his strength.

Our bodies growing vigorous with this plenty, we took new courage,
and resolv'd (as many as were able) to attempt the finding out of *Virginia*. We guess'd the distance could not be great, and that it bore from
us S. by W. to S.W. Our ignorance of the latitude we were in, was some

discouragement to us; but we were confident, from what the seamen discoursed, we were to the southward of the *Menados,* then a *Dutch* plantation, now *New York:* Fair weather and full stomachs made us willing to be gone. To that end we laid out for a quantity of pone; and for our surer conduct we resolved to procure an *Indian* to be our pilot through the wilderness, for we were to expect many remora's[28] in our way, by swamps and creeks, with which all those sea-coasts do abound.

The king remarking our more than ordinary care to procure more bread than amounted to our usual expence, gathered thence our design to leave him, and shift for ourselves. To prevent the rashness and folly of such attempt, he made use of all his silent rhetorick to put us out of conceit of such design, and made us understand the peril and difficulty of it by many obstacles we must meet with. He shew'd us the danger we should expose ourselves unto, by rain and cold, swamps and darkness, unless we were conducted by other skill than we could pretend to: He pointed to his fires and shocks of corn, of which he had enough, and made it legible to us in his countenance, that we were welcome to it. All the signs the king made upon this occasion, we were content to understand in the best sense; and taking for granted our sojourning there was renewed to another day, we retired to our quarters.

About midnight following, the king sent to invite me to his fire. He placed me near him as before, and in the first place shewing me quarters of a lean doe, new brought in. He gave me a knife to cut what part of it I pleased, and then pointing to the fire, I inferr'd, I was left to my own discretion for the dressing of it. I could not readily tell how to shew my skill in the cookery of it, with no better ingredients than appear'd in sight; and so did no more but cut a collop[29] and cast it on the coals. His majesty laugh'd at my ignorance, and to instruct me better, he broach'd the collop on a long scewer, thrust the sharp end into the ground (for there was no hearth but what nature made) and turning sometimes one side, sometimes the other, to the fire, it became fit in short time to be served up, had there been a dining-room of state such as that excellent king deserved.

I made tender of it first to the king, and then to his nobles, but all refused, and left all to me, who gave God and the king thanks for that great meal. The rest of the doe was cut in pieces, stewed in a pipkin,[30] and then put into my hands to dispose of amongst my company.

Assoon as I had dispatch'd this midnight venison feast, and sent the
rest to my comrades, the king was greatly desirous to make me comprehend, by our common dialect of signs and motions, the ingenious stratagem
by which they use to take their deer in the winter season, especially when
the surface of the earth is cover'd with snow. He shewed me in the first
place a small leather thong, in which (said he) any kind of deer should be
invited to hamper himself and lie fast ti'd on his back, until the engineer
(or some body else for him) should take quiet possession of him.
I could not conceive the particular structure of this machine, so as to
direct the making of it elsewhere; but this much in the general I did understand; they would fasten a pine green branch at the end of a pole (such as
hops grow upon) which should lie athwart an oak, like the pole of a turn-
er's lath, and the green hanging dingle-dangle at the pole end, fastened
by a string; it should be set at a heighth for a deer to reach, but not without mounting and resting on his hinder legs, that so in pulling the branch,
as at a trigger, the machine discharging, his heels are struck up to fly in
the air, and there he remains on his back so straitly hamper'd, that the
least child may approach to touch and take him.

Before I parted, the king attack'd me again, with reiterated attempts
to be understood, and I thought by these three or four days conversation, I had the air of his expression much more clear and intelligible than
at first. His chief drift for the first essay seemed to be a desire to know
which way we were bound, whether north or south; to which I pointed
to the south. This gave him much satisfaction, and thereupon steps in the
little grotman before described, who by the motion of his hand seemed
to crave my regard to what he was going about. He took up a stick, with
which he made divers circles by the fireside, and then holding up his finger
to procure my attention, he gave to every hole a name; and it was not hard
to conceive that the several holes were to supply the place of a sea-chart,
shewing the situation of all the most noted *Indian* territories that lay to
the southward of *Kickotank*.

That circle that was most southerly, he called *Achomack*, which, tho'
he pronounc'd with a different accent from us, I laid hold on that word
with all demonstrations of satisfaction I could express, giving them to
understand, that was the place to which I had a desire to be conducted.

The poor king was in a strange transport of joy to see me receive satisfaction, and did forthwith cause a lusty young man to be called to him, to

whom, by the earnestness of his motions, he seemed to give ample instructions to do something for our service, but what it was we were nor yet able
to resolve. In two or three days time, seeing no effect of what he had so
seriously said, we began again to despond, and did therefore resume our
former thoughts of putting ourselves in posture to be gone; but the king
seeing us thus ready at every turn to leave him, shewed in his looks a
more than ordinary resentment; still describing (as he could) the care he
had taken for us, and impossibility of accomplishing our ends by ourselves, and that we should surely faint in the way and die without help,
if we would not be ruled by him.

He shewed me again his stores of corn, and made such reiterated signs,
by the chearfulness of his countenance, that we should not want, whilst
he had such a plenty, as made us lay aside all thoughts of stirring till he
said the word. But as oft as he look'd or pointed to the coast of *Achomack,*
he would shake his head, with abundance of grimmaces, in dislike of our
design to go that way till he saw it good we should do so. I was abundantly convinced of our folly in the resolution we were ready to take of going
away without better information of the distance from *Achomack,* and
way that led to it; and having so frank a welcome where we were, we
resolved to stay till the king should approve of our departure, which he
was not able to determine till the messenger came back, that he had sent
to *Achomack,* who, it now seemed more plainly, was dispatched upon
my owning that place to be our home, tho' we knew it not from any
cause we could rely upon, before we saw the effect.

While we lived in this suspense, the king had a great mind to see our
fire-arms, and to be acquainted with the use and nature of them. That
which best did please his eye I presented to him, and shew'd him how to
load and discharge it. He was very shy at first essay, fearing it might hurt
him, but I made him stand upon his lodging place, and putting him in
a posture to give fire, he presented the mouth of his gun to the chimney
hole, and so let fly. The combustible nature of the king's palace not well
considered, the fabrick was endangered by the king's own hand, for the
flashing of the powder having taken hold of the roof at the smoke-hole,
all was in a flame; but a nimble lad or two ran up to quench it, and did
soon extinguish it without considerable damage to the building, which
was of mat and boughs of oak as aforesaid.

The king's eldest son, of about eighteen years of age, was hugely en-
amour'd with our guns, and look'd so wistfully on me, when he saw what

wonders they would do, that I could not forbear presenting him with a birding-piece. Some of our company, who knew that by the laws of *Virginia,* it was criminal to furnish the *Indians* with fire-arms, gave me caution in this case, but I resolved, for once, to borrow a point of that law; for tho' it might be of excellent use in the general, yet as our condition was, I esteemed it a much greater crime to deny those *Indians* any thing that was in our power, than the penalty of that law could amount to.

Father and son abundantly gratified in this manner, the king thought himself largely requited for the cost we put him to in our entertainment. I taught his son to shoot at fowls, to charge his gun and clean it, insomuch that in a few minutes, he went among the flocks of geese, and firing at random he did execution on one of them to his great joy, and returned to his father with the game in his hand, with such celerity, as if he had borrowed wings of the wind.

About three o'clock this afternoon, the king was pleased in great condescension to honour me with a visit, a favour which I may (without vanity) assume to myself, and my better habit, from the many particular applications that he made to me, exclusive of the rest of the company. He thought I was too melancholy, (for the *Indians,* as has been observ'd, are great enemies to that temper) and shewed me by his own chearful looks, what humour he would have me put on; he would not have me in the least apprehensive of wanting any thing his country afforded, as his mien and gesture witnessed; and for the higher proof of his reality, he found me out a divertisement, that was very extraordinary. He came at this time attended by his young daughter, who had done us the good offices before-mentioned, and having first by kind words and pleasant gestures given us renewed assurance of hearty welcome, he singled me out, and pointed with his hand to a way he would have me take, but whither, or to what end, I was at liberty to guess; upon that he produced his little daughter for my conductrix to the place to which I should go, and shewed his desire that I should follow her where-ever she should lead me.

Major *Stephens,* not yet enough convinc'd of the *Indians* fidelity, would have discouraged me from leaving the company in that manner, unreasonably fancying that this was a contrivance in the king to take away my life in a private way; but this I thought did so much out-strip all his other senseless jealousies, that after I had acknowledged the obliga-

tion I had to his care of my person, his needless caution had no other
effect on me than to turn it into ridicule. These inordinate fears of this
major in three foregoing instances, might (I confess) have been very well
omitted, as not worthy the mention, and so they should have been, had
his humour and constitution in prosperous times been any way suitable
to this wary temper; but because his habits on shore were scandalously
vicious, his mouth always belching oaths, and his tongue proving him the
vainest hector I had seen, I thought it was pity to lose such a strong con-
firmation of that known truth, (*viz.*) That true innate courage does seldom
reside in the heart of a quarrelling and talking hector.

The weather (as I have said) was excessive cold, with frost, and the
winds blowing very fresh upon my face, it almost stopt my breath. The
late condition I had been in, under a roof, with great fires, and much
smoke, did conduce to make me the more sensible of the cold air: but in
less than half an hour that pain was over; we were now in sight of the
house whereto we were bound, and the lady of the place was ready to
receive us, (who proved to be the mother of my conductrix) and to shew
me my apartment in the middle of her house, which had the same accommodation to sit and rest upon, as before has been described in other
instances.

The lusty rousing fire, prepared to warm me, would have been noble
entertainment of itself, but attended (as it was quickly) with good food
for the belly, made it to be that compleat good chear I only aimed at;
a wild turkey boiled, with oysters, was preparing for my supper, which,
when it was ready, was served up in the same pot that boiled it. It was
a very flavoury mess, stew'd with muscles, and I believe would have passed
for a delicacy at any great table in England, by palates more competent
to make a judgment than mine, which was now more gratified with the
quantity than the quality of what was before me.

This queen was also of the same mould of her majesty whom we first
met at our landing place, somewhat ancient (in proportion to the king's
age) but so gentle and compassionate, as did very bountifully requite all
defects of nature; she passed some hours at my fire, and was very desirous
to know the occasion that brought us there (as her motion and the emphasis of her words did shew), but I had small hopes to satisfy her curiosity therein, after so many vain attempts to inform the king in that
matter. In fine, I grew sleepy, and about nine o'clock every one retired

to their quarters, separated from each other by traverses of mat, which (besides their proper vertue) kept the ladies from any immodest attempts, as secure as if they had been bars of iron.

Assoon as the day peeped in, I went out and felt the same cold as yesterday, with the same wind, N.W. I was not forward to quit a warm quarter, and a frank entertainment, but my young governess, who had her father's orders for direction, knew better than myself what I was to do: she put herself in a posture to lead the way back from whence we came, after a very good repast of stew'd muscles, together with a very hearty welcome plainly appearing in the queen's looks.

My nimble pilot led me away with great swiftness, and it was necessary so to do; the weather still continuing in the violent sharpness, nothing but a violent motion could make our limbs useful. No sooner had I set my foot in the king's house to visit my comrades, but a wonderful surprize appeared to me in the change of every countenance, and as every face did plainly speak a general satisfaction, so did they with one voice explain the cause thereof, in telling me the messengers of our delivery were arriv'd, and now with the king.

I hastened to see those angels, and addressing myself to one of them in *English* habit, ask'd him the occasion of his coming there? He told me his business was to trade for furs, and no more; but assoon as I had told him my name, and the accidents of our being there, he acknowledg'd he came under the guidance of the *Kickotank Indian* (which I imagin'd, but was not sure the king had sent) in quest of me and those that were left on shore, sent by the governor's order of *Virginia* to enquire after us, but knew not where to find us till that *Indian* came to his house; he gave me a large account of the ship's arrival, and the many dangers and difficulties she encountered before she could come into *James* river, where she ran ashore, resolving there to lay her bones. His name was *Jenkin Price*,[31] he had brought an *Indian* of his neighborhood with him that was very well acquainted in those parts, for our conduct back to *Achomack,* which *Indian* was called *Jack.*

The king was very glad of this happy success to us, and was impatient to learn something more of our history than hitherto he had been able to extract from signs and grimaces. *Jenkin Price* with his broken *Indian,* could make a shift to instruct *Jack* to say any thing he pleased, and *Jack* was the more capable to understand his meaning by some sprinklings of

English, that he had learnt at our plantations. Betwixt them both they were able to satisfy the king in what he pleased to know. *Jack* told them of himself what a mighty nation we were in that country, and gave them caution not to imbezil any goods we had brought with us, for fear of an after-reckoning. I wondered, upon this serious discourse he had with the king, to see guns and stockings, and whatever trifles we had given, offer'd to be return'd, and being told the reason of it by *Jenkin Price,* I was very much ashamed of *Jack's* too great zeal in our service, which, tho' it did proceed from a principal of honesty, and good morality in him, we were to consider that our dearest lives, and all we could enjoy in this world, was (next to divine providence) owing to the virtue and charity of this king, and therefore not only what they had in possession, but whatever else he should desire that was in my power, would be too mean an acknowledgment for so high obligations. I took care to let them know that I had no hand in the menace by which *Jack* brought them to refund what they had got of us; the right understanding whereof increased our good intelligence, and became a new endearment of affection betwixt us.

By better acquaintance with these our deliverers, we learn'd that we were about fifty *English* miles from *Virginia:* That part of it where *Jenkin* did govern, was call'd *Littleton's Plantation,*[32] and was the first *English* ground we did expect to see. He gave me great encouragement to endure the length of the way, by assuring me I should not find either stone or shrub to hurt my feet thorow my thin-soaled boots, for the whole colony had neither stone nor underwood; and having thus satisfi'd my curiosity in the knowledge of what *Jenkin Price* could communicate, we deferred no longer to resolve how and when to begin our journey to *Achomack.*

The *Indian* he brought with him (who afterwards lived and died my servant) was very expert, and a most incomparable guide in the woods we were to pass, being a native of those parts, so that he was as our sheet-anchor in this our peregrination. The king was loth to let us go till the weather was better-tempered for our bodies; but when he saw we were fully resolved, and had pitch'd upon the next morning to begin our journey, he found himself much defeated in a purpose he had taken to call together all the flower of his kingdom to entertain us with a dance, to the end that nothing might be omitted on his part for our divertisement, as well as our nourishment, which his small territory could produce. Most of our company would gladly have deferred our march a day longer, to see this masquerade, but I was wholly bent for *Achomack,* to which place I was to dance almost on my bare feet, the thoughts of which took off the edge I might otherwise have had to novelties of that kind.

When the good old king saw we were fully determined to be gone the next day, he desired as a pledge of my affection to him, that I would give him my camblet coat, which he vowed to wear whilst he lived for my sake; I shook hands to shew my willingness to please him in that or in any other thing he would command, and was the more willing to do myself the honour of compliance in this particular, because he was the first king I could call to mind that had ever shew'd any inclinations to wear my old cloaths.

To the young princess, that had so signally obliged me, I presented a piece of two-penny scarlet ribbon, and a *French* tweezer I had in my pocket, which made her skip for joy, and to shew how little she fancy'd our way of carrying them concealed, she retired apart for some time, and taking our every individual piece of which it was furnish'd, she tied a snip of ribbon to each, and so came back with scissars, knives and bodkins hanging at her ears, neck and hair. The case itself was not excus'd, but bore a part in this new dress: and to the end we might not part without leaving deep impressions of her beauty in our minds, she had prepared on her forefingers, a lick of paint on each, the colours (to my best remembrance) green and yellow, which at one motion she discharged on her face, beginning upon her temples, and continuing it in an oval line downwards as far as it would hold out. I could have wished this young princess would have contented herself with what nature had done for her, without this addition of paint (which I thought, made her more fulsome than handsome); but I had reason to imagine the royal family were only to use this ornament exclusive of all others, for that I saw none other of her sex so set off; and this conceit made it turn again, and appear lovely, as all things should do that are honour'd with the royal stamp.

I was not furnish'd with any thing upon the place, fit to make a return to the two queens for the great charity they used to feed and warm me; but when I came into a place where I could be suppli'd, I was not wanting that way, according to my power.

Early next morning we put our selves in posture to be gone, (*viz.*) major *Stephens,* myself, and three or four more, whose names are worn out of my mind. Major *Morrison* was so far recovered as to be heart-whole, but he wanted strength to go thro' so great a labour as this was like to prove. We left him with some others to be brought in boats that the governor had order'd for their accommodation; and with them the two weak women, who were much recover'd by the good care and nourishment they receiv'd in the poor fisherman's house.

Breakfast being done, and our pilot *Jack* ready to set out, we took a solemn leave of the good king. He inclosed me in his arms with kind embraces, not without expressions of sorrow to part, beyond the common rate of new acquaintance. I made *Jack* pump up his best compliments, which at present was all I was capable to return to the king's kindness; and so, after many *Hana baes,* we parted.

We were not gone far till the fatigue and tediousness of the journey discovered itself in the many creeks we were forc'd to head, and swamps to pass; (like *Irish* bogs) which made the way at least double to what it would have amounted to in a strait line: and it was our wonder to see our guide *Jack* lead on the way with the same confidence of going right, as if he had had a *London* road to keep him from straying. Howbeit he would many times stand still and look about for landmarks; and when on one hand and the other his marks bore right for his direction, he would shew himself greatly satisfied. As to the purpose, an old deform'd tree that lay north-west, opposite to a small hammock of pines to the south-east, would evidence his going right in all weathers. It is true, they know not the compass by the loadstone, but, which is equivalent, they never are ignorant of the north-west point, which gives them the rest; and that they know by the weather-beaten moss that grows on that side of every oak, different from the rest of the tree, which is their compass. Towards evening we saw smoak (an infallible sign of an *Indian* town) which *Jack* knew to arise from *Gingo Teague.* We went boldly into the king's house (by advice of his brother of *Kickotank*) who was also a very humane prince. What the place and season produc'd was set before us with all convenient speed, which was enough to satisfy hunger, and to fit us for repose.

I was extremely tir'd with this tedious journey; and it was the more irksome to me, because I perform'd it in boots (my shoes being worn out) which at that time were commonly worn to walk in; so that I was much more sleepy than I had been hungry. The alliance I had newly made at *Kickotank* did already stand me in some stead, for that it qualified me to a lodging apart, and gave me a first taste of all we had to eat, tho' the variety was not so great as I had seen in other courts.

And yet (as we see in all wordly honours) this grandeur of mine was
not without its allay; for as it gave me accommodation of eating and
sleeping in preference to my comrades, so did it raise the hopes of the
royal progeny of gifts and presents, beyond what I was either able or
willing to afford them: for when I would have taken my rest, I was
troubled beyond measure with their visits, and saw by their carriage what
they would be at; wherefore, to free myself of further disturbance, and to
put myself out of the pain of denials, I resolv'd to comply with the necessities of nature, which press'd me hard to sleep; and to that end I took the
freedom by *Jack,* to desire they would all withdraw until I found myself
refresh'd.

I passed the night 'till almost day-break in one intire sleep; and when
I did awake (not suddenly able to collect who, or where I was) I found
myself strangely confounded, to see a damsel plac'd close to my side,
of no meaner extract than the king's eldest daughter, who had completely
finish'd the rape of all the gold and silver buttons that adorn'd the king
of *Kickotank*'s coat, yet on my back. When I was broad awake, and saw
this was no enchantment (like those trances knights-errant use to be in)
but that I was really despoiled of what was not in my power to dispense
withal, I called for *Jack,* and made him declare my resentment and much
dislike of this princess's too great liberty upon so small acquaintance,
which made me have a mean opinion of her. *Jack* shew'd more anger
than myself to see such usage by any of his country, and much more was
he scandaliz'd, that one of the blood royal should purloin.

But the king, upon notice of the fact and party concerned in it, immediately caused the buttons to be found out and returned, with no
slight reprimand to his daughter, and then all was well, and so much the
better by the gift of such small presents as I was able to make to the king
and princess. Breakfast was given us, and we hasten'd to proceed in our
journey to *Achomack.*

The uneasiness of boots to travel in, made me by much the more weary
of the former day's journey, and caus'd me to enter very unwillingly upon
this second day's work. We reckon'd our selves about twenty-five miles
distant from *Jenkin*'s house. It pleased God to send us dry weather, and
not excessive cold. We had made provision of *Pone* to bait on by the way,
and we found good water to refresh us; but all this did not hinder my
being tired and spent almost to the last degree. *Jack* very kindly offer'd
his service to carry me on his shoulders (for I was brought to a moderate

weight by the strict diet I had been in) but that would have been more uneasy to me, in contemplation of his more than double pains, and so I resolved to try my utmost strength, without placing so great a weight on his shoulders.

The hopes of seeing *English* ground in *America,* and that in so short a time as they made us expect, did animate my spirits to the utmost point. *Jack* fearing the worst, was of opinion, that we should call at his aunt's town, the queen of *Pomumkin,* not far out of the way: but *Jenkin Price* opposed that motion, and did assure me our journey's end was at hand. His words and my own inclination carried the question, and I resolved, by God's help, that night to sleep at *Jenkin's* house.

But the distance proving yet greater than had been described, and my boots trashing me almost beyond all sufferance, I became desperate, and ready to sink and lie down. *Jenkin* lull'd me on still with words that spurr'd me to the quick; and would demonstrate the little distance betwixt us and his plantation, by the sight of hogs and cattle, of which species the *Indians* were not masters. I was fully convinc'd of what he said, but would however have consented to a motion of lying without doors on the ground, within two or three flights shot of the place, to save the labour of so small a remainder.

The close of the evening, and a little more patience (thro' the infinite goodness of the Almighty) did put a happy period to our cross adventure. A large bed of sweet straw was spread ready in *Jenkin's* house for our reception, upon which I did hasten to extend and stretch my wearied limbs. And being thus brought into safe harbour by the many miracles of divine mercy, from all the storms and fatiques, perils and necessities to which we had been exposed by sea and land for almost the space of four months, I cannot conclude this voyage in more proper terms, than in the words that are the burthen of that psalm of providence, *O that men would therefore praise the Lord for his goodness, and for his wondrous works unto the children of men!*

Our landlord *Jenkin Price,* and conductor *Jack,* took great care to provide meat for us; and there being a dairy and hens, we could not want. As for our stomachs, they were open at all hours to eat whate'er was set before us, assoon as our wearied bodies were refresh'd with sleep. It was on *Saturday* the _ day of *January,* that we ended this our wearisome pilgrimage, and entred into our king's dominions at *Achomat,* called by the

English, Northampton county, which is the only county on that side of
the bay belonging to the colony of *Virginia,* and is the best of the whole
for all sorts of necessaries for human life.

Having been thus refresh'd in *Jenkin*'s house this night with all our
hearts could wish, on the next morning, being *Sunday,* we would have
been glad to have found a church for the performance of our duty to
God, and to have rendred our hearty thanks to him in the publick assembly, for his unspeakable mercies vouchsafed to us; but we were not yet
arrived to the heart of the country where there were churches, and
ministry perform'd as our laws direct, but were glad to continue our own
chaplains, as formerly. As we advanced into the plantations that lay thicker
together, we had our choice of hosts for our entertainment, without money
or its value; in which we did not begin any novelty, for there are no inns
in the colony; nor do they take other payment for what they furnish to
coasters, but by requital of such courtesies in the same way, as occasion
offers.

When I came to the house of one *Stephen Charlton,*[33] he did not only
outdo all that I had visited before him, in variety of dishes at his table,
which was very well order'd in the kitchen, but would also oblige me to
put on a good farmer-like suit of his own wearing cloaths, for exchange
of my dirty habit; and this gave me opportunity to deliver my camlet
coat to Jack, for the use of my brother of *Kickotank,* with other things
to make it worth his acceptance.

Having been thus frankly entertain'd at Mr. *Charlton*'s, our company
were in condition to take care for themselves. We took leave of each other,
and my next stage was to esquire *Yardly,*[34] a gentleman of good name,
whose father had sometimes been governor of *Virginia.* There I was received and treated as if I had in truth and reality been that man of honour
my brother of *Kickotank* had created me. It fell out very luckily for my
better welcome, that he had not long before brought over a wife from
Rotterdam, that I had known almost from a child. Her father (*Custis*[35]
by name) kept a victualling house in that town, lived in good repute, and
was the general host of our nation there. The esquire knowing I had the
honour to be the governor's kinsman, and his wife knowing my conversation in *Holland,* I was recciv'd and caress'd more like a domestick and
near relation, than a man in misery, and a stranger. I stay'd there for a
passage over the bay, about ten days, welcomed and feasted not only by

the esquire and his wife, but by many neighbours that were not too
remote.

About the midst of *February* I had an opportunity to cross the bay in
a sloop, and with much ado landed in *York* river, at esquire *Ludlow*'s[36]
plantation, a most pleasant situation. I was civilly receiv'd by him, who
presently order'd an accommodation for me in a most obliging manner.
But it fell out at that time, that captain *Wormly*[37] (of his majesty's council)
had guests in his house (not a furlong distant from Mr. *Ludlow*'s) feasting
and carousing, that were lately come from *England,* and most of them
my intimate acquaintance. I took a sudden leave of Mr. *Ludlow,* thank'd
him for his kind intentions to me, and using the common freedom of the
country, I thrust myself amongst captain *Wormly*'s guests in crossing the
creek, and had a kind reception from them all, which answered (if not
exceeded) my expectation.

Sir *Thomas Lundsford,* Sir *Henry Chickly,* Sir *Philip Honywood,* and
colonel *Hammond*[38] were the persons I met there, and enjoyed that night
with very good chear, but left them early the next morning, out of a passionate desire I had to see the governor, whose care for my preservation
had been so full of kindness.

Captain *Wormly* mounted me for *James Town,* where the governor
was pleased to receive and take me to his house at *Greenspring,* and there
I pass'd my hours (as at mine own house) until *May* following; at which
time he sent me for *Holland* to find out the king, and to sollicite his
majesty for the treasurer's place of *Virginia,* which the governor took to
be void by the delinquency of *Claybourne,*[39] who had long enjoy'd it.
He furnish'd me with a sum of money to bear the charge of this sollicita-
tion; which took effect, tho' the king was then in *Scotland.* He was not
only thus kind to me (who had a more than ordinary pretence to his
favour by our near affinity in blood) but, on many occasions, he shew'd
great respect to all the royal party, who made that colony their refuge.
His house and purse were open to all that were so qualifi'd. To one of my
comrades (major *Fox*) who had no friend at all to subsist on, he shew'd
a generosity that was like himself; and to my other (major *Morrison*) he
was more kind, for he did not only place him in the command of the fort,
which was profitable to him whilst it held under the king, but did advance
him after to the government of the country, wherein he got a competent
estate.

And thus (by the good providence of a gracious God, who helpeth us in our low estate, and causeth his angels to pitch tents round about them that trust in him) have I given as faithful an account of this signal instance of his goodness to the miserable objects of his mercy in this voyage, as I have been able to call to a clear remembrance.

NOTES

1. *Isle of Wight; Whitehall.* King Charles I was imprisoned on the Isle of Wight from November 1647 to December 1648. On January 30, 1649, he was executed in front of the royal palace at Whitehall.

2. *Surinam.* Dutch colony on the northeast coast of South America.

3. *Barbadoes.* Island and British colony in the Lesser Antilles, West Indies.

4. *Antigua.* Island of eastern West Indies, two hundred and sixty miles east of Puerto Rico.

5. *Leeward Islands.* Chain of Caribbean islands from Dominica on the south to the Virgin Islands on the north; includes Antigua, Montserrat, St. Kitts-Nevis, and St. Thomas, St. Croix, and St. John in the Virgin Islands.

6. *William Barkeley.* Or Berkeley, 1606-77. Governor of Virginia, 1642-76. During the interregnum Berkeley offered asylum to royalists like Norwood, for which action he was forced to resign the governorship. At the Restoration, however, he was restored to office.

7. Cargaroon. Cargosoon. Literally, cargo.

8. *Royal-Exchange.* In Cornhill, London, the trading exchange, the commercial center of the city.

9. *Gravesend.* Borough on Thames estuary, twenty-two miles southeast of London.

10. *Downs.* Roadstead in the English Channel, along the east coast of Kent, about nine miles long and six miles wide; affords excellent anchorage, protected by a natural breakwater, the Goodwin Sands.

11. *Deal.* A card game.

12. *Fyall.* Faial or Fayal, westernmost island of the center group of the Azores.

13. *Teneriff.* Largest of the Canary Islands, off the northwest coast of Africa.

14. *Hatteras.* A long, narrow sandbar, off the coast of North Carolina; a dangerous navigation point.

15. Cape *Henry.* Cape of northeast coast of Princess Anne County, Virginia; the southern point of the entrance to Chesapeake Bay.

16. *Achomat.* Present-day Accomack is the northernmost of two counties on Virginia's eastern shore.

17. Hum-works. Hummockes. Low, rounded hills, or a clump of trees as seen from the sea.

18. *Malaga* sack. A sweet white wine of Málaga, Spain.

19. *Oxeyes. Squatarola squatarola,* the black-bellied plover.

20. Stabcast. Quirk of fortune.

21. *Chaldean.* From the Chaldeans, an ancient semitic people in the region of Babylonia, famous for their learning, particularly in astrology and prophecy.

22. Camlet. A fabric of silk and wool in imitation of the Asian camel and angora weave.

23. Galoon. Galloon, a narrow ornamental strip of lace or embroidery scalloped on both edges.

24. *Kickotank.* Kikotan, the northern region of present-day Accomack County, Virginia, on the Atlantic side of the eastern shore, near the Maryland-Virginia line.

25. Mr. Smith's travels. *The True Travels, Adventures, and Observations of Capt. John Smith in Europe, Asia, Africa, and America, from Anno Domini 1593 to 1629, together with a Continuation of his General History of Virginia . . .* (London, 1630).

26. Sir *William Waller.* (1597?-1668), English Parliamentary general in the Civil War, although he later opposed the Commonwealth and supported the Restoration.

27. Pokickery. Hickory.

28. Remora. Any of several fishes with a highly developed suctorial disk on the top of the head; in legend the Remora was said to guide ships through perilous seas.

29. Collop. A small piece or slice of meat.

30. Pipkin. A small earthenware pot.

31. *Jenkin Price.* In October 1650 the Virginia Assembly awarded fur trader Price five thousand pounds of tobacco for his kindness to Norwood's party.

32. *Littleton's Plantation.* Colonel Nathaniel Littleton, of Shropshire; the plantation was near Nandua Creek. Littleton was chief magistrate of Accomack in 1640 and a burgess in 1652.

33. *Stephen Charlton.* The owner of a plantation styled the "Glebe," about three miles from Bridgetown.

34. *Yardly.* Argoll Yeardley, born at Jamestown in 1621, son of former Governor George Yeardley; the plantation was at Mattawaman.

35. *Custis.* Ann, daughter of John and Joan Custis; the parents later followed the daughter and son-in-law to Virginia.

36. *Ludlow.* George Ludlow, a member of the Governor's Council after 1655.

37. *Wormly.* Ralph Wormeley, who arrived in Virginia in 1636 and first settled along the York River; later built an elegant plantation, "Rosegill," on the Rappahannock.

38. *Lundsford, Chickly, Honywood,* and *Hammond.* Like Norwood, these four were all Royalist émigrés. Lundsford had been appointed lieutenant of the Tower of London by Charles I in 1641. Sir Henry Chicheley was appointed deputy-governor of Virginia by the king in 1647; later Sir Henry married the widow of Ralph Wormeley. After the Restoration Honywood returned to England where he was named a prize sub-commissioner for the Port of London as a reward for his services to the Royalist cause. Robert Hammond was commander of the troops under whose guard Charles I was kept a prisoner on the Isle of Wight. At first a supporter of the parliamentary forces, Hammond later openly sympathized with the king.

39. *Claybourne.* William Claiborne, whose patent for the Virginia treasurer's post was dated April 6, 1643.

Benjamin Bartholomew

A relation of the Wonderful Mercies of God Extended hunto us the 19 of October 1660 in the Ship Exchang being bound from Newingland to Barbadoes

On the 19th of October 1660, the ship *Exchange,* on a passage from Boston to Barbadoes, found itself in a violent gale and in danger of foundering. Disaster was averted largely through the skill and perseverance of the captain, who in the midst of the panic that gripped passengers and crew maintained his presence of mind and kept the vessel afloat. Seven months later, one of those aboard, Benjamin Bartholomew, commemorated the deliverance in a poem addressed to Thomas Rigges of Gloucester, Massachusetts.

Bartholomew's poem (or at least the version that survives) was either dictated to or copied by a man named Mordecay Hunton. Hunton was a less than skillful scribe, as his many errors, cancellations, and inconsistencies attest, and Bartholomew himself may have been an illiterate versifier whose oral compositions were transcribed by whoever was handy at the moment. In any event, the lives of these nearly anonymous men have proven untraceable, and the *Relation* remains their only memorial.

Despite its faults, Bartholomew's poem is an interesting and attractive piece. There is suprising power in the description of the ship's peril, and the development of the narrative is, despite the overt didacticism, competently handled. Bartholomew was evidently a staunch Puritan, although his providential interpretation of the storm and deliverance is entirely typical of the period.

Harrison Meserole first called attention to Bartholomew's work in "New Voices from Seventeenth-Century America," in *Discoveries and Considerations: Essays on Early American Literature and Aesthetics Presented to Harold Jantz,* ed. Calvin Israel (Albany: State University of New York Press, 1976), pp. 24-45.

The *Relation* has never before been printed.

TEXT: Manuscript in the Houghton Library, Harvard University.

This littil scrid of paper doth containe
A sea of mercies it may be cald the name
An ochan[1] we beleve it may be cald
That doth reduce againe our lives Enthrald[2]
For when we did expect to be devoured   5
By winds and seas whome god most strong empoured
Yet by the providence of god at last
Into a hopefull posture we ware Cast:

The thing was thus we sald from boston towne
Being from Newengland to barbadous bound—   10
The twelth day of October we first sailde
The nineteenth day we had a storme prevaild
At foure a cloke winds dredfuly did blow
And ast[3] Grew night Sease higer still did Growe
All sailes but mainsaile by us handed ware: 15
For dredfull wether we did greatly fear
And by our masters order we lay by:

Fearing sume dredfull strom would us draw nigh
But mighty winds and seas did Rage and roare
Our mainsaile we wore furct to hand therfore   20
Our Ship now lies a hull in dolfull plite
Alas sayd we this is a dolfull night
The sight of Seas and winds did us dismay
We wisht ifft[4] ware gods will that it ware day:
With force of winds our ship lay one a side: 25
All meanse then posible was by us tried
To right our Ship but when no help we had
And soe we ware in a condition sad:
That then which sered the beast course in our eies
Was for to cut our mast our Ship might rise   30
Our mainmast then we cut with out delay
And cast into the sea to pas a way
But presantly it would not go away
But beat against the ship and long did stay
Till at the last our rudor it did breake   35
And in our quarter it did Make a leake
Yet more and more the winds increased ware:
We war almost out our wits end with feare
And which much aded to our dolfull case
Then ten foote water in the hould their was   40
Our mison Mast we fain would have left stood
But seeing that it did more hurt then good
We did it cut and cast into the sea:
And what would we not doe in misire:
Our sciffe and Oares into the sea we threw   45
With our sheat ancer we the same did doe.
There nothing was that troubled us that past
All that combered into the sea ware cast:
Our water still did us increas upon:
Yet we had still som expectation   50
When it would seas but litel hopes their wase
When as the seas soe over us did pas
All means then possible was by [us] usd
And counsel we then in noe case refewsd
O fears and doupts increasing more and more   55
Winds being violent and rayging sore

Yet at the last seas sweling mountain like
Terror into our harts extream did strike.
Alas sade we what hopes are to us Left
We shall of all our comforts be bereft: 60
Our ship by Noe Means Used we can ware
Now we poore harts for sartain dead Men are
It is not long that we our lives shall have
The sea and Nothing als will be our Grave
Twase God alone that in our state did Move   65
What for to render doth it us Behove:
O let us tel abrod his wondrous acts
Lets Glorifie his Name for all his facts[5]
Who bringeth loe and raiseth up againe
God surly doth not these great things in vaine   70
He is expecting from us som Great thing
And lookes more prayes we to his name should bring
It may be we have bin in stormes before:
And God our lives hath thretened very sore
And we in dangers voues to God hath vowd   75
And god at last his ear to us hath bowd:
But when we have our lives in safty had
We have forgote the vows that we have Made:
And now againe God has put us in mind
How we ourselves by voues doe use to bind   80
And how oft those voues neglected have
And now againe god brings us to the Grave
Therfore let us be warnd and great heed take:
Our Caling and election sure to Make
Make sure of Christ Noe longer make delay   85
To Morow is none of yours this is your day
When at the dore of your harts Criste doth knoke
Open unto him unloke unloke
Let him have free and large Rome in your Soules
And then you apon him your selves may roule: 90
Alwaies rely upon him on him trust:
Tis he which rased you out of the dust
Consider that Great Love he to us bore:
Who brought us out of perils great and sore: ·
Twas not for any thing that we desevrd   95

For day by day we from his law have swervd.
Yet he hath sade in dangers Great we Live
[line missing]
Blessed is he whose sines are now forgiven
Who has acounts twixt Christ and him made even: 100
Whose sines In that Redemors blood washed are:
If soe, com life or death he need not fear
For when he breath from his shall pased be
He dwels with saints to all eternity
The thoughts of death did strike into our minds   105
And fear of death the worst to pray Now binds
If thou O Lord wilt turn againe thy hand:
And death revoke well folow thy command
We will thy Statuts headfuly Observe
And from thy presepts we will niver Swerve   110
To set our feat one shoere we could then parte
With all we did posses with a free hart:
We could Have Gladly bin the shoore upon
Though we had had not one Ragge too put one
If we a world of treshewre then had had   115
Yea a thousand world offt yet we would have bin Glad.
For to have lost it all soe we had bin
Amoung the living ones yet once againe
Some sent unto the master and did say
All hopes of living Longers fled away   120
Theirfore whiles that we Live and whilst that we may
Unto Our God though Angery Let us pray
He then replied to pray I would agree
Yet for our lives Let all means used be:
Therfore I think tis beast to hoyse foreyarde.   125
Who knowes but God to us may have regard
Now I resolved am with Greatest care
If posible I can the shipe to ware
To hoyse foreyard at last we did consent:
Five men noe more to hoyse him forward went   130
The reson why to hoyse him ware but five
The rest ware at the pump for all our lives
At length thay hoysed him altho soe few
Five men to hoyse him soe we niver knew

Forthwith we did our helm put hard awether   135
And did forsheat hall aft then alltogether.
Now let us all unto the pump be gone
For what is posible to doe is done
We all unto the pump did then retier
And pumpt with a good stomak and desier[6]   140
Till at the last that glad sound we did hear
Which did revive us almost dead with fear
Pump on good harts the ship now round doth ware
Some hopes at last though litil left their are:
The seas soe high we thought we should not steare   145
But god did wondrowesly for us apeare
And gided us that we did stear along
Yee us that war then weeke he did make strong
And now at last the water did decrease:
Which in our minds created wondrous pease: 150
Our fainting harts that ware before soe sad
In a Great measure are revived and glad
And Now before we could wele se the day
The force of winds and seas our God did Lay
We that noe light of any other day   155
Had thoughts to see yet now we see it may
Twas eight a Clocke in th['] morn before that we
Our ship soe full of water quite did free
And afterwards our rudor we did mend
And in our quarter we the leake soond kend[7]   160
Twas god alone that us to help was neer
Twas he alone that did remove oure feare
Twas god alone that us with fear amasd:
Tis he alone that us from death hath rasd,
Of thanks and prayes lets niver Cease to Give: 165
O let this great diliverance we have past:
Who our lives thretened yet did not them end
If this will not what will our lives amend

Made By Benjemin Bartholmew
Righten by Mordecay Hunton
    for thomas Rigges this 11 of April 1661

NOTES

1. Ochan. Ocean.
2. Reduce againe our lives Enthrald. Lead us out of sin.
3. Ast. As it.
4. Ifft. If it.
5. Facts. The works of God.
6. Stomak and desier. Stomach and desire, that is, with enthusiasm.
7. Kend. Saw, understood.

Anonymous

A Description of a Great Sea-Storm, That happened to some Ships in the Gulph of Florida, in September last; Drawn up by one of the Company, and sent to his Friend at London

The anonymous author of this short verse narrative was emigrating to the New World—probably to Virginia—when the fleet in which he was sailing was struck by a hurricane off Florida's Atlantic coast.

Of the writer himself we know nothing other than what his poem reveals. He was, clearly, a man possessed of a lively sense of humor. One suspects he was a Restoration wit set out to find his fortune in a new land. Internal evidence in the poem also suggests he was something of a rake, well-acquainted with the seamier side of London tavern life. In any event, his comic spirit is evident throughout the poem, and he observes all goings on (and his own poetic efforts) with a certain wry detachment and a well-developed sense of fun. A charming bit of verse, the *Description* celebrates human foible and confusion (including the author's) in an amusing and engaging way.

The author's friend in London to whom the verses were sent arranged to have them published, and the *Description* appeared as a broadside in 1671, printed by Thomas Milbourn for Dorman Newman.

TEXT: John Carter Brown Library facsimile of the original in the British Library, London.

THE PREFACE

THe blustring Winds are husht into a Calme;
No Air stirs now, but what my Muse Embalm'd,
Breaths forth to thee, dear Friend; Heaven smiles upon
My Paper, and the Sea turnes Helicon;[2]
The Mermaids *Muses all, the* Sea-Nymphs, *bring*   5
Aid to my Genius, whilst to thee I Sing
Of Storms, Gusts, Tempests, if compar'd to these,
Bermoodus *Winds are but a Gentle Breez;*
And to express them fully, I am faine
To raise in Verse *a kind of* Hurrycane.   10

THE STORM

NOthing but Air and Water is in sight;
    (I am no Poet here, since Truth I wright.)
When *Eolus*[3] with his Iron whistle Rouzes
    The blustring breathings from their Airy houses,
Which like to *Libertines* let loose, will know   15
    No Law to guide them, but begin to blow
The Sea to swell her teaming Womb, brings forth
    Wave after wave, and each of greater birth:
Waves grow to Surges, Surges Billowes turn;
    The Ocean is all *Timpany*,[4] the *Urn*   20
Of water is a brimmer; *Neptune* drinks
    So full a Cup it over-runs the brinks.
To *Amphetrites*[5] Health, the proud waves dash
    At Heaven as though its Cloudy Face t'would wash:
Or sure the lower Water now was bent   25
    To mix with that above the Firmament;
Or the cold Element did go about
    To put the Element of Fire out.
Our Ship now under water seems to sayle
    Like to a drowned Tost in *John Cook's* Ale.[6]   30
The Sea rould up in Mountains: O! 'tis such
    Your *Cottsall-Hill's*[7] a Wart, if't be so much,

Which fall again into such hollow Vales
 I thought I'de crost the Sea by *Land* ore *Wales;*
And then to add Confusion to the Seas,   35
 The Saylers speak such *Babel* words as these:
Hale in maine Bowlin, Mizen tack aboard;
 A Language, like a Storm, to be abhorr'd:
I know not which was loudest, their rude Tongues,
 Or the Bigg Winds with her whole Cards of *Lungs.* 40
So hideous was the Noise, that one might well
 Fancy himself to be with Souls in Hell;
But that the Torments differ, those Souls are
 With Fire punisht, we with Water here.
Our Helme that should our *Swimming-Colledge* sway, 45
 We lash'd it up, lest it should run away.
Have you a Hedge seen hung with Beggars Fleeces?
 So hung our tattered *Mainsaile* down in pieces.
Our *Tackling* crack't as if it had been made
 To string some *Fiddle,* not the *Sea-mans* Trade. 50
Whilst her own *Knell* the Sea-sick *Vessel* Rings,
 In breaking of her *Ropes,* the Ships Heart-string
As to repent, but never to amend;
 So we pumpt th' Ship, even to as little end;
For all the water we pumpt out with pain,   55
 The Sea returns with scorne, and more again.
The Guns we carry'd to be our Defence,
 Heaven thunder'd so, it almost scar'd them thenc[e]
And yet to Heaven for this give thanks we may,
 But for it's Lightning we had had no Day.   60
The dropy Clouds drinking Salt-water sick,
 Did spew it down upon our Heads so thick;
That twixt the low'r and upper Seas that fell,
 Our Ship a *Vessel* seem'd, and we *Mackrell.*
Pickl'd in Brine, and in our Cabines lye   65
 Soust up for Lasting Immortality.
The Fear of being drowned, made us wish
 Our selves transpeciated into *Fish.*
Indeed this Fear did so possess each one,
 All look't like *Shotten-Herring,*[8] or *Poor-John:*[9] 70

Nay of our Saving, there was so much doubt,
   The Masters *Faith* begun to tack about;
And had he perish't in this doubtful Fit,
   His Conscience sure (with his own Ship) had [split]
For which way into Heaven could his Soul Steer,   75
   Starboard or *Larbord* that still cries, *No neer?*
But we were in great Danger, you will say,
   If *Sea-men* once begin to *Kneele,* and *Pray;*
What *Holy Church* ne're could, Rough Seas hav[e done]
   Made *Sea-men* buckle to Devotion,   80
And force from them their *Letany,* whilst thus
   They whimper out, *Good Lord deliver us!*
So pray I too, good Lord deliver thee,
   Dear Friend, from being taught to Pray at S[ea]
Be wise, and keep the *Shoar* then, since you m[ay]   85
   Go in by *Land* to your *VIRGINIA.*

NOTES

1. *Gulph* of *Florida.* That portion of the ocean lying between the Bahamas and the Atlantic coast of Florida.

2. Helicon. The largest mountain in Boetia, in east central Greece, and the sanctuary of the Muses.

3. *Eolus.* Aeolus, the god of winds.

4. *Timpany.* Swollen, puffed-up.

5. *Amphetrites.* Amphitrite, goddess of the waves.

6. *John Cook's* Ale. A general term for the common, low-quality beverage of taverns and public houses.

7. *Cottsall-Hill.* Cotswold or Cotteswolds, a range of hills in Gloucestershire, England.

8. *Shotten-Herring.* Herring of poor quality.

9. *Poor-John.* Hake or other fish, dried and salted; poor fare.

Richard Steere

A Monumental Memorial of Marine Mercy Being An Acknowledgment of an High Hand of Divine Deliverance on the Deep in the Time of distress, In a Late Voyage from Boston in New-England to London, Anno 1683

A trading master of the Cordwainers guild (and hence "Citizen of London"), Richard Steere came to America in 1683 at the age of forty, the emigration hastened by his involvement in politics as a writer of satirical verses that attacked the government of Charles II. When Steere returned to England briefly the following year, he found the political situation still uncongenial, but the stormy ocean crossing had provided occasion for his poem, *A Monumental Memorial of Marine Mercy,* a lively and fast-paced narrative of the ship *Adventure*'s near disaster in the North Atlantic.

Steere's poem not only gives us a vivid picture of the manifold distresses of a ship caught in a violent storm at sea, it also provides a perceptive psychological portrait of the fickle attitudes of the passengers and crew. *A Monumental Memorial* is also a didactic poem, allegorically portraying the voyage of the Christian pilgrim, a spiritual passage that parallels the temporal crossing. Yet the moral dimension of the poem is handled skillfully. The doctrinal purpose develops naturally in the narrative and is never allowed to impede the dramatic progress of the poem.

In 1685 Steere settled in New London, Connecticut, where he was for many years a merchant of the coasting and West Indies trade. In 1695 he wrote and signed, along

with three others, an eloquent defense of religious freedom.
In 1710 he moved across the Sound to Southold, Long
Island. A second volume of his poems to appear in
America, *The Daniel Catcher,* was published in Boston
in 1713. Steere died in Southold in 1721.

A Monumental Memorial was first printed by Richard
Pierce for James Cowse in Boston in 1684. A facsimile was
produced in George E. Littlefield's *Early Massachusetts
Press* (Boston: Odd Volumes, 1907), and more recently
Harrison T. Meserole edited it for his *Seventeenth-
Century American Poetry* (New York: New York Uni-
versity Press, 1968). For further information on Steere,
see Donald P. Wharton, *Richard Steere, Colonial Merchant
Poet* (University Park: Pennsylvania State University Press,
1978).

TEXT: Facsimile of Massachusetts Historical Society
first edition in Littlefield, corrected by Evans Microcard
(E377).

TO THE READER

Reader

I Here present thee with an Impartial Narrative, Collected from a
Diurnall,[1] *and other Credible Information of some Persons who had a
share in this so* never to be forgotten *a Deliverance, and at whose Importunity it was Reduced into this small* Tract, *and shrouded in the modern
Attire of* Measure *and* Cadency, *whose even and easie Pace being more
Alluring and Captivating (Especially with youth, or the Crittically Ingenious of this Age) than the Elaborate* Volumns *of* Prose *left to us by
our Worthy Ancestors, may probably the sooner* Decoy *or Invite thy
Perusal.*

I could not Conveniently avoyd the use of some Sea phrases *The Subject being a* Sea Deliverance, *tho they may seem improper and unintelligible to a* Land Capacity. *And if I have erred in missapplying those*
Termes *of* Art, *I hope thé Ingenious* Mariner *will attribute it to the want
of Experience in the* Tarpolin *Tongue:*

But to put a period to this Epistle,

Read and Admire the Mercy,—*Tho' the Stile*
May make thee think it hardly worth the while.

SInce Every *Quill* is silent to Relate
What being known must needs be wonder'd at
I take the boldness to present your *Eye*
With Safty's *Prospect* in Extremity,
Which tho not Cloath'd with *Academick* Skill,   5
Or lofty Raptures of a *Poet's* Quill;
But wrapt in *raggs,* through which your eyes may see
The *Naked* Truth in plain simplicitee.
   I without further prologue *Lanch with* Ink
With Captain *Balston* in th' *Adventure Pinck;*   10
Who in *December* on the fourteenth day,
His Anchors *weigh'd* in *Massachusetts BAY,*
New-England's Chiefest *Port,* and *sayling* on,
Soon *lay'd the Land* below the *Horizon.*
   The *Sea* was kind, the Sky serene and clear,   15
All seem to smile, no threating Frowns appear;
Yet sometimes Clouds of Rain, of Hail, of Snow,
Sometimes the *winds* more lofty, sometimes low,
   The *Mariners* and *Passengers a'board,*
Enjoying what the Vessel did afford   20
With Satisfaction, and in full Content:
This good beginning was Encouragement
Of good success, in hope and expectation
The Ship might prove an *Ark* of preservation;
Her *swelling sayls* gave her a nimble motion,   25
Making her *Keel* to *plough* the Yeilding *Ocean,*
Whose little *Billows* still her *Bow* out braves,
Glideing Tryumphant o're the *Curled waves.*
   Thus for five weeks the gentler winds did play
Upon the *Oceans* Surface to convey   30
Our little *Pinck,* filling her plyant Sayles
With easie *Breezes,* sweet *Topgallant Gailes:*
And now the *Mariners* by Judgment found
We did approach nigh to *Great Brittains* ground
And therefore *heav'd* the *Deep-sea lead* to *sound,*   35

Woodcut from Richard Steere's *Monumental Memorial of Marine Mercy* (Boston, 1684).
Courtesy of the Massachusetts Historical Society, Boston, Massachusetts.

Which tho they *Fathom'd* not did Truth afford,
For the same night a *Land bird* came *a'board*,
And the next morning we beheld two more
Which made the Judgment good they gave before
    Had we continu'd *thus* upon the Deep   40

We had bin Charm'd into a drowsie sleep
Of calme Security, nor had we known
The Excellence of *PRESERVATION;*
We had been Dumb and silent to Express
Affectedly the Voy'ges good success.   45
    But to awake and Rowse our sleepy minds,
The *Po'wrs* above let loose th' unruly winds,
Heav'ns milder *Puffs* with violence at last
Let fly more fierce, and *blow* a stronger *Blast:*
The dark'ned Sky with gloomy *Clouds* o're spread,   50
Whose moist'ned *fleeces* have *Enveloped*
Tempestous Flaws[2] which Issue more and more
In *Thunder*'s Language, or as *Cannons* roar:
The weighty Seas Roul from the *Deeps* beneath.
Hill stands on *hill* by force of Heav'n blown breath,   55
And from the *rocks foundations* do arise
As tho resolv'd to *storm* th' *Impending* Skyes;
Flaws from those lofty *Battlements* are hurld,
As to *a Chaos* they would shake the world:
Thus as between a warr of *Sea* and *Heaven,*   60
From place to place our little *Ship* is driven;
And by the Seas tost like a ball in sport,
From *wave to wave* in *Neptunes Tennis Court.*
    While thus the *winds & seas* their pow'rs dispute
A neighb'ring object did our Eyes salute,   65
A Sayle to windward; (in Distress no doubt)
Who *Fir'd a Gun* and *heav'd* their *Colours* out;
We *made* her *English,* but no help could give,
The Lofty Seas found each enough to *live*
But in the morning we *to windward* were   70
And *Bearing down* resolv'd to *speak with her,*
And understood she from *East India* came,
Under Command of Captain *Hide* by Name
Burden *six hundred Tuns* and *Ninety Men*
Having about ten *months* from *India* been,   75
And had bin *Beating* six weeks on the *Coast*
Wanting *Provis'on,* almost spent and Lost:

An Interval of *storms* became their friend,
And gave us leave some little help to lend;
The *storm* renewing its *Impetuous Force*   80
Did Each from Other further off Divorce,
Yet we might see them two or three dayes more,
But since have heard that they were drave *a'shore*
Somewhere in *Cornwall,* on the *Western Coast,*
And ev'ry *Soul* except two *Boyes* were lost.   85
   Still the resistless *winds* rebellious grow,
As they the *Universe* would Overthrow,
The pondrous *seas* like Rowling *Mountains* still,
Each *Billow* seeming an *Alpean* hill
By its prodigious Altitude: Despair   90
And fear of Danger, moves all lips to *pray'r*
Mixt with *Industry,* but *Industry* failes,
The *Pumps* are now in use but not the *Sayles,*
The Artist's *Quadrants* now are useless grown,
For *Darkness* dwells upon our *Horizon;*   95
Thus we for sev'ral days upon the *Ocean*
Did *Ly a Hull,* keeping our *Pumps* in motion;
Till *January twenty sixth* at night,
A mighty *Sea* did *Overwhelm* us quite,
Which falling down with a resistless stroke   100
Both our Ships *Waste* (or well built *Gunwalls*) broke
And carr'd away: now seeming like a *Wreck*
From the *Fore-castle* to the *Quarter Deck,*
The *Long boat, Windless, Captstern,* with the blow
Besides two weighty *Anchors* from the *Bow,*   105
With *Ropes,* & *Ring-bolts* (where ye *Boat* was fast,
And we constrain'd to cut our *Mizen mast,*)
All lost at once: Afflictions now prevail,
And each mans heart and strength begins to fail;
Sometimes we seem to *sink* sometimes to *float,*   110
The *Masters mate* tear's from his back his Coat
And stuffs between the *Timbers;* then they cry
For *Bedding, Ruggs, and Blankets* eagerly,
Which when obtain'd they Crowd into each place

Where *streames* of *water* Issu'd in apace: 115
But all Industry seems without success,
The *Rageing storm* grows rather more than Less;
Over those *Ruggs* they added *skins* of Bears,
And two new *Clothes* which our new *mainsail* spares;
Here may the hand of providence be Ey'd, 120
The *sayl* was made by those two *clothes* too wide,
Which by so much, we had made so much less
But a few dayes before our great Distress;
Ropes *Fore and Aft* were *streched* to secure
The *Mariners,* who scarcely could endure 125
Those *Big-swel'd Billows,* (what are feeble men?)
So oft wash'd in, and out and in agen,
Sometimes upon, sometimes within the Ocean;
The *Pumps* nev'r *sucking* tho in Constant motion;
Whilst all the men and women then *on board* 130
With earnest Cryes did call upon the *LORD*
The *Seas* did frequently *o'erflow* the *ship,*
And we were often buri'd in the *Deep:*
The Chests *between Decks swim* as in a *flood,*
Where men up to their *knees* in water stood, 135
Expecting ev'ry Moment *grim look'd Death*
With that cold Element would stop their breath.
    When suddenly a voice salutes our ears,
With Joy unspeakable amidst our Fears,
One of the PUMPS *does* SUCK! who can believe 140
What unexpected Comfort a *Repreive*
Brings a Condemned *Convict:* So that Voice
Caused each Cast down spirit to Rejoyce.
    But on the *Fifth* of *February* we
Ship'd a prodigious *Mountain of a sea,* 145
Which with a pondrous and resistless Stroke
The Fixed *Table* and the Benches broke,
And with its Force Op'ned the *Cabbin* Door.
A weighty *Chest of Tooles* away it bore,
Then with loud Ecchos ev'ry Tongue declares 150
Our Period come, our Hopes were now Despaires,

For we lay buri'd in the Oceans Womb,
And might conclude it was our wat'ry Tomb;
But an Almighty power became our Freind,
Causing our *buri'd Vessel* to Ascend,   155
And by degrees climb up the *Mountain waves,*
From whence our *eyes* might view our *fluid Graves;*
Thus the Great God did Snatch us from below,
Unto whose pow'r we all our safeties owe.
    Some few dayes after we a Ship might see,   160
Which *Coming up with* understood to be
For *England bound,* and from *Virginia* came,
Gregory Sugar was her *Captains* Name;
So *Leaky* (that tho they did what they could)
Sh' had *six* or *sev'n foot water in the Hould,*   165
The Safety of their *Lives* they only sought,
For to preserve their *Vessel* they could not,
And *Hoysting* out their *Boat* to come *a'board*
Which could not Safety to them all afford,
Yet *Thirteen* of them soon into it prest: 170
And *putting off,* promis'd to fetch the Rest:
When they came nigh our *Side* such fear was shown,
None sought the good of *others* but his *own,*
Each striving to preserve himself with hast,
Without regard to *make the Painter fast;*   175
(Had they Endeavour'd, it had bin in vain)
The *Boat* such wrong and dammage did sustain:
In *Laying us aboard* her *Bows* were *Stav'd,*
That t'was meer *Mercy* any man was sav'd:
Soon the Disabled *Boat was gon a drift,*   180
And now no hope of preservat'on left
For those behind, who were in number five,
For 'twas not possible the Ship should *Live,*
Nor with our Vessel did we dare come nigh,
For still the troubled Sea *ran mountains high,*   185
Tho their Intreaties, Peircing Cries and Grones,
Might even draw Remorsness out of Stones;
And now because of the approaching night,

We did advise them to *hang out a Light,*
Which but till eight a Clock appear'd in Sight,   190
After which time it did no more appear,
And we concluded (as we well might fear)
They then went down: Tho we could not *relieve*
Their *wants,* their *loss* we could not choose but *grieve.*
    And now some Comfort we begin to find,   195
The *winds* are *Calmer* and the *Seas* more kind,
Now Heav'ns alscourging hand its strokes withdrew
And former Consolations did Renew,
By giving us at length the *Sight* of *Land,*
By an Or'e ruling providential hand: 200
Our Cloudy cares appear to fly apace,
And Comforts seemingly supply their place;
The fourteenth day at *Plymouth* we Arrive,
With those thirteen we had preserv'd alive:
The nineteenth day for *London* we *set sayle,*   205
With not too much *wind,* but a mod'rate Gale.
But as if *Heav'n* with anger should reprove,
That we those mercies did not well Improve;
Its *Breath* comes forth with *Fury* as before,
And we tho in the *Downes*[3] and nigh the *Shore,*   210
Must feel more *strokes* of the chastising *Rod*
Of our offended of our angry GOD.
    The Two and twentieth day much *wind* did blow,
When in the *Downs* we let our *Anchor* goe,
But it *came home:* we our *Shift Anchor Cast,*   215
Which (*insignificant*) *came home* as fast,
And we were driven up *alongst* the *Side*
Of a *Ship* there, which did at *Anchor ride,*
Our *Anchor* took her *Cable,* and did pass
Up with a speedy motion to her *Hass,*   220
Which at their *Bows* they *Cutting* from the *Cable,*
And t'other *Anchor* being too unable
To bring us up, broke in the *shank,* and we
Again (by Violence) *Drove out to Sea;*
We thought to *Anchor* then in *Poulstone Bay,*[4]   225

And let our *small Bower go* without delay,
Which like a rotten stick was quickly broke
(When once it came to strain) both *flewks* & *stock,*
Neither *Shift-Anchor, Best* nor yet *Small Bower*
To *Bring us up* had strength enough or power;   230
And in the Afternoon the *winds* Restrain
Their furious *Blasts,* now only did remain
Our small *Cedge Anchor,* (unto which we must
Our *Lives,* our *Ship,* and all her *Cargo* trust,)
Which *Letting go,* Heav'ns care did so provide,   235
That we that *Ebb* secure in safety *Ride;*
From which our apprehensions may Inspect,
How the *Great* God by *Small* meanes doth protect,
Whose strength can make our strongest *cables* weak,
Our *Cobwebs* strong, no earthly strein can break,   240
That we might put no Trust in *Earthen* Powers:
For weak is all the *Fortitude* of Ours.
An *Anchor* we that night from *Shore* obtain.
And so Return into the *Downs* again,
And *weighing* thence, favour'd with *winds* & *floods,*   245
Our *selves* in Safety with our *ship* and *goods,*
The *Twenty fifth* (assisted by the Lord)
Arriv'd at *London* and at *Ratcliff Moor'd.*
   Thou God of this great Vast, *that aloft Command*
             With thy Almighty Hand,   250
            Water, Earth, Air, and Fire
(The Elements:) the Sun, *the* Moon, *and* Stars
          Act not their own affaires,
           But what thou dost require:
O who can view thy pow'r, & not thy pow'r admire.   255
Tis thou Alone art our alone support,
          Thy Mercy's our strong fort,
          Thou giv'st us length of dayes,
To thee th' Almighty and Tri-une *JEHOVE,*
          Dwelling in Heav'en *above;*   260
          Be Everlasting Praise;
O who can tast thy Good, & *not* Thanksgiving *Raise.*

NOTES

1. Diurnall. A daybook or journal.
2. *Flaws.* Lightning.
3. *Downes.* Roadstead in the English Channel, along the east coast of Kent, about nine miles long and six miles wide; affords excellent anchorage, protected by a natural breakwater, the Goodwin Sands.
4. *Poulstone Bay.* Undoubtedly this should be Folkstone Bay in Kent, six miles southwest of Dover. Poulstone is a landlocked village in Gloucestershire.

John Dean and Christopher Langman
The Voyage of the *Nottingham Galley*

The wreck of the *Nottingham Galley* of London on
Boon Island on December 11, 1710, may well be the most
famous eighteenth-century shipwreck in New England.
The reasons are not far to seek. After nearly three weeks
on a rock where their only provisions were a few bits of
cheese, some beef bones, seaweed, and a single sea gull,
the crew began to eat their dead. A few days later the
castaways were sighted from the shore and later taken
off the island.

Cannibalism is not a unique phenomenon in the history
of sailing (there are in fact three instances of it in the
narratives of this edition). Yet the proximity of Boon
Island made news of the tragedy there which shocked
the coastal communities of New England and even created
a stir in England. In Massachusetts Cotton Mather promptly
appended a version of the story (apparently gathered from
Samuel Penhallow, a magistrate of Portsmouth) to a sermon
written in response to the occasion. Well aware that a market
for their story also awaited them in England, the Dean
brothers hurried back to London where two editions were
run off, one intended for distribution in Northern Ireland
and Scotland, the other (with Jasper Dean's preface) for
England.

The continuing popularity of Dean's narrative is attested
to by the numerous printings and reprintings. In addition to

the editions already noted, new editions appeared in 1722, 1730, 1738, and 1762. Other American editions were printed with the sermons of William Shurtleff in 1727 and Samuel Wilson in 1735. In the nineteenth century Dean's narrative found its way into several anthologies, including Archibald Duncan's *Mariner's Chronicle* (1804) and R. Thomas's *Remarkable Shipwrecks* (1835). Mason P. Smith edited the 1762 edition for separate publication (Portland, Maine: Provincial Press, 1968) and Keith Huntress reprinted the 1727 edition in his *Narratives of Shipwrecks and Disasters, 1586-1860* (Ames, Ia.: Iowa State University Press, 1974).

Ironically, the very popularity of Dean's narrative has tended to obscure the other version of what took place aboard the *Nottingham Galley* and on Boon Island. After Dean's first London edition appeared in 1711, the first mate of the *Nottingham Galley*, Christopher Langman, and two other members of the crew, Nicholas Mellen and George White, published their story. Langman and the others contradict Dean's account in several respects and throughout their narrative blame the captain for the wreck. Dean stoutly maintained his innocence in later editions, even using the narrative as an occasion for moralizing on the wayward lives of sailors. However, in light of Langman's accusations it does seem that the captain protests a bit too much. Langman for his part entertained a hearty dislike for Dean even in the best of circumstances, and his antipathy strongly colors his account. As is usual in such cases, the truth probably lies somewhere in between.

In later years Dean served as His Majesty's consul for the Port of Flanders. Christopher Langman and his shipmates, having neither position nor influence, disappeared from public view. Their story has not been printed since 1711.

TEXT: Dean's first London edition by R. Tookey and S. Popping (1711) in the Houghton Library, Harvard University; Langman's 1711 edition, also by Tookey and Popping, in the Library of Congress.

John Dean

A Narrative of the Sufferings, Preservation and Deliverance, Of Capt. John Dean and Company; In the *Nottingham-Gally* of London, cast away on Boon-Island, near New England, December 11, 1710.

THE PUBLISHER TO THE READER

A *Few Months past, I little expected to appear in Print (especially on* such Occasion) *but the frequent Enquiries of many* curious *Persons (as also the Design of others, to publish the Account without us) seem to lay me under an* absolute Necessity, *least others less acquainted, prejudice the Truth with an* imperfect *Relation. Therefore, finding my self oblig'd to expose this small Treatise to publick View and Censure, I perswade my self, that what's here recorded will be* entirely *credited, by all* candid, ingenious Spirits; *for whose kind Opinion* [I] *am* really *sollicitous.*

I presume, any Person acquainted with my Brother, will readily believe the Truth hereof: And for the Satisfaction *of others, I woud hope need only offer, that both his Character and my own may be easily gain'd by Enquiry: Likewise several of his Fellow Sufferers being now in Town, their Attestations might be procur'd, if saw a real Necessity.*

I have in the whole endeavour'd a plain smooth, unaffected *stile, suitable to the Occasion, carefully avoiding* unnecessary *Enlargements, and relating only* Matters *of* Fact.

I must acknowledge to have (in composing from my Brothers Copy) omitted many lesser *Circumstances, least shou'd swell this Narrative beyond it's* first *Design, and thereby exceed the Bounds of* common *Purchase.*

It's almost needless to intimate what Approbation the Copy has reciv'd, from many Persons, of the most curious *and* discerning *Judgments who have done me the Favour to view it, urging its Publication, and (at least) flattering me with an Expectation of a general Acceptance, considering it both as* Novel *and* Real.

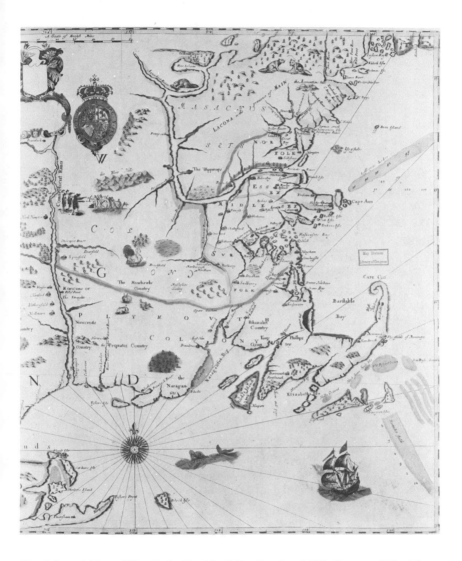

Detail from *A Mapp of New England* by John Seller (London, 1686). Courtesy of The Library of Congress, Washington, D.C.

I cannot but also take Encouragement from the Value and Esteem it met with when appearing under much greater Disadvantages, as to Particulars and Dress in New England, North Britain, &c. So that adventure it into the the World, to receive its Applause or Censures, according to its Demerrits or the Fancy of the Reader.

The Account I have receiv'd of those worthy New England Gentlemens Kindness to the poor Men in their Extremities, affected me in the most near and sensible manner, and which to omitt making honourable mention of, wou'd be the highest Ingratitude (an evil I hope, forreign to my Temper.)

How generous, Christian-like, and worthy of Immitation, have these Gentlemen behav'd themselves, to such Objects of Commiseration who must otherwise (in all Probability) have been render'd unable to serve their Families (methinks I am glad such a noble compasionate humane Temper is still found amongst Men) and how happy wou'd it be for us, did this kind and publick Spirit more prevail among us, as on the contrary, how much to be lamented is that barbarous and salvage Custom of murdering fellow Creatures (shipwrackt on our Coasts) in Order to plunder and rifle them with the greater Ease: A Crime so brutish and agravated (and yet so frequently practic'd as to be the common Disgrace of a Christian Nation.

I might offer Abundance more Thoughts (pertinent enough) on these and other subjects in this Preface, but I am fearfull least shou'd make the Porch too large for the House; therefore conclude, subscribing my self (candid Reader) thine in all Friendly Offices,

Jasper Dean.

THE *Nottingham Gally,* of and from *London,* 120 Tons, 10 Guns, and 14 Men, *John Dean Commander;* having taken in Cordage[1] in *England,* and Butter and Cheese, &c. in *Ireland,* sail'd for *Boston* in *New England,* the 25th of *September,* 1710. But meeting with contrary Winds and bad Weather, 'twas the Beginning of *December* when first made Land to the Eastward of *Piscataqua,*[2] and haling *Southerly* for the *Massachuset's-Bay,* under a hard gale of Wind at *North-East,* accompanied with Rain, Hail and Snow, having no Observation for 10 or 12 Days. We on the Eleventh handed all our Sails, except our Fore-Sail, and Main-Top-Sail double reeft, ordering one Hand forward to look out: Between 8 and 9 going forward my self, I saw the *Breakers* a Head, whereupon I call'd out to put the

Helm hard a Starboard, but 'ere the Ship cou'd wear, we struck upon the East End of the Rock called *Boon-Island,* 4 Leagues to the Eastward of *Piscataqua.*

The Second or Third Sea heav'd the Ship along Side of it, running likewise so very high, and the Ship labouring so excessively that we were not able to stand upon Deck, and notwithstanding it was not above 30 or 40 Yards, yet the Weather was so thick and dark we cou'd not see the Rock, so that we were justly thrown into a Consternation, at the sad Prospect of immediately perishing in the Sea. I presently call'd down all Hands to the Cabin, where we continu'd a few Minutes earnestly supplicating Mercy; but knowing Prayers without Endeavours are vain, I order'd all up again, to cut the Masts by the board, but several sunck so under Racks of Conscience, that they were not able to stir: However, we upon Deck cut the Weather-most Shrouds, and the Ship heeling towards the Rock, the Force of the Sea soon broke the Masts, so that they fell right towards the Shore.

One of the Men went out on the Boltspright, and returning, told me he saw something black a Head, and wou'd adventure to get on Shore, accompanied with any other Person; upon which I desir'd some of the best Swimmers (my Mate and one more) to go with him, and if they recover'd the Rock, to give Notice by their Calls, and direct us to the most secure Place; and remembring some Money and Papers that might be of use, also Ammunition, Brandy, &c. I went down and open'd the Place in which they were, but the Ship bulging, her Decks opening, her Back broke, and Beams giving Way, so that the Stern sunk almost under Water, I was oblig'd to hasten forward, to prevent immediate perishing: And having heard nothing of the Men gone before, concluded them lost; yet notwithstanding, I was under a Necessity to make the same Adventure upon the Fore Mast, moving gradually forward betwixt every Sea, 'till at last quitting it, I cast my self with all the Strength I had toward the Rock, and it being dead low Water and the Rock exceeding slippery I cou'd get no Hold, but tore my Fingers, Hands and Arms in a most lamentable Manner; every Wash of the Sea fetching me off again, so that it was with the utmost Peril and Difficulty that I got safe on Shore at last. The Rest of the Men running the same Hazard yet thro' Mercy we all escap'd with our Lives.

After endeavouring to discharge the Salt-Water, and creeping a little Way up the Rock, I heard the Three Men mentioned before, and by Ten all met together; where with joyfull Hearts we return'd humble Thanks to

Providence for our Deliverance from so eminent a Danger; we then endeavour'd to gain Shelter to the Lee-ward of the Rock, but found it so
small and inconsiderable, that it wou'd afford none (being but about 100
Yards long, and Fifty broad) and so very craggy, that we cou'd not walk
to keep our selves warm, the Weather still continuing extream cold, with
Snow and Rain.

As soon as Day-light appear'd, I went towards the Place where we
came on Shoar, not questioning but we should meet with Provisions
enough from the Wreck for our Support, but found only some Pieces of
the Masts and Yards, amongst some old Junk and Cables conger'd together, which the Anchors had prevented from being carried away, and
kept moving about the Rock at some Distance: Part of the Ships Stores
with some Pieces of Plank and Timber, old Sails and Canvas &c. drove
on Shoar, but nothing to eat, except some small Pieces of Cheese we pick'd
up from among the Rock-Weed[3] (in the whole, to the Quantity of three
small Cheeses).

We used our utmost Endeavour to get Fire, (having a Steel and Flint
with us, also by a Drill with a very swift Motion) but having nothing but
what had been long water-soak'd, we could not effect it.

At Night we stow'd one upon another (under our Canvas) in the best
Manner possible, to keep each other warm; and the next Day the Weather
a little clearing, and inclining to Frost, I went out, and seeing the main
Land knew where we was, therefore encouraged my Men with Hopes of
being discover'd by fishing Shallops &c. requiring them to go about, and
fetch up what Planks they could get, (as also Carpenters Tools and Stores
&c.) in order to build a Tent and a Boat: The Cook then complaining he
was almost starv'd, and his Countenance discovering his Illness, I ordered
him to remain with 2 or 3 more the Frost had seiz'd: About noon the
Men acquainted me that he was dead, so laid him in a convenient Place
for the Sea to carry him away; none mentioning eating of him, tho' several
with my self afterwards acknowledged, had Tho'ts of it.

After we had been there 2 or three Days, the Frost being very severe,
and the Weather extream cold, it seized most of our Hands and Feet to
such a Degree, as to take away the Sence of Feeling, and render them almost useless; so benumbing and discolouring them, as gave us just Reason
to fear Mortifications. We pull'd off our Shoes, and cut off our Boots,
but in getting off our Stockings, many whose Legs were blister'd, pull'd
off Skin and all, and some the Nails of their Toes; we wrap'd up our Legs
and Feet as warm as we could in Oakum and Canvas.

We now began to build our Tent in a triangular Form, each Angle about 8 Foot, covered with what Sails and old Canvas came on Shoar, having just Room for all to lie down each on one Side, so that none cou'd turn except all turn'd, which was about every two Hours, upon Notice given: We also fix'd a Staff to the Top of our Tent, upon which (as often as Weather wou'd permit) we hoisted a Piece of Cloth in the Form of a Flag, in order to discover our selves to any Vessels that might come near.

We began now to build our Boat of Plank and Timber belonging to the Wreck; our Tools the Blade of a Cutlash (made into a Saw with our Knives) a Hammer and a Caulking Mallet: Some Nails we found in the Clifts of the Rock, others we got from the Sheathing; we laid 3 Planks flat for the Bottom, and Two up each Side fix'd to stauchings, and let into the bottom Timbers, with two short Pieces at each End, also one Breadth of new Holland Duck round the Sides, to keep out the Spr[a]y of the Sea: We cork'd all we could with Oakum drawn from the old junk, and in other Places, fill'd up the Distances with long Pieces of Canvas, all which we secured in the best Manner possible; we found also some Sheet Lead and Pump Leather, which proved of use; we fix'd a short Mast and square Sail, with Seven Padles to row, and another longer to stear; but our Carpenter who now should have been of most use to us, was (by reason of Illness) scarce able to affoard us either Assistance or Advice; and all the Rest so benumb'd and Feeble as not able to stir, except my self and 2 more, also the Weather so extream cold, that we could seldom stay out of the Tent above 4 Hours in the Day, and some Days do nothing at all.

When we had been there about a Week without any manner of Provisions, except the Cheese before mentioned and some Beefe Bones, which we eat (first beating them to Pieces); we saw 3 Boats about 5 Leagues from us, which may be easily imagined rejoyced us not a little, believing our Deliverance was now come: I made all creep out of the Tent, and hollow together (so well as our Strength would allow) making also all the Signals we could, but alass all in vain; they neither hearing nor otherwise discovering us: however we receiv'd no small Encouragement from the Sight of 'em, they coming from S. West, and the Wind at N.E. when we were cast away, gave us reason to conclude our Distress might be known, by the Wreck driving on Shoar, and to presume were come out in search of us, and that they would Daily do so when Weather would permit; thus we flatter'd our selves in hopes of Deliverance tho' in vain.

Just before we had finished our Boat, Providence so ordered it, that the Carpenter's Ax was cast on the Rock to us, whereby we were enabled

to compleat our Work; but then we had scarce Strength enought to get
her into the Water.

About the 21st (*December*) the Boat just perfected, a fine Day, and
the Water smoother than I had ever yet seen it since we came there, we
consulted who shou'd attempt getting on Shore, I offering my self as one
to adventure, which they agreed to, because I was the strongest, and therefore fittest to undergoe the Extremities we might be reduc'd to. My Mate
also offering himself, and desiring to accompany me, I was allow'd him
with my Brother, and four more; so committing our Enterprize to Divine
Providence, all that were able came out, and with much Difficulty we
got our poor patch'd-up Boat to the Water Side; and the Surf running
very high, was oblig'd to wade very deep to launch her, which being done,
and my self and one more got into her, the Swell of the Sea heav'd her
along Shore, and overset her upon us, (whereby we again narrowly escap'd drowning) and stav'd our poor Boat all to pieces: Totally disappoint-
ing our Enterprize and destroying all our Hopes at once.

And as that which still heighten'd our Afflictions, and serv'd to aggravate our miserable prospects, and render our Deliverance less practicable:
We lost with our Boat, both our Ax and Hammer, which wou'd have been
of great Use to us if we should hereafter attempt to build a Raft, yet had
we reason to admire the Goodness of God, in over-ruling our Disappointment, for our Safety; for that Afternoon, the Wind springing up it blew
very hard, so that had we been at Sea in the imitation of a Boat, in all
probability we must have perish'd, and the rest left behind had no better
Fare, because unable to help themselves.

We were now reduc'd to the most deplorable and mallancholy Circumstance imaginable, almost every Man but my self, weak to an Extremity,
and near starved with Hunger and Cold; their Hands and Feet frozen and
mortified, with large and deep Ulcers in their Legs (the very smell offensive
to those of us, who could creep into the Air) and nothing to dress them
with, but a Piece of Linnen that was cast on Shoar. No Fire, and the
Weather extream cold; our small Stock of Cheese spent, and nothing to
support our feeble Bodies but Rock-weed and a few Muscles, scarce and
difficult to get (at most, not above 2 or 3 for each Man a Day). So that
we had our miserable Bodies perishing, and our poor disconsolate Spirits
overpowerd, with the deplorable Prospect of starving, without any Appearance of Relief: Besides, to heighten (if possible) the Agravation, we had
reason to apprehend, least the approaching Spring-Tide (if accompanied

with high Winds) should totally overflow us. How dismal such a Circumstance must be, is imposible to express; the pinching Cold and Hunger, extremity of Weakness and Pain, Racks and Horror of Conscience (to many) and Foresight of certain and painful (but lingring) Death, without any (even the most remote) views of Deliverance. How heighten'd? How agravated? Is such Misery! and yet alass such was our deplorable Case: insomuch that the greater Part of our Company were ready to die with Horror and Despair, without the least Hopes of Escaping.

For my own Part, I did my utmost to encorage my self, and exhort the rest to trust in God and patiently wait for his Salvation; and Providence, a little to aleviate our Distress, and encourage our Faith, directed my Mate to strike down a Sea Gull, which he joyfully brought to me, and I equally divided every one a Proportion; and (tho' raw and scarce every one a Mouthful) yet we received and eat thankfully.

The last Method of Safety we could possibly propose, was, the fixing a Raft that might carry Two Men, which was mightily urged by one of our Men, a Sweed, a stout brave Fellow, but had since our Distress lost both his Feet by the Frost; he frequently importun'd me, to attempt our Deliverance in that Way, offering himself to accompany me, or if I refused him, to go alone: After deliberate Thoughts and Consideration, we resolv'd upon a Raft, but found abundance of Labour and Difficulty in clearing the Fore-Yard (of which it was chiefly to be made) from the Junk, by reason our working Hands were so few and weak.

That done, we split the Yard, and with the two Parts made Side Pieces, fixing others, and adding some of the lightest Plank we cou'd get, first spiking and afterwards seizing them firm, in Breadth 4 Foot: We likewise fix'd a Mast, and of two Hammocks that were drove on Shoar we made a Sail, with a Paddle for each Man and a spare one in Case of Necessity. This Difficulty thus surmounted and brought to a period, he wou'd frequently ask me whether I design'd to accompany him, giving me also to understand that if I declin'd, there was another ready to embrace the Offer.

About this Time we saw a Sail come out of *Piscataqua* River, about 7 Leagues to the Westward, we again made all the signal we cou'd, but the Wind being at N. West, and the Ship standing to the Eastward, was presently out of sight, without ever coming near us, which prov'd a very great Mortification to our Hopes; but the next Day being moderate, and in the Afternoon a small Breze right on Shoar, also the Raft wholy finish'd, the two Men were very solicitous to have it launch'd, and the Mate as strenuously oppos'd it, on account 'twas so late (being 2 in the Afternoon) but they urging the light Nights, beg'd of me to have it done, to which at last I agreed, first commiting the Enterprize to God's Blessing; they both got upon it, and the Swell rowling very high soon overset them as it did our Boat; the Sweed not minding it swam on Shoar, but the other (being no Swimmer) continu'd some Time under Water, and as soon as appear'd, I caught hold of him and sav'd him, but was so discourag'd, that he was afraid to make a second Attempt.

I desir'd the Sweed to wait a more favourable Oportunity, but he continuing resolute, beg'd of me to go with him, or help him to turn the Raft, and would go himself alone.

By this Time another Man came down and offer'd to adventure, so getting upon the Raft I launch'd 'em off, they desiring us to go to Prayers, also to watch what became of them; I did so, and by Sunset judg'd them half Way to the Main, and that they might reach the Shoar by 2 in the Morning: But I suppose they fell in with some Breakers, or the Violence of the Sea overset them and they perish'd; for two Days after, the Raft was found on Shoar, and one Man dead about a Mile from it, with a Paddle fastned to his Wrist; but the Sweed who was so very forward to adventure, was never heard of more.

We upon the desolate Island not knowing what had befallen them, waited daily for Deliverance, and our expectations was the more heightend by a smoak we saw in the Woods, two Days after (the Signal appointed if arriv'd safe) which continuing every Day, and being willing to believe it made on our Account, tho' saw no appearance of any thing towards our Relief, yet suppos'd the Delay was occasion'd, by their not being able to procure a Vessel so soon as we desir'd; and this Hope under God, serv'd to bear our Spirits and Support us much.

But still our great Want was Provisions; having nothing to eat but Rockweed and a very few Muscles, and the Spring-Tide[4] being (thank God safely over) we cou'd scarce get any at all. I have gone my self (no other Person being able) several Days at low Water, and cou'd get no more than 2 or 3 a Piece, and have frequently been in Danger of losing my Hands and Arms by putting them so often in the Water, which when got, my Stomach refus'd, and rather chose Rockweed.

At our first coming saw several *Seals* upon the Rock, and supposing they might harbour there in the Night, I walkt round at Midnight, but cou'd never get any Thing: We also saw a great many Fowls, but they perceiving us daily there, wou'd never come on the Rock to lodge, so that we caught none.

Which Disappointment was very greivous and still serv'd to irritate our Miseries, but it was more especially afflicting to a Brother I had with me, and another young Gentleman, who had never (either of 'em) been at Sea, or endur'd any Severities before; but were now reduc'd to the last Extreamities, having no assistance but what they receiv'd from me.

Part of a Green Hide[5] being thrown up by the Sea, (fasten'd to a Peice of the Main-Yard) the Men importun'd me to bring it to the Tent, which being done we minc'd it small and swallow'd it down.

About this Time, I set the Men to open Junck, and with the Rope-Yarn (when Weather wou'd permit) I thatcht the Tent in the best Manner my Strength wou'd allow; that it might the better shelter us from Extreamities of Weather: And it prov'd of so much Service as to turn 2 or 3 Hours Rain, and preserve us from the cold pinching winds which were always very severe upon us.

About the latter End of this Month (viz. *December*) our Carpenter (a fat Man, and naturaly of a dull, heavy, Phlegmatick Constitution and Disposition, aged about 47) who from our first coming on Shore, had been always very ill, and lost the Use of his Feet, complain'd of an excessive Pain in his Back, and Stiffness in his Neck: being likewise almost choakt with Phlegm (for Want of Strength to discharge it) so that to our Aprehension he drew near his End. We praied over him, and us'd our utmost Endeavours to be serviceable to him in his last Moments; he shew'd himself sensible tho' speechless, and that Night died: We suffered the Body to remain with us 'till Morning, when I desir'd them who were best able, to remove it; creeping out my self, to see if Providence had yet sent us any thing, to satisfie our extreamly craving Appetites: Before Noon returning and not seeing the dead Body without, I ask'd why they had not remov'd it? And receiv'd for Answer, they were not all of them able: Whereupon fastening a Rope to the Body, I gave the Utmost of my Asistance, and with some Difficulty we got it out of the Tent. But the Fategue and Consideration of our Misery together, so overcame my Spirits, that being ready to faint I crept into the Tent, and was no sooner got in there, but (as the highest Addition of Trouble) the Men began to request of me the dead Body to eat, the better to support their Lives.

This, of all I had met with, was the most greivous and shocking to me, to see my self and Company, who came thither laded with Provisions but three Weeks before, now reduc'd to such a deplorable Circumstance, as

to have two of us absolutely starv'd to Death, other two we knew not
what was become of, and the Rest of us at the last Extreamity and (tho'
still living, yet) requiring to eat the Dead for Support.

After Abundance of mature Thought and Consultation about the Law-
fullness or Sinfullness on the one Hand, and absolute Necessity on the
other; Judgment, Conscience, &c. were oblig'd to submit to the more
prevailing Arguments of our craving Appetites; so that at last we determined to satisfie our Hunger and support our feeble Bodies with the
Carkass in Possession: first ordering his Skin, Head, Hands, Feet and
Bowels to be buried in the Sea, and the Body to be quarter'd for Conveniency of drying and carriage, to which I again receiv'd for Answer,
that they were not all of them able, but entreated I wou'd perform it for
them: A Task very greivous, and not readily comply'd with, but their
incessant Prayers and Intreaties at last prevail'd, and by Night I had perform'd my Labour.

I then cut Part of the Flesh in thin Slices, and washing it in Saltwater,
brought it to the Tent, and oblig'd the Men to eat Rockweed along with
it, to serve instead of Bread.

My Mate and two others, refus'd to eat any that Night, but next
Morning complied, and earnestly desir'd to partake with the Rest.

I found they all eat abundance and with the utmost Greediness, so
that I was constrain'd to carry the Quarters farther from the Tent, (quite
out of their Reach) lest they shou'd prejudice themselves by overmuch
eating, as also expend our small Stock too soon.

I also limited each Man to an equal Proportion, that none might quarrel,
or entertain hard thoughts of my self, or one another, and I was the more
oblig'd to this Method, because I found (in a few Days) their very natural
Dispositions chang'd, and that affectionate, peacable Temper they had
all along hitherto, discover'd totally lost; their Eyes staring and looking
wild, their Countenances fierce and barbarous, and instead of obeying
my Commands (as they had universally and readily done before) I found
all I cou'd say (even Prayers and Entreaties vain and fruitless) nothing
now being to be heard but brutish Quarrels, with horrid Oaths and Imprecations, instead of that quiet submissive Spirit of Prayer and Supplica-
tion we had before enjoy'd.

This, together with the dismal Prospect of future Want, oblig'd me to
keep a strict Watch over the Rest of the Body, least any of 'em shou'd
(if able) get to it, and this being spent, we be forc'd to feed upon the

living: Which we must certainly have done, had we staid a few Days longer.

But now the Goodness of God began to appear, and make Provision for our Deliverance, by putting it in the Hearts of the good People on Shore, where our Raft drove, to come out in Search of us; which they did the 2d of *January* in the Morning.

Just as I was creeping out of the Tent, I saw a Shallop half Way from Shore, standing directly towards us, which may be easily imagin'd was Life from the Dead; how great our Joys and Satisfactions were, at the Prospect of so speedy and unexpected Deliverance, no Tongue is able to express, nor Thoughts to conceive.

Our good and welcome Friends came to an Anchor to the *South-West*, at about 100 Yards distance, (the Swell not suffering them to come nearer) but their Anchor coming home, oblig'd them to stand off 'till about Noon, waiting for smoother Water upon the Flood: Mean Time our Passions were differently mov'd, our Expectations of Deliverance, and Fears of Miscarriage, hurry'd our weak and disorder'd Spirits strangely.

I gave them Account of our Miseries in every Respect, except the Want of Provisions (which I did not mention, least I shou'd not get them on shore for fear of being constrain'd by the Weather to tarry with us): Earnestly entreating them to attempt our immediate Deliverance; or at least (if possible) to furnish us with Fire, which with the utmost Hazard and Difficulty they at last accomplished, by sending a small Cannoe with one Man, who with Abundance of Labour got on Shore.

After helping him up with his Canoe, and seeing nothing to eat, I ask'd him if he cou'd give us Fire, he answer'd in the Affirmative, but was so affrighted, (seeing me look so thin and meagre) that could hardly at first return me an Answer: But recollecting himself, after several Questions askt on both Sides, he went with me to the Tent, where was surpriz'd to see so many of us in so deplorable Condition.

Our Flesh so wasted, and our Looks so gastly and frightful, that it was really a very dismal Prospect.

With some Difficulty we made a Fire, determining to go my self with the Man on Board, and after to send for the Rest, one or two at a Time, and accordingly got both into the Canoe, but the Sea immediately drove it with such Violence against the Rock, that overset us into the Water; and I being very weak, 'twas a great while before cou'd recover my self, so that I had again a very narrow Escape from Drowning.

The good Man with very great Difficulty, got on Board himself without me, designing to return the next Day with better Conveniences if Weather wou'd permit.

'Twas a very uncomfortable Sight to see our worthy Friends in the Shallop stand away for the Shore without us: But God who orders all our Affairs (by unseen Movements) for the best, had doubtless Designs of Preservation towards us, in denying us that Appearance of present Deliverance: For that Night the Wind coming about to *South-East,* blowing hard and being dark Weather, our good Friends lost their Shallop, and with extream Difficulty sav'd their Lives: But, in all Probability, had we been with them, we must have perish'd, not having Strength sufficient to help our selves.

Immediately after their getting on Shore, they sent an Express to *Portsmouth* in *Piscataqua,* where soon as Weather wou'd allow: But to our great Sorrow, and for further Trial of our Patience, the next Day continu'd very stormy, so that, tho' we doubted not, but the People on Shore knew our Condition, and wou'd assist us as soon as possible, yet our Flesh being near spent, no fresh Water, nor any Certainty how long the Weather might continue thus, render'd our Circumstance still miserable, tho' much advantag'd by the Fire, for now we cou'd both warm our selves, and broil our Meat.

The next Day, our Men urging me vehemently for Flesh, I gave them a little more than usual, but not to their Satisfaction, for they wou'd certainly have eat up the whole at once, had I not carefully watch'd 'em, designing to share the rest next Morning, if the Weather continu'd bad: But it pleased God that Night the Wind abated, and early next Morning a Shallop came for us, with my much esteemed friends Captain *Long* and Captain *Purver* and three more Men, who brought a large Canoe, and in two Hours Time got us all on Board to their Satisfaction and our great Comfort: Being forc't to carry almost all the Men on their Backs, from the Tent to the Canoe, and fetch us off by two or three at a Time.

When we first came on Board the Shallop, each of us eat a Bit of Bread and drank a Dram of Rumm, and most of us were extreamly Sea sick; but after we had cleans'd our Stomachs, and tasted warm nourishing Food, we became so exceeding hungry and ravenous, that had not our worthy Friends dieted us (and limited the Quantity for about two or three Days) we shou'd certainly have destroy'd our selves with eating.

We had also two other Vessels came off for our Assistance, if there had been any Necessity (so generous and charitable were the good People of *New-England,* in our Distress) but seeing us all on Board the shallop made the best of their Way Home again.

At Eight at Night we came on Shore, where we were kindly entertain'd my self and another at a private House (having Credit sufficient to help us) all the Rest at the Charge of the Government, who took such care that the poor Men knew not the least want of any thing their necessitys call'd for or the kind and generous *Gentlemen* cou'd furnish them with (the care Industry and Generosity of my much honoured Friends *John Plaisted,* Esq; and Captain *John Wentworth,* in serving both my self and these poor Men being particularly eminent) providing them a good Surgeon and Nurses 'till well, bearing the Charge, and afterwards allowing each Man sufficient Cloathing; behaving themselves in the whole, with so much Freedom, Generosity and Christian Temper, that was no small Addition to their other Services, and render'd the whole worthy both of Admiration and Imitation; and likewise was of the last Consequence to the poor Men in their Distreses.

Two Days after we came on Shore, my Apprentice lost a great Part of one Foot, the rest all recover'd their Limbs, but not their perfect Use. Very few (beside my self) escaping without losing the Benefit of Fingers or Toes, &c. tho' thank God all otherwise in perfect Health; some sailing one Way and some another: My Mate and two or three more now in *England* at the Publication hereof.

Postcript.

HAving two or three spare Pages, we think it our Duty to the Truth, and our selves, to obviate *a barbarous and scandelous Reflection, industriously spread abroad and level'd at our ruine, by some unworthy, malicious Persons (viz.)* That we having ensur'd more than our Intrest in the Ship *Nottingham,* agreed and willfully lost her, first designing it in *Ireland,* and afterwards effecting it at *Boon Island.*

Such a base and villanous Reflection, scarse merrits the Trouble of an Answer, were not Truth and Reputation so much concern'd: Therefore, as to the Business of Ireland, *'tis really preposterous (the Commander not knowing there was one Penny ensur'd) but being chac'd by two large Privateers, in their Passage North-about the* Killibegs,[6] *and standing in betwixt the Islands of* Arran[7] *and the Main, to prevent being taken; the Commander, and Mr.* Whitworth *agreed (if it came to the last Extremity) to run the Ship on Shore and burn her (first escaping themselves*

*and Men, with what else they cou'd carry in the Boat) rather than be
carry'd into* France *and lose all. But being near, they recover'd their Port,
and proceeded on their Voyage.*

And as for the other Part of the Charge, of willfully losing her at Boon
Island, *one wou'd wonder Malice it self cou'd invent or suggest any thing
so ridiculous, and which wou'd certainly be credited by no body, that
considers the extream Hazards and Difficulties suffer'd by the Commander
himself, as well as his Men, where 'twas more than Ten Thousand to one,
but every Man had perish'd: And wou'd certainly have chose another
Place to have effected it, if we had such a Design: But alas, what will not
vain impotent Malice say, when it intends Injury? Were the Persons reflecting, but to suffer the like Extremities (we can't but think) they'd
be* feelingly *convinc't. But this Matter speaking so plainly for it self, we
think it needless to add more, therefore proceed to the last part of the
Charge (viz.)* Ensurance.

We presume Interest *only can induce Men to such Villanies, (indeed
thats pretended in this Case) therefore to let the World see how little
we gain (or rather how much we lose) by the Matter in Hand, as also
further to expose the malicious and injurious Scandal, we fairly and voluntarily offer. If any Person can make out, that* Jasper Dean *(who own'd
7/8 of the said Ship, besides considerable in Cargoe) or* Miles Whitworth
(who own'd the other 8th part) or John Dean *Commander of the said
Ship, they jointly or seperatly, or any others for (or on) their Accounts,
or for their (or any of their) Use or Advantage, directly or indirectly,
or they (or any of them,) for the Use or Benefit of any others, in any
others, in any Manner whatsoever, have ensur'd or caus'd to be ensur'd,
in Britain or elsewhere, any more than 250 1. to* Ireland *(which was not
paid the Ship arriving safe) and 300 1. from there to* Boston *in* New
England *(which paid, and Premium and Office Charges deducted, was no
more than 226 1. 17s) if any Person can make out more, they are desired
to publish it by Way of Advertisement in some* common News Paper
*and we undernam'd do hereby promise to make the utmost Satisfaction,
and stand convict to be the* greatest Villains *in the Universe.*

*And now, let the World judge whether 'tis reasonable to imagine, we
shou'd willfully lose a good Ship of* 120 *Tuns, besides a valuable Interest
in Cargoe in such a Place, where the Commander (as well as the Rest)
must unavoidably run the utmost Hazard of perishing in the most miserable Manner, and all this to recover 226 1. 17s. how absurd and ridicu-*

lous is such a Supposition, and yet this is the Reproach we at present labour under, so far, as to receive daily ignominious Scandals upon our Reputations, and injurious Affronts and Mobbings to our Faces: Yet we solemnly profess, we are not conscious of the least Guilt; nor even in this Account, of the least Errours in Representation.

Jasper Dean.
John Dean.
Miles Whitworth.
(*lately dead*)

NOTES

1. Cordage. Rope, especially for the rigging of ships.
2. *Piscataqua.* Harbor and district of Portsmouth, New Hampshire, so called for the river of the same name.
3. Rock-Weed. A coarse seaweed growing attached to rocks, especially the genera *Fucus* and *Ascophyllum.*
4. Spring-Tide. A tide of greater than average range between high and low tide that occurs twice each synodic month around the times of the new and full moon when the tidal action of the sun and moon are nearly in the same direction.
5. Green Hide. A fresh, or untanned hide.
6. Killibegs. In northwest Ireland, fifteen miles west of Donegal, on the Bay.
7. Arran. Arranmore Island, northwest Ireland, twenty-five miles northwest of Donegal. Not to be confused with the Aran Islands off Galway Bay to the south.

Christopher Langman

A True Account Of The Voyage Of The *Nottingham-Galley*
of London John Dean Commander, From The River Thames
to New-England

THE PREFACE

WE *having been Sufferers in this unfortunate Voyage, had reason to be-*
lieve, from the Temper of our Captain, who treated us barbarously both
by Sea and Land, that he would misrepresent the Matter, as we now find
he has done in a late Pamphlet by him publish'd, intituled, A Narrative of
the Sufferings, Preservation, and Deliverance of Captain *John Dean,* and
Company, in the *Nottingham* Galley of *London,* &c. London, *Printed by*
R. Tooky, *and Sold by* S. Popping *at the* Raven *in* Pater-noster-Row,
and at the Printing-Press *under the* Royal-Exchange.

   Our Apprehensions of this made us refuse the Encouragement which
was offered us in New England, *and resolve to come home that we might*
have an Opportunity to lay before the World, and before those Gentle-
men and others who have lost their Estates and Relations in this unhappy
Voyage, the true Causes of our own and their Misfortunes, and how they
might, humanely speaking, have been easily avoided, had Captain Dean
been either an honest or an able Commander. This we think ourselves
oblig'd to do in common Justice, and to prevent others from suffering
by him in the like manner.

   We cannot but in the first place take notice of a notorious Falshood
he asserts in his Preface, That he might have had the Attestation of several
of his Fellow Sufferers now in Town to the Truth of what he has wrote,
since he very well knows that Two of us did positively refuse it in publick
Company, after reading a part of it, and told him to his Face, that it was
not true.

   In the next place, as to what he says of the Encouragement his Narrative met with in *New England* and *North Britain,* where it appeared under much greater Disadvantages as to the Particulars and Dress, *We think fit to reply, That the Acceptance it met with in* New England *was occasion'd by our being confined from appearing in publick during our Sickness, and that he compell'd us to sign what our Illness made us uncapable to understand; but when it pleas'd God that we recover'd our Health, and made our Affidavits here subjoin'd before Mr.* Penhallow, *a Justice of Peace, and Member of Council at* Portsmouth *in the Province of* New Hampshire, New England, *in the Presence of the said* Dean, *who had not the Face to deny it, his Character appear'd in a true Light, and he was cover'd with Shame and Confusion.*

The Captain has reason indeed to commend the Charity of the Gentlemen of New England, *which is no more than their due, both from him and us, tho' we were unhappily deprived of the chief Effects of it by the Captain's Brother; who being the Person that received it, took care not to be wanting to the Captain and himself, whereas we had nothing but what was fit for such miserable Wretches, who were glad of any thing, since we were then uncapable of working for better.*

As to what he says in his Postscript about Insurance, we know nothing further of that matter than what we heard on Board, as will appear by our Narrative, viz. That there were great Sums insured upon the Ship, *the truth of which is more proper for the Inquiry of others than us who are only Sailors.*

We come now to the Narrative, wherein we shall represent nothing but the Truth, of which we our selves had the Misfortune to be Witnesses, to our great Sorrow, and the manifest Danger of our Lives.

And since what we deliver is upon Oath, we hope it will obtain Credit sooner than the bare Word of Captain Dean, *his Brother, and Mr.* Whitworth, *who were all Three interested Persons, and but One of them acquainted with all the Matter of Fact, which for his own Reputation and Safety he has been obliged to set off in false Colours. Besides, Mr.* Whitworth *is since dead, so that the Captain has no Vouchers but himself and his Brother; and how little Credit they deserve, will sufficiently appear by what follows.*

THE NARRATIVE

THE *Nottingham-Galley* of 120 Tons, 10 Guns, and 14 Men, *John Dean* Commander, took in part of her Lading in the River *Thames,* which

was Cordage, and the rest in Butter and Cheese, at *Killybags*[1] in *Ireland.*
But Captain *Dean* in his Narrative has omitted to acquaint the World
that 4 of the Guns were useless, and that not above 6 of the Men were
capable to Serve in the Ship, in case of bad Weather. She Sail'd from
Gravesend[2] the 2d Day of *August,* 1710. to the *Nore,*[3] and from thence
on the 7th, with 2 Men of War, and several Merchant-Men under their
Convoy, towards *Scotland.* When we came off of *Whitby,*[4] the Fleet
brought to, and several of the Ships were a-stern. We having a fine Gale,
the Captain said he would Run it, and make the best of his way for
Ireland, which we did. And when we were on that Coast, the 12th of
August, we saw 2 Ships in a Bay, towards whom the Captain would have
bore down, but the Men would not consent to it, because they perceiv'd
them to be *French* Men of War. Upon this we stood off to Sea till 12 at
Night; when the Captain coming upon Deck, we Sail'd easily in towards
the Shore, by the Mate's Advice, till Daylight, and came so near Land
that we were forced to stand off. The next Day we saw the two Privateers
again, and the Captain propos'd to stand down towards them, or to come
to an Anchor; but the Mate and the Men oppos'd it. The Captain was
seconded in this by *Charles Whitworth* the Merchant, who said in the
hearing of the Boatswain, and others, *That he had rather be taken than
otherwise, tho' he had an Eighth Part of the Ship, because he had Insured*
200 1. And the Captain said, *He had rather run the Ship ashore than perform his Voyage, if he thought he could be safe with the Insurers, because his Brother had insur'd* 300 1. *upon her.* Accordingly he put in
towards the Shore, to find out a proper Place for that purpose, and ordered
the Boatswain to get the Tackle upon the Boat and hoist her overside,
that she might be in readiness to go ashore. At the same time the Captain and *Charles Whitworth* went to the Cabbin to get out the best of
their Goods in order to carry them with them; and putting them up in a
Chest, commanded the Men to carry them into the Boat, which they did.
The Captain promis'd that we should want for nothing, and resolv'd to
go ashore; so that we all plainly saw he was resolv'd to lose the Ship. But
he was opposed by the Mate *Christopher Langman,* who wrought the
Vessel through between the Main and an Island, and she arriv'd safely at
Killybags in *Ireland* that same Night.

    We took in the rest of Lading there the 25th of *September,* being 30
Tons of Butter, and above 300 Cheeses, and sail'd for *Boston* in *New-
England;* which we were very uncapable to do, because the Captain, by

his barbarous Treatment of our Men, had disabled several of 'em, and particularly two of our best Sailors were so unmercifully beat by him, because they oppos'd his Design above mention'd, that they were not able to work in a Month. This gave us a very melancholy Prospect of an unfortunate Voyage, since we perceiv'd he would either lose the Ship, or betray her to the *French*, because she was insured for much above the Value. Besides, he put us to short Allowance, so that we had but one Quart of Water *per* Head in twenty four Hours, and had nothing to eat but salt Beef, which made us so dry that we were forc'd to drink the Rain Water that run off the Deck. And the Captain was so barbarous that he knock'd down one of our Men for dead, because when he found the Hold open, he went and drew a Gallon of Water to quench our Thirst. In the mean time he wanted nothing himself, tho' he pretended to us that he confin'd himself also to short Allowance, yet we knew the contrary.

When we came to the Banks of *Newfoundland* we saw a Ship which made all the Sail she could towards us, and soon came up with us. The Captain and Mr. *Whitworth* hoping she was a *Frenchman*, put on their best Apparel, and gave us as much strong Beer and Brandy as we could drink: But it prov'd to be the *Pompey* Galley of *London*, Captain *Den* Commander, at which we rejoic'd, tho' our Captain was melancholy. We continu'd our Course towards *New England;* and the first Land we made was *Cape Sables,* which is about 50 Leagues from *Boston* in that Country.

We made the best of our way for that Port, but the Wind blew hard, so that we were several Days without sight of Land, and were forced to hand all our Sails, and lie under our Mizzen-Ballast till Daylight; when the Boatswain having the Morning Watch discover'd Land to the Leeward, with which he acquainted the Captain and the Mate, who both came upon Deck. The Captain said that was the first Land we had made, wherein he was justly contradicted by the Mate, which caus'd some Words between 'em: For in Truth we made Cape *Sables*[5] a Week before; and if we had kept our Course then, according to the Opinion of the Mate and Ship's Company, we had, in all Probability, arriv'd safe the next Day at *Boston,* but the Master laying the Ship by, and the next Day proving moderate Weather, and the Wind coming to the West, we stood away to the North, and so it was a Week before we made Cape *Porpus,*[6] which was the same Day we were lost; so untrue is it what the Captain says, that the first Land we made was to the East of *Piscataqua.*[7] After those Words had pass'd with the Mate, the Captain went down to serve us with Water, according to Custom, and in the mean time the Captain's Brother took a Bottle of Water from the Mate, and struck him; upon which the Captain coming out of the Hold, he took up a Perriwig Block, with which he came behind the Mate, and struck him three Blows on the Head, upon which he fell down and lay as dead for several Minutes, all in Blood. This was very discouraging to the Seamen, who durst not speak to him for fear of the like Treatment. Soon after this barbarous Action we perceiv'd the Ship in Danger by being so near Land; upon which the Boatswain being on the Watch call'd the Captain, and the Mate, who being scarce recovered came on the Deck all in Gore, and told the Captain he had no Business so near the Land, except he had a Mind to lose the Ship, and therefore desir'd him to hawl further off, or else he would be ashore that Night. The Captain answer'd, *That he wou'd not take his Advice though the Ship should go to the Bottom, threatned to shoot the Mate with a Pistol,* and told him, *he would do what he pleas'd except they confin'd him to his Cabbin.* It fell out according as the Mate had said; we run ashoar that Night, being the 11*th* of *December,* between 8 and 9 a Clock, when the Ship struck upon *Boon Island,* a Rock three or four Leagues East from *Piscataqua.* And here the Captain is false again in his Narrative, when he says *p. 2. that he saw the Breakers ahead, upon which he call'd out to put the Helm hard on the Starboard;* for he was then undressing himself to go to Bed, according to his usual Custom. When the Ship struck, the Boatswain told the Captain, *he had made his Words good, and lost the Ship on purpose, whereas had he taken the Mate's Advice, he might in all probability have been safe at* Boston *Ten Days before.* The Captain bid him hold his Peace, *He was sorry for what had happen'd, but we must now all prepare for Death, there being no Probability to escape it.* Upon this several of our Men went on the Deck, but cou'd not stay there, because the Sea broke in all over the Ship. Then the Captain, who had been Cursing and Swearing before, began to cry and howl for Fear of losing his Life. The Boatswain and another went into the Hold to see if there was any Water there, and finding there was, we went all into the Cabbin to Prayers, being in hopes the Ship would lie whole till Daylight. Soon after this the Mate, though hardly able, went with some others above Deck; for this Surprize made him forget his Pain. He spoke to the Captain, and told him, *It was his Business to encourage the Men, and not to dishearten them:* Yet still he insisted it was impossible for us to save our Lives. However, the Mate with three others cut down the Main-Mast and Fore-Mast, which by God's Assistance prov'd the Means of our Preservation; for the Fore-Mast fell on the Rock with one End, and the other rested on the Ship. The Mate went afterwards into the Cabbin, and desired the Captain to use his Endeavours to save the Men, for the Ship would immediately sink, and it was not time to think of saving any thing, but to get ashore as light as we cou'd. By this Time the Water came out of the Hold, and the Sea beat over the Deck, so that there was no standing upon it. The Mate got first on the Mast, and with great Difficulty escap'd to the Rock. He was follow'd by two others, who like wise got on Shore, but were scarce able to stand on the Rock, from whence they hallow'd to us to follow them, and we not hearing them any more than once, were afraid they were wash'd off by the Waves. This put us into a mighty Consternation, so that we knew not whether it were best to follow them, or to stay on board till it was Day. The Captain was for the latter; but it being dead low Water, the Tide of Flood coming on, and the Wind beginning to blow hard, the Sea beat into the Cabbin while we were at Prayers, which forced us to go upon Deck: Some more of our Men escap'd to the Shore by help of the Mast, as the others had done, and call'd to us to make haste and follow them, which we did, and by the Blessing of God got safe to the Rock, though not without much Danger, being forced to crawl upon our Hands and Knees we were so heavy with Water, and the Rock so slippery.

Here again the Captain is false in the second Page of his Narrative; for he neither call'd us down to Prayers, nor order'd us up again, nor did he either command or assist at cutting down the Mast. We know not whom he points at, where he says, several of the Company did so sink under Racks of Conscience, that they were not able to stir; for he himself had as great Reason to be under Terror of Conscience as any Man, since he was the Cause of all our Misfortunes. Accordingly he cryed heartily, and begg'd the Mate to do what he cou'd to save us, for he himself cou'd do nothing. Nor was the Captain ever upon the Deck but once, when he held by the Long Boat, cryed out, and presently went down again, which greatly discouraged us, so that had it not been for the Mate, &c. who cut down the Shrowds, &c. as above-mention'd, we had all perish'd. He is also unjust to the Mate in his third Page, where he says, *That one of the Men went out on the Bowsprit, and returning, told the Captain he saw something black ahead, and would adventure to get on Shore, accompanied with any other Person;* upon which the Captain pretends he desired

some of his best Swimmers, the Mate and one more, to go with him, and
if they recover'd the Rock, to give Notice by their Calls, and direct the
rest to the most secure Place; for it was the Mate who went on the Boltsprit and discover'd the Land. After which he desired the Captain and the
rest to go ashore before he attempted it himself; but finding them all
dead-hearted, the Mate, who cou'd not swim, as the Captain alledges, got
on Shore by the Mast as above-mention'd. The Captain is also false in
asserting that he attempted to save his Money, Brandy, Ammunition,
&c. for our Relief, since he had not the Value of one Guinea aboard in
Money. It is equally false that he tore his Arms and Fingers in such a
lamentable manner in climbing up the Rock; for not one Man was hurt
in getting ashore. Nor was the Captain in danger of being wash'd off from
the Yard, the Water there being no deeper than our Middle.

When we got ashore we found it to be a desolate small Island, without
any Shelter; and being wet, and having but few Cloathes, some began to
despair of being able to live there till the Morning; and besides, we were
not certain but it might be over flow'd at high Tide. We comforted our
selves however, the best we cou'd, and though we expected to perish
there, return'd God Thanks for giving us some more Time to repent. In
this dismal Condition we continued till next Morning, without any thing
to refresh us: But being in hopes that the Wreck would remain till Day-
light, and that we might recover some of our Provisions, we sent a Man
down to see what was become of her, but he brought us Word that he
cou'd see nothing of her. When Daylight came we went to look for the
Wreck in a cold and hungry Condition; but found nothing except one
half Cheese, entangled in a Piece of a Rope, and this we equally distributed among us. Soon after we found a Piece of fine Linnen and Canvas,
of which we endeavour'd to make a Tent, and effected it at last by the
help of the Boatswain the second Day, and this preserv'd us from being
all frozen to Death, as our Cook was in a little Time to our very great
Grief, since we look'd upon it as a certain Presage that we should all have
the same Fate. We carried the Corpse to the Seaside, from whence it was
soon wash'd off by the Flood. Here the Captain publishes another Falshood in his fifth Page, when he says *he knew where he was;* for he declared to us that he knew not: Nor is there any more Truth in the Compassion he there alledges that he shew'd to the Cook when he was a dying.

When the Weather clear'd we discover'd the main Land, which we suppos'd to be about a League from us. This fill'd us with Hopes that by the

Providence of God we should soon be deliver'd, for which we return'd him Thanks, and immediately set about building a Boat out of part of the Wreck which was drove ashore, and heartily pray'd, that God would give us Success. We were so cold, hungry and feeble, that it was scarce possible for us to do any thing, nor could we walk on the Rock in order to keep us warm, it was so craggy, uneven and slippery. We made shift however to finish our Boat, the Bottom of which was made of Three Planks, and the Side was Half a Plank High. We cork'd and lin'd it with Canvas the best we could, and made it about Twelve Foot Long and Four Foot Wide, thinking it sufficient to hold Six of us.

After this some Controversie happen'd who the Six should be. The Carpenter pleaded his Right to be one, because he build it; the Captain pleaded to be another, which was agreed to; and the Boatswain was thought fit to be one, because he spoke the *Indian* Language; but at last it was concluded that the Mate, the Captain's Brother, *Charles Whitworth,* and *George White,* should be the Men; and we carried the Boat to the Shore, where we launch'd her, putting on Board such of the Carpenter's Tools as we had sav'd from the Wreck, in order to build a better when we came on Shore. We begg'd the Assistance and Direction of God, and some of our Company went into the Boat, taking leave of the rest, and promising to bring them Relief as soon as possible. But the Boat overset, by which our Men were almost drown'd, and narrowly escaped again to the Rock. The Boatswain held the Boat almost an Hour with a Rope in hopes to save her till the Weather grew more calm, and the Gunner came to his Assistance, but soon after she was stav'd to pieces, which was a great Mortification to us. We thank'd God however that he was pleas'd again to preserve so many of us, tho' the Time for our Relief was not yet come. The Captain is out in his Account, *pag.* 7. when he says, our Boat had a Mast and a Sail, for she had neither.

The Wind blowing hard, and there being a great Snow, we betook our selves to Prayer, and earnestly begg'd that God would have mercy on us, and consider our deplorable Condition. Being wet with our Endeavours to launch the Boat, our Cloaths freezed to our Backs, which proved fatal to our Carpenter, who died a few Days after. The next Day prov'd fair Weather, so that we could see the Houses on the main Land, and several Boats rowing to and fro, which rejoyc'd us very much; and after praying that God might direct some of them to us, we shew'd our selves on several Places of the Rock, and hallow'd to them, but they could not hear us.

This quite discourag'd us again, for we had no Provisions but some small pieces of Cheese, four or five pieces of Beef, and one Neats Tongue[8] that we recover'd our of the Wreck, and a small quantity of this was distributed among us every Morning when we went round the Rock to see if it would please God to send us any further Provisions. At last *George White,* one of our Number, found some Muscles at Low Water, for which we return'd God Thanks, and we found about as many for two or three days as six or seven came to each Man's share; but the Weather was so cold, and the Tides fell out so late in the Night that we could get no more. The Captain then told us, *We must shift for our selves, there being nothing now for us to trust to but the Merci[e]s of God.* There being a piece of a Cows Hide on the Fore Yard of the Wreck, we cut it into small pieces and swallow'd it down, which reviv'd us a little. Some of our Company got Sea Weed, which was also shar'd among us, and this was all the Entertainment we had for several Days; but still we liv'd in hopes of being deliver'd from this dismal Place; and the Captain told us, *If we were, he would sell the Cables, Anchors and Guns that were cast ashore, for our Maintenance.* In this Distress our Mate perceiving a large Sea Gull in a Hole of the Rock, he knock'd it down with the Handle of a Sawce Pan, brought her into the Tent, and shar'd her among us, to our great Relief.

Perceiving no hopes of any Boats coming to us, a stout *Dutchman,* one of our Company, propos'd the making of a Raft, and proffer'd to endeavour to get ashore with it himself, if no body else would. This Proposal being well relish'd, such of us as were able clear'd the Fore Yard of the Rigging with a great deal of Trouble, for want of sufficient Strength and necessary Instruments; and having split it in two to make the Sides of the Raft, and fastning the End pieces with Nails, we put a Plank in the Middle, with a Mast, and a Sail made of two Hammocks, and accordingly launch'd her, with *George White* and the *Dutchman* upon it, giving them Orders, if they got ashore, to acquaint the People with our Distress, and to beg their hastening to our Assistance. But the Raft overset, by which the Men were almost drown'd, so that none would venture upon it again except the *Dutchman* and another. We pray'd heartily for their Success, and saw them paddle along till the Sun was down, and they appear'd to us to be so near the Shore, that we hoped they might Land safely.

That Night it blew very hard, and the next Day our Carpenter died as above-mention'd, and in the Morning we hawl'd him out of the Tent. That same Day the Captain and *George White* went out to see what they could find, but return'd empty handed.

Upon this the Captain propos'd the fleying and eating of the Carpenter's dead Body, and told us, *It was no Sin, since God was pleas'd to take him out of the World, and that we had not laid violent Hands upon him.* He ask'd the Boatswain to help to skin and cut him up, which he refus'd because of his Weakness; whereupon one *Charles Gray* help'd the Captain to do it, and brought in several pieces of the Corps into the Tent, where some of our Men eat of it; but the Mate, the Boatswain, and *George White* would not touch any of it till next Day that they were forced to it by Extremity of Hunger.

Here the Captain is guilty of several Heads, and particularly *pag.* 11, &c. for he was so far from offering to go ashore on the Raft, that he said, *Let who will go 'twas all one to him.* Nor did the *Dutchman* or *Swede* ever desire the Captain to go with him or help him to turn the Raft; nor did the Captain assist *George White* to get ashore when he was overset in the Raft. It is likewise false, that the other Man who went off in the Raft was found dead with a Paddle fastned to his Wrist, for his Corps was found about 300 Yards from the Shore, and no Paddle to his Wrist. 'Tis likewise false, that the Captain went several times out alone to look for Provisions, for *George White* was always with him. Nor is it true, that the piece of Cow's Hide beforemention'd was brought into the Tent by the Captain's Order, for George White brought it without his Knowledge. It is likewise false, that the Men first requested the Carpenter's dead Body of the Captain to eat, for he himself was the first that propos'd it, and the Three Deponents refus'd to eat any of it until the next Morning that the Captain brought in some of his Liver and intreated 'em to eat of it; so that the Captain's Pretensions of being moved with Horror at the Thoughts of it, are false, for there was no Man that eat more of the Corps than himself. It is likewise false, that any of the Men removed the dead Body from the Place where they laid it at first. It is also untrue, that the Captain order'd his Skin, Head, Hands, &c. to be buried in the Sea, for these we left on the Island when we came off. Nor is there any more Truth in the Care which the Captain ascribes to himself, in hindring us to eat too much of the Corps lest it should prejudice our Health, for we all agreed, the Night before we come off, to limit our selves, lest our Deliverers should be detain'd from coming to us. And as to our Tempers being alter'd after the eating of humane Flesh, as the Captain charges us, *p.* 16. we can safely declare, that tho' he says, *There was nothing to be heard among us but brutish Quarrels, with horrid Oaths and Imprecations,* all the Oaths we heard were between the Captain, his Brother, and Mr. *Whitworth,* who

often quarrel'd about their Lying and Eating. And whereas the Captain
often went to Prayers with us before we had the Corps to eat, he never,
to our hearing, pray'd afterwards, but behav'd himself so impiously, that
he was many times rebuked by the Mate and others for profane Swearing.

Having agreed with the Men we sent off on the Raft, that they should
kindle a Fire if they got safe on Shore, we were rejoic'd upon the sight
of a Smoke, hoping that had been the Signal they promis'd, but it was
not. Soon after that we perceiv'd a Boat coming towards us, which made
our Hearts leap for Joy, and we return'd Thanks to God for the Prospect
of a speedy Deliverance. The Boat came to an Anchor along the side of
the Rock, but could not get ashore; and we call'd to 'em for Fire, which
the Master sent us by one of his Men in a small Canoe, but no Provisions.
This was the 22d Day after we had been on this desolate Rock, so that
the Man was frighten'd at the sight of so dismal a Spectacle. We all got
about him, and cryed for Joy. He told us, that the Reason of their coming to the Rock to see for us, was their finding a Raft on the Shore, with
one Man frozen to Death about Two or Three Hundred Yards from it,
but they heard nor saw nothing of the other, from whence 'twas supposed
that the Man found dead ashore having landed there in the Night Time,
and not knowing where to go, he was frozen to Death under a Tree where
they found him. After this Discourse, our Captain went to go off in the
Boat, but it overset, so that we were forc'd to take up the Canoe, and
carry it all over the Rock, to seek for a smooth Place to put her off again,
which we did after the Man had staid with us Two or Three Hours. He
promised to come with a better Boat to carry us off, but lost his Vessel
as he came near the Shore, and narrowly escaped with his own and his
Mens Lives; upon which he sent an Express to *Piscataqua* for Relief to
us. This Night we had a prodigious Storm, but kept a great Fire, which
was seen on the Shore, and prov'd very comfortable to us, both for its
Warmth, and by Broiling Part of the Dead Corps, which made it eat with
less Disgust.

The next Day it blowed very fresh, so that no Relief could come to
us; but on the 4th of *January* in the Morning, the Weather being fair,
several Sloops came towards us, and one Canoe came ashore with Four
Men, Two of which were Captain *Long* and Captain *Forbe,* Commanders
of Ships, and soon carried us all off on board their Vessel; for several of
us had our Legs so frozen, and were so weak that we could not walk.

These Gentlemen took great Care of us, and would not suffer us to eat or drink but a little at a time, lest it should do us hurt. [That] Night we arrived at *Piscataqua* in *New England,* where we were all provided for, and had a Doctor appointed to look after us. We were Ten who came ashore, Two of us having died on the Island, and Two being lost that were sent off on the Raft. The Names of those that were sav'd are *John Dean,* Captain; *Christopher Langman,* Mate; *Christopher Gray,* Gunner; *Nicholas Mellan,* Boatswain; *George White, Charles Whitworth, Henry Dean, Charles Graystock, William Saver,* and the Captain's Boy, who had Part of his Foot cut off to prevent a Mortification, and several others were lame. Thus we were delivered by the Goodness of God (for which we praise his Name) after we had been Twenty Four Days upon that Desolate Island in the Distress abovementioned, having nothing to shelter us but a sorry Tent that could not keep us from wet, and was once in Danger of being carryed off by the high Tide, which obliged us to remove it to the highest Part of the Rock. We had nothing to lie on but the Stones, and very few Cloathes to cover us; which, together with our Hunger, made our Lives a Burden to us.

Some Days after our Arrival, the Captain drew up a Protest, which was sign'd by the Mate, being then very ill of a Flux and Fever; and also by the Boatswain *Geo. White,* who was also ill, and declared that he did it for fear of being put out of his Lodgings by the Captain, while he was both sick and lame. But as soon as the Deponents recover'd, they declar'd the Captain's Protest to be false, &c. as may been seen by the Depositions hereunto annex'd.

The Captain falsly ascribes to himself, *p.* 17. the first Discovery of the Sloop that came to relieve us, whereas it was first discover'd by *Christopher Gray,* the Gunner, he being sent out on purpose by the Mate, who the Night before had dreamt of the Sloop's Arrival. The Captain likewise falsly magnifies his own Danger of being drowned, when the Canoe was overset, since the Water then was scarce half a Yard deep; and instead of being thankful to God for his own and our Deliverance, he returned with the Dog to his Vomit, and behav'd himself so brutishly, that his Friend Captain *Purver* was obliged to turn him out of his House. He was so little sensible of the Merciful Deliverance from the Danger he had escaped, that he barbarously told the Children in his Lodging, he would have made a Frigasy of them if he had had 'em in *Boon Island;* which frighten'd the

People that heard him, and made them esteem him a Brute, as he was. He likewise wrong'd us of what the Good People gave us towards our Relief, and applyed it to his own and his Brother's Use; and particularly when Captain *John Wentworth* gave several of our Men good Cloaths, Captain *Dean* came and order'd them the worst that could be had; and was likewise so barbarous as to get us turn'd out of our Lodgings, before we were able to shift for our selves.

All this we avouch to be Truth, and have no other End in publishing it, but to testify our Thankfulness to God for his Great Deliverance, and to give others Warning not to trust their Lives or Estates in the Hands of so wicked and brutish a Man.

For the Truth of what we have deliver'd, we refer to the Affidavits subjoined, which we made concerning this Matter both in *New England,* and since our Arrival at *London.*

NOTES

1. *Killybags.* Killibegs, in northwest Ireland, fifteen miles west of Donegal, on the Bay.

2. *Gravesend.* Borough on Thames estuary, twenty-two miles southeast of London.

3. The *Nore.* A sandbank in the center of the Thames estuary, forty-seven miles below London.

4. *Whitby.* A district and ancient cathedral in North Riding, Yorkshire, at the mouth of the Esk River.

5. Cape *Sables.* Southern point of Cape Sable Island, just off the southwest tip of Nova Scotia.

6. Cape *Porpus.* On the southern coast of Maine, approximately four miles north of the mouth of the Kennebunk River.

7. *Piscataqua.* Harbor and district of Portsmouth, New Hampshire, so called for the river of the same name.

8. Neats Tongue. The tongue of an ox or cow.

Philip Ashton and John Barnard

Ashton's Memorial. An History Of The Strange Adventures,
And Signal Deliverances, Of Mr. Philip Ashton, Who, after
he had made his Escape from the Pirates, liv'd alone on a
Desolate Island for about Sixteen Months, & c.

Ashton's Memorial is one of America's first "as told
to" stories—a journalistic arrangement in which the teller
or celebrity, himself without literary ability or pretensions, has his story written by someone more practiced
in the craft. The writer in this case was the Reverend
John Barnard (Harvard, 1700), minister of Marblehead.
When Barnard first came to Marblehead from Boston in
1715, he found the inhabitants to be mainly fishermen
"of low Life and uncultivated Minds." Whether this estimate included the fisherman Philip Ashton we do not know,
but Barnard saw at once that the young man who had been
captured by pirates had an extraordinary tale to tell. He
saw, too, that Ashton's adventures might be used to promote
a valuable lesson in the Providence of God.

Barnard wrote quickly, and even though he complained
that "Mr. Ashton has necessarily been so much absent, that
I have not been able to get the opportunity of Conferring
with him, more than two or three times," the *Memorial*
(including the minister's own sermon) was ready for the
press on August 3, 1725, just three months after Ashton's
return.

Ashton's Memoiral is one of the most fascinating narratives in colonial American literature. Its subjects are perennial
favorites. Who, after all, is not intrigued by tales of pirates
and desert islands? The latter aspect of the *Memorial* invites

comparison with *Robinson Crusoe,* published six years
earlier. It is instructive to observe, however, that Ashton had
none of the fortuitously placed provisions and implements
that enabled Crusoe to transform his island into a thriving
economy. The young fisherman from Marblehead endured
an exile of impoverishment and privation.

Just how much of the narrative's style belongs to Ashton
and how much to Barnard is difficult to estimate, although
some portions are clearly Barnard's. Ashton was probably
not quite so pious or prudish as Barnard sometimes makes
him out to be. The occasional incidence of sentimentality,
such as occurs in the story of Low's wife and children, probably also belongs to Barnard, a consequence of his acquaintance
with the literary fashion of the age in England. By and large,
however, Barnard renders Ashton's adventures with immedi-
acy and skill.

The *Memorial* has long been a popular narrative. Its original
appearance in Boston (printed by Samuel Gerrish) in 1725
was followed by a London edition the next year. In addition
to several printings in the nineteenth and early twentieth centuries, Russel W. Knight produced a fine edition in 1975 for
the Peabody Museum.

TEXT: Massachusetts Historical Society first edition
on Evans microcard (E2602). Barnard's preface and sermon,
as well as the narrative of Nicholas Merritt, have been omitted.

UPON *Friday, June* 15*th.* 1722. After I had been out for some time
in the Schooner *Milton,* upon the Fishing grounds, off *Cape Sable*[1] Shoar,
among others, I came to Sail in Company with *Nicholas Merritt,* in a
Shallop, and stood in for *Port-Rossaway,*[2] designing to Harbour there,
till the Sabbath was over; where we Arrived about Four of the Clock in
the Afternoon. When we came into the Harbour, where several of our
Fishing Vessels had arrived before us, we spy'd among them a Brigantine,
which we supposed to have been an Inward bound Vessel, from the *West
Indies,* and had no apprehensions of any Danger from her; but by that
time we had been at Anchor two or three Hours, a Boat from the Brigan-

tine, with Four hands, came along side of us, and the Men Jumpt in upon
our Deck, without our suspecting any thing but that they were Friends,
come on board to visit, or inquire what News; till they drew their Cut-
lashes and Pistols from under their Clothes, and Cock'd the one and
Brandish'd the other, and began to Curse & Swear at us, and demanded
a Surrender of our Selves and Vessel to them. It was too late for us to
rectify our Mistake, and think of Freeing our selves from their power:
for however we might have been able, (being Five of us and a Boy) to have
kept them at a Distance, had we known who they were, before they had
boarded us; yet now we had our Arms to seek, and being in no Capacity
to make any Resistance, were necessitated to submit our selves to their
will and pleasure. In this manner they surprised *Nicholas Merritt,* and 12
or 13 other Fishing Vessels this Evening.

When the Boat went off from our Vessel, they carried me on board the
Brigantine, and who should it prove but the Infamous *Ned Low,*[3] the
Pirate, with about 40 Hands, 2 Great Guns, and 4 Swivel Guns. You may
easily imagine how I look'd, and felt, when too late to prevent it, I found
my self fallen into the hands of such a mad, roaring, mitcheivous Crew;
yet I hoped, that they would not force me away with them, and I purposed to endure any hardship among them patiently, rather than turn
Pirate with them.

Low presently sent for me Aft, and according to the Pirates usual Custom, and in their proper Dialect, asked me, *If I would sign their Articles,
and go along with them.* I told him, *No;* I could by no means consent to
go with them, I should be glad if he would give me my Liberty, and put
me on board any Vessel, or set me on shoar there. For indeed my dislike
of their Company and Actions, my concern for my Parents, and my fears
of being found in such bad Company, made me dread the thoughts of
being carried away by them; so that I had not the least Inclination to
continue with them.

Upon my utter Refusal to joyn and go with them, I was thrust down
into the Hold, which I found to be a safe retreat for me several times
afterwards. By that time I had been in the Hold a few Hours, they had
compleated the taking the several Vessels that were in the Harbour, and
the Examining of the Men; and the next Day I was fetched up with some
others that were there, and about 30 or 40 of us were put on board a
Schooner belonging to Mr. Orn of *Marblehead,* which the Pirates made

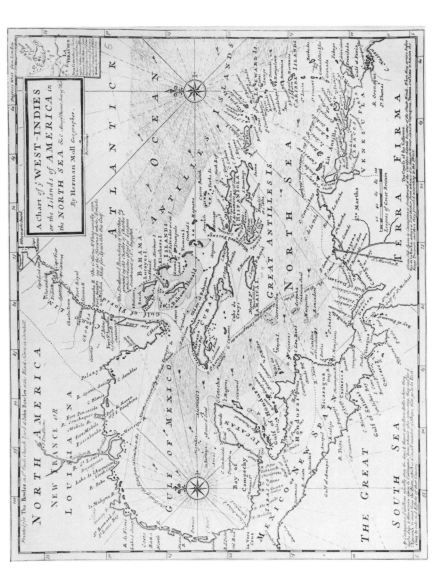

A Chart of the West Indies by Herman Moll (London, 1709). Courtesy of the John Carter Brown Library, Brown University, Providence, Rhode Island.

use of for a sort of Prison, upon the present occasion; where we were all confined unarm'd, with an armed Guard over us, till the *Sultan*'s pleasure should be further known.

The next Lord's Day about Noon, one of the Quarter Masters, *John Russel* by Name, came on board the Schooner, and took six of us, *(Nicholas Merritt, Joseph Libbie, Lawrence Fabins,*[4] and *my self,* all of *Marblehead,* the Eldest of us, if I mistake not, under 21 Years of Age, with two others) and carried us on board the Brigantine; where we were called upon the Quarter Deck, and *Low* came up to us with Pistol in hand, and with a full mouth demanded, *Are any of you Married Men?* This short and unexpected Question, and the sight of the Pistol, struck us all dumb, and not a Man of us dared to speak a word, for fear there should have been a design in it, which we were not able to see thro'. Our Silence kindled our new Master into a Flame, who could not bear it, that so many Beardless Boyes should deny him an Answer to so plain a Question; and therefore in a Rage, he Cock'd his Pistol, and clapt it to my Head, and cryed out, *You D-g! why don't you Answer me?* and Swore vehemently, he would shoot me thro' the Head, if I did not tell him immediately, whether I was married or no.

I was sufficiently frightned at the fierceness of the Man, and the boldness of his threatning, but rather than lose my Life for so trifling a matter, I e'en ventured at length to tell him, *I was not Married,* as loud as I dar'd to speak it; and so said the rest of my Companions. Upon this he seemed something pacified, and turned away from us.

It seems his design was to take no Married Man away with him, how young soever he might be, which I often wondred at; till after I had been with him some considerable time, and could observe in him an uneasiness in the sentiments of his Mind, and the workings of his passions towards a young Child he had at *Boston* (his Wife being Dead, as I learned, some small time before he turned Pirate) which upon every lucid interval from Revelling and Drink he would express a great tenderness for, insomuch that I have seen him sit down and weep plentifully upon the mentioning of it; and then I concluded, that probably the Reason of his taking none but Single Men was, that he might have none with him under the Influence of such powerful attractives, as a Wife & Children, lest they should grow uneasy in his Service, and have an Inclination to Desert him, and return home for the sake of their Families.

Low presently came up to us again, and asked the Old Question, Whether we would Sign their Articles, and go along with them? We all told him No; we could not, so we were dismissed. But within a little while we were call'd to him Singly, and then it was demanded of me, with Sterness and Threats, whether I would Joyn with them? I still persisted in the Denial; which thro' the assistance of Heaven, I was resolved to do, tho' he shot me. And as I understood, all my Six Companions, who were called in their turns, still refused to go with him.

Then I was led down into the Steerage, by one of the Quarter-Masters, and there I was assaulted with Temptations of another kind, in hopes to win me over to become one of them; a number of them got about me, and instead of Hissing, shook their Rattles, and treated me with abundance of Respect and Kindness, in their way; they did all they could to sooth my Sorrows, and set before me the strong Allurement of the Vast Riches they should gain, and what Mighty Men they designed to be, and would fain have me to joyn with them, and share in their Spoils; and to make all go down the more Glib, they greatly Importuned me to Drink with them, not doubting but this wile would sufficiently entangle me, and so they should prevail with me to do that in my Cups, which they perceived they could not bring me to while I was Sober: but all their fair and plausible Carriage, their proffered Kindness, and airy notions of Riches, had not the Effect upon me which they desired; and I had no Inclination to drown my Sorrows with my Senses in their Inebriating Bowls, and so refused their Drink, as well as their Proposals.

After this I was brought upon Deck again, and *Low* came up to me, with his Pistol Cock'd, and clap'd it to my Head, and said to me, *You D-g you! if you will not Sign our Articles, and go along with me, I'll shoot you thro' the Head;* and uttered his Threats with his utmost Fierceness, and with the usual Flashes of Swearing and Cursing. I told him, *That I was in his hands, and he might do with me what he pleased, but I could not be willing to go with him:* and then I earnestly beg'd of him, with many Tears, and used all the Arguments I could think of to perswade him, not to carry me away; but he was deaf to my Cryes, and unmoved by all that I could say to him; and told me, *I was an Impudent D-g,* and Swore, *I should go with him whether I would or no.* So I found all my Cryes, and Entreaties were in vain, and there was no help for it, go with them I must, and as I understood, they set mine, and my Townsmens Names down in their Book, tho' against our Consent. And I desire to mention it with due

Acknowledgements to GOD, who withheld me, that neither their promises, nor their threatnings, nor blows could move me to a willingness to Joyn with them in their pernicious ways.

Upon *Tuesday, June 19th.* they changed their Vessel, and took for their Privateer, as they call'd it, a Schooner belonging to Mr. *Joseph Dolliber* of *Marblehead,* being new, clean, and a good Sailer, and shipped all their hands on board her, and put the Prisoners, such as they designed to send home, on board the Brigantine, with one——[5] who was her Master, and ordered them for *Boston.*

When I saw the Captives were likely to be sent Home, I thought I would make one attempt more to obtain my Freedom, and accordingly *Nicholas Merritt,* my Townsman and Kinsman, went along with me to *Low,* and we fell upon our Knees, and with utmost Importunity besought him to let us go Home in the Brigantine, among the rest of the Captives: but he immediately called for his Pistols, and told us we should not go, and Swore bitterly, if either of us offered to stir, he would shoot us down.

Thus all attempts to be delivered out of the hands of unreasonable Men (if they may be called *Men*) were hitherto unsuccessful; and I had the melancholly prospect of seeing the Brigantine sail away with the most of us that were taken at *Port-Rossaway,* but my self, and three Townsmen mentioned, and four Isle of Shoal-men detained on board the Schooner, in the worst of Captivity, without any present likelyhood of Escaping.

And yet before the Brigantine sailed, an opportunity presented, that gave me some hopes that I might get away from them; for some of *Low's* people, who had been on shoar at *Port-Rossaway* to get water, had left a Dog belonging to him behind them; and *Low* observing the Dog a shoar howling to come off, order'd some hands to take the Boat and fetch him. Two Young Men, *John Holman,* and *Benjamin Ashton,* both of *Marblehead,* readily Jumpt into the Boat, and I (who pretty well knew their Inclination to be rid of such Company, & was exceedingly desirous my self to be freed from my present Station, and thought if I could but once set foot on shoar, they should have good luck to get me on board again) was geting over the side into the Boat; but Quarter Master *Russel* spy'd me, and caught hold on my Shoulder, and drew me in board, and with a Curse told me, Two was eno', I should not go. The two Young Men had more sense and virtue than to come off to them again, so that after some time of waiting, they found they were deprived of their Men, their Boat, and their Dog; and they could not go after them.

When they saw what a trick was play'd them, the Quarter Master came up to me Cursing and Swearing, that I knew of their design to Run away, and intended to have been one of them; but tho' it would have been an unspeakable pleasure to me to have been with them, yet I was forced to tell him, I knew not of their design; and indeed I did not, tho' I had good reason to su[s]pect what would be the event of their going. This did not pacifie the Quarter-Master, who with outragious Cursing and Swearing clapt his Pistol to my Head, and snap'd it; but it miss'd Fire: this enraged him the more; and he repeated the snapping of his Pistol at my Head three times, and it as often miss'd Fire; upon which he held it over-board, and snap'd it the fourth time, and then it went off very readily. (Thus did GOD mercifully quench the violence of the Fire, that was meant to destroy me!) The Quarter-Master upon this, in the utmost fury, drew his Cutlash, and fell upon me with it, but I leap'd down into the Hold, and got among a Crowd that was there, and so escaped the further effects of his madness and rage. Thus, tho' GOD suffered me not to gain my wished-for Freedom, yet he wonderfully preserved me from Death.

All hopes of obtaining Deliverance were now past and gone; the Brigantine and Fishing Vessels were upon their way homeward, the Boat was ashore, and not likely to come off again; I could see no possible way of Escape; and who can express the concern and Agony I was in, to see my self, a Young Lad not 20 Years Old, carried forcibly from my Parents, whom I had so much reason to value for the tenderness I knew they had for me, & to whom my being among Pyrates would be as a Sword in their Bowels, and the Anguishes of Death to them; confined to such Company as I could not but have an exceeding great abhorrence of; in Danger of being poisoned in my morals, by Living among them, and of falling a Sacrifice to Justice, if ever I should be taken with them. I had no way left for my Comfort, but earnestly to commit my self and my cause to GOD, and wait upon Him for Deliverance in his own time and way; and in the mean while firmly to resolve, thro' Divine Assistance, that nothing should ever bring me to a willingness to Joyn with them, or share in their Spoils.

I soon found that any Death was preferible to being link'd with such a vile Crew of Miscreants, to whom it was a sport to do Mischief; where prodigious Drinking, monstrous Cursing and Swearing, hideous Blasphe-

mies, and open defiance of Heaven, and contempt of Hell it self, was the
constant Employment, unless when Sleep something abated the Noise
and Revellings.

Thus Confined, the best course I could take, was to keep out of the
way, down in the Hold, or whereever I could be most free from their
perpetual Din; and fixedly purpose with my self, that the first time I
had an opportunity to set my Foot on shore, let it be in what part of
the World it would, it should prove (if possible) my taking a final leave
of *Low* and Company.

I would remark it now also (that I might not interrupt the Story with
it afterwards) that while I was on board *Low*, they used once a Week, or
Fortnight, as the Evil Spirit moved them, to bring me under Examination, and anew demand my Signing their Articles, and Joyning with them;
but Blessed be GOD, I was enabled to persist in a constant refusal to become one of them, tho' I was thrashed with Sword or Cane, as often as
I denyed them; the fury of which I had no way to avoid, but by jumping
down into the Hold, where for a while I was safe. I look'd upon my self,
for a long while, but as a Dead Man among them, and expected every Day
of Examination would prove the last of my Life, till I learned from some
of them, that it was one of their Articles, Not to Draw Blood, or take
away the Life of any Man, after they had given him Quarter, unless he
was to be punished as a Criminal; and this emboldned me afterwards, so
that I was not so much affraid to deny them, seeing my Life was given
me for a Prey.

This *Tuesday,* towards Evening, *Low* and Company came to sail in the
Schooner, formerly called the *Mary,* now the *Fancy,* and made off for
Newfoundland; and here they met with such an Adventure, as had like
to have proved fatal to them. They fell in with the Mouth of *St. John's*[6]
Harbour in a Fogg, before they knew where they were; when the Fogg
clearing up a little, they spy'd a large Ship riding at Anchor in the Harbour, but could not discern what she was, by reason of the thickness of
the Air, and concluded she was a Fish-Trader; this they look'd upon as a
Boon Prize for them, and thought they should be wonderfully well ac-
commodated with a good Ship under Foot, and if she proved but a good
Sailer, would greatly further their Roving Designs, and render them a
Match for almost any thing they could meet with, so that they need not
fear being taken.

Accordingly they came to a Resolution to go in and take her; and

imagining it was best doing it by St[r]atagem, they concluded to put
all their Hands, but Six or Seven, down in the Hold, and make a shew
as if they were a Fishing Vessel, and so run up along side of her, and surprise her, and bring her off; and great was their Joy at the distant prospect how cleverly they should catch her. They began to put their designs
in Execution, stowed away their Hands, leaving but a few upon Deck,
and made Sail in order to seise the Prey; when there comes along a small
Fisher-Boat, from out the Harbour, and hailed them, and asked them,
from whence they were? They told them, from *Barbadoes,* and were
laden with Rhum and Sugar; then they asked the Fisherman, What large
Ship that was in the Harbour? who told them it was a large Man of War.

The very Name of Man of War struck them all up in a Heap, spoil'd
their Mirth, their fair Hopes, and promising Design of having a good Ship
at Command; and lest they should catch a Tartar, they thought it their
wisest and safest way, instead of going into the Harbour, to be gone as
fast as they could; and accordingly they stretched away farther Eastward,
and put into a small Harbour, called *Carboneur,*[7] about 15 Leagues distance; where they went on Shoar, took the Place, and destroyed the
Houses, but hurt none of the People; as they told me, for I was not suffered to go a shore with them.

The next Day they made off for the Grand Bank, where they took
seven or eight Vessels, and among them a French Banker, a Ship of about
350 Tuns, and 2 Guns; this they carried off with them, and stood away
for *St. Michaels.*[8]

Off of *St. Michaels* they took a large *Portugueze* Pink, laden with
Wheat, coming out of the Road, which I was told was formerly call'd
the *Rose-Frigat.* She struck to the Schooner, fearing the large Ship that
was coming down to them; tho' all *Low's* Force had been no Match for
her, if the Port[u]gueze had made a good Resistance. This Pink they soon
observed to be a much better Sailer than their French Banker, which went
heavily; and therefore they threw the greatest part of the Wheat over
board, reserving only eno' to Ballast the Vessel for the present, and took
what they wanted out of the Banker, and then Burnt her, and sent the
most of the *Portugueze* away in a large Lanch they had taken.

Now they made the Pink, which Mounted 14 Guns, their Commodore,
and with this and the Schooner Sailed from *St. Michaels,* to the *Canaries,*[9]
where off of *Teneriff,*[10] they gave Chase to a Sloop, which got under the

Command of the Fortress, and so escaped falling into their Hands; but
stretching along to the Western end of the Island, they came up with a
Fishing Boat, and being in want of Water, made them Pilot them into a
small Harbour, where they went a shore and got a supply.

After they had Watered, they Sailed away for *Cape de Verde* Islands,[11]
and upon making the Isle of *May,* they descry'd a Sloop, which they took,
and it proved to be a Bristol-man, one *Pars* or *Pier* Master; this Sloop they
designed for a Tender, and put on board her my Kinsman *Nicholas Merritt*
with 8 or 9 hands more, and Sailed away for *Bonavista,*[12] with a design
to careen their Vessels.

In their Passage to *Bonavista,* the Sloop wronged both the Pink and
the Schooner; which the Hands on board observing, being mostly Forced
Men, or such as were weary of their Employment, upon the *Fifth* of
September, Ran away with her and made their Escape.

When they came to *Bonavista,* they hove down the Schooner, and
careen'd her, and then the Pink; and here they gave the Wheat, which
they had kept to Ballast the Pink with, to the *Portugueze,* and took
other Ballast. After they had cleaned and fitted their Vessels, they steered
away for *St. Nicholas,*[13] to get better Water: and here as I was told, 7 or
8 hands out of the Pink went a shore a Fowling, but never came off
more, among which I suppose *Lawrence Fabins* was one, and what became of them I never could hear to this Day. Then they put out to Sea,
and stood away for the Coast of *Brasil* hoping to meet with Richer
Prizes than they had yet taken; in the Passage thither, they made a Ship,
which they gave chase to, but could not come up with; and when they
came upon the Coast, it had like to have proved a sad Coast to them:
for the Trade-Winds blowing exceeding hard at South East, they fell in
upon the Northern part of the Coast, near 200 Leagues to the Leeward
of where they designed; and here we were all in exceeding great Danger,
and for Five Days and Nights together, hourly feared when we should be
swallowed up by the violence of the Wind and Sea, or stranded upon some
of the Shoals, that lay many Leagues off from Land. In this time of Extremity, the Poor Wretches had no where to go for Help! For they were
at open Defiance with their Maker, & they could have but little comfort
in the thoughts of their Agreement with Hell; such mighty Hectors as
they were, in a clear Sky and a fair Gale, yet a fierce Wind and a boisterous Sea sunk their Spirits to a Cowardly dejection, and they evidently

feared the Almighty, whom before they defied, lest He was come to Torment them before their expected Time; and tho' they were so habituated to Cursing and Swearing, that the Dismal Prospect of Death, & this of so long Continuance, could not Correct the Language of most of them, yet you might plainly see the inward Horror and Anguish of their Minds, visible in their Countenances, and like Men amazed, or starting out of Sleep in a fright, I could hear them ever now and then, cry out, *Oh! I wish I were at Home.*

When the Fierceness of the Weather was over, and they had recovered their Spirits, by the help of a little *Nantes,*[14] they bore away to the *West Indies,* and made the three Islands call'd the *Triangles,*[15] lying off the Main about 40 Leagues to the Eastward of *Surinam.*[16] Here they went in and careened their Vessels again; and it had like to have proved a fatal Scouring to them.

For as they hove down the Pink, *Low* had ordered so many hands upon the Shrouds, and Yards, to throw her Bottom out of Water, that it threw her Ports, which were open, under Water; and the Water flow'd in with such freedom that it presently overset her. *Low* and the *Doctor* were in the Cabbin together, and assoon as he perceived the Water to gush in upon him, he bolted out at one of the Stern-Ports, which the *Doctor* also attempted, but the Sea rushed so violently into the Port by that time, as to force him back into the Cabbin, upon which *Low* nimbly run his Arm into the Port, and caught hold of his Shoulder and drew him out, and so saved him. The Vessel pitched her Masts to the Ground, in about 6 Fathom Water, and turn'd her Keel out of Water; but as her Hull filled, it sunk, and by the help of her Yard-Arms, which I suppose bore upon the Ground, her Masts were raised something out of Water: the Men that were upon her Shrouds and Yards, got upon her Hull, when that was uppermost, and then upon her Top-Masts and Shrouds, when they were raised again. I (who with other light Lads were sent up to the Main-Top-Gallant Yard) was very difficulty put to it to save my Life, being but a poor Swimmer; for the Boat which picked the Men up, refused to take me in, & I was put upon making the best of my way to the Buoy, which with much ado I recovered, and it being large I stayed my self by it, till the Boat came along close by it, and then I called to them to take me in; but they being full of Men still refused me; and I did not know but they meant to leave me to perish there; but the Boat making way a head very slowly because of her deep load, and *Joseph Libbie* calling to me to put off from the

Buoy and Swim to them, I e'en ventured it, and he took me by the hand
and drew me in board. They lost two Men by this Accident, viz. *John
Bell,* and one they called *Zana Gourdon.* The Men that were on board
the Schooner were busy a mending the Sails, under an Auning, so they
knew nothing of what had happened to the Pink, till the Boat full of Men
came along side of them, tho' they were but about Gun-Shot off, and We
made a great out-cry; and therefore they sent not their Boat to help take
up the Men.

And now *Low* and his Gang, having lost their Frigate, and with her the
greatest part of their Provision and Water, were again reduced to their
Schooner as their only Privateer, and in her they put to Sea, and were
brought to very great straits for want of Water; for they could not get a
supply at the *Triangles,* and when they hoped to furnish themselves at
Tobago,[17] the Current set so strong, & the Season was so Calm, that they
could not recover the Harbour, so they were forced to stand away for
Grand Grenada,[18] a French Island about 18 Leagues to the Westward of
Tabago, which they gained, after they had been at the hardship of half a
pint of Water a Man for Sixteen Dayes together.

Here the French came on board, and *Low* having put all his Men down,
but a sufficient number to Sail the Vessel, told them upon their Enquiry,
Whence he was, that he was come from *Barbadoes,*[19] and had lost his
Water, and was oblig'd to put in for a recruit; the poor People not suspecting him for a Pyrate, readily suffered him to send his Men ashoar
and fetch off a supply. But the *Frenchmen* afterwards suspecting he was
a Smugling Trader, thought to have made a Boon Prize of him, and the
next day fitted out a large *Rhode-Island* built Sloop of 70 Tuns, with 4
Guns mounted, and about 30 Hands, with design to have taken him. *Low*
was apprehensive of no danger from them, till they came close along side
of him and plainly discovered their design, by their Number and Actions,
and then he called up his hands upon Deck, and having about 90 Hands
on board, & 8 Guns mounted, the Sloop and Frenchmen fell an easy prey
to him, and he made a Privateer of her.

After this they cruised for some time thro' the *West Indies,*
in which excursion they took 7 or 8 Sail of Vessels, chiefly Sloops; at
length they came to *Santa Cruz,*[20] where they took two Sloops more,
& then came to Anchor off the Island.

While they lay at Anchor here, it came into *Low's* Head, that he wanted
a Doctor's Chest, & in order to procure one, he put four of the French-

men on board one of the Sloops, which he had just now taken, & sent
them away to *St. Thomas*'s,[21] about 12 Leagues off where the Sloops belonged, with the promise, that if they would presently send him off a good
Doctors Chest, for what he sent to purchase it with, they should have
their Men & Vessels again, but if not, he would kill all the Men & burn
the Vessels. The poor People in Compassion to their Neighbours, & to
preserve their Interest, readily complyed with his Demands; so that in
little more than 24 Hours the four Frenchmen returned with what they
went for, & then according to promise, they & their Sloops were Dismissed.

From *Santa Cruz* they Sailed till they made *Curacao*,[22] in which Passage they gave Chase to two Sloops that out sailed them & got clear;
then they Ranged the Coast of *New Spain*,[23] and made *Carthagena*,[24]
& about mid-way between *Carthagena* and *Port-Abella*,[25] they descry'd
two tall Ships, which proved to be the *Mermaid* Man of War, & a large
Guinea-Man.[26] *Low* was now in the *Rhode-Island* Sloop, & one *Farring-
ton Spriggs* a Quarter-Master, was Commander of the Schooner, where I
still was. For some time they made Sail after the two Ships, till they came
so near that they could plainly see the Man of War's large range of Teeth,
& then they turned Tail to, and made the best of their way from them,
upon which the Man of War gave them Chase & overhalled them apace.
And now I confess I was in as great terrour as ever I had been yet, for I
concluded we should be taken, & I could expect no other but to Dye for
Companies sake; for true is what *Solomon* tells us, *a Companion of Fools
shall be destroyed.* But the Pirates finding the Man of War to overhale
them, separated, & *Low* stood out to Sea, & *Spriggs* stood in for the
Shoar. The Man of War observing the Sloop to be the larger Vessel much,
and fullest of Men, threw out all the Sail she could, & stood after her,
and was in a fair way of coming up with her presently: But it hapened
there was one Man on board the Sloop, that knew of a Shoal Ground
thereabouts, who directed *Low* to run over it; he did so; and the Man of
War who had now so forereached him as to fling a Shot over him, in the
close pursuit ran a Ground upon the Shoal, and so *Low* and Company
escaped Hanging for this time.

Spriggs, who was in the Schooner, when he saw the Danger they were
in of being taken, upon the Man of War's out sailing them, was afraid of
falling into the hands of Justice; to prevent which, he, and one of his
Chief Companions, took their Pistols, and laid them down by them, and
solemnly Swore to each other, and pledg'd the Oath in a Bumper[27] of

Liquor, that if they saw there was at last no possibility of Escaping, but
that they should be taken, they would set Foot to Foot, and Shoot one
another, to Escape Justice and the Halter. As if Divine Justice were not
as inexorable as Humane!

But, as I said, he stood in for the Shoar, and made into *Pickeroon Bay,*
about 18 Leagues from *Carthagena,* and so got out of the reach of Danger.
By this means the Sloop and Schooner were parted; and *Spriggs* made
Sail towards the Bay of *Honduras,* and came to Anchor in a small Island
called *Utilla,* about 7 or 8 Leagues to Leeward of *Roatan,*[28] where by the
help of a small Sloop, he had taken the Day before, he haled down, and
cleaned the Schooner.

While *Spriggs* lay at *Utilla,* there was an Opportunity presented, which
gave occasion to several of us to form a design, of making our Escape out
of the Pirates Company; for having lost *Low,* and being but weak handed,
Spriggs had determined to go thro' the Gulf, and come upon the Coast
of *New-England,* to encrease his Company, and supply himself with Provision; whereupon a Number of us had entred into a Combination, to take
the first fair advantage, to Subdue our Masters, and Free our selves. There
were in all about 22 Men on board the Schooner, and 8 of us were in the
Plot, which was, That when we should come upon the Coast of *New-
England,* we would take the opportunity when the Crew had sufficiently
dozed themselves with Drink, and had got sound a Sleep, to secure them
under the Hatches, and bring the Vessel and Company in, and throw ourselves upon the Mercy of the Government.

But it pleased GOD to disappoint our Design. The Day that they came
to Sail out of *Utilla,* after they had been parted from *Low* about five
Weeks, they discovered a large Sloop, which bore down upon them.
Spriggs, who knew not the Sloop, but imagined it might be a *Spanish*
Privateer, full of Men, being but weak handed himself, made the best of
his way from her. The Sloop greatly overhaled the Schooner. *Low,* who
knew the Schooner, & thought that since they had been separated, she
might have fallen into the hands of honest Men, fired upon her, & struck
her the first Shot. *Spriggs,* seeing the Sloop fuller of Men than ordinary,
(for *Low* had been to *Honduras,* & had taken a Sloop, & brought off
several Baymen, & was now become an Hundred strong) & remaining still
ignorant of his old Mate, refused to bring to, but continued to make off;
and resolved if they came up with him, to fight them the best he could.
Thus the Harpies had like to have fallen foul of one another. But *Low*
hoisting his Pirate Colours, discovered who he was; and then, hideous

was the noisy Joy among the Piratical Crew, on all sides, accompanied
with Firing, & Carousing, at the finding their Old Master, & Companions,
& their narrow Escape: and so the design of Crusing upon the Coast of
New-England came to nothing. A good Providence it was to my dear
Country, that it did so; unless we could have timely succeeded in our
design to surprise them.

Yet it had like to have proved a fatal Providence to those of us that
had a hand in the Plot; for tho' our design of surprising *Spriggs* and Company, when we should come upon the Coast of *New-England,* was carried
with as much secrecy as was possible, (we hardly daring to trust one another, and mentioning it always with utmost privacy, and not plainly,
but in distant Hints) yet now that *Low* appeared, *Spriggs* had got an account of it some way or other; and full of Resentment and Rage he goes
aboard *Low,* and acquaints him with what he called our Treacherous design, and says all he can to provoke him to Revenge the Mischief upon us,
and earnestly urged that we might be shot. But GOD who has the Hearts
of all Men in His own Hands, and turns them as He pleases, so over ruled,
that *Low* turned it off with a Laugh, and said he did not know, but if it
had been his own case, as it was ours, he should have done so himself; and
all that *Spriggs* could say was not able to stir up his Resentments, and
procure any heavy Sentence upon us.

Thus *Low's* merry Air saved us at that time; for had he lisped a Word
in compliance with what *Spriggs* urged, we had surely some of us, if not
all, have been lost. Upon this he comes on board the Schooner again,
heated with Drink, but more chafed in his own Mind, that he could not
have his Will of us, and swore & tore like a Mad-man, crying out that four
of us ought to go forward, & be shot; and to me in particular he said,
You D-g, Ashton, *deserve to be hand'd up at the Yards-Arm, for designing to cut us off.* I told him, I had no design of hurting any man on board,
but if they would let me go away quietly I should be glad. This matter
made a very great noise on board for several Hours, but at length the
Fire was quenched, and thro' the Goodness of GOD, I Escaped being consumed by the violence of the Flame.

The next Day, *Low* ordered all into *Roatan* Harbour to clean, and
here it was that thro' the Favour of GOD to me, I first gained Deliverance
out of the Pirates hands; tho' it was a long while before my Deliverance
was perfected, in a return to my Country, and Friends; as you will see in
the Sequel.

Roatan Harbour, as all about the Gulf of *Honduras,* is full of small

Islands, which go by the General Name of the Keys. When we had got in here, *Low* and some of his Chief Men had got a shoar upon one of these small Islands, which they called *Port-Royal Key,* where they made them Booths, and were Carousing, Drinking, and Firing, while the two Sloops, the *Rhode-Island,* and that which *Low* brought with him from the Bay were cleaning. As for the Schooner, he loaded her with the Logwood which the Sloop brought from the Bay, & gave her, according to promise, to one *John Blaze,* and put four men along with him in her, and when they came to Sail from this Place, sent them away upon their own account, and what became of them I know not.

Upon *Saturday* the 9*th* of *March,* 1723, the Cooper with Six hands in the Long-Boat were going ashore at the Watering place to fill their Casks; as he came along by the Schooner I called to him and asked him, if he were going a shoar? he told me Yes; then I asked him, if he would take me along with him; he seemed to hesitate at the first; but I urged that I had never been on shoar yet, since I first came on board, and I thought it very hard that I should be so closely confined, when every one else had the Liberty of going ashoar at several times, as there was occasion. At length he took me in, imagining, I suppose, that there would be no danger of my Running away in so desolate uninhabited a Place, as that was.

I went into the Boat with only an Ozenbrigs Frock and Trousers on, and a Mill'd Cap upon my Head, having neither Shirt, Shoes, nor Stockings, nor any thing else about me; whereas, had I been aware of such an Opportunity, but one quarter of an Hour before, I could have provided my self something better. However thought I, if I can but once get footing on *Terra Firma,* tho' in never so bad Circumstances, I shall count it a happy Deliverance; for I was resolved, come what would, never to come on board again.

Low had often told me (upon my asking him to send me away in some of the Vessels, which he dismissed after he had taken them) that I should go home when he did, and not before, and Swore that I should never set foot on shoar till he did. But the time for Deliverance was now come. GOD had ordered it that *Low* and *Spriggs,* and almost all the Commanding Officers, were ashoar upon an Island distinct from *Roatan,* where the Watering place was; He presented me in sight, when the Long Boat came by, (the only opportunity I could have had) He had moved the Cooper to take me into the Boat, and under such Circumstances as rendred me least lyable to Suspicion; and so I got ashoar.

When we came first to Land, I was very Active in helping to get the

Casks out of the Boat, & Rowling them up to the Watering place; then I lay down at the Fountain & took a hearty Draught of the Cool Water; & anon, I gradually strol'd along the Beach picking up Stone & Shell, & looking about me; when I had got about Musket Shot off from them (tho' they had taken no Arms along with them in the Boat) I began to make up to the Edge of the Woods; when the Cooper spying me, call'd after me, & asked me where I was going; I told him I was going to get some Coco-Nuts, for there were some Coco-Nut Trees just before me. So soon as I had recovered the Woods, and lost sight of them, I betook my self to my Heels, & ran as fast as the thickness of the Bushes, and my naked Feet would let me. I bent my Course, not directly from them, but rather up behind them, which I continued till I had got a considerable way into the Woods, & yet not so far from them but that I could hear their talk, when they spake any thing loud; and here I lay close in a very great Thicket, being well assured, if they should take the pains to hunt after me never so carefully they would not be able to find me.

After they had filled their Cask and were about to go off, the Cooper called after me to come away; but I lay snug in my Thicket, and would give him no Answer, tho' I plainly eno' heard him. At length they set a hallooing for me, but I was still silent: I could hear them say to one another, *The D-g is lost in the Woods, and can't find the way out again;* then they hallooed again; and cried, *he is run-away and won't come again;* the Cooper said, if he had thought I would have served him so, he would not have brought me ashoar. They plainly saw it would be in vain to seek for me in such hideous Wood, and thick Brushes. When they were weary with hallooing, the Cooper at last, to shew his good Will to me, (I can't but Love and Thank him for his Kindness) call'd out, *If you don't come away presently, I'll go off and leave you alone.* But all they could say was no Temptation to me to discover my self, and least of all that of their going away and leaving me; for this was the very thing I desired, that I might be rid of them, and all that belonged to them. So finding it in vain for them to wait any longer, they put off with their Water, without me; and thus was I left upon a desolate Island destitute of all help, and much out of the way of all Travellers; however this Wilderness I looked upon as Hospitable, and this Loneliness as good Company, compared with the State and Society I was now happily Delivered from.

When I supposed they were gone off, I came out of my Thicket, and drew down to the Water side, about a Mile below the Watering place,

where there was a small run of Water; and here I sat down to observe
their Motions, and know when the Coast was clear; for I could not have
some remaining fears lest they should send a Company of Armed Men
after me; yet I thought if they should, the Woods and Bushes were so
thick that it would be impossible they should find me. As yet I had nothing to Eat, nor indeed were my Thoughts much concerned about living
in this Desolate Place, but they were chiefly taken up about my geting
clear. And to my Joy, after the Vessels had stayed five Dayes in this Harbour, they came to Sail, and put out to Sea, and I plainly saw the Schooner
part from the two Sloops, and shape a different Course from them.

When they were gone and the Coast clear, I began to reflect upon my
self, and my present Condition; I was upon an Island from whence I could
not get off; I knew of no Humane Creature within many scores of Miles
of me; I had but a Scanty Cloathing, and no possibility of getting more;
I was destitute of all Provision for my Support, and knew not how I
should come at any; every thing looked with a dismal Face; the sad prospect drew Tears from me in abundance; yet since GOD had graciously
granted my Desires, in freeing me out of the hands of the Sons of Violence,
whose Business 'tis to devise Mischief against their Neighbour, and from
whom every thing that had the least face of Religion and Virtue was in-
tirely Banished (unless that *Low* would never suffer his Men to work upon
the Sabbath, (it was more devoted to Play) and I have seen some of them
sit down to Read in a good Book) therefore I purposed to account all the
hardship I might now meet with, as Light, & Easy, compared with being
Associated with them.

In order to find in what manner I was to Live for the time to come, I
began to Range the Island over, which I suppose is some 10 or 11 Leagues
Long, in the Latitude of 16 *deg.* 30 *min.* or thereabouts. I soon found
that I must look for no Company, but the Wild Beast of the Field, and
the Fowl of the Air; with all of which I made a Firm Peace, and GOD
said Amen to it. I could discover no Footsteps of any Habitation upon
the Island; yet there was one walk of Lime Trees near a Mile long, and
ever now & then I found some broken Shreds of Earthen Pots, scattered
here and there upon the Place, which some say are some remains of the
Indians that formerly Lived upon the Island.

The Island is well Watered, and is full of Hills, high Mountains, and
lowly Vallies. The Mountains are Covered over with a sort of shrubby
black Pine, & are almost inaccessible. The Vallies abound with Fruit Trees,

and are so prodigiously thick with an underbrush, that 'tis difficult passing.

The Fruit were *Coco-Nuts,* but these I could have no advantage from, because I had no way of coming at the inside; there are *Wild-Figs,* and *Vines* in abundance, these I chiefly lived upon, especially at first; there is also a sort of Fruit growing upon Trees somewhat larger than an Orange, of an Oval shape, of a brownish Colour without, and red within, having two or three Stones about as large as a Walnut in the midst: tho' I saw many of these fallen under the Trees, yet I dared not to meddle with them for sometime, till I saw some Wild Hogs eat them with safety, and then I thought I might venture upon them too, after such Tasted, and I found them to be a very delicious sort of Fruit; they are called *Mammees Supporters,*[29] as I learned afterwards. There are also a sort of small *Beech-Plumb,* growing upon low shrubs; and a larger sort of Plumb growing upon Trees, which are called *Hog-Plumbs;* and many other sorts of Fruit which I am wholly a Stranger to. Only I would take notice of the Goodness of GOD to me, in preserving me from destroying my self by feeding upon any Noxious Fruit, as the *Mangeneil Apple,*[30] which I often took up in my hands, and look'd upon, but had not the power to eat of; which if I had, it would have been present Death to me, as I was informed afterwards, tho' I knew not what it was.

There are also upon this Island, and the Adjacent Islands, and Keys, *Deer,* and *Wild Hogs;* they abound too with *Fowl* of diverse sorts, as *Ducks, Teil, Curlews, Galdings,* (a Fowl long Legged, and shaped somewhat like a *Heron,* but not so big) *Pellicans, Boobys, Pigeons, Parrots, &c.* and the Shoars abound with *Tortoise.*

But of all this Store of Beast, and Fowl, I could make no use to Supply my Necessities; tho' my Mouth often watered for a Bit of them; yet I was forced to go without it; for I had no Knife, or other Instrument of Iron with me, by which to cut up a *Tortoise,* when I had turned it; or to make Snares or Pitts, with which to entrap, or Bows & Arrows with which to kill any Bird or Beast withal; nor could I by any possible means that I knew of, come at Fire to dress any if I had taken them; tho' I doubt not but some would have gone down raw if I could have come at it.

I sometimes had thoughts of Digging Pits and covering them over with small Branches of Trees, & laying Brush and Leaves upon them to take some Hogs or Deer in; but all was vain imagination, I had no Shovel, neither could I find or make any thing that would answer my end, and

I was presently convinced, that my Hands alone, were not sufficient to make one deep and large eno' to detain any thing that should fall into it; so that I was forced to rest satisfied with the Fruit of the Vine, and Trees, and looked upon it as good Provision, and very handy for one in my Condition.

In length of time, as I was poking about the Beach, with a Stick, to see if I could find any *Tortoise* Nests, (which I had heard lay their Eggs in the Sand) I brought up part of an Egg clinging to the Stick, and upon removing the Sand which lay over them, I found near an Hundred & Fifty Eggs which had not been laid long eno' to spoil; so I took some of them and eat them: And in this way I sometimes got some Eggs to Eat, which are not very good at the best; yet what is not good to him that has nothing to Live upon, but what falls from the Trees.

The *Tortoise* lay their Eggs above High Water Mark, in a hole which they make in the Sand, about a Foot, or a Foot and half deep, and cover them over with the Sand, which they make as smooth & even as any part of the Beech, so that there is no discerning where they are, by any, the least sign of a Hillock, or Rising; and according to my best observation, they Hatch in about 18 or 20 Days, and as soon as the Young Ones are Hatch'd they betake themselves immediately to the Water.

There are many *Serpents* upon this, and the Adjacent Islands. There is one sort that is very Large, as big round as a Man's Wast, tho' not above 12 or 14 Feet long. These are called *Owlers*.[31] They look like old fallen Stocks of Trees covered over with a short Moss, when they lye at their length; but they more usually lye coiled up in a round. The first I saw of these greatly surprised me; for I was very near to it before I discovered it to be a Living Creature, and then it opened it's Mouth wide eno' to have thrown a Hat into it, and blew out its Breath at me. This Serpent is very slow in its motion, and nothing Venemous, as I was afterwards told by a Man, who said he had been once bitten by one of them. There are several other smaller Serpents, some of them very Venemous, particularly one that is called a *Barber's Pole*,[32] being streaked White and Yellow. But I met with no *Rattle-Snakes* there, unless the Pirates, nor did I ever hear of any other being there.

The Islands are so greatly infested with vexatious *Insects,* especially the *Musketto,* and a sort of small *Black Fly,* (something like a *Gnat*) more troublesome than the *Musketto;* so that if one had never so many of the comforts of Life about him, these Insects would render his Living here very burthensome to him; unless he retired to a small Key, destitute of Woods and Brush, where the Wind disperses the Vermin.

The Sea hereabouts, hath a variety of *Fish;* such as are good to Eat, I could not come at, and the *Sharks,* and *Alligators* or *Crocodiles,* I did not care to have any thing to do with; tho' I was once greatly endangered by a *Shark,* as I shall tell afterwards.

This was the Place I was confined to; this my Society and Fellowship; and this my State and Condition of Life. Here I spent near Nine Months, without Converse with any Living Creature; for the *Parrots* here had not been taught to Speak. Here I lingred out one Day after another, I knew not how, without Business, or Diversion; unless gathering up my Food, rambling from Hill to Hill, from Island to Island, gazing upon the Water, and staring upon the Face of the Sky, may be called so.

In this Lonely and Distressed Condition, I had time to call over my past Life; and Young as I was, I saw I had grown Old in Sin; my Transgressions were more than my Days; and tho' GOD had graciously Restrained me from the Grosser Enormities of Life, yet I saw Guilt staring me in the Face; eno' to humble me and forever to vindicate the Justice of GOD in all that I underwent. I called to mind many things I had heard from the Pulpit, and what I had formerly Read in the *Bible,* which I was now wholly Destitute of, tho' I thought if I could but have one now, it would have sweetned my Condition, by the very Diversion of Reading, and much more from the Direction and Comfort it would have afforded me. I had some Comforts in the midst of my Calamity. It was no small Support to me, that I was about my Lawful Employment, when I was first taken; and that I had no hand in bringing my Misery upon my self, but was forced away solely against my Will. It wonderfully aleviated my Sorrows, to think, that I had my Parents approbation, and consent in my going to Sea; and I often fancied to my self, that if I had gone to Sea against their will and pleasure, and had met with this Disaster, I should have looked upon it as a designed Punishment of such Disobedience, and the very Reflection on it would have so aggravated my Misery, as soon to have put an end to my Days. I looked upon my self also, as more in the way of the Divine Blessing now, than when I was linked to a Crew of Pirates, where I could scarce hope for Protection and a Blessing. I plainly saw very signal Instances of the Power & Goodness of GOD to me, in the many Deliverances which I had already experienced, (the least of which I was utterly unworthy of) and this Encouraged me to put my Trust in Him; and tho' I had none but GOD to go to for help, yet I knew that He was able to do more for me than I could ask or think; to Him therefore I committed my self, purposing to wait hopefully upon the *Lord* till he should send Deliverance to me: Trusting that in his own time and way, he would find out means for my safe Return to my Fathers House; and earnestly entreating that he would provide a better place for me.

It was my Daily Practice to Ramble from one part of the Island to an other, tho I had a more special Home near to the Water side. Here I had built me a House to defend me from the heat of the Sun by Day, and the great Dews of the Night. I took some of the best Branches I could find fallen from the Trees, and stuck them in the Ground, and I contrived as often as I could (for I built many such Huts) to fix them leaning against the Limb of a Tree that hung low; I split the *Palmeto* Leaves and knotted the Limb & Sticks together; then I covered them over with the largest and best *Palmeto* Leaves I could find. I generally Situated my Hut near the Water side, with the open part of it facing the Sea, that I might be the more ready upon the look out, and have the advantage of the Sea Breez, which both the Heat and the Vermin required. But the Vermin, the *Muskettos* and *Flys,* grew so troublesome to me, that I was put upon contrivance to get rid of their Company. This led me to think of getting over to some of the Adjacent Keys, that I might have some Rest from the disturbance of these busy Companions. My greatest difficulty lay in getting over to any other Island; for I was but a very poor Swimmer; and I had no Canoo, nor any means of making one. At length I got a peice of Bamboe, which is hollow like a Reed, and light as a Cork, and having made tryal of it under my Breast and Arms in Swimming by the shoar; with this help I e'en ventured to put off for a small *Key* about Gun-shot off, and I reached it pretty comfortably. This *Key* was but about 3 or 400 Feet in compass, clear of Woods & Brush, & lay very low; & I found it so free from the Vermin, by the free Passage of the Wind over it, that I seemed to be got into a New World, where I lived more at ease. This I kept as a place of Retreat, whither I retired when the Heat of the Day rendred the Fly-kind most troublesome to me: for I was obliged to be much upon *Roatan* for the sake of my Food, Water, & House. When I swam backward & forward from my Day Island, I used to bind my

Frock & Trousers about my Head, but I could not so easily carry over Wood & Leaves to make a Hut of; else I should have spent more of my time upon my little Day Island.

My Swimming thus backward & forward exposed me to some Danger. Once I Remember as I was passing from my Day to my Night Island, the *Bamboe* got from under me 'er I was aware, & the Tide or Current set so strong, that I was very difficultly put to it to recover the Shoar; so that a few Rods more distance had in all probability landed me in another World. At another time as I was Swimming over to my Day Island, a *Shovel nos'd Shark,* (of which the Seas thereabouts are full, as well as *Alligators*) struck me in the Thigh just as I set my Foot to Ground, & so grounded himself (I suppose) by the shoalness of the Water, that he could not turn himself to come at me with his Mouth, & so, thro' the Goodness of GOD, I escaped falling a Prey to his devouring Teeth. I felt the Blow he gave me some hours after I had got ashoar. By accustoming my self to Swim, I at length grew pretty dexterous at it, and often gave my self the Diversion of thus passing from one Island to another among the *Keys.*

One of my greatest difficulties lay in my being Bare-foot, my Travels backward & forward in the Woods to hunt for my Daily Food, among the thick under-brush, where the Ground was covered with sharp Sticks & Stones, & upon the hot Beech among the sharp broken Shells, had made so many Wounds and Gashes in my Feet, & some of them very large, that I was hardly able to go at all. Very often as I was treading with all the tenderness I could, a sharp Stone or Shell on the Beech, or pointed Stick in the Woods, would run into the Old Wounds, & the Anguish of it would strike me down as suddenly as if I had been shot thro', & oblige me to let down and Weep by the hour together at the extremity of my Pain: so that in process of time I could Travel no more than needs must, for the necessary procuring of Food. Sometimes I have sat leaning my Back against a Tree, with my Face to the Sea, to look out for the passing of a Vessel for a whole Day together.

At length I grew very Weak & Faint, as well as Sore and Bruised; and once while I was in this Condition, a Wild *Boar* seemed to make at me with some Fierceness; I knew not what to do with my self, for I was not able to defend my self against him if he should attack me. So as he drew nearer to me, I caught hold of the Limb of a Tree which was close by me, & drew my Body up by it from the Ground as well as I could; while I was in this Hanging posture, the *Boar* came and struck at me, but his Tushes only took hold on my shattered Trousers & tore a piece out; and then he went his way. This I think was the only time that I was assaulted by any Wild Beast, with whom I said I had made Peace; and I look upon it as a Great Deliverance.

As my Weakness encreased upon me, I should often fall down as tho' struck with a dead sleep, and many a time as I was thus falling, and sometimes when I lay'd my self down to Sleep, I never expected to wake or rise more; and yet in the midst of all GOD has Wonderfully preserved me.

In the midst of this my great Soreness & Feebleness I lost the Days of the Week, & how long I had layn in some of my numb sleepy Fits I knew not, so that I was not able now to distinguish the Sabbath from any other Day of the Week; tho' all Days were in some sort a Sabbath to me. As my Illness prevailed I wholly lost the Month, and knew not where abouts I was in the Account of Time.

Under all this Dreadful Distress, I had no healing Balsames to apply to my Feet, no Cordials to revive my Fainting Spirits, hardly able now & then to get me some *Figs* or *Grapes* to Eat, nor any possible way of coming at a Fire, which the Cool Winds, & great Rains, beginning to come on now called for. The Rains begin about the middle of *October,* & continue for Five Months together, and then the Air is Raw Cold, like our North East Storms of Rain; only at times the Sun breakes out with such an exceeding Fierceness, that there is hardly any enduring the Heat of it.

I hard often heard of the fetching Fire by Rubbing of two Sticks together; but I could never get any this way, tho' I had often tried while I was in Health and Strength, untill I was quite tired. Afterwards I learned the way of getting Fire from two Sticks, which I will Publish, that it may be of Service to any that may be hereafter in my Condition.

Take Two Sticks, the one of harder the other softer Wood, the dryer the better, in the soft Wood make a sort of Mortice or Socket, point the harder Wood to fit that Socket; hold the softer Wood firm between the Knees, take the harder Wood between your Hands with the point fixed in the Socket, and rub the Stick in your Hands backward & forward briskly like a Drill, and it will take Fire in less than a Minute; as I have sometimes since seen, upon experiment made of it.

But then I knew of no such Method (and it may be should have been difficultly put to it to have formed the Mortice and Drill for want of a

Knife) and I suffered greatly without a Fire, thro' the chillness of the Air,
the Wetness of the Season, and Living only upon Raw Fruit.

Thus I pass'd about Nine Months in this lonely, melancholy, wounded,
and languishing Condition. I often lay'd my self down as upon my last
Bed, & concluded I should certainly Dye alone, & no Body knew what
was become of me. I thought it would be some relief to me if my Parents
could but tell where I was; and then I thought their Distress would be exceeding great, if they knew what I under went. But all such thoughts were
vain. The more my Difficulties encreased, and the nearer prospect I had
of Dying, the more it drove me upon my Knees, and made me the more
earnest in my Crys to my Maker for His favourable regards to me, and to
the Great Redeemer to pardon me, and provide for my after well being.

And see the surprising Goodness of GOD to me, in sending me help in
my time of trouble, & that in the most unexpected way & manner, as tho'
an Angel had been commissioned from Heaven to relieve me.

Sometime in *November* 1723, I espied a small Canoo, coming towards
me with one Man in it. It did not much surprise me. A Friend I could not
hope for; and I could not resist, or hardly get out of the way of an Enemy,
nor need I fear one. I kept my Seat upon the Edge of the Beech. As he
came nearer he discovered me & seemed greatly surprised. He called to me.
I told him whence I was, & that he might safely venture ashoar, for I was
alone, & almost Dead. As he came up to me, he stared & look'd wild with
surprise; my Garb & Countenance astonished him; he knew not what to
make of me; he started back a little, & viewed me more thorowly; but
upon recovering of himself, he came forward, & took me by the Hand &
told me he was glad to see me. And he was ready as long as he stayed with
me, to do any kind offices for me.

He proved to be a *North-Britain,* a Man well in Years, of a Grave and
Venerable Aspect, and of a reserved Temper. His Name I never knew, for
I had not asked him in the little time he was with me, expecting a longer
converse with him; and he never told me it. But he acquainted me that
he had lived with the *Spaniards* 22 Years, and now they threatned to
Burn him, I knew not for what Crime: therefore he had fled for Sanctuary
to this Place, & had brought his Gun, Amunition, and Dog, with a small
quantity of Pork, designing to spend the residue of his Days here, & support himself by Hunting. He seemed very kind & obliging to me, gave me
some of his Pork, and assisted me all he could; tho' he conversed little.

Upon the Third Day after he came to me, he told me, he would go out

in his Canoo among the Islands, to kill some Wild Hogs & Deer, and would
have had me to go along with him. His Company, the Fire and a little
dressed Provision something recruited my Spirits; but yet I was so Weak,
and Sore in my Feet, that I could not accompany him in Hunting: So he
set out alone, and said he would be with me again in a Day or two. The
Sky was Serene and Fair, and there was no prospect of any Danger in his
little Voyage among the Islands, when he had come safe in the small Float
near 12 Leagues, but by that time he had been gone an Hour, there arose
a most Violent Gust of Wind and Rain, which in all probability overset
him, so that I never saw nor heard of him any more. And tho' by this
means I was deprived of my Companion, yet it was the Goodness of GOD
to me, that I was not well eno' to go with him; for this I was preserved
from that Destruction which undoubtedly overtook him.

Thus after the pleasure of having a Companion almost Three Days, I
was as unexpectedly reduced to my former lonely Condition, as I had
been for a little while recovered out of it. It was grievous to me to think,
that I no sooner saw the Dawnings of Light, after so long Obscurity, but
the Clouds returned after the Rain upon me. I began to experience the
Advantage of a Companion, and find that Two is better than One, and
flattered my self, that by the help of some fresh Hogs Grease, I should
get my Feet well, and by a better Living recover more Strength. But it
pleased GOD to take from me the only Man I had seen for so many
Months after so short a Converse with him. Yet I was left in better Circumstances by him than he found me in. For at his going away he left
with me about Five Pound of Pork, a Knife, a Bottle of Powder, Tobacco,
Tongs and Flint, by which means I was in a way to Live better than I had
done. For now I could have a Fire, which was very needful for me, the
Rainy Months of the Winter; I could cut up some *Tortoise* when I had
turned them, and have a delicate broiled Meal of it: So that by the help
of the Fire, and dressed Food, and the Blessing of GOD accompaning it,
I began to recover more Strength, only my Feet remained Sore.

Besides, I had this Advantage now, which I had not before, that I could
go out now and then and catch a Dish of Crab-Fish, a Fish much like a
Lobster, only wanting the great Claws. My manner of Catching them was
odd; I took some of the best pieces of the old broken small Wood, that
came the nearest to our Pitch Pine, or Candle-Wood, and made them up
into a small Bundle like a Torch, and holding one of these lighted at one
End in each hand, I waded into the Water upon the Beech up to my Wast:

the Crab-Fish spying the Light at a considerable distance, would crawl away till they came directly under it, and then they would lye still at my Feet. In my other hand I had a Forked Stick with which I struck the Fish and tossed it ashoar. In this manner I supplyed my self with a Mess of Shell-Fish, which when roasted is very good Eating.

Between two and three Months after I had lost my Companion, as I was ranging a long shoar, I found a small Canoo. The sight of this at first renewed my Sorrows for his Loss; for I thought it had been his Canoo, and it's coming ashore thus, was a proof to me that he was lost in the Tempest: but upon further Examination of it I found it was one I had never seen before.

When I had got this little Vessel in possession, I began to think my self Admiral of the Neighbouring Seas, as well as Sole Possessor and Chief Commander upon the Islands; and with the advantage hereof I could transport my self to my small Islands of Retreat, much more conveniently than in my former Method of Swimming. In process of time I tho't of making a Tour to some of the more distant and larger Islands, to see after what manner they were inhabited, and how they were provided, and partly to give my self the Liberty of Diversions. So I lay'd in a small parcel of *Grapes* and *Figs,* and some *Tortoise,* & took my Fire-Works with me, and put off for the Island of *Bonacco,* an Island of about 4 or 5 Leagues long, and some 5 or 6 Leagues to the Eastward of *Roatan.*

As I was upon my Voyage I discovered a Sloop at the Eastern End of the Island; so I made the best of my way, and put in at the Western End; designing to travel down to them by Land, partly because there ran out a large point of Rocks far into the Sea, and I did not care to venture my self to far out in my little Canoo as I must do to head them: & partly because I was willing to make a better discovery of them, before I was seen by them; for in the midst of my most deplorable Circumstances, I could never entertain the thoughts of returning on board any Pirate, if I should have the opportunity, but had rather Live and Dye as I was. So I haled up my Canoo, and fastned her as well as I could, and set out upon my Travel.

I spent two Days, and the biggest part of two Nights in Travelling of it; my Feet were yet so sore that I could go but very slowly, and sometimes the Woods and Bushes were so thick that I was forced to Crawl upon my Hands and Knees for half a Mile together. In this Travel I met with an odd Adventure that had like to have proved fatal to me, and my preservation was an eminent Instance of the Divine Conduct and Protection.

As I drew within a Mile or two of where I supposed the Sloop might be, I made down to the Water side, and slowly opened the Sea, that I might not discover my self too soon; when I came down to the Water side I could see no sign of the Sloop, upon which I concluded that it was gone clear, while I spent so much time in Traveling. I was very much tired with my long tedious March, and sat my self down leaning against the Stock of a Tree facing to the Sea, and fell a Sleep. But I had not slept long before I was awakned in a very surprising manner, by the noise of Guns. I started up in a fright, and saw Nine Periaguas, or large Canooes, full of Men firing upon me. I soon turned about and ran as fast as my sore Feet would let me into the Bushes; and the Men which were *Spaniards,* cryed after me, *O Englishman, we'll give you good Quarter.* But such was the Surprise I had taken, by being awakned out of Sleep in such a manner, that I had no command of my self to hearken to their offers of Quarter, which it may be at another time under cooler thoughts I might have done. So I made into the Woods, and they continued Firing after me, to the Number of 150 small Shot at least, many of which cut off several small twigs of the Bushes along side of me as I went off. When I had got out of the reach of their Shot, into a very great Thicket, I lay close for several Hours; and perceiving they were gone by the noise of their Oars in Rowing off, I came out of my Thicket, and Travelled a Mile or two along the Water side, below the place where they Fired upon me, and then I saw the Sloop under English Colours, Sailing out of the Harbour, with the Periaguas in tow; and then I concluded that it was an English Sloop that had been at the Bay, whom the *Spaniards* had met with and taken.

The next Day I went up to the Tree, where I so narrowly Escaped being taken Napping, and there to my surprise I found 6 or 7 Shot had gone into the Body of the Tree, within a Foot or less of my Head as I sat down; & yet thro' the wonderful goodness of GOD to me, in the midst of all their Fire, and tho' I was as a Mark set up for them to shoot at, none of their Shot touched me. So did GOD as yet signally preserve me.

After this I Travelled away for my Canoo at the Western End of the Island, and spent near three Days e're I reached it. In this Long March backward and forward, I suffered very much from the Soreness of my Feet, & the want of Provision; for this Island is not so plentifully stored

with Fruit as *Roatan* is, so that I was very difficultly put to it for my
Subsistence, for the 5 or 6 Days that I spent here; and besides the *Muskettoes* and *Black Flys* were abundantly more numberous, and vexatious
to me than at my old Habitation. The Difficulties I met with here made
me lay aside all thoughts of tarrying any time to search the Island. At
length much tired and spent I reached my Canoo, and found all safe there,
to my great Joy; and then I put off for *Roatan,* which was a Royal Palace
to me in comparison of *Bonacco,* where I arrived to my great Satisfaction
about Ten a Clock at Night, & found all things as I left them.

Here I Lived (if it may be called Living) alone for about Seven Months
more, from the time of my loosing my *North British* Companion; and
spent my time after my usual manner in Hunting for my Food, and Ranging the Islands; till at length it pleased GOD, to send some Company to
me with whom I could Converse, and enjoy somewhat more of the Comforts of Life.

Sometime in *June,* 1724, as I was upon my small Island, where I often
retired for Shelter from the pestering Insects, I saw two large Canooes
making into the Harbour; as they drew near they saw the Smoak of the
Fire which I had kindled, and wondring what it should mean came to a
stand. I had fresh in my Memory what I met with at *Banacco,* and was
very loth to run the risque of such another firing, and therefore steped
to my Canoo upon the back side of my small Island, not above 100 feet
off from me, and immediately went over to my great Mansion, where I
had places of safety to Shelter me from the Designs of an Enemy, and
Rooms large and spacious eno' to give a kindly welcome to any ordinary
number of Friends. They saw me cross the Ferry of about Gun shot over,
from my little to my great Island, and being as much afraid of Spaniards,
as I was of Pirates, they drew very cautiously towards the shoar. I came
down upon the Beech shewing my self openly to them; for their caution
made me think they were no Pirates, and I did not much care who else
they were; however, I thought I could call to them, and know what they
were; before I should be in much danger from their shot; and if they
proved such as I did not like, I could easily retire from them. But before
I called, they, who were as full of fears as I could be, lay upon thir Oars
and hallooed to me, enquiring who I was, and whence I came; I told them
I was an English Man, and had Runaway from the Pirates. Upon this they
drew something nearer and enquired who was there besides my self; I
assured them I was alone. Then I took my turn, and asked them who they
were, and whence they came. They told me they were Bay-men, come

from the *Bay*. This was comfortable News to me; so I bid them pull ashoar,
there was no danger, I would stop for them. Accordingly they put ashoar,
but at some distance from me, and first sent one Man ashoar to me, whom
I went to meet. When the Man came up to me he started back, frighted
to see such a Poor, Ragged, Lean, Wan, Forlorn, Wild, Miserable Object
so near him: but upon recovering himself, he came and took me by the
hand, and we fell to embracing one another, he with surprise and wonder,
I with a sort of Extasy of Joy. After this was over he took me up in his
Arms and carried me down to their Canooes, where they were all struck
with astonishment at the sight of me, were glad to receive me, and expressed a very great tenderness to me.

I gave them a short History how I had escaped from *Low,* and had
lived here alone for Sixteen Months, (saving three days) what hardship
I had met with, and what danger I had run thro'. They stood amazed!
they wondred I was alive! and expressed a great satisfaction in it, that
they were come to relieve me. And observing I was weak, and my Spirits
low, they gave me about a Spoonful of Rhum to recruit my fainting
Spirits. This small quantity, thro' my long disuse of any Liquor higher
Spirited than Water, and my present weakness, threw my Animal Spirits
into such a violent Agitation, as to obctruct their Motion, and produced
a kind of Stupor, which left me for sometime bereft of all Sense; some
of them perceiving me falling into such a strange Insensibility, would
have given me more of the same Spirit to have recovered me; but those
of them that had more wit, would not allow of it. So I lay for some small
time in a sort of a Fit, and they were ready to think that they should
lose me as soon as they had found me. But I revived.

And when I was so thorowly come to my self as to converse with them,
I found they were Eighteen Men come from the Bay of *Honduras,* the
chief of which were, *John Hope,* and *John Ford.* The occasion of their
coming from the Bay was, a Story they had got among them, that the
Spaniards had projected to make a descent upon them by Water, while
the *Indians* were to assault them by Land, and cut off the *Bay;* and they
retired hither to avoid the Destruction that was designed. This *John
Hope* and *Ford* had formerly, upon a like occasion, sheltred themselves
among these Islands, and lived for four Years together upon a small Island
called *Barbarat,* about two Leagues from *Roatan,* where they had two
Plantations, as they called them; and being now upon the same design
of retreating for a time for Safety, they brought with them two Barrels
of Flower, with other Provisions, their Fire-Arms, Ammunition and Dogs

for Hunting, and Nets for Tortoise, and an *Indian* Woman to dress their
Provision for them. They chose for their chief Residence a small Key
about a quarter of a Mile Round, lying near to *Barbarat,* which they called
the *Castle of Comfort,* chiefly because it was low, and clear of Woods and
Bushes, where the Wind had an open passage, and drove away the pestering *Muskettoes* and *Gnats.* From hence they sent to the other Islands
round about for Wood and Water, and for Materials, with which they
Built two Houses, such as they were, for Shelter.

And now I seemed to be in a far more likely way to Live pretty toller-
ably, than in the Sixteen Months past; for besides the having Company,
they treated me with a great deal of Civility, in their way; they Cloathed
me, and gave me a large sort of Wrapping Gown to lodge in a Nights to
defend me from the great Dews, till their Houses were Covered; and we
had plenty of Provision. But after all they were Bad Company, and there
was but little difference between them and the Pirates, as to their Common
Conversation; only I thought they were not now engaged in any such bad
design as rendred it unlawful to Joyn with them, nor dangerous to be
found in their Company.

In process of time, by the Blessing of GOD, & the Assistance I received from them, I gathered so much Strength that *I* was able sometimes
to go out a Hunting with them. The Islands hereabouts, I observed before,
abound with *Wild Hogs* and *Deer,* and *Tortoise.* Their manner was to go
out a number of them in a Canoo, sometimes to one Island, sometimes
to another, and kill what Game they could meet with, and *Jirk* their Pork,
by beginning at one end of a *Hog* and cutting along to the other end, and
so back again till they had gone all over him, and free the flesh in long
strings off from the Bones; the Venison they took whole or in quarters,
and the *Tortoise* in like manner; and return home with a load of it; what
they did not spend presently, they hung up in their House a smoak drying; and this was a ready supply to them at all times.

I was now ready to think my self out of the reach of any danger from
an Enemy, for what should bring any here? and I was compassed continually with a Number of Men with their Arms ready at hand; and yet
when I thought my self most secure, I very narrowly escaped falling again
into the hands of the Pirates.

It happened about 6 or 7 Months after these Bay-men came to me,
That three Men and I took a Canoo with four Oars, to go over to *Bonacco,*
a Hunting and to kill *Tortoise.* While we were gone the rest of the Bay-

men haled up their Canooes, and Dryed and Tarred them, in order to go
to the *Bay* and see how matters stood there, and to fetch off their Effects
which they had left behind them, in case they should find there was no
safety for them in tarrying. But before they were gone, we, who had met
with good Success in our Voyage, were upon our return to them with a
full load of *Tortoise* and *Jirkt Pork.* As we were upon entring into the
Mouth of the Harbour, in a Moon-light Evening, we saw a great Flash of
Light, and heard the report of a Gun, which we thought was much louder
than a Musket, out of a large Periagua, which we saw near our *Castle of
Comfort.* This put us into a great Consternation, and we knew not what
to make of it. Within a Minute or two we heard a Volley of 18 or 20 small
Arms discharged upon the shoar, and heard some Guns also fired off from
the shoar. Upon which we were satisfied that some Enemy, Pirates or
Spaniards were attacking our People, and being cut off from our Companions, by the Periaguas which lay between us and them, we thought it
our wisest way to save our selves as well as we could. So we took down
our little Mast and Sail, that it might not betray us, and rowed out of the
Harbour as fast as we could; thinking to make our Escape from them un-
discovered, to an Island about a Mile and half off. But they either saw us
before we had taken our Sail down, or heard the noise of our Oars as we
made out of the Harbour, and came after us with all speed, in a Periagua
of 8 or 10 Oars. We saw them coming, & that they gained ground upon
us apace, & therefore pull'd up for Life, resolving to reach the nearest
shoar is possible. The Periagua overhaled us so fast that they discharged a
Swivel Gun at us, which over-shot us; but we made a shift to gain the
shoar before they were come fairly within the reach of their small Arms;
which yet they fired upon us, as we were getting ashoar. Then they called
to us, and told us they were Pirates, and not Spaniards, and we need not
fear, they would give us good Quarter; supposing this would easily move
us to surrender our selves to them. But they could not have mentioned
any thing worse to discourage me from having any thing to do with them,
for I had the utmost dread of a Pirate; and my first aversion to them was
now strengthened with the just fears, that if I should fall into their hands
again, they would soon make a Sacrifice of me, for my Deserting them.
I therefore concluded to keep as clear of them as I could; and the Bay-
men with me had no great inclination to be medling with them and so
we made the best of our way into the Woods. They took away our Canoo
from us, and all that was in it; resolving if we would not come to them,

they would strip us, as far as they were able, of all means of Subsistance where we were. I who had known what it was to be destitute of all things, and alone, was not much concerned about that, now that I had Company, and they their Arms with them, so that we could have a supply of Provision by Hunting, and Fire to dress it with.

This Company it seems were some of *Spriggs* Men, who was Commander of the Schooner when I Ran-away from them. This same *Spriggs,* I know not upon what occasion, had cast off the Service of *Low;* and set up for himself as the Head of a Party of Rovers, and had now a good Ship of 24 Guns, and a *Barmuda* Sloop of 12 Guns, under his Command, which were now lying in *Roatan* Harbour, where he put in to Water and Clean, at the place where I first made my Escape. He had discovered our People upon the small Island, where they Resided, and sent a Periagua full of Men to take them. Accordingly they took all the Men ashoar, and with them an *Indian* Woman and Child; those of them that were ashoar abused the Woman shamefully. They killed one Man after they were come ashore, and threw him into one of the Baymens Canooes where their Tar was, and set Fire to it, and burnt him in it. Then they carried our People on Board their Vessels, where they were barbarously treated.

One of the Baymen *Thomas Grande,* turned Pirate; and he being acquainted that Old Father *Hope* (as we called him) had hid many things in the Woods, told the Pirates of it, who beat poor *Hope* unmercifully, and made him go and shew them where he had hid his Treasure, which they took away from him.

After they had kept the Bay-men on board their Vessels for five Days, then they gave them a *Flat,* of about 5 or 6 Tons to carry them to the *Bay* in, but they give them no Provision for their Voyage; and before they sent them away, they made them Swear to them, not to come near us, who had made our Escape upon another Island. All the while the Vessels rode in the Harbour, we kept a good look out, but were put in some difficulties, because we did not dare to make a Fire to dress our Victuals by, least it should discover whereabouts we were, so that we were forced to live upon Raw Provisions for five Days. But as soon as they were gone, Father *Hope* with his Company of Bay-men, (little regarding an Oath that was forced from them; and thinking it a wicked Oath better broken, than to leave four of us in such a helpless Condition) came to us, and acquainted us who they were, and what they had done.

Thus the watchful Providence of GOD, which had so often heretofore appeared on my behalf, again took special care of me, and sent me out of the way of danger. 'Tis very apparent that if I had been with my Companions, at the usual Residence, I had been taken with them; and if I had, it is beyond question (humanely speaking) that I should not have escaped with Life, if I should the most painful and cruel Death, that the Madness and Rage of *Spriggs* could have invented for me; who would now have called to mind the design I was engaged in while we were parted from *Low*, as well as my final Deserting of them. But Blessed be GOD, who had designs of favour for me, and so ordered that I must at this time be absent from my Company.

Now Old Father *Hope* and his Company are all designed for the *Bay;* only one *John Symonds,* who had a Negro belonging to him, purposed to tarry here for some time, and carry on some sort of Trade with the *Jamaica* Men upon the Main. I longed to get home to *New-England,* and thought if I went to the Bay with them, it was very probable that I should in a little while meet with some *New-England* Vessel, that would carry me to my Native Country, from which I had been so long a poor Exile. I asked Father *Hope,* if he would take me in with him, and carry me to the *Bay.* The Old Man, tho' he seemed glad of my Company, yet told me the many Difficulties that lay in the way; as that their *Flat* was but a poor thing to carry so many Men in for near 70 Leagues, which they must go before they would be out of the reach of Danger; that they had no Provision with them, and it was uncertain how the Weather would prove, they might be a great while upon their Passage thither, & their *Flat* could very poorly endure a great Sea; that when they should come to the *Bay,* they not how they should meet with things there, and they were Daily in Danger of being cut off; and it may be I should be longer there, in case all was well, than I cared for e'er I should meet with a Passage for *New-England;* for the *New-England* Vessels often Sailed from the *Bay* to other Ports: so that all things considered, he thought I had better stay where I was, seeing I was like to have Company; whereas rather than I should be left alone he would take me in.

On the other hand, *Symonds,* who as I said designed to spend sometime here, greatly urged me to stay and bear him Company. He told me that as soon as the Season would permit he purposed to go over to the Main to the *Jamaica* Traders, where I might get a Passage to *Jamaica,*

and from thence to *New-England,* probably quicker, and undoubtedly
much safer than I could from the *Bay;* and that in the mean while I should
fare as he did.

I did not trouble my self much about fareing, for I knew I could not
fare harder than I had done; but I thought, upon the Consideration of
the whole, that there seemed to be a fairer Prospect of my getting home
by the way of *Jamaica,* than the *Bay;* and therefore I said no more to
Father Hope about going with him, but concluded to stay. So I thanked
Father *Hope* and Company for all their Civilities to me, wished them a
good Voyage, and took leave of them.

And now there was *John Symonds,* and I, and his Negro left behind;
and a good Providence of GOD was it for me, that I took their Advice
and stayed; for tho' I got not home by the way of *Jamaica* as was proposed,
yet I did another and quicker way, in which there was more evident Inter-
positions of the Conduct of Divine Providence, as you will hear presently.

Symonds was provided with a Canoo, Fire-Arms, and two Dogs, as well
as a Negro; with these he doubted not but we should be furnished of all
that was necessary for our Subsistence; with this Company I spent between two and three Months, after the usual manner in Hunting and
Ranging the Islands. And yet the Winter Rains would not suffer us to
hunt much more than needs must.

When the Season was near approaching for the *Jamaica* Traders to be
over at the Main, *Symonds* proposed the going to some of the other Islands that abounded more with *Tortoise,* that he might get the Shells of
them, and carry to the Traders, and in Exchange furnish himself with
Ozenbrigs and Shoes and such other necessaries as he wanted. We did so,
and having got good store of *Tortoise* Shell, he then proposed to go first
for *Bonacco,* which lies nearer to the Main than *Roatan,* that from thence
we might take a favourable Snatch to run over.

Accordingly we went to *Bonacco,* and by that time we had been there
about Five Days there came up a very hard *North,* which blew exceeding
Fierce, and lasted for about three Days; when the heaft of the Storm was
over, we saw several Vessels standing in for the Harbour; their number
and largeness made me hope they might be Friends, and now an opportunity was coming in which Deliverance might be perfected to me.

The Larger Vessels came to Anchor at a great Distance off; but a
Brigantine came over the Shoals, nearer in against the Watering place
(for *Bonacco* as well as *Roatan* abounds with Water) which sent in her

Boat with Cask for Water; I plainly saw they were Englishmen, and by
their Garb & Air, and number, being but three Men in the Boat, concluded
they were Friends, and shewed my self openly upon the Beech before
them: as soon as they saw me they stop'd rowing, and called out to me to
know who I was. I told them, and enquired who they were. They let me
know they were honest Men, about their Lawful Business. I then called
to them to come ashoar, for there was no Body here that would hurt
them. They came ashoar, and a happy meeting it was for me. Upon enquiry I found that the Vessels were the *Diamond* Man of War, and a Fleet
under his Convoy, bound to *Jamaica,* (many whereof she had parted with
in the late Storm) which by the violence of the *North* had been forced to
far Southward; and the Man of War wanting Water, by reason of the Sickness of her Men which occasioned a great Consumption of it, had touched
here, and sent in the Brigantine to fetch off Water for her. Mr. *Symonds,*
who at first kept at the other end of the Beech, about half a Mile off,
(lest the three Men in the Boat should refuse to come ashoar, seeing two
of us together,) at length came up to us and became a sharer in my Joy,
and yet not without some very considerable reluctance at the Thoughts
of Parting. The Brigantine proved to be of *Salem,* (within two or three
Miles of my Fathers House) Capt. *Dove* Commander, a Gentleman whom
I knew. So now I had the prospect of a Direct Passage Home. I sent off
to Capt. *Dove,* to know if he would give me a Passage home with him,
and he was very ready to comply with my desire; and upon my going on
Board him, besides the great Civilities he treated me with, he took me
into pay; for he had lost a hand, and needed me to supply his place. The
next Day the Man of War sent her Long Boat in, full of Cask, which they
filled with Water, and put on Board the Brigantine, who carried them off
to her. I had one Difficulty more to encounter with, which was to take
leave of Mr. *Symonds,* who Wept heartily at parting; but this I was forced
to go thro' for the joy of getting Home.

So the latter end of *March* 1725, we came to Sail, and kept Company
with the Man of War, who was bound to *Jamaica:* the first of *April* we
parted, and thro' the good hand of GOD upon us came safe thro' the
Gulf of *Florida,*[33] to *Salem*-Harbour, where we Arrived upon *Saturday-*
Evening, the first of *May:* Two Years, Ten Months and Fifteen Days,
after I was first taken by the Pirate *Low;* and Two Years, and near two
Months after I had made my Escape from him upon *Roatan* Island. I went
the same Evening to my Father's House, where I was received, as one

coming to them from the Dead, with all Imaginable Surprise of Joy.

Thus I have given you a Short Account, how GOD has Conducted me thro' a great variety of Hardships and Dangers, and in all appeared Wonderfully Gracious to me. And I cannot but take notice of the strange concurrence of Divine Providence all along, in saving me from the Rage of the *Pirates,* and the Malice of the *Spaniards,* from the *Beasts* of the Field, and the *Monsters* of the Sea; in keeping me alive amidst so many Deaths, in such a lonely and helpless Condition; and in bringing about my Deliverance: the last Articles whereof are as peculiarly Remarkable as any;—I must be just then gone over to *Bonacco;* a Storm must drive a Fleet of Ships so far Southward; and their want of Water must oblige them to put in at the Island where I was;—and a Vessel bound to my own Home must come and take me in.—*Not unto Men and means, but unto thy Name, O Lord, be all the Glory!* Amen.

NOTES

1. *Cape Sable.* Southern point of Cape Sable Island, just off the southwest tip of Nova Scotia.

2. *Port-Rossaway.* On the southeastern coast of Nova Scotia, near present-day Shelburne.

3. *Ned Low.* Edward Low had a well-deserved reputation for ferocity. Among his other atrocities, he had a habit of cutting off the ears of his prisoners and then demanding that the victim eat them. His own crew finally mutinied and set him adrift in a small boat. He was subsequently picked up by a French warship, whereupon he was promptly tried and hanged.

4. *Nicholas Merritt, Joseph Libbie, Lawrance Fabins.* Merritt escaped from the pirates as Ashton relates, but was imprisoned on St. Michaels for four months. Released, he made his way to Lisbon and finally back to New England. Libbie and Fabins were held by pirates for several months; Libbie ultimately joined with his captors and was later captured and hanged at Newport, Rhode Island.

5. Brigantine, with one ——. Russel Knight identifies the vessel as the *Rebecca;* James Flucker, master.

6. *St. John's.* Port city, southeast coast of Newfoundland.

7. *Carboneur.* West shore of Conception Bay, twenty-eight miles west-northwest of St. John's.

8. *St. Michaels.* São Miguel, largest of the Azores.

9. *Canaries.* Island group in the Atlantic, off the northwest coast of Africa, 823 miles southwest of Spain.

10. *Teneriff.* Largest of the Canary Islands.

11. *Cape de Verde* Islands. Volcanic group five hundred miles off the west coast of Africa, one thousand miles south-southwest of the Canaries.

12. *Bonavista.* Boa Vista, in the Cape Verde Islands.

13. *St. Nicholas.* Sao Nicolau, in the Windward group of the Cape Verde Islands.

14. *Nantes.* French Brandy, from the city of that name on the Loire.

15. *Triangles.* A reef of several islands off the coast of Dutch Guina, South America.

16. *Surinam.* Dutch Guiana on the northeastern shoulder of South America.

17. *Tobago.* West Indian island adjacent to Trinidad, off the northern coast of South America.

18. *Grand Grenada.* Southernmost of the Windward Islands, West Indies, ninety miles north of Trinidad.

19. *Barbadoes.* West Indian island, two hundred and fifty miles northeast of Trinidad.

20. *Santa Cruz.* Saint Croix, largest of the Virgin Islands, West Indies.

21. *St. Thomas.* Island of the Virgin Islands, forty miles east of Puerto Rico.

22. *Curacao.* Largest Island of the Netherlands Antilles, sixty miles north of northwest Venezuela.

23. *New Spain.* Central America, Mexico, and the West Indies.

24. *Carthagena.* Port city, northwest coast of Columbia.

25. *Port-Abella.* Portobelo. Village on Caribbean coast of Panama, twenty miles northeast of Colón.

26. Guinea-Man. A ship of the west African trade, possibly a slaver.

27. Bumper. A large glass or cup. also signifies a toast.

28. *Utilla; Roatan.* Two of the three (the other is Bonacca) islands that together form the Bay Islands, off the coast of Honduras.

29. *Mammes Supporters. Mammee sapota* [obs.] or *Lucuma Mammosa,* the Marmalade tree.

30. *Mangeneil Apple.* Poisonous, applelike fruit of *Hippomane Mancinella,* the Manchineel tree.

31. *Owlers.* Probably *Epicrates angulifer,* the Cuban Boa.

32. *Barber's Pole.* Probably *Elaps Lemniscatus,* one of several South American coral snakes.

33. Gulf of *Florida.* That portion of the ocean between the Bahamas and the Atlantic coast of Florida.

William Walling

The Wonderful Providence of God Examplified in the Preservation of William Walling, Who was drove out to Sea from Sandy Hook near New-York, in a leaky Boat and taken up by a Whaling Sloop and brought into Nantucket, after he had floated on the Sea eight Days without Victuals or Drink.

A native of Middletown, New Jersey, William Walling was typical of many colonial Americans to whom travel by small boat for both business and transportation was nearly as usual as walking or horseback riding. So it was that Walling left his coastal home in the spring of 1726 to travel to New York on business. Having remained in the city longer than he had anticipated, he expected to find another boat passage home even as we might today decide to take a later plane or train. When he did leave Manhattan, Walling arranged (on the condition of a reduced fare) to accompany another man in a leaky boat and to man the pumps on the short trip from New York to Middletown.

The tragedy that overtook Walling and his companion has long held a special terror for travelers of the sea. Adrift in a small boat without food or water, the two men faced drowning, starvation, frostbite, and, perhaps most frightening of all, madness. Walling renders all of this in a style that is understated but compelling, and the delirious antics of Gardner are evoked in an atmosphere that is positively eerie.

A plain, honest man, Walling afterwards suffered the anguish of "survivor guilt," and as if his tribulations at sea were not enough, he was made to endure the rigors of eighteenth-century medical practice and a shrewish nursemaid to boot.

The *Wonderful Providence* was probably first printed in
1726 or 1727 and most likely in New York, although possibly
in London. In 1730 it was reprinted for Francis Skinner of
Boston. No copy of the first edition is known to exist.

TEXT: the second edition in the John Carter Brown Library,
Brown University. The affidavits of Coffin and Davis have
been deleted.

I *William Walling* of *Middletown* in *Monmouth* County, in the Province
of *New-Jersey,* took Passage with *Abraham Watson* to go to *New-York,*
on Thursday the ninth of *March,* 1726 in the Evening, and arrived there
safely the next Day; but being hindred by the Weather from doing any
Business, I went over to *Gravesend* on *Long-Island,* on Saturday I returned
with an Intention to do my Business, in order to go home with *Abraham
Watson.* On Monday Morning *Abraham Watson* was ready to go home, and
because I had not finished my Business, he was forc'd to go without me.
On Tuesday morning I met with one *Tys Deriks,* who was bound to the
same Shore, about ten Miles from *Middletown,* and I desiring to be at
home took Passage with him. There were also three Women Passengers on
Board. We left the City of *New-York* about Noon; and when we came to
the Narrows,[1] one *Nathaniel Gardner,* who together with another Man
was hired to go in a Boat belonging to this *Tys Dericks,* called to us and
came off in a Canoe; when he came on Board he told *Tys Dericks,* That
the Boat had lost the great Anchor, and that s[he] had been upon the
Rocks and was so leaky th[at] he knew not how to get home with her,
for h[is] Companion had left the Boat. Then *Tys D[e]ricks* asked him
if he though that he could g[et] home in her safely? Gardner answered
that h[e] thought he could, if one kept pumping continually; thereupon
Tys Dericks asked me to go an[d] help him home with the Boat, saying
that h[e] would give me over and above my Passage fi[ve] Shillings. I
consented and went on Shore with *Gardner* in the Canoe, and found the
Boat aground. Then I repented that I had not gone with *Tys Dericks,*
for I began to fear that [we] should have a tedious Passage. Here we wer[e]
oblig'd to stay still *Thursday* before the Boa[t] floated, and then it blew
so hard that we coul[d] not go; but on *Fryday,* the wind being moderate
and pretty fair, we ventured to set Sail i[n] Company with another small
Boat that was going the same Way. When we were got abou[t] half way

over to the *Neversink*[2] Shore the Win[d] dyed away, and it continued
stark calm for a little while; Then the Wind sprung up at Sout[h] and blew
very fresh. We turn'd it to windwar[d] with great Difficulty for some
time, but whe[n] we saw the other Boat turn back we followe[d] her, to
go round *Statten Island,* and so home b[y] the Way of Amboy: But on
the North Side o[f] *Statten-Island* we run a-ground, and did not ge[t]
off till Saturday Night.

On Sunday Morning we set Sail again, fetch'd all our Provisions and
we ate all. [We we]re not satisfied, for I had not brought above [tw]o
Meals for both of us on Board when we [lef]t *Long-Island:* But with the
Beginning of [th]e Ebb the Wind dyed away and we drove a [st]ern, so
we turn'd about with an Intention to [go] through the Narrows; but before we got out [of] the Narrows the Wind Sprung up at South [W]est
and blew pretty hard; however we laid it [al]ong, the Tyde of Ebb helping us: But when we [w]ere got about half Way over to the *Neversinks,*
[it] began to blow so hard that the Boat lay with [he]r Gunel under
Water sometimes; we lower'd [th]e Mainsail, and *Gardner* was for turning back [ag]ain, but I wanting to be at home, would not [co]nsent to
it; for I told him, if he could but [ge]t within the Hook,[3] I could lay her
into *Sper[m]a-Caeta-Cove,*[4] then we could walk home on [fo]ot, he told
me he thought that he could get [w]ithin the Hook. Thus through an
over great [d]esire of being at Home I brought my self into [e]xtream
great Sufferings. We laid it along, as [w]ell as we could, till we came within
about [th]ree or four Hundred Yards of the Hook, and [th]en he told
me that he could not get within [th]e Hook, so I told him to run her a-
ground [a]ny where: But whilst we were talking a very [h]ard Flaw overtook us, which almost overset us, [fo]r the Mast just touch'd the Water,
I immedi[at]ely let fly the Main-Hall-Yards, (for I held [th]em in my
Hands for more Security) & pulled [d]own the Main-Sail as fast as I
could, which [he]lped her to rise again, but the Foresail was [pu]ll[ed
in] Pieces and blown away. As soon as she was righted we bore away and
scudded bfore the Wind, and by this time she was half full of Water. Now
the Fear of Death began to come hard upon he, for I did not expect to
live an Hour longer, and my Companion was so affected with seeing himself blown away from shore in a leaky Vessel, half full of Water, that he
cryed out with a loud Voice, *We are drowned!* However thinking my self
oblig'd to make the best of all Means for our Preservation, I went to Pumping, and encouraged him to mind the Helm; I laboured very hard, both in

Body and Mind: For the Tho'ts of being drove out to Sea in a leaky Boat, without a Morsel of any kind of Victuals or a drop of Drink, affected me very sorely. Add to this, that I tho't my self the Author, not only of my own, but another Man's Misfortune's also because I hindred *Gardner* from going back when it was in his Power. I repented very much that I did not let him take his won Course, as being more us'd to the Water than I, and consequently saw the Danger we were in sooner. In short it is impossible to describe the Horrour & anguish of my Mind. My Companion also was very much dejected, And I believe labouring with the same Thoughts. After I had pumpt some time the Pump stopt, so that I could do nothing with it, then I took the Bucket and went to Bailing. The Wind blew so hard that we lost Sight of Land in about two Hours after we had the hard Flaw of Wind. Some time in the Afternoon it began to snow very hard and continued for some time. About Sun-set I began to get the upperhand of the Water, this with the Hopes of striking upon some Part of *Long-Island* was some Comfort to us. Some time in the Night I got the Water out pretty clean, & after that Time I took care to pump or bail before there was too much Water in her.

All this Night the Wind continued, and on *Monday* it was the same, so that we had enough to do to keep the Boat afloat and before the Wind, for she began to be so leaky now, that I think she would have been full in less than 12 Hours Time.

On *Tuesday* some time before Noon the Wind began to Moderate, and in the Afternoon the Weather was so moderate that we could let the Boat drive without steering. My Companion, for want of Sleep, now begun to talk idle, and among other silly Things said, he was sure we were bewitch'd, I told him that I believ'd no such thing, and perswaded him to go to sleep, for we had neither of us slept since Saturday night, and he seemed to want Sleep very much; but before he went down into the Cabin I desired him to show me how to clear the Pump, for I wet my self so much with bailing that I was never dry; and whilst he was doing that there appeared a Vessel in sight, but at so great a Distance that we could not see her when we lay in the Trough of the Sea; we lost sight of her in less than half an Hours Time, then my Companion laid himself down to sleep, and when I Pumpt the water out of the Boat I laid my self down also. After I had slept a little while I heard the Wind blow harder and the Boat tumbled so much that I awaked and got up, and fel[t] my self something refreshed with the little Slee[p] I had got, but extremely hungry; I

guessed tha[t] it was about three a Clock then: I freed the Boa[t] of the
Water again and then I took the Helm and steer'd before the Wind as well
as I could till about five a-Clock, and then there was much Water in her
Hold, so I called to *Nathaniel* to take the Helm, for the Wind blew hard,
and the Sea was so rough that I was afraid a Sea migh[t] break in upon
her broad side and sink her if I should let her drive; as soon as I had called
him he came up hastily and in a Consternation, telling me that he had seen
two Spirits on Board in Shape of Women, and would have me go down
into the Hold to see them, I reproved him and told him that he should
not give way to such idle Fancies; But he persisted in the Notion tha[t]
he had seen them, and I could not satisfy him without going down into
the Cabin to see them so I went down, (not that I believ'd I should see
any thing, but only to satisfy him) when I came up again he asked me
whether I had seen them? I answered No, and that I did not believe that
he had. Then he said, that they would not let me see them, but as soon
as he should come on Shore he would go to a Justice of the Peace and
take his Oath that he had seen them. When I had freed the Boat of the
Water I took the Helm again, then he pull'd off his Coat and Jacket, and
wrapt a Piece of an old Blanket about his Waste [and] C[hest in] Fashion
of Indian Women; I asked him what he did that for? He answered *The*
Spirits told me, that all those that wear Peticoats they wont hurt, and
all those that do not they will kill, and this is the best Peticoat I have,
I hope they will be contented with it. I told him that these were only
Imaginations, and perswaded him to put on his Cloaths, for he shivered
very much with the Cold, and about Sun set he put on his Cloaths again.
About two hours in the Night I asked him to stand to the Helm again,
and I freed her of the Water; then I steer'd till about Midnight, and there
being a great deal of Water in her, I called to *Nathaniel* to take the Helm
that I might free her, but he was very unwilling to come up again, telling
me I might pull out the Tiller and let her drive; I told him that the Wind
blew too hard and the Sea run too high to let her drive, for every Wave
seemed high enough to run over the Mast, and if a Sea should break in
upon her broad side, she would surely be stav'd and sink. Thus I argued
with him a long Time before he would come; however at length he came,
and then I freed her of the Water again. As soon as I had done Bailing I
crept through the Bulk Head into the Cabin to get a Blanket to wrap about
me, for I was wet and cold, and the Blankets were wet also; but as soon
as he perceived that I was in the Cabin he called me to take the Helm,

I desired him to hold it so long that I might get a Blanket, he said that he
would let it go if I did not come up pre[sently, w]hereupon I stept up
to him hastily and took the Helm, for I fear'd that the Sea would take her
broad side if he should let her go: Then I asked him, why he would neither
steer nor pump, nor throw water out of the boat (for he had neither
pump'd nor bail'd so long as we were drove away, tho' he had steer'd
two Days and two Nights constantly) he answer'd, he wanted to go into
the Cabin, so I stood aside that he might go in, for we always stood upon
a Plank in the Cabbin Door to Steer. When I had stood there about half
an hour, I heard a very unusal strangling noise, which struck me immediately with a fear and concern for him lest he should make Way with himself; and as soon as I had rais'd the Sea that was coming after me, I stoopt
down, calling upon him & put my hand back into the Cabbin, so far till
I catch'd hold of his hair, & pull'd him right to me, talking to him all the
while, but he made me no Answer, neither could he, for I found, upon
feeling that he had made a Noose into one Corner of his Handkerchief,
and put the other corner thro' it, & drawn it together about his naked
neck (for, he had unbutton'd his Coller) that he was past Speaking or
Breathing by all that I could perceive. I made all the haste I could to un-
tie the Handkerchief; but before I got it loose our Boat came too and a
Sea broke in over her Quarter with such Violence that I expected her to
be stove to Pieces and filled and going down, tho' it pleas'd God to order
it otherwise. As soon as I had untied the Handkerchief he begun to Cough,
& soon after to Vomit, and then to Speak; as soon as he begun to speak
I asked him why he went to murder himself thus both Body and Soul &
he said, that he wanted to cut his throat just now, but the Knife was so
dull that he could not cut with it, but he had cut two Gashes into his
Neck. I told him again sharply, *that if he did kill himself, he would ex-*
pect nothing but Damnation and eternal Misery for his poor Soul, as
soon as it Departed from his Body. Why, said he, *the Devil told me that*
he would carry me away alive, if I did not kill my self. Then said I, *the*
Devil's ends in persuading you to Self-Murder are, that he might have
Power over your poor Soul, he well knows Self-Murder to be the worst
Murder, for there is no Repentance to the Grave. Ah! (said he) do you
take a Rope and hang me, then I shall not be guilty of so heinous a Crime.
I answered him, *that in so doing I should be guilty not only of Murder-*
ing him, but also of burying his Soul to eternal Destruction, and he could
not be guiltless because he desired it. Then he ask'd me, *What he should*

do? for the Devil told him, he would carry him away alive, and he was re-solved he should not, for he would kill himself first. But I admonished him to think otherwise and not to give so much way to those Destructive Whiles, but rather to put his Trust in God, and Call upon him for assistance. While I was yet talking to him, he cryed out saying, *Look! how he stands in the Hold of the Vessel, telling me to kill myself or he will carry me away alive; don't you hear him?* Then I asked him where he was? He answered, *In the Hold of the Vessel, don't you [see him]? No* said I *and ho[w] can you see him since it is so very dark? Why,* says he, *he stands all of a light Fire, Laughing and Grinning at me, and are not you afraid? No,* said I, *and if all the Devils in Hell were in the Hold, I should not be afraid, nor entertain the least thought of their hurting me, for I believed that God would preserve and protect me from the Devil.* And herein I was confirmed by the Raging of the Sea, since one Wave was enough to make an end of us, if the Almighty did not preserve us. After some Time he Burst out in Tears and bemoan'd himself sadly, calling very often on the name of the *Lord Jesus Christ,* seeming to be very much Terrified in his mind for Fear the Devil should carry him away, and I believe that he began to Repent of his Sins, for all this Day (*Wednesday*) he Cry'd and Groan'd under the Weight of them very much Confessing and Praying for forgive-ness, notwithstanding all this and my Comforting of him as well as I could (for God knows I needed Comfort my Self) he was so very much afraid, that if I went from the Quarter-deck to the Fore-castle he would follow me and hold me fast, and if I went down into the Hold he would lie down upon Deck and look down to keep me in sight. This Day he drank abun-dance of Salt Water, tho' I spoke against it very much.

On *Thursday* he was taken violently with a Fever and Flux, & about Noon he was Speechless. My Condition now began to be very dismal, for my Strength decay'd & I was no more able to do as I was used to do, my Companion lay as tho' every breath would be his last; ye[t] I trusted in God that he would deliver me, and therefore I did my utmost to keep the Boat afloat. I was now alone, and so spent the most of my Time in Prayer and Meditation.

Friday and *Saturday* nothing particular happened to me, it being good weather.

On *Sunday* Morning I began to pump about the dawning of the Day, and got her clear'd about Sun rising, then I sat my self down on Deck, poor and low in Body, (tho' strong in Spirit, thro' the Grace of God.)

After I had sat about two Hours musing on my desperate State, I thought
to get up to pump again, but I found my Strength so wasted that I was
not able to rise, I made several efforts but to no purpose, for then with
much Labour I was got upon my Legs, I was not able to stand, nor is it
to be wondered at, for this was the eighth Day that I had had no manner
of Sustenance but three black Walnuts, and my own Water, of which I
could hardly make enought to wet my Mouth at last, tho' I mixt Salt
Water with it. Then I crept down into the Cabbin and laid me down in
one of the Cuddies upon the Boards, for there was no Bed in it, and began
to compose my self to meet my Fate, which I thought approaching. In
this Posture I lay till about Noon and then I was overcome by Sleep, after
I had slept some time, how long I know not, I awak'd and saw the Water
pouring in at the Cabbin Window, and then I began afresh to recommend
my Soul to the Almighty, as expecting no other than to be reliev'd by
Death in a short time. I had not been thus employ'd long before I heard
a Cock crow, and four o[r] five Men hallowing, this revived me very much
and I got up upon Deck as if I was well, tho' I was truly an object of Pity,
and saw a Sloop sailing by, I call'd to them in the Name of the Lord
Jesus to relieve me! and they answered that they could. Then they immediately hoisted out their Boat and fetch'd me and my Companion,
whom I had given over for dead, and carried us on board of their Sloop,
my poor Companion they laid into a warm Bed, but I being more able to
help my self than he, desir'd that I might go down into the Fore-castle
where the Mate gave me some dry Cloaths. I had not been long by the
Fire before I fainted, so they brought me a little Water and Wine & a little
Sugar in it, of which they gave me about a Mouthful, and then they gave
me a little Victuals, and put me into the Mates Cabbin, where he began
to examine my Feet and found that they were frozen; at first I could not
believe him, but he went and warm'd a Stone and put it to my feet, but
when they began to be warm, I felt a most exquisite pain in them. The
next Day they roasted Turnips and laid on my Feet, this they continued
for four or five Days and then their Turnips were spent. As for my Companion, after they had shifted him, & laid him into the Captains Cabbin,
(where the Captain like a good charitable Christian tended him himself)
they gave him a little Victuals and Drink, which so revived him that he
recovered [h]is Senses and Speech and talk'd very sensibly [f]or about
three Hours, & then his Speech fail'd [a]gain, and the next Day he departed to Eter[n]ity. Now altho' this Man was but a Stran[g]er to me,

yet it griev'd me sore when he died. The next Day they sow'd him up in
a Rug, [a]nd Buried him in the Sea.

After all their Turnips were gone, the Mate, who had skill in frozen
Feet, made Poultises[5] of [I]ndian Meal and continued that for fourteen
Days, and by that time all the skin and Nails [c]ame off of my Feet,
then he made an Ointment and applied to them which gave me some ease.

Fourteen Days after I was taken up I was brought to *Nantucket,* and
two Days after the People hearing of my Misfortunes, gathered together
to consult what to do with me, at length [t]hey concluded that I should
be brought to the House of one *Isaac Coleman,* whose Wife had some
skill in frozen Feet, and because they had no Children they tho't that the
properst House for me; the next Day I was carried thither in a Calash and
staid there six Weeks, and then I began to walk about upon Crutches, but
one *Nathaniel Starbuck* told me I should stay there no longer for they
must be paid, and if I would come to his House I should be very welcome:
He was a good and just Man, and feared God. The next Day several of the
principal Men came to me and advised me to ask her what I had to pay,
and they would lend me the Money to [p]ay her (tho' their design was
to give it, as they told me afterwards) but they knew he[r] to be a Woman
of no Conscience, or a very evil one, and therefore made use of that Device
to the end that she might not ask me too much. When I asked her what
she must have, she told me she would have thirteen Pounds and no less;
when I had told my Friends what she Demanded, they told me, I should
have nothing to do with her, for they would pay her, which they did,
giving her seven Pounds ten shillings. She was a very slanderous Woman,
for while [I] was in her House she always had something or other to say
of every one that came to the House, for this Reason I did not like her,
for I tho't she did not do as a Christian ought to do.

I continued here till the second Day of *June,* and when I was going
away, I had about five Pounds given me towards defraying the Charges
of my going home, by several well disposed People. I went on Board one
Capt. *Bush* of *New-York,* who gave me my Passage to *New-Port* on
Rhode-Island, where we arrived in a very short Time. Here I met with
Capt. *Watson* and another Neighbour, the seeing of my Neighbours once
more on this side of the Grave, perfectly rejoyced me. Capt. *Watson* immediately offered me Assistance, if I wanted either Money or any other
Thing that he could help me to, for which I thank'd him, and told him
that I wanted to go home with him, to which he replied very affection-

ately, that he would carry me home thro' the help of God. We left *New-Port* the eleventh of *June* and [on the] ninetee[n]th I arrived at *Monmouth* County in *New-Jersey*, to the great Joy of all my Friends who had given me over for lost. I was drove out to Sea on a *Sunday*, I was taken up on a *Sunday*, I was brought into *Nantucket* on a *Sunday*, and I arrived at my own home, on a *Sunday*.

NOTES

1. Narrows. The strait between the west end of Long Island and the eastern side of Staten Island.

2. *Neversink*. Navesink, a range of hills in northeast New Jersey, extending from Sandy Hook to Raritan Bay.

3. Hook. Sandy Hook, New Jersey, a six-mile peninsula in northeast New Jersey, fifteen miles south of Manhattan.

4. *Sper[m]a-Caeta-Cove*. On Sandy Hook.

5. Poultises. Plasters.

Joseph Bailey

God's Wonders in the Great Deep: Or, A Narrative Of The Shipwreck of the Brigantine *Alida and Catharine,* Joseph Bailey, Master, On the 27th of December, 1749. Bound from New-York to Antigua.

Captain Joseph Bailey came of a seafaring family, a family that had suffered the afflictions common to those who trafficked in ships. The master of the *Alida and Catharine* had lost both his father and brother to the sea, and in the hour of his own greatest peril he grimly contemplated the anguish his own imminent death would cause his widowed mother.

Leaving his residence in Antigua, Bailey sailed to New York in the late fall of 1749. There he took on a cargo for the return voyage and weighed anchor on December 20. The weather was bad, but Bailey gambled that he could outsail the winter storms as he fled southward toward the West Indies. They had not been out long when he regretted his decision, but as he says, "the Wind being notherly, there was no going back." On Christmas Eve a howling gale overtook Bailey's brigantine, beating the vessel about for three days and ultimately oversetting her.

A pious man, Bailey charges his language with the force of his Puritan convictions. Nevertheless his is one of the more dramatic narratives, taut and well-executed. The wealth of detail combined with a matter-of-fact tone contributes much to the tense excitement of his relation.

The Shipwreck of the Alida and Catharine was first printed in New York by James Parker in 1750. A second

edition, undated but probably brought out within a year
or two of the first, was printed in Boston by Samuel Knee-
land.
TEXT: Massachusetts Historical Society first edition
on Evans Microcard (E6458), corrected by another original
issue in the John Carter Brown Library, Brown University.

I *Joseph Bailey,* being Master of the Brigantine *Alida* and *Catharine,*
of the Island of *Antigua,* and consigned to Mr. *Peter Van Brugh Livingston,*
Merchant in *New-York,* I arrived there about the 21st Day of *November,*
1749; and meeting with such Dispatch as the Season of the Year would
permit, about the 18th Day of *December* was ready to sail, except some
few Trifles; however they were sufficient to detain us, till such Time as
we had lost our Wind, which then presented; the Weather looking very
dubious, kept us till Wednesday the 20th of *December,* when the Wind
being notherly, was willing to embrace the last Opportunity; the Pilot
came on board, and we got under sail; we ran down to the Hook.[1] But
before I got there I repented I had left *York;* however the Wind being
notherly, there was no going back, nor any safety riding in the Hook,
so that I stood out to Sea. (Our Vessel's Company consisting of myself,
Master, *Edward Vaughan,* Mate, *Samuel Parsons* and *Mathew Finn,*
Mariners, *John Baxter* and *Lawrence Mason,* Boys, and *Anthony Suga,*
a Negro Man belonging to myself.) Before we had lost Sight of the Land,
it began to look very dismal, and lightned all round. In the Night it blew
very fresh, cold and Snow; we had like to have lost our Main-
Boom, and Main-Sail; the Toping-Lift getting off the Boom, and the
Boom falling unhook'd in the Goose-Neck, we had much ado to save the
Boom and Sail, in doing which some of our People froze themselves, in
particular the Negro Man had all his Fingers froze. Our Vessel being very
deep in the Water, and deep wasted, we were continually full to our main
Deck, and our People very much exposed at the Pump: The Weather continued so Bad that we had little or no Use of our Main-Sail afterwards, and
for some Time lay by; after which scudded under bare Poles, the Wind
veering round the Compass once in twenty-four Hours, and always blowing hard.

On Saturday the 23d of *December* we had a violent Gale at S.E. which
obliged us to scud under bare Poles, till we run on Soundings, and got

into cold Water again, which proved very bad to our People, as they were obliged to keep the Pump continually working, and being likewise up to the Knees in Water; but as the Wind veer'd round to the Southward and Westward, and we continually scudding before the Wind, we run on Soundings again: It continued one constant Series of bad Weather; sometimes both Pumps were at Work, occasioned by her being constantly under Water; and the Deck being Prime out,[2] the backs of the Timber were all open, and no coming at them to make them tight.

On Sunday the 24th of *December,* the Sea hove our Boat out of her Chocks, and we had like to have lost her, but secur'd her again. The badness of the Weather drowned most of our Stock upon Deck; and the Weather continued with very little Alteration, still veering round once in 24 Hours, till Wednesday the 27th of *December.* Towards Noon [we] reeft our Fore-Sail, and settled our Fore-Yard, but the bad Weather coming on, oblig'd us to hand and scud a hull before Night. A terrible hard Gale ensu'd, that wash'd our Deck of every thing that was moveable, Lumber, Coops, and Water-Casks; and for some Time the People were up to their Necks in Water at the Pump. Night came on and the Weather increas'd; and about 8 Clock in the Evening a Sea poopt us, and drove in our two Larboard Lights in the Cabbin, which almost fill'd it and the Steerage, putting out all our Lights below, and spoil'd our Tinder; but by the Help of a Pistol with some Powder I got Light again. I found the Sea had carry'd away one dead Light, so that to supply the Deficency, was obliged to put my Bed into one of the Windows, and secur'd it in the best Manner I was capable. I then set the Boys to bailing the Water out of the Steerage with Buckets as fast as they could, and call'd for the Broad-Ax and plac'd it at the Cabbin-Door, so that I might readily find it in Case she broach'd too, to have cut away her Main-Mast.

After Things were in this Posture, I went up on the Quarter-Deck, the Weather appear'd with a terrible Aspect, and a monstrous Sea follow'd us; but the Vessel steering exceeding well, and the Mate and *Sam. Parsons* both at the Helm, I was in Hopes that we should have done well: I stood over the Scuttle on the Quarter-Deck for some Time and observ'd the Sea: at length it struck her on the Starboard-Quarter and hove her something too, although the Helm was hard a Starboard: the Wind being about four Points on the Quarter, then she immediately overset; and by the Time I could get hold of the Weather Gunnel, her Mast was flat in the Water, and there she lay. *Sam. Parsons* and my Self recovered the Weather Side

near upon the Instant she overset. Providence so order'd it that I had
two Knives in my Pocket, I gave *Parsons* one, and employ'd the other
with all Speed in order to cut the Lanyards of the Main-Shrouds, which
we immediately did, and then made the best of our Way to the Fore-
Shrouds, and cut them likewise; The Fore-Mast immediately broke off
close by the Deck, and by that Time the Vessel had winded so that her
Deck came to the Wind, which taking in her Gunnel she immediately
righted, and soon fell down on her Starboard Broad-Side. We immediately
got on board as she righted, and fell on our Knees, desiring God to spare
us: But as she fell down again we were oblig'd to shift for our selves, to
get on the Weather Bow, where the Fore-Mast Yard and Rigging prevented
my getting up for some Time, so that the Sea struck me back several
Times, that I could scarce recover to secure my self from being drowned,
till at length I got hold. In the mean Time *Sam. Parsons* got aft on the
Larboard Gunnel, and with the Assistance of the Mate cut the Lanyards
of the Main-Shroud, and came forward. By that Time she righted the
second Time, and immediately fell over again on her Larboard Side, and
in my getting over I found the Fore Scuttle to blow up under my Feet,
and the Vessel to be full of Water.

I expected nothing less than that she would immediately sink under
us, knowing that we had considerable of Shingle Ballast under our Cargo,
and our lading of heavy Flour, which I thought impossible to support
the Weight. But some small Time after she had fell over the third Time,
Mathew Finn recovered the Bow where *Parsons* and my Self were; soon
after *Lawrence Mason* call'd out for help, and we help'd him up along
Side; after which *John Baxter* came swimming along amongst the Rubbish of Boat and other Things, they being both in the Steerage when she
overset, and with much Difficulty got out: The Mate and Negro were
all this Time abaft, and I know not in what Manner Providence secured
them; for every Thing was swept clean off the Quarter-Deck with the
Sea, at which Time I held myself fast by the Fluke of the Sheet Anchor,
which was stow'd on the Bow.

By the Time we were in this Situation, I perceiv'd the Main Mast to
be going, and the Vessel begin to right; on which I call'd out with a good
Voice, and a strong Confidence in God, seeing she did not Sink after she
was full of Water, *Have Courage, my dear Souls, her Masts are gone, she
rights, and will not sink; for God will deliver us yet; he is All-sufficient,
if we put our Trust in Him,* (or to that Effect:) By this Time she was got

pretty Up-right, and we all got into the Bow on the Starboard Side, when
the Negro came to us, but no News of the Mate; we lamented him, as we
still thought to the Eye of Reason he was gone but a few Minutes before,
and we should soon follow. The Negro inform'd us that both the Pumps
were Dead, it being so dark we could not perfectly desearn any Thing
five Foot from us, nor know one another only but by our Voices. The
Gale continued, and the Sea made fair Breaches over us, insomuch that
we were obliged to hold for our Lives, lest we should wash away. Our
People shelter'd themselves under the Bow, and though the Sea wash'd
continually amongst them, it was more tolerable than the Sharpness of
the Air, which was attended with prodigious hard Rain and Hail, that as
I stood and watch'd the Sea, and held fast, my Hands were so numb'd
with the Cold, I was glad to dip them into the Sea to warm them, and
keep me from quite losing the Use of them.

Some considerable Time after we heard the Mate halloe, which we
answer'd, and it was something of a Surprize to us, not doubting but that
he was drowned; but upon our Answers he came to us, which was a great
joy to us, to think God was so wonderfully kind and merciful to preserve
us all in this terrible Overthrow: We blessed God, and put up our earnest
Prayer to Him in the best Manner we were capable, and waited patiently
for the Return of the Day; at which Time the Weather was something
abated, and presented to our View the most terrible Sight that any Mortal
can imagine, or Tongue can express! The Stern Lights were beat in, and
the Bulk-Heads, and the Cabbin were all blown up, and every Thing wash'd
out that was necessary for the Support of Life: We were naked and cold,
no Cloaths to put on, nor Victuals to satisfy our craving and hungry
Appetites: Our Water that was lash'd on Deck in the best Manner, was
gone: Our Boat, that might have been of some Help to us in Case we discover'd a Vessel, was likewise gone: In short every Thing that was above
our Main Deck was gone, only our Quarter Deck remain'd, and the Main-
Boom over it, which was confin'd by the Main-Sheet.

But one Thing I am short in, that was, that towards Day, after the
Weather moderated, our People went aft on the Quarter Deck, where
they thought to be more out of the Sea, being almost drowned, and where
they secured an old Stay-Sail, and wrap'd themselves up as well as they
could under the Starboard netting Rail. I could not trust the Quarter
Deck for fear it should blow up, but stood forward till almost Day, and
then went aft, holding by the Starboard Gunnel in the Waist, where the

Sea made a constant Breach. On my coming aft, I perceiv'd the Helm was lash'd hard a Starboard, which I imagin'd made her lay broad off the Wind, and caused the Sea to break more upon; I endeavour'd to remove the Helm to Leward, but in getting a Rope to secure it, a Sea came in over the Boom, and wash'd me from the Windward Part of the Stern quite forward to the Waist, and in my Passage struck one of my Hips against one of the Stanchions of the Barrocado, as I imagine; for I was entirely wash'd from the feeling of any Part of the Vessel, and under Water, when I felt the Lee-Gunnel near the Main Chains with my foot, with which I gave my self a Send-up, and paddl'd with my Hands till my Head came out of Water, when I found my Face towards the Bow of the Vessel, and with the Send of the Sea discovered the Main-Hatches partly bare. I struggled for Life and recovered the Hatches, and from thence to one of the Top-Sail-Sheet Bitts that appeared, (the Windless and Bitts being gone before.) I recovered my old Station in the Bow, where I held fast till Day-Light, still begging of God to deliver me, or fit me for his good Will and Pleasure. After this *Sam. Parsons,* endeavouring to cut the Clew of the Main-Sail from the Boom, in order to cover them the better on the Quarter-Deck to keep them from the Cold, was struck over-board from the Vessel, but happen'd to hang by some Part of his Coat, which split the same up the Back, and gave him an Opportunity to recover himself.

Soon after, as the Morning came on, they came forward, and discovering the old Fore-Sail floating between Deck, not wash'd over, they ventured to get hold and draw it forward to cover themselves, (wet as it was), where with much Difficulty they kept it from washing from them. Some of the People ventured into the Cabbin, where they found a Bottle of Wine whole, the others were all wash'd out of the Locker or broke.

We spent the Remainder of the Day without any Thing remarkable, except the removing some Wood out of the Fore-Scuttle, where the Negro had a Bundle of Fish, which being secured was very welcome to us, and as thankfully received. We then spent our Time in reflecting on our miserable State, being the 28th Day of *December,* in the Lat. of $34°$ $40'$ N. nearest, and the Long. $65°$ $30'$ W. Bermudas being the nearest Land, and which I judg'd to be 70 or 80 Leagues Distance; no Hopes of Assistance from any Human Creature, and an Impossibility of our subsisting long in that miserable Condition. And although we had two Hogsheads of Water in the Hold, we could not come at either without breaking up the Decks; and then our terrible Apprehensions were such, that if once the Hold was broke up, and the Goods came out, that the Ballast in her would immediately sink her; besides, we had Nothing to do it withall. Under those and such like terrible Apprehensions we pass'd the Day, sending up our most humble and fervent Desires to God to pardon our sins, and deliver us, or at least to fit and prepare us for his Holy Will and Pleasure, for Jesus Christ's Sake.

Thus the Day was spent in almost a profound Fast, not having any Thing to subsist upon only as I mention'd before; Though the Weather moderated, yet a long and tedious Night coming, and the refreshing Heat of the Sun withdrawn, we being constantly in the Water, were almost perished. That Night *Sam. Parsons,* my self, and Negro *Tony,* fix'd ourselves on the Windward Side of the Quarter-Deck, having strech'd some Ropes along the same in Case the Sea should wash us away, that we might catch by: We lay up close under the Sails, and covered our Heads as well as we could with an old Stay-Sail we had, the Water continually washing over and under us: But we knew no better Place, the Bow being taken up with the Rest, who had the old Fore-Sail to cover them; and it was terrible to hear the Lamentations and Moans that they made.

In this Manner we pass'd the second Night; and on Friday Morning the 29th Day of *December,* the Weather had moderated very much, we began to exert ourselves to see what we could save; we found the Pump Hook twisted with some Oznabrigs and Cloaths, Ropes and Part of an Old Sail; we cleared it; The Mate and *Sam. Parsons* went into the Cabbin, and with the Hook got up a Hogshead, and several Pieces of Beef out of the Run of the after Scuttle; a Box with Six Caggs of Oysters, mark'd B. S. and a Barrel of Apples, which when open had like to have swam away from us; our Broad-Ax, Iron Crow and Hand-Saw, which proved useful to us; an old Cutlass, Bayonet, and sundry other Things we might have got, but thought it would be Madness and Folly for Men under our Circumstances to save and incumber ourselves with unnecessary Things, though never so valuable.

After our People had fatigued themselves, and saved what is above mentioned, together with two large Silver Spoons belonging to me, one of the Boys began to make heavy Complaints for want of Drink, notwithstanding the Apples we had just got were very refreshing to us: This put us upon Thoughts how to came at our Water, and having recovered our Saw and Broad-Ax, *Sam. Parsons* went to work, and cut off the Beams of the fore'Part of the fore Scuttle, in order to make room, if possible, to get the Cask out; which to our great Comfort he soon effected, and then secured it in the Bow, on the Starboard Side of the Bowsprit; we likewise got up the best Part of the Bundle of Fish before mentioned. We then seemed to be, through God's good Providence, enabled to continue some considerable Time, if it pleased God to continue the Weather moderate. We broach'd the Water, and found it to be very brackish, the Bung not being very tight: however we were heartily thankful for that Mercy, as bad as it was, and were as well satisfied as People could possibly be in such miserable Circumstances. After which the People wrap'd themselves in the old Fore-Sail, as being very much fatigu'd; and I went to work with my small Knife with a Piece of Oznabrigs and a Rope-yarn, and sew'd up a Bag in the best Manner I could, and counted two hundred and twenty eight fine large Apples into it, putting my two Silver Spoons in the Middle thereof, thinking it to be the most safest Place, and then lath'd it well fast to the Starboard Crotch on the Quarter Deck; and after having secured what Meat and Fish we had, in the best Manner possible, I continued to return Thanks to God for his Mercies, and endeavoured to compose myself as well as I could. Towards the Afternoon I observ'd the Winds begin to rise again, and the Sea ran very high, that it had like to have taken the Sail from the People forward, several Times washing them from the Bows, so that it was with Difficulty they recovered; at length were obliged to remove aft, and hale the Sail after them, and with Difficulty got it on the Quarter Deck. We divided the Sail as well as we could, and stretch'd a Loos-Tackle fore and aft the Quarter Deck to prevent our washing over board, and then placed ourselves in the best Manner possible, my self being next to the Stern. The Sea presently came near us, and soon rouz'd me up, when to my great Grief I perceived a very hard Gale near at Hand, the Wind as I imagin'd being at S. E. I stood some Time and consider'd, then look'd at the Bowsprit; our Flying-jib, Fore-stay-Sail and Spritsail being tangled with the Rigging and Boom lay under our Bowsprit ever since we had been wreck'd; and our Fore-Mast and Fore-top-Masts, with the Yards and all the Sails thereto belonging, was hanging under our Starboard-Bow, held By the Fore-stay and some of the Rigging belonging to it: We cut neither the Sails away that hung at the Bowsprit, nor the Wreck under our Bows, by reason the Sail was the only Thing we had left that could show us at a Distance, and the Wreck was very necessary to keep our Vessel to the Wind, and was a Means of securing us. I now went forward and consider'd some Time,

at length concluded to go out on the Bowsprit, the Sail being dry, and
if possible to secure myself out of the Way of the Sea; accordingly went
out, and hung myself under the Bowsprit in the best Manner I could. I
had not been there long before a violent Gale came on; and, together
with the flying of Part of the Spritsail, and the sudden Twinges of the
Wreck hanging by our Fore-stay, Imagin'd the Bowsprit might go away,
having Nothing to secure it but the Strap at the Heel. I frequently looked
to see how they fared a-baft, at length a Sea struck them and carry'd them
all to Leward, and like to have carry'd them all overboard; it took the
Fore-Sail quite from them, but happily lodg'd about the Leward Stanchions
of the Quarter Deck, the Rails being before gone: They recovered themselves, and some of them came forward; at the same Time I endeavoured
to stop the troublesome Part of the Spritsail which was flying, but could
not, although the Negro came to my Help: I therefore try'd to split the
Sail with my Knife, which when done, stopt it in some Measure: The Negro
remain'd on the Bowsprit with me some Time, but with much Difficulty,
by reason of the sudden Jerks the Wreck gave; so that he left me and went
in. I saw *Parsons* bring the Bag of Apples forward, expecting the Quarter
Deck would go every Minute; but they still continued on it: The Storm
increased exceedingly, and prodigious Rains; I expected every Moment
to hear them cry out from a-baft for being wash'd overboard; the dismal
Night came on, and the Storm continued; the Vessel labour'd much, and
dipt me several Times into the Sea; but still could not be worsted, altho'
I was just perish'd with the cold Rain and Wind. By frequent looking aft,
I discovered the main Hatches to be burst open, and the Bread and Flour
floating out, which put me under terrible Apprehension of our immediate
sinking; though I cannot say I ever once despaired of God's Mercy, or
was quite void of Hopes: At length, after some sharp Thunder and Lightning, the Weather began to abate the latter Part of the Night; and I, being
chill'd and benumb'd with cold Rain and Wind, crawl'd in, and stood
some Time in the Water, which warm'd me; then I crawl'd aft to see how
they did there, where I found them in a miserable Condition, and could
find no Place to set or lay down with them: I stood a while and bemoan'd
our lamentable Circumstance; my Heart was ready to burst: I beg'd
Heartily of God to deliver us, if it was his blessed Will, and Strove as
much as possible to resign my self to his Providence. I went forward
again, and there stood in the Water as much as I could out of the Wind,
to keep my self warm: I was so worn out for Want of Rest and Sleep,

I was obliged to hold my self up by my Hands (or I should have fell into the Sea) till they were so cold that I was oblig'd to put them into the Water to warm them.

At length the Day came on, being Saturday the 30th of December: The Sun being above the Horizon, warmed the Air; though it did not shine upon us, it was very comfortable: We blessed God for the Mercies of the Night past, and sincerely pray'd for Deliverance, though nothing appear'd to our Relief, yet we had great Hopes, being so plentifully supply'd with what was necessary for Life, as long as the Weather lasted moderate. This Day the Hatch being open, the People went to work, and got a Cask of Gammons[3] out of the Hold, and secur'd them; likewise a Barrel of Flour unheaded,[4] and set it up forward, together with a Cask of seventy Gallons of Water, and our other Provisions, which we had secured the last Storm (although to our Sorrow we lost the Bag of Apples the last Night.) We had sufficient to have lasted us three Weeks, should it please God to continue the Weather moderate, and not to let the Vessel sink under us; which put us in great Hopes that God would perfect our Deliverance, who had hitherto so wonderfully preserved us, and so plentifully provided for us, contrary to the Eye of Reason and our Deserts. This Day we had a comfortable One, and some Rest; we got our Sail up again that the Sea took from us last Night; we still continued our Addresses to God for his Assistance, and possess'd a more comfortable Night than any we had had, with some Rest; and inthe Morning, being

Sabbath-Day, the 31st of *December,* a fine smooth Sea and a warm pleasant Morning, I got up; and after addressing my self to God, I crawl'd forward on our Starboard Gunnel, being dry, and got a Rope, and stretch'd it from the Cat-head to to the Quarter-Deck Rail, so that we could walk forward for Water without wetting up to our Necks. This Day to our great Grief found ourselves begin to swell, and the Wounds and Bruises we got in the Wreck became very sore and troublesome. Yesterday I contriv'd a Method whereby we could make Use of our Flour; I took an Oyster-Keg that we had empty'd, and mix'd the Flour with fresh Water, so that we could eat it off a Stick; We saved a Pitcher that I had Pickles in which held three Quarts, and as there was Seven of us, he that went for Water drank at the Cask: I then cut another Oyster-Barrel to the Bigness of a Pint: The Pitcher holding three Quarts, being fill'd with Water, and thicken'd up with Flour so that we could drink it, serv'd us for both Victuals and Drink, the Flour taking away the Saltness of the Water, and

made it of a pleasant Taste; so that three of them Pitchers of Water in a
Day, satisfy'd us very well, and enabled us to eat our Meat (raw as it was)
with a good Stomach. We rubbed our Wounds and Sores with some of the
Fat of the Bacon, and ripp'd the thin Lining of the Sails and bound them
up in the best Manner we could. This Day dryed ourselves, the Sun shining out, began to feel comfortable, though very sore and worn out with
Watching and Fatigue. I began to think it impossible we should continue
long in that Condition, our Hands and Feet being so swell'd they became
almost useless to us, and with much Difficulty got forward for Water. I
thought it would be a terrible Thing should we all perish in that miserable
Condition, and no Soul be able to give an Account of us; especially considering that my Father was lost, with the only Brother I had, within a
Day or two of 31 Years before, being bound from *Piscataqua*[5] to *Madeira,*[6]
and never heard of after; consequently they suffer'd much in that Condition; the Storm, as near as I can remember, happening about the 2d
or 3d Day of *January,* 1718, 19: I was therefore strongly possess'd, that
about that Time my Dissolution or Deliverance would be fix'd; I likewise consider'd my poor Mother, who I expect is now living, I being her
only Son; and upon Consideration of the Whole, resolved (lame as I was
in my Right Hand) to cut Out in the best Manner I could, on a Barrel
Stave, with my Knife, an Account of the Name of the Brigantine, where-
unto she belonged, from whence she came, and when and where she
over-set, together with my own Name, as being Master; which I was resolved to keep secure, and fasten it to some Part of the Vessel where it
might be found, in Case we should all perish, and the Vessel afterwards
taken up. Accordingly this Day I began, altho' it was Sabbath-Day, my
Hands being very much swell'd, and particularly my Right-One, having
a Wound on the Inside, occasion'd by the Prick on a Nail the Day before
we overset: I finish'd two Lines, but my Hand failing me very much I
could do no more, without great Pain: However it being fair pleasant
Weather, we kept a wishful sharp Look-out; but Nothing appeared. Towards
Evening we contriv'd to fix our Lodging in a more commodious Way than
we had before, making a Sort of Tent and Weather Cloth, tacking the Sail
out-side with some Nails we had got from wherever we could pull them
out, and bringing the other Part over the Rail, stretching a Rope along the
Deck fore and aft, so that we could set pretty Up-right when the Water
came in, or we were tired with laying down. Thus pass'd the Day, and

likewise Monday the first Day of *January,* nothing remarkable happened,
but that a few Barrels of Flour work'd themselves loose and came out;
we saved what Nails we could out of the Hoops, to secure our Tent and
keep ourselves as dry as we could, for as we had recovered our natural
Health, and constantly soaking in the Water, our Flesh became very sore,
and our Feet swell'd, not one of us having any Shoes; we could do Nothing but implore the Assistance of Almighty God, beg his Mercy, and
recommend ourselves to his kind Providence, which had protected us
hitherto. Towards Evening, considering our deplorable Condition, I proposed to the People, to keep the next Day as a Day of Fasting and Prayer,
to humble ourselves before the Lord, and beg his divine Assistance; which
was consented to by most of the People. This Afternoon I perceiv'd the
Wind to freshen, and look squally to the Eastward; the Water began to
come over our Quarter, and I perceiv'd the Fashion-Piece on our Quarter
throw the Sea with a Re-bound over the Deck; I went to work with the
Broad-Ax and Crow, and got it off, drawing two large Bolts and several
Nails that held it: We then plac'd ourselves, and after recommending ourselves to the Almighty, endeavour'd to rest; but the Water coming in,
soon disconcerted me, and made me get up and try to wipe up the Water,
but to no Purpose, it constantly coming in, so that it oblig'd me to get
the Piece I had pull'd off our Quarter into my Birth, to sit on and keep
me out of the Water; on which I sat and lean'd all Night. The Morning
came on, being Tuesday the second Day of *January,* I being fatigued did
not rise as soon as some of our People, who to my great Grief I found
had begun to eat; Whether they heard me when I propos'd the Fast, or
whether it was Forgetfulness, I cannot tell; however I reprimanded them,
and desir'd they would keep the Day as we proposed; accordingly we
fasted and lamented our Sins before the Lord, and humbled ourselves;
But towards Noon some of the young Lads desired I would let them
have Water, I upbraided them, giving them a sharp Reprimand, charging
them not to taste any Thing till the Evening, but beg God for his Mercy.
Some of them began to draw forward near the Water Cask; but as I could
see it from the Quarter-Deck, I was very jealous, and kept a sharp Look-
out on them and promis'd them, if I caught any of them meddling with
Water until Night, I would take Care they should have none all the next
Day. Soon after I found my self much affected, so that I poured out my
Soul to God in a publick Manner, for the general Cause, and was so over-

come that I could scarce utter myself for Sobs and Tears: begging of the
Almighty he would feed us immediate Deliverance in his own Way that
would tend most to his Honour and Glory; and that he would enlarge our
Hearts to call upon and praise his holy Name for the Mercies he had been
pleased to favour us with hitherto; and that he would please to continue
the moderate Weather that he was pleased to bless us with; and in all
Things submitting ourselves to his divine Providence. I this Fore-noon had
finished my third Line on my Stave, with a Design not to meddle with it
any more till such Time as we were at the last Extremity, and not able to
help ourselves any more, and then to set down the Time we had been on
the Wreck; after which to secure myself, and that on the Wreck in the
best Manner I could, so that I might not wash from her. Soon after I found
my Mind to be very calm, and was sitting with the Mate on the Tiller,
discoursing, when on a sudden he starts up and cries out, *a Sail!* Joyful
News! We were ready to hug one another for Joy, and was inspir'd as it
were with new Life; immediately it cast in our Mind which way the Vessel
was bound, and how we should discover ourselves to them; I remember'd
I had sav'd an old white Shirt, which I had secured on the Bowsprit ever
since the Night we rode out the Storm; I took a small Pole (being a Mop
handle we had lash'd a Cutlass to which we made a Hook of to hale up
Things after the Loss of our Pump hook) and spread the Shirt thereon,
and set on the End of the Bowsprit and display'd it in the best Manner
I could to show us, holding the Tail of the Shirt in my Hand that the Sun
might shine on it, being white, could be discovered a long Way off: We
perceiv'd the Vessel to draw near sensibly. Our People fell to and eat and
drank heartily, not considering that though we saw the Vessel, she might
not see us, or at least not discover our Distress, and so pass by; especially
Night coming on and little Wind. I sat till I was tired; the Mate got the
Tiller out, and tail'd a Piece of Canvas and lash'd it to the Windward
Crotch, and then came and gave me a Spell; We would fain persuade ourselves that she made the best of her Way towards us, she being to Leward
of us, and little Wind, though at the same Time it seem'd to me that she
made the best of her Way to the Southward without regarding us, as she
never shew'd us any Colours, not ever attempted to tack while Day-Light
lasted. We began again to be under sensible Apprehensions of being left,
and some of the People began to bemoan themselves; I still retain'd a
strong Confidence in the Almighty that he would deliver us by this
Vessel, and therefore answered to this Purpose, *My dear Souls, never*

distrust the Providence of the Almighty, who is able to save to the last Moment them that put their Trust in him; and as he has been so wonderfully kind to us, and has us all hitherto, I do not doubt but that he will compleat his Mercies by our Deliverance, and in particular by this Vessel. They objected, the Vessel was gone by and took no Notice of us, and a long Night coming on: I acknowledg'd it; but at the same Time insisted, if it was the Pleasure of the Almighty (as I was strongly of the Belief it was) that they could not leave us were they ever so much a Mind to; and that God would in his Providence send them back (though unwilling) and they would be obliged to take us off: With this and such like Discourses I comforted them as well as I could. We made up our Lodging, and every Man plac'd himself in his Station; after which we sung the Hundredth Psalm, all but the four last Lines, which I could not remember; and then put up our hearty Prayers to God for his Mercy, that he would compleat our Deliverance, as he had given us a Glimpse of Hopes; and that he would not suffer us to be deceiv'd; and that in particular he would send us Deliverance by that Vessel we had seen this Day, altho' she had passed us; and that he would be pleas'd in his Providence to send her back to our Relief: Thus after recommending ourselves to his kind Providence, and begging Protection for the Night, we endeavour'd to repose ourselves as well as we could. Soon after we discover'd it to be a flat Calm, and towards Mid-Night a small Breeze southerly, which gave us great Hopes that the Vessel would be in Sight, in the Morning, whether they endeavour'd or not: We had the comfortablest Night of any we had whilst on the Wreck, considering the different Motions in our Hearts of Hope and Despair.

At Length the Morning came on, when I, being awake very much in the Night, did not rise as soon as some of the Rest of the People, who, between sleeping and waking, I heard bemoaning their woeful Condition, the Vessel not appearing: But as the Day-Light came on, to our great Joy we espied her laying under her Jib, right to Windward of us, the Wind being then S.W. or thereabouts: We imagin'd she had discover'd our Condition over Night, and was lying too, expecting to relieve us in the Morning, though we were much deceiv'd. However, in the Sense of God's divine Providence, we fell on our Knees all of us, and with the utmost Sincerity of Heart and Humility returning humble and hearty Thanks to Almighty God, for all the Acts of his kind Providence towards us, and that he then gave us so lively Hopes of a speedy Deliverance; still begging he would compleat it, and give us a due Sense of all the Mercies he had be-

stowed upon us; and that he would give us Grace to make a right Improve-
ment thereof; that we might amend our Lives, and live to shew forth his
wonderful Acts of Providence, and loving Kindness to us the sinful Children of Men. We then waited with great Impatience, and wonder'd the
Reason she did not bear down upon us, which was above an Hour after
we saw them; we was so near them we could plainly see their Hull. At
length to our great Joy and Satisfaction, we see her bearing away for us,
and hoist all the Sail they could make, and came down to us. No one can
express or imagine the Joy and Satisfaction we conceiv'd, only them that
felt it. They came under our Stern and spake with us, and immediately
hoisted out the Boat, and took us off. It proved to be the sloop *Dove*,
from *Boston*, Capt. *David Ford*, bound to *Surranam*,[7] who never discover'd our Distress till the Moment they bore away to take us off, taking
us for two Sail at a great Distance, and had no Thought of our being in
Distress, so that their being staid all Night was a pure Act of Providence!
The Wind soon brees'd up, and the Night following had a strong Gale of
Wind, and great Sea, that according to the Eye of Reason it would have
been impossible for us to have secur'd ourselves on the Wreck, (if she
had not sunk under us) in the Condition we then were reduc'd to, being
seven Nights and six Days on the Wreck in that miserable Condition; in
all which Time I cannot say, I once despaired of God's Mercy and Providence towards me; for which I desire forever to bless and praise his glorious Name.

NOTES

1. Hook. Sandy Hook, New Jersey, a six-mile peninsula in northeast
New Jersey, fifteen miles south of Manhatten.
2. Prime out. Uncaulked.
3. Gammons. Hams.
4. Unheaded. Without yeast.
5. *Piscataqua.* Harbor and District of Portsmouth, New Hampshire,
so called for the river of the same name.
6. *Madeira.* Principal island of a group 338 miles off the west coast of
Africa, famous for wines.
7. *Surranam. Surinam,* Dutch colony on the northeast coast of South
America.

Nathaniel Peirce

An Account of the Great Dangers and Distresses, And The
remarkable Deliverance Of Capt. Nathanael Peirce, Who
sail'd from Portsmouth, in New-Hampshire, bound for
Louisbourg; And Being taken up at Sea, was Carried to
Oporto.[1]

Both the vessel and the variegated crew commanded by
Nathaniel Peirce were in many ways typical of those ships
and men who plied the shipping lanes between New England,
Canada, and the West Indies during the eighteenth century.
A seasoned captain and a long-time resident of Portsmouth,
New Hampshire, Peirce was well acquainted with the waters
of the North Atlantic when he took his cargo of lumber
aboard the *Portsmouth* and sailed north for Louisbourg on
November 22, 1752. However, the winter storms that
buffeted the vessel and caused so much suffering among the
crew (three of whom had just returned from Jamaica) finally
persuaded him to change course and make for Antigua. At
the time the *Portsmouth* put about, Peirce estimated her
position at no more than thirty-five miles from Louisbourg.
Unfortunately, by that time serious damage to the brigantine
had already been done. The stress of the storm off Cape
Breton had weakened the ship's timbers, and when a second
storm overtook her two days later, the vessel sprung a fatal
leak.

Even in the company of narratives in which instances of
great courage and endurance are common, Peirce's story is
unusually compelling. His style is at once manly and direct,
yet rich in active detail. A plain-spoken ship's captain, Peirce
had no pretensions to literature, and his inexperience with
the narrative form shows up in one curious and noticeable

way. Halfway through his narrative he suddenly shifts from
a third- to first-person description, a change the captain apparently felt his circumstances aboard the wreck necessitated.
At that point in the story he was obviously reluctant to go
back and revise the portion already composed.

Nathaniel Peirce died in Portsmouth in the fall of 1762.

His *Account* was printed in Boston by the firm of Edes
and Gill in 1756, three years after the captain's return to
New England.

TEXT: American Antiquarian Society first edition on
Evans Microcard (E7747). The brief introduction "by another
hand" has been omitted.

THE Brigantine called the *Portsmouth,* NATHANAEL PEIRCE, Master,
belonging to Mr. *Robert Odiorne,* and others, of *Portsmouth* in *New-
England,* sail'd from thence the 22d Day of *November* 1752, bound to
Louisbourg; with a Cargo chiefly of Lumber. The Crew, besides the Master,
consisting of the following Persons, *viz. Nathaniel Barns* Mate, *David
Brown* Cooper, *William Langdon, Timothy Cotton, Langford* a Negro
Man, all Residents of *Portsmouth* aforesaid; *William Williams* of *Liverpool,*
and *Thomas Chambers* of some Part of the North of *England,* and *John
Olson* a Dutchman; in all Nine in Number.

They proceeded for some Days on their intended Voyage, without
any uncommon Accident. *December* the first, the Wind having been for
three or four Days so much to the Northward, with Snow Squals and exceeding cold, and the Brigant [i] ne being deep loaded, and at best a heavy
Sailor, they could not get in with the Land; saw it at a Distance, and supposed it to be the Land between Island Harbour[2] and White-Head.[3] The
Night before the Wind came to North West by West, by the Favour of
which they made the Land at Day-Light, and judg'd it to be about 10
Leagues to the Westward of *Louisbourg,* and stood close in with it. At
Noon, the Wind veering to the Eastward, and no Harbour near that they
could get into, and a Storm at East North East coming on, thick with
Snow, and very cold; they tack'd and stood off Shore till four in the
Afternoon, and then lay by under the Foresail, with the Head to the
Southward. The three last mentioned of the Crew, were very much dis-
couraged at the Severity of the Season, being but just arrived from

Jamaica, and badly cloath'd. They and all the Rest at different Times, were confin'd to their Cabbins by some slight Indisposition, and often beg'd the Master to go off the Coast, which he was very loath to do, as his Vessel and Cargo were disposed of at *Louisbourg* to good Advantage if he could get in there. But the Weather continuing very cold, the People still solliciting, and considering that the Cargo on board would suit the West India Market, He at last consented to go off the Coast; and at Eight in the Morning, the second Day of *December,* order'd the Helm a Weather, and bore away, designing to go for the Island of *Antigua,* and slop'd a Course accordingly.

They sail'd off the Coast under the Foresail till Noon; the Weather being moderate, they made more Sail; making the best of their Way to the Westward of the Island of Sables,[4] and then going to the Southward as the Winds and Weather would permit. It continued moderate till *December* the fourth at Night, when a Storm arose at West North West. They continued before the Wind the remaining Part of the Night, the next Day being the 5th of *December,* the Storm not abating, about 4 o'Clock in the Afternoon the Pump was suck'd. About five, the Master and Crew found She had sprung a Leak, and required both Pumps, which were set to work accordingly; but notwithstanding all they could do, the Water gain'd upon them so fast, that about eight in the Evening the Water was above the lower Deck; upon the Discovery of which they ceased Pumping, as finding that of no Manner of Service. The Master then went into the Cabbin which was very full, to endeavour to get some of his Papers and Things of Value out of his Chest (if haply he might be saved) but before he had Time to open it, the Things in the Cabbin began to fleet,[5] and shifted forward, and prest too the Door, that it was with very great Difficulty that he got out. They were now in the utmost Consternation imaginable, expecting the Vessel would be soon full of Water and then over-set.

They had no Sail set since the Gale began, but the Fore-sail: As soon as they could resolve what to do, the Ax was secured; the fore Jears were cut, and the Fore-Yard got close down. At the same Time some were employ'd in geting some Salt Pork and Beef upon Deck; which at first, as fast as they threw upon Deck was wash'd overboard, till it was proposed that some of it should be strung, which was done accordingly, and made fast to the aftermost Stantion of the quarter Deck and the Horse-piece. The Master took a Spell to cut away the Main-mast, but for want of

Strength, and some one to second him, did not accomplish it. The Rest
of the Crew were employed in clearing the Decks of Hoops, Hen-coops,
and Lumber, which the Sea in a great Measure facilitated, as by that
Time the Vessel was full of Water, and the Sea continually running over
them, which washed away the Boats, Caboose & Windless; so that before
Morning they had nothing remaining upon Deck, save the Main-top-sail,
Yard and Sail, bent and furl'd to the Yard, which had not been dry
enough to put down, altho' unrig'd some Days before; and now happen'd
to be so jamm'd between the Main-mast and Pumps, that the Sea could
not wash it away.

They attempted at first to steer the Vessel before the Wind, but she
soon broach'd too, with her Head to the Northward, which though bad
on one Account, was good on another. As they reckon'd themselves between the Latitude of 4° 1 and 4° 2 North Latitude (having had no Observation for several Days) and about South from the Island Sables, her
Head being to the Northward she would naturally gain more to the Northward; if so, they thought that they should be more out of the Way of
Vessels meeting with them, at that Season of the Year. But then on the
other Hand, the Vessel having a Lift to Starboard, the other being the
Weather Side (as the Winds for the most Part at that Season of the Year
are to the Westward) she was for that Reason the higher out of Water;
and this was the only Position to lay in for Safety, as will hereafter appear.

They past this Night in great Distress, and horrible Apprehensions of
every Moments being their last, and their State fixt to all Eternity. And
having so sudden a Call, what must be the Consternation of such miserable
unthinking Wretches as the generality of Seamen are?

When the Day came on, there was a new Scene of Terror; the Negro
Man *Langford* was missing; suppos'd to be wash'd over-board in the
Night; and enquiring for the Ax to cut the Main-mast away, it was not
to be found, being lost in the Night; and no one could be blamed, as it
was with very great Difficulty that they kept themselves on the Wreck,
the Sea continually breaking over them. Every Thing in the Cabin and
Steerage, such as Casks, Chests, Scrutores,[6] and likewise the Lumber,
was by the violent Surges of the Sea stove in Pieces; so that the ruinous
State to which these Things were reduc'd, is almost incredible.

The Crew attended at the Companion, to catch what should come in
Sight, that might be' of Service. They recovered some Apples, and Part
of three Cheeses; but to their great Mortification, could not meet with

any of their Cloaths or Bedding. They began now to consider of some
Way to obtain Rest; and the first Thing to be done, was to unbend the
Main-top-sail, and get it aft on the Poop, (which was a Rise of about six
Inches from the Quarter-deck, and about eight from the Taffril, and being short Plank, did not blow up, as did most Part of the Quarter-deck
afterwards, when she overset.) This they effected; and then fastning the
Robins to the Rail, from the Crutch aft to the after Stantion, (which was
the only Place free from Water) they laid down Side by Side, and hauling
the other Part of the Sail over them, they obtain'd some Rest; altho' the
Sea would much disturb them by breaking over them; and when it did so,
which was very often, they got up to wring their Cloaths, and laid down
again. In this Posture they continued as long as any one remained on the
Wreck, save when employed on necessary Occasions.

December the 7th, proved a moderate and fine clear Day, with but
little Wind. Perceiving the Lee Water-way Plank, and that next to it, of
the foremast Part of the Quarter-deck was blown up, and some small
Things washing out, they attended to get what they could there; but
could meet with nothing that was of any Service to them, excepting one
of the Captain's Sheets, and a large Part of the Ensign, which proved of
great Service, as will appear hereafter. Every Thing was stove to Pieces in
the Steerage and Cabbin, as above; but observing the Bulk of Boards that
was stowed before the Main-mast, between Deck, to remain fast, they concluded if they could get Water any where, it must be in the Fore-castle,
which was stowed full; upon which Account the Water-Casks and other
Things there, were more likely to be preserv'd.

They went to work, and broke open the Fore-castle, and hawling out
the spare Rigging, Wood, Staves, and Shingles, &c. as it came to the Scuttle,
which was for the most Part under Water; they at last obtained what they
aim'd at, which was one Barrel, and another half full of Apples, and a
French Hogshead[7] of Fresh Water; all which they got aft on the Quarter-
deck, and secured them in the best Manner they possibly could. The Water
stunk very much, being in Rum Casks, but they tho't it a great Relief in
their present Necessity. When they were at Work getting these Things out
of the Fore-castle, as large a Shark as they had ever seen, attempted to
come in upon Deck to them; but the Master perceiving it, beat him off
with a Hogshead Stave; however, he attended about the Wreck for several
Days, as a horrible Sepulchre for them that should fall into his Power.
They now tho't themselves in a Condition to subsist for some Days; and

had some Hope that God, would of his infinite Mercy, grant them Relief, by sending some Vessel in their Way, to take them off; of which there was but a bare Possibility; however, it was earnestly desired of the Almighty.

The Water, Cheese, and Apples they used with Discretion; every one taking a little at certain Times: But they were deprived of every Thing commonly used to drink out of, and so were obliged to make Use of one of their Shoes.

It continued moderate 'till the Ninth Day of *December,* but blowing hard all that Day, about the Dusk of the Evening, in a very severe Squall, the Vessel fell on her starboard Broadside, with her Masts in the Water. The Crew got on the Broadside to Windward, in the best Manner they could, and some of them crawl'd forward on the Outside, and cut away the Lanyards of the Weather-Main and Fore-Shrouds, in Hopes the Masts would go away by the Board, and the Vessel right on her Bottom as before. But the Masts proved too good to be got rid of so easily, and the Vessel remain'd on her Broadside, the Sea continually running over them, and the Weather very cold; and one large Sea in particular, wash'd the Master from the main Chains of the Wreck to Leeward, but by a kind Providence, he happen'd to fall on the Main-mast, where the Sea left him; by the Help of which and the Barricado, he got again on the Windward Side, and was securing himself to the main Chains when the Squall abated, and the Vessel righted on her Bottom as before.

They then got within Board, and mustering their Number, *William Langdon* and *John Olson* the Dutchman were lost, and all the Fresh Water, Apples and Cheese gone; the Companion and most Part of the Quarter-deck blown up. and the greatest Part of the loose Stuff in the Steerage and Cabbin floated out; and nothing left them to subsist upon, but the raw Salt Pork secured as above. From this Time they had never a drop of Water, but what the Heavens, at Times, aforded them. It was now that the Sheet and Piece of the Ensign, mentioned above, became serviceable; first, by dividing to each a Piece, to catch Rain Water with; and to some to wrap their sore Legs in, of which some were very bad; and to others, to bind round their Head that had no Cap or Wigg. The Manner they got Water was, by standing up when it rained, and spreading out their Cloth with their Arms, leaning on the Rail for Safety, and facing the Rain 'till the Squall was over, or the Cloth full of Water; then each, to make the most of what he had got, laid down, and wringing the Cloth between his Teeth, suck'd out what Water he could. But at first using the Cloth, they

were oblig'd to wring out the Water several Times to wash it, for it was
so impregnated with Salt, having been soak'd so long in Salt Water, that
they could not drink it. And often, to their great Mortification, when
they thought they had a Mouth-full of Water in their Cloth, the Spray
of the Sea would fly on it, and render the Water unfit for Use; so that it
would take two or three Showers to freshen them again. But what will
not a Man attempt to save Life? and no Man knows what Hardship he can
bear, 'till he is bro't to the Test.

Either the 12th or 13th Day, *David Brown*, the Cooper, proved delirious; which was first discovered by his asking idle and ridiculous Questions,
for which he was reproved at first; but it had no other Effect on him, than
to make him whisper instead of calling aloud for Beer, Cyder, and other
Liquors, and contriving how he would go and get them. And the next
Morning he was missing, and they supposed that he went overboard in
the Night.

About this Time, i.e. the 13th Day of *December, Thomas Chambers,*
the ablest and best Seaman on board, went up and cut the Fore-top-sail-
Yard away, Sail and all, to prevent the Vessel's oversetting, of which they
were very much afraid, it blowing hard, and looking likely for a bad Storm,
of which they had several. During this Time, to the 15th, they had several
light Showers of Hail, but could save only a very small Quantity, which
each as soon as they got it, eagerly devoured, tho' it gave but small Relief.

The 16th, *Nathaniel Barns* the Mate, by his Behaviour, shew'd that he
was delirious; talking and behaving much as *Brown* had done; and for
Fear that he should steal from them in the Night, as *Brown* had done,
they with a Reef Plat took a Turn round his Body, under his Arms, and
made the Ends fast to the Crutch, which was between the Master's Birth
and *Timothy Cotton;* and before Night they tho't he was struck with
Death by some Signs in his Countenance, and Motion of his Body; but
when Night came on, he lay still and soon died, without any Struggle,
that they could perceive; and the next Day in the Afternoon they threw
him into the Sea.

From the 9th to this Day, being the 17th, they endeavoured all they
could, to get some loose Boards and Plank that were washing about the
Steerage and Cabbin overboard, which this Day they accomplished; when
it was hoped that some of the Tools, that were in the Mate's Cabbin in
the Steerage, might be found to Leeward, which was considerably under
Water.

The Crew was now reduc'd to the Master, *Timothy Cotton, Thomas Chambers,* and *William Williams.* It was ask'd, Who could swim, and venture to dive down to the Lee-side in the Steerage, and search for some of the Tools, to cut the Main-Mast away? The three last could not swim, and when they knew the Master could, they let him have no Rest 'till he complied with their Request. But first he made them promise that they would take Spell and Spell with such Tools as he should find, 'till the Mast should fall. He then strip'd off his Cloaths, and soon recovered a new Cooper's Ax, that was never ground, an Iron Crow, and Part of a Bar of Lead. He then split a Stave, and with his Knife made a Handle for the Ax, with which, and the Iron Crow, they took Spell and Spell, according to their Promise, and in about three or four Hours, they got the Mast to fall, when they tho't the Vessel in no Danger of being overset by any Storm. The Bar of Lead they cut to chew and roll about in their Mouths, which they tho't in some Measure allay'd their Thirst, which was at Times very great; and especially about this Time, when they were tempted to drink their own Urine, which one of them had often done before. In this great Distress, the Master not standing upon Niceties, borrow'd one of the Men's Shoes, urin'd in it, and drank it off, which, as he tho't, soon purged him; for which Reason he never repeated it, and endeavoured to diswade others from doing it, as well as from chewing Tobacco, which they would do, altho' wet with Salt Water: Which Advice he had Reason to think was too much slighted. The Reason he borrowed one of the Men's Shoes to drink out of was, because he saw them drink in the same Manner; and had none of his own, since the second Day after the Vessel filled with Water, when his Feet swell'd and were so painful, that he was obliged to pull them off, and there being no Place of Safety, they were soon wash'd overboard.

In the Evening of this Day *Timothy Cotton* shewed great Signs of a Delirium, by insisting on the Master's giving him some Drink; and when reason'd with upon the Impossibility of complying with his Request, he insisted on going ashore, and nothing should persuade him out of it; for he said he could easily get ashore, but would not go without Leave from the Master. But upon the Master's telling him, if he would stay till next Day, if he liked the Opportunity he would go with him; he sat down in his Birth, and seem'd to be in the full Exercise of his Reason in a Moment; and ask'd the Master if he thought there was any Likelihood of a Vessels meeting with them. This he had encouraged them before to hope for, but now told them that there was only a Possibility of such a Thing's happening; all Things being possible to the Almighty, and that it might so happen in the Course of his Providence. But at the same Time he advis'd them not to think much of this, or any Thing in the present Life, but to endeavour to secure their eternal Happiness in the next, by looking unto Jesus Christ their merciful Redeemer for sincere Repentance of all their Sins, and Salvation thro' his Blood, and to let that take up all their Thoughts, as they had nothing before their Eyes, but Death, and an Eternity of Joy or Misery. They then earnestly supplicated God to wash away all their Sins, and to receive them into his Favour for the Sake of Jesus Christ; and beg'd for the Continuance of their Reason till their appointed Time should come; and that they might not be left to destroy themselves, or be any Way accessary to their own End; and so humbly submitted themselves to his Will and Pleasure.

Timothy Cotton continued very calm and rational till towards the next Evening, which was the eighteenth Day of *December,* when he fell into a more violent Fit than the Day before; and after insisting on having some Drink, in ha[r] sher Terms then he had done; and the Master refusing to go with him, as he desir'd, he in a sudden, and violent Manner threw himself into the Sea, and they saw no more of him.

The Master and two Men that remained with him, were in great Distress for want of Water till this Night, when it pleased God to send a very plentiful Rain, of which by the Use of their Cloths, they got as much as they desired, and drank rather more than did them good. The nineteenth was moderate, but unsettled Weather, and at Night it began to blow hard, and the Sea to run high. Some Time in the Night, the two Men that were left with the Master, while he was asleep, shifted the Helm, which occasioned the Vessel to ware round on the other Tack, which they had often done before, being very much affraid she would overset. And while they had the Forestay-sail and Strength, they hoisted it, and so wore her round again. But now that Sail was render'd useless; and if it were not, they had no Strength to hoist it. Laying on the Starboard Tack, as was observed before, was much the best both for Safety and Ease; whenever the Vessel was about on the other Tack, then every Sea would run over her as it would over a Rock that is but just above Water. At this Time, no sooner was She about, then the Sea came over them with the utmost Violence. The first Sea very narrowly mist washing the Master over-board, and of Course thoroughly awakened him. When he perceived what was the Matter, he crawled out of the Sail to the Tiller, unlash'd it from the Place where the Men had fastned it, and lash'd it to the Place where it was before, which was then the Weather Side, and returned as soon as possible to his Birth in the Sail, in hopes that the Vessel would ware round on the other Tack. But all he could say to the two Lads could not persuade them to get into their Births in the Sail for Safety. They were weak, and discovered some Signs of a Delirium; and the Sea having free Passage over them, they were wash'd away, and the Master saw no more of them, and expected every Moment to follow them.

But it pleased God in about a quarter of an Hour, that the Wreck wore round on the other Tack, when the Difference was so great, that I thought it very comfortable Lodging to what it was before, altho' exposed to the Winds and Weather as much as if I had been in the open Field. The Weather was cold, but not enough to freeze. I was now sensible of a general Decay or Weakness in all my Faculties: my Eyes weak and dazzling; my Limbs hardly enabled me to get on my Feet; at the same Time, I had bad Sores on my Ancles, Knees, Hips, Elbows and Sholders and Joynts of my Fingers. But nevertheless I was obliged to get up when it rain'd, or I could get no Water, which proved to be very scarce, seldom being able to get a mouthful for the last four Days; and was so reduc'd, that I could not have held out above twenty-four Hours longer, having had no Bread from the beginning, and no other Provisions, than as mentioned above: and indeed the Cry of Thirst was so great, that we had very little Desire for Eating, in Comparison for that of Drink, of which we had so scanty a Supply, that we never but once had, as we thought, enough.

I was alone from the Nineteenth to Christmas Eve, expecting to starve to Death, and at the same Time earnestly begging God's Mercy in the Forgiveness of my Sins, and a Preservation of my Senses until my Time should come, trusting in the Merits and Satisfaction of Jesus Christ for Acceptance unto Salvation; at the same Time praying for a sincere Submission to the divine Will. But it pleased God that I should continue longer in this World (than I expected) a Monument of his Mercy; and to grant me a wonderful Deliverance, by sending Capt. *Thomas Martin,* in the Snow *Elizabeth* from *Hallifax,* loaded with *Fish* bound to *Oporto* in *Portugal,* to take me off the Wreck, the 24th Day of *December* 1752, at Noon, when they were in 41° 1′ 5 North Latitude, and 112 Leagues to the Eastward of *Halifax.*

It had blown hard, according to the Account they gave me, the Night before, and they had reef'd their Top-sails; and in the Morning it growing moderate, they went up to let their Reefs out; and while they were about it, as it is common, they looked round to see what they could see; and spied as they thought a Sloop lying a Hull. But they soon alter'd their Opinion, and believed it to be a Top-sail Vessel with but one Mast standing. They immediately alter'd their Course, and came close to Windward. And seeing the Water run in and out at the Cabbin Windows, and the Hatches and Deck blown up, they concluded that there could be no Body alive on the Wreck; so made what Observations and Remarks on the Vessel they could, and then made Sail and shot a-head. But as they fell under the Lee-bow, they saw a Sailor's Jacket hanging on one of the Crotches, and a Sail fastned as above, and thought some Body was in it, but doubted if alive. However, they resolved to take their Speaking-trumpet and hail; which they did accordingly; and I think they told me they repeated it three Times. But being asleep, I heard them but once, and they said they heard me answer them. As soon as I open'd my Eyes I saw a Vessel close by me, under the Lee-bow, I immediately took the Peice of the Ensign I had in my Bosom (which I kept there to preserve free from Salt Water, being what I catch'd fresh Water with) and lifted up my Arm as high as I could, and swung it to them; which they answered with their Hats; telling me they would send their Boat immediately, which they did as soon as possible. I lay still all the While in my Birth, and saw them hoist out their Boat, and perceived her advancing towards me. All this While I was ruminating in my Mind, whether what I saw was real. I thought I could not be deceived with false Appearances, as I was thoroughly sensible of my Condition; and how I came into this Situation; and so resolved to trust to the Reality of it.

As soon as the Boat came near, they called to me, and asked me, if I could help myself; I told them I could; and as the Boat advanced, I got myself down to the Lee-quarter, ready to throw myself into her; and when a smooth Time offer'd, they back'd the Boat to the Side, when with the Help of the Man that was in the Stern of her, I tumbled myself into the Bottom of the Boat, where I had not above two or three Feet to fall; and so was rowed along Side the Hospitable Snow that received me. The Sea was very rough, and I thought there was Danger in getting out the Boat, especially for one so weak as I was, so desired them to throw me a Rope, which they did, and I fastned it round under my Arms, by the Help of which I got safe upon Deck. As soon as I had fallen on my Face, and thanked Almighty God for so merciful a Deliverance, I was help'd down into the Cabbin, where they had prepared a little hot Wine, of which they gave me a Glass to drink, which I thought very comfortable, and a Bit of white Bisquet, but I could not eat it, by Reason all my Teeth were very loose. The Wine soon coming out of my Stomack, I took a little more with a Bit of Bisquet soaked in it, which stay'd by me. They strip'd me of all my Cloaths, which were dirty and ragged; my Shirt being rotten in some Places; and what was left of it, as still as Buckrum, by being frequently wet with Salt Water; and put me on a new clean check'd Shirt, Drawers, and Stockings. They got me also the biggest Pair of Shoes they could find, but my Feet were so swell'd, I could not put my Toes into them. I committed myself to the Care of the Captain, and begged he would be careful of what was given me to Eat and to Drink; for that I was reduced to the Weakness of a Child. They then put me to Bed, or Cabbin in the Steerage; for as the Vessel was small, and several Passengers in the great Cabbin, there was no Room for me there.

I no sooner was laid in the Bed assign'd me, than I was in a Delirium, which was so constant, that I know not what I did, or what they gave me to Eat or Drink for some Days. But when I recovered my Reason, I was sensible that Capt. *Martin* must have taken a great Deal of Care of me, and that I must have been no small Trouble to him; and what I had Occasion for of his Stores, was at my Service: And till I have it in my Power to make him another Return, can only say, I am greatly oblig'd to him.

He proceeded on his intended Voyage for *Oporto,* without any uncommon Accident, till we made the Coast of *Portugal.* We were about a Week before we could get in with the Barr, which was occasion'd by little Winds and Calms, and was more tedious than all the Passage besides. The Nights I thought were very sharp and cold; and the scorbutick Habit[8] that I had contracted on the Wreck was now purging off by Urin, which obliged me to go upon Deck three or four Times a Night, for Want of a Conveniency below. This exposed me to the Weather very much; and as I have been told by able Physicians, it was a very extraordinary Providence that I should recover from so low and starved a Condition; for I was so weak that I was often ready to faint before I could get to my Cabbin again. And once in particular, just as I got down to the Foot of the Ladder in the Steerage, I fainted away, and fell with my Face to the Ladder; and as I was coming to myself again, I heard one of the Sailors say, what is the Matter with the old Man? I answered, that I had fainted away, and then got to my Cabbin. As I had a long Beard, and was so much ematiated, their distinguishing me by that Name, is not to be wonder'd at.

About the twentieth Day of *January* we got in with the Barr of *Oporto*.
It being a proper Time of Tide and smooth Water, we sail'd directly in,
tho' poop'd by three Seas; And that Night and the next Day, warpt the
Snow up to *Merigiah*,[9] and had Protick;[10] tho' on my Account the Visit-
Boat made much Difficulty. But at last the Captain obtain'd it, and then
he went ashore with the Passengers. I desired them to procure me a Lodging, which they endeavour'd, as they told me when they came on Board,
without Success.

Had I not been deliver'd from such Extremity of Distress, I should
now have tho't myself very unhappy; in a strange Country; without any
Habitation; without Friends or Money; with little or no Cloaths to my
Back, and them very dirty and lousy; and hardly able to stand on my
Feet, having several loathsome Sores about me, and no Dressing for
them. I desired Capt. *Martin,* when he went ashore the next Day, that
he would make my Case know[n] on Change,[11] and acquaint the Consul
with it, that I might get Relief like other Beggers—By Change Time we
got up to the Key, but outside another Fish Vessel that was then discharging.

Captain *Martin* was telling my Story on Change, when it came to the
Ears of my good Friend Captain *William Morris,* whose Humanity led him
to come directly to see me. When I was call'd, and told that Capt. *Morris*
wanted to see me, I had no Notion of its being any Man that I had ever
seen; but when I came upon Deck, and saw my old Acquaintance, I had
Hopes of Relief. But his seeing me in that Condition, gave him so much
Concern, that he could not help showing it in his Countenance; and I
being sensible of this at the same Time, could not refrain from Tears,
and turn'd about to wipe them away with my Sleeve; and turning again,
found he was gone. I was sorry that he went away so abruptly, tho' I did
not doubt but it was for my good.

I was such a miserable Object to look at, I thought it best to go to my
Cabbin, which I did; but was no sooner there, than Capt. *Morris* came
down the Steerage, and his Steward, with a Bag of Cloaths, with which
he desired me to dress myself. I soon shifted from Head to Foot, and
threw all my dirty, lousey Cloaths into the Cabbin I had so long slept
in, and went ashore with Capt. *Morris,* and Mr. *Welkinson,* Merchant
there, to his House and drank Tea; and he was so good as to send for
Dr. *Henry Nickols,* Physician to the English Factory at *Oporto,* who
kindly came, and gave me his best Advice and Assistance. It was then

agreed that I should go on board the *Julius Cesar,* Capt. *William Morris*'s
Ship, till he had acquainted the Consul, Mr. *Jackson,* with my Misfortune,
and could provide a Lodging for me ashore.

The Consul, who is a most human Gentleman, and very much beloved
by the Factory, when he heard my Story (as I was informed) said he
would have a Lodging for me near his own House; that he might often
hear from me; and had provided one accordingly in a Portugee's House.
But at my Friend *Morris*'s Desire, I was lodged at Mr. *Nicholas Webber*'s
at *Villa-Nova,*[12] where I met with all the kind Treatment I could expect,
or a Person in my weak Circumstances desire—Here, by Order of the
Consul and Factory, I was attended by a Taylor, Perriwig-maker, Shoe-
maker, &c. who furnished me with a Suit of Cloaths from Head to Foot,
as also with Shirts, Crevats, Handkerchiefs, Stockings, &c.—And when
I was able to take my Passage for *England,* they procured a Passage for
me, in the *Mary* Capt. *Francis Smith,* for *London,* and laid in all Manner
of Stores necessary for a Gentleman, and five Moidores[13] in my Pocket,
all at their own Cost & Charge. Nor must I forget the Kindness of Dr.
Bromley, who was so good as to attend me every Day that I was at
Oporto, to dress my sore Ancles, and gave me proper Dressing for them,
to use in the Passage to *England.* Nor can I omit to mention the Present
made me by the Masters of the Ships then at *Oporto;* in which kind Affair,
Capt. *Knowler,* and my Friend *Morris,* were exceeding active.

We sail'd over the Barr of *Oporto* the 3d of *March* 1753, and arrived
at *Dover* the 13th of the same Month.

By the Assistance of some Friends in *London,* and the Owners of the
Britania Capt. *George Spender* in particular, in which I took Passage from
London, I have had an Opportunity of seeing once more my native Place
Portsmouth in *New-England.*

On the 15th Day of *July,* 1753, I arrived at *Boston,* in *New-England,*
an affecting Instance, more especially to my Friends, of the Goodness of
that Being, *who is the Confidence of the Ends of the Earth; and of them
that are afar off upon the Sea.*

NOTES

1. *Oporto.* Porto, northwest coast of Portugal; principal city after
Lisbon and the home of port wine.

2. Island Harbour. Probably New Harbor, fifteen miles north of White-
head.

3. White-Head: On the west coast of Nova Scotia, seventy-five miles southeast of Louisbourg.

4. Island of Sables. A long, sandy island off Nova Scotia, one hundred and twenty miles west of Halifax.

5. Fleet. To move or change position.

6. Scrutores. Small chests or lockers.

7. French Hogshead. A barrel of forty-six gallons; as opposed to the usual British hogshead of sixty-three gallons.

8. Scorbutick Habit. Scurvy.

9. *Merigiah.* Apparently a district of Porto on the Douro River.

10. Protick. Evidently a diplomatic and/or commercial inspection by Portuguese officials.

11. Change. Of tide.

12. *Villa-Nova.* Villa Nova de Gaia, across the Douro River from Porto.

13. Moidores. Portuguese coin; in the eighteenth century valued at approximately twenty-seven shillings.

Briton Hammon

A Narrative Of the Uncommon Sufferings, And Surprizing Deliverance Of Briton Hammon, A Negro Man,—Servant to General Winslow, Of Marshfield, in New-England; Who returned to Boston, after having been absent almost Thirteen Years.

Briton Hammon's relation is attractive on its own merits, but it is also remarkable for its being the work of a slave, a black man owned by General John Winslow of Marshfield, Massachusetts. But Briton Hammon was no ordinary man. He was literate and well-read, especially in the Scriptures. He also seems to have had the complete trust of Winslow, who allowed him time and opportunity to go to sea.

From a man sensitive and pious by nature, Hammon's *Narrative* is a tale of patient suffering and perseverance, of hardship matched by gritty determination. His style is terse yet emotionally charged, his story spare and economical. The *Narrative* is also one of the more important works of black American writers in the colonial period, and students accustomed to the poetry of Jupiter Hammon (apparently no relation) and Phillis Wheatley will find considerable merit in Briton Hammon's sturdy prose.

Hammon's *Narrative* was printed and sold by Green and Russel in Boston in 1760.

TEXT: Library of Congress first edition on Evans Microcard (E8611).

ON Monday, 25th Day of *December,* 1747, with the leave of my Master, I went from *Marshfield,* with an Intention to go a Voyage to Sea, and the next Day, the 26th, got to *Plymouth,* where I immediately ship'd myself on board of a Sloop, Capt. *John Howland,* Master, bound to *Jamaica* and the *Bay.*[2] —We sailed from *Plymouth* in a short Time, and after a pleasant Passage of about 30 Days, arrived at *Jamaica;* we was detain'd at *Jamaica* only 5 Days, from whence we sailed for the *Bay,* where we arrived safe in 10 Days. We loaded our Vessel with Logwood, and sailed from the *Bay* the 25th Day of *May* following, and the 15th Day of *June,* we were cast away on *Cape-Florida,*[3] about 5 Leagues from the Shore; being now destitute of every Help, we knew not what to do or what Course to take in this our sad Condition:—The Captain was advised, intreated, and beg'd on, by every Person on board, to heave over but only 20 Ton of the *Wood,* and we should get clear, which if he had done, might have sav'd his Vessel and Cargo, and not only so, but his own Life, as well as the Lives of the Mate and Nine Hands, as I shall presently relate.

After being upon this Reef two Days, the Captain order'd the Boat to be hoisted out, and then ask'd who were willing to tarry on board? The whole Crew was for going on Shore at this Time, but as the Boat would not carry 12 Persons at once, and to prevent any Uneasiness, the Captain, a Passenger, and one Hand tarry'd on board, while the Mate, with Seven Hands besides myself, were order'd to go on Shore in the Boat, which as soon as we had reached, one half were to be Landed, and the other four to return to the Sloop, to fetch the Captain and the others on Shore. The Captain order'd us to take with us our Arms, Ammunition, Provisions and Necessaries for Cooking, as also a Sail to make a Tent of, to shelter us from the Weather; after having left the Sloop we stood towards the Shore, and being within Two Leagues of the Same, we espy'd a Number of Canoes, which we at first took to be Rocks, but soon found our Mistake, for we perceiv'd they moved towards us; we presently saw an English Colour hoisted in one of the Canoes, at the Sight of which we were not a little rejoiced, but on our advancing yet nearer, we found them, to our very great Surprize, to be *Indians* of which there were Sixty; being now so near them we could not possibly make our Escape; they soon came up with and boarded us, took away all our Arms Ammunition, and Provision. The whole Number of Canoes (being about Twenty,) then made for the Sloop, except Two which they left to guard us, who order'd us to follow on with them; the Eighteen which made for the Sloop, went so much faster than we that they got on board above Three Hours before we came along side, and had kill'd Captain *Howland,* the Passenger and

the other hand; we came to the Larboard side of the Sloop, and they
order'd us round to the Starboard, and as we were passing round the
Bow, we saw the whole Number of *Indians,* advancing forward and load-
ing their Guns, upon which the Mate said, *"my Lads we are all dead
Men,"* and before we had got round, they discharged their Small Arms
upon us, and kill'd Three of our hands, viz. *Reuben Young* of *Cape-Cod,*
Mate; *Joseph Little* and *Lemuel Doty* of *Plymouth,* upon which I immediately jump'd overboard, chusing rather to be drowned, than to be
kill'd by those barbarous and inhuman Savages. In three or four Minutes
after, I heard another Volley which dispatched the other five, viz. *John
Nowland,* and *Nathaniel Rich,* both belonging to *Plymouth,* and *Elkanah
Collymore,* and *James Webb,* Strangers, and *Moses Newmock,* Molatto.
As soon as they had kill'd the whole of the People, one of the Canoes
padled after me, and soon came up with me, hawled me into the Canoe,
and beat me most terribly with a Cutlass, after that they ty'd me down,
then this Canoe stood for the Sloop again and as soon as she came along
side, the *Indians* on board the Sloop betook themselves to their Canoes,
then set the Vessel on Fire, making a prodigious shouting and hallowing
like so many Devils. As soon as the Vessel was burnt down to the Water's
edge, the *Indians* stood for the Shore, together with our Boat, on board
of which they put 5 hands. After we came to the Shore, they led me to
their Hutts, where I expected nothing but immediate Death, and as they
spoke broken English, were often telling me, while coming from the Sloop
to the Shore, that they intended to roast me alive. But the Providence of
God order'd it otherways, for He appeared for my Help, *in this Mount of
Difficulty,* and they were better to me then my Fears, and soon unbound
me, but set a Guard over me every Night. They kept me with them about
five Weeks, during which Time they us'd me pretty well, and gave me
boil'd Corn, which was what they often eat themselves. The Way I made
my Escape from these Villains was this; A Spanish Schooner arriving there
from *St. Augustine,*[4] the Master of which, whose Name was *Romond,*
asked the *Indians* to let me go on board his Vessel, which they granted,
and the Captain* knowing me very well, weigh'd Anchor and carry'd me
off to the *Havanna,*[5] and after being there four Days the *Indians* came
after me, and insisted on having me again, as I was their Prisoner;—They

*The Way I came to know this Gentleman was, by his being taken last
  War by an *English* Privateer, and brought into *Jamaica,* while I was
  there. [*Hammon's note.*]

made Application to the Governor, and demanded me again from him; in answer to which the Governor told them, that as they had put the whole Crew to Death, they should not have me again, and so paid them Ten Dollars for me, adding, that he would not have them kill any Person hereafter, but take as many of them as they could, of those that should be cast away, and bring them to him, for which he would pay them Ten Dollars a-head. At the *Havanna* I lived with the Governor in the Castle[6] about a Twelve-month, where I was walking thro' the Street, I met with a Press-Gang[7] who immediately prest me, and put me into Goal,[8] and with a Number of others I was confin'd till next Morning, when we were all brought out, and ask'd who would go on board the King's Ships, four of which having been lately built, were bound to *Old-Spain,* and on my refusing to serve on board, they put me in a close Dungeon, where I was confin'd *Four Years and seven months;* during which Time I often made application to the Governor, by Persons who came to see the Prisoners, but they never acquainted him with it, nor did he know all this Time what became of me, which was the means of my being confin'd there so long. But kind Providence so order'd it, that after I had been in this Place so long as the Time mention'd above the Captain of a Merchant-man, belong to *Boston,* having sprung a Leak was obliged to put into the *Havanna* to refit, and while he was at Dinner at Mrs. *Betty Howard's,* she told the Captain of my deplorable Condition, and said she would be glad, if he could by some means or other relieve me; The Captain told Mrs. *Howard* he would use his best Endeavours for my Relief and Enlargement.

Accordingly, after Dinner, [he] came to the Prison, and ask'd the Keeper if he might see me; upon his Request I was brought out of the Dungeon, and after the Captain had Interrogated me, told me, he would intercede with the Governor for my Relief out of that miserable Place, which he did, and the next Day the Governor sent an Order to release me; I lived with the Governor about a Year after I was delivered from the Dungeon, in which Time I endeavour'd three Times to make my Escape, the last of which proved effectual; the first Time I got on board of Captain *Marsh,* an *English* Twenty Gun Ship, with a Number of others, and lay on board conceal'd that Night; and the next Day the Ship being under sail, I thought myself safe, and so made my Appearance upon Deck, but as soon as we were discovered the Captain ordered the Boat out, and sent us all on Shore—I intreated the Captain to let me, in particular, tarry on board, begging, and crying to him, to commiserate my unhappy Condition, and added, that I had been confin'd almost five Years in a close Dungeon, but the Captain would not hearken to any Intreaties, for fear of having the Governor's Displeasure, and so I was obliged to go on Shore.

After being on Shore another Twelvemonth, I endeavour'd to make my Escape the second Time, by trying to get on board of a Sloop bound to *Jamaica,* and as I was going from the City to the Sloop, was unhappily taken by the Guard, and ordered back to the Castle, and there confined. —However, in a short Time I was set at Liberty, and order'd with a Number of others to carry the *Bishop*** from the Castle, thro' the Country, to confirm the old People, baptize Children, &c. for which he receives large Sums of Money.—I was employ'd in this Service about Seven Months, during which Time I lived very well, and then returned to the Castle again, where I had my Liberty to walk about the City, and do Work for my self;—The *Beaver,* an *English* Man of War then lay in the Harbour, and having been informed by some of the Ship's Crew that she was to sail in a few Days, I had nothing now to do, but to seek an Opportunity how I should make my Escape.

Accordingly one Sunday Night the Lieutenant of the Ship with a Number of the Barge Crew were in a Tavern, and Mrs. *Howard* who had before been a Friend to me, interceded with the Lieutenant to carry me on board: the Lieutenant said he would with all his Heart, and immediately I went on board in the Barge. The next Day the *Spaniards* came along side the *Beaver,* and demanded me again, with a Number of others who had made their Escape from them, and got on board the Ship, but just before I did; but the Captain, who was a true *Englishman,* refus'd them, and said he could not answer it, to deliver up any *Englishmen* under *English* Colours. —In a few Days we set Sail for *Jamaica,* where we arrived safe, after a short and pleasant Passage.

After being at *Jamaica* a short Time, we sail'd for *London,* as convoy to a Fleet of Merchantmen, who all arrived safe in the Downs,[9] I was turned over to another Ship, the *Arcenceil,* and there remained about a Month. From this Ship I went on board the *Sandwich* of 90 Guns; on board the *Sandwich,* I tarry'd 6 Weeks, and then was order'd on board the *Hercules,* Capt. *John Porter,* a 74 Gun Ship, we sail'd on a Cruize,

**He is carried (by Way of Respect) in a large Two-arm Chair; the Chair
   is lined with crimson Velvet, and supported by eight Persons. [*Hammon's note.*]

and met with a French 84 Gun Ship, and had a very smart Engagement,*** in which about 70 of our Hands were Kill'd and Wounded, the Captain lost his Leg in the Engagement, and I was Wounded in the Head by a small Shot. We should have taken this Ship, if they had not cut away the most of our Rigging; however, in about three Hours after, a 64 Gun Ship, came up with and took her.—I was discharged from the *Hercules* the 12th Day of *May* 1759 (having been on board of that Ship 3 Months) on account of my being disabled in the Arm, and render'd incapable of Service, after being honourably paid the Wages due to me. I was put into the *Greenwich* Hospital where I stay'd and soon recovered.—I then ship'd myself a Cook on board Captain *Martyn,* an arm'd Ship in the King's Service. I was on board this Ship almost Two Months, and after being paid my Wages, was discharg'd in the Month of *October.*—After my discharge from Captain *Martyn,* I was taken sick in *London* of a Fever, and was confin'd about 6 Weeks, where I expended all my Money, and left in very poor Circumstances; and unhappy for me I knew nothing of my *good Master's* being in *London* at this my very difficult Time. After I got well of my sickness, I ship'd myself on board of a large Ship bound to *Guinea,*[10] and being in a publick House one Evening, I overheard a Number of Persons talking about Rigging a Vessel bound to *New-England,* I ask'd them to what Part of New-England this Vessel was bound? they told me, to *Boston*; and having ask'd them who was Commander? they told me, Capt. *Watt;* in a few Minutes after this the Mate of the Ship came in, and I ask'd him if Captain *Watt* did not want a Cook, who told me he did, and that the Captain would be in, in a few Minutes; and in about half an Hour the Captain came in, and then I ship'd myself at once, after begging off from the Ship bound to *Guinea;* I work'd on board Captain *Watt's* Ship almost Three Months, before she sail'd, and one Day being at Work in the Hold, I overheard some Persons on board mention the Name of *Winslow,* at the Name of which I was very inquisitive, and having ask'd what *Winslow* they were talking about? They told me it was *General Winslow*; and that he was one of the Passengers, I ask'd them what *General Winslow?* For I never knew *my good Master,* by that Title before; but after enquiring more particularly I found it must be *Master,* and in a few Days Time the Truth was joyfully verify'd by a happy Sight

***A particular Account of this Engagement, has been Publish'd in the *Boston* News-Papers. [*Hammon's note.*]

of his Person, which so overcome me, that I could not speak to him for some Time—*My good Master* was exceeding glad to see me, telling me that I was like one arose from the Dead, for he thought I had been Dead a great many Years, having heard nothing of me for almost Thirteen Years.

I think I have not deviated from Truth, in any particular of this my Narrative, and tho' I have omitted a great many Things, yet what is wrote my suffice to convince the Reader, that I have been most grievously afflicted, and yet thro' the Divine Goodness, as miraculously preserved, and delivered out of many Dangers; of which I desire to retain a *grateful Remembrance,* as long as I live in the World.

And now, That in the Providence of that GOD, who delivered his Servant David out of the Paw of the Lion and out of the Paw of the Bear, *I am freed from a* long *and* dreadful Captivity, among worse Savages than they; *And am return'd to my* own Native Land, to Shew how Great Things the Lord hath done for Me; *I would call upon all Men, and Say,* O Magnifie the Lord with Me, and let us Exalt his Name together!—O that Men would Praise the Lord for His Goodness, and for his Wonderful Works to the Children of Men!

NOTES

1. General Winslow. John Winslow (1703-74), colonial army officer, on several campaigns in the French and Indian War.

2. *Bay.* Of Honduras.

3. *Cape-Florida.* Point, southeast end of Key Biscayne, Florida.

4. *St. Augustine.* Spanish fort and settlement on the northeast coast of Florida, thirty-five miles southeast of Jacksonville.

5. The *Havanna.* Havana, Cuba. Chief naval station of Spain in the new world; in 1762, four years after Hammon was imprisoned there, Havana was captured by the British but was returned to Spain in 1763.

6. *Castle.* El Morro Castle, at the entrance to the harbor.

7. Press-Gang. A company of sailors under orders to seize forceably or "impress" men for service aboard a ship.

8. Goal. Jail.

9. Downs. Roadstead in the English Channel, along the east coast of Kent, about nine miles long and six miles wide; affords excellent anchorage, protected by a natural breakwater, the Goodwin Sands.

10. *Guinea.* Name generally applied to the coastal region of west Africa in an area roughly between modern Gambia and Angola. Also variously the Slave Coast, Gold Coast, Ivory Coast.

David Harrison

The Melancholy Narrative Of The Distressfull Voyage And Miraculous Deliverance Of Captain David Harrison, Of The Sloop, *Peggy,* Of New York, on his Voyage from Fyal,[1] one of the Western Islands, to New York

When David Harrison of New York City sailed for home from the Azores on October 24, 1765, he could have had no idea of the particular horror that would befall his vessel, or that his story would later figure in a novel by Edgar Allan Poe. Yet both happened.

Much of Harrison's bizarre narrative bears the marks of the effusive piety and sentiment fashionable in English and American literature in the latter half of the eighteenth century. In this Harrison differs from the other authors of colonial sea-deliverances, the majority of whom wrote a plain and fairly restrained style. A more important difference occurs with respect to the uses for which Harrison's sea-deliverance was intended. Like the other writers, Harrison offered his narrative as an example of the goodness of Providence. However, he also directs his story to "Those who read for mere amusement," an indication of the writer's awareness of the growing novel-reading public in England and America. *The Melancholy Narrative* thus shows evidence of literary influences not found in the earlier colonial sea-deliverances.

The *Narrative* was first printed by James Harrison in London in 1766. Early in the nineteenth century it appeared in a severely abbreviated version in Archibald Duncan's *Mariner's Chronicle* (1804) and from thence was reprinted several times, including an appearance in R. Thomas's *Remarkable Shipwrecks* (1835). The latter is probably the version Poe read about the time he began to compose *The*

Narrative of Arthur Gordon Pym. Poe used instances from
several shipwreck narratives and tales to assist the plot of
his novel, and no single work may be said to be the source for
Pym, but the events of chapters eleven to thirteen of the
novel bear more than a little resemblance to incidents aboard
the crippled, famine-haunted *Peggy.*

For a further study of the relationship between Harrison's
Narrative and Poe's *Pym,* see Keith Huntress, "Another
Source for Poe's *Narrative of Arthur Gordon Pym,*" *American
Literature* 16 (1944): 19-25. In his *Narratives of Shipwrecks
and Disasters, 1586-1860* (Ames: Iowa State University
Press, 1974), Huntress reprints the nineteenth-century version of the *Peggy*'s voyage, an edition that is only one-half
the size of the first, which is printed here for the first time
since 1766.

TEXT: First edition in the Library of Congress. Harrison's
affidavits (which simply recount the events of the voyage in
shorter space) have been deleted.

THE occurrences of my late unfortunate voyage, are of a nature so
extraordinary, and my preservation is a circumstance so miraculous, that,
sensible as I am at present of the Divine goodness, it would look like a
want of gratitude to the great disposer of all things, if I neglected to employ a few hours in the recital of some particulars, where his Providence
has been singularly manifested, and where he has given an incontestible
lesson to all his creatures, to dread the impiety of despair, since his assistance may be nearest at hand when they are least in expectation of relief.

THE solemnity of this sentiment will not, I hope, terrify a reader of
elegance from the perusal of the following pages.—Those who read for
mere amusement, will probably find something to entertain them, unless
they are too refined to put up in real distress with those circumstances
which would possibly yield them most satisfaction in a work of mere
imagination,—while those who are actuated by a more serious turn, will
possibly exclaim in the exalted language of the Psalmist, "How wonderful
are the works of the Lord, how great in wisdom all."

WITHOUT farther preface, I weighed anchor at NEW-YORK, on the
25th of August, 1765, and came to sail from SANDY HOOK[2] on the

27th with a cargo consisting of lumber, staves, bees-wax, fish, &c. and proceeded on my intended voyage, with a small breeze of wind, at S.S.W.—Nothing remarkable occurred on the outward bound part of my passage, and arrived safe at FYAL on the 5th of October following—where I immediately addressed myself to the British consul at that place, Mr. Richard Gathorne, and his partner, Mr. Alexander Graham, pursuant to my instructions, and after clearing my ship in the customary mercantile course, I got a cargo of wine, brandy, &c. for NEW-YORK, by the 22d of October, which I had no sooner completed, than I went immediately on shore for my letters and dispatches; apprehensive of the consequences of coming on the coast of AMERICA, in a single deck vessel, in the winter season, a time in which these seas are uncommonly dangerous.

EVERY thing being ready by the 24th,—I set sail about half after eleven in the morning from FYAL, with a fine breeze of wind at S.E. and at six o'clock in the evening the body of the island bearing from me North, three leagues, I lost sight of land, and began to flatter myself with the hopes of a very expeditious voyage. On the 29th, however matters put on quite a different aspect; the wind blowing pretty fresh, my standing jib, a very old one indeed, was split, and as we had no other on board, we unbent and put it into as good a condition as the nature of our circumstances would admit.—The violence of the weather still continuing, we went under an easy sail, a double-reefed mainsail and jib.—Nevertheless on Wednesday the 6th of November, two pair of my foremost mainshrouds, on the larboard side, were carried away, being old and unable to resist the severity of the weather.—On this we immediately set up stoppers; and got a runner and tackle as a support to the mast; lying too under a ballanced mainsail, as it blew extremely hard.—The next day the wind shifting to the W.N.W. and blowing more violently, we wore ship, and laid her head to the Southward; but about eight o'clock in the morning, my two fore main shrouds, on the starboard side, were carried away, which obliged us to get up another runner and tackle for the additional security of the mast.—Till the 12th of November, the weather was intolerably bad, the seas excessively heavy, and the continued peals of thunder joined to our incapacity of carrying any sail, unless for a few hours, threw a horror over our situation, which is not to be conceived by any but those who have unhappily experienced something like our circumstances.

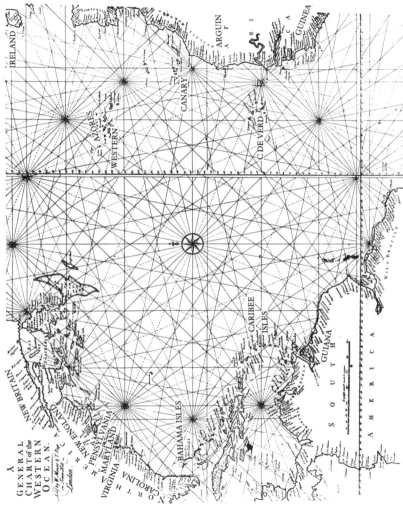

A General Chart of the Western Ocean, from *The English Pilot, the Fourth Book* (London, 1745). Courtesy of the John Carter Brown Library, Brown University, Providence, Rhode Island.

ON Tuesday, the 12th of November, the weather seemed more moderate, though the change did not carry the appearance of any great dura-
tion; and, indeed, next day, to our unspeakable mortification, it came
on to blow as hard as ever at W.N.W. so that my fore-stay and fore-sheets
were not only torn away, but the fore-sail itself rent in pieces; and what
added considerably to the loss, was my not having any other to put in
it's place.—In this situation we lay too, as before, under a ballanced reefed
main-sail, the impetuosity of the storm still continuing, and the seas rolling mountains high, all of us expecting that the vessel would prove leaky,
as she strained inconceivably hard.

SCUDDING away, however, on the 16th or 17th, under the square sail
head, about two in the morning, the tack unfortunately happening to
give way, this sail was torn all to tatters, so that we were obliged to cut
it from the yard, and to heave too immediately under bare poles till the
mainsail was ballanced reefed.—One misfortune is generally the forerunner of another; at least we found it so; for while we lay too in the
same gale of wind, which destroyed our square sail, the flying jib blew
overboard, from a new set of points, although it was a new sail, and made
of top-gallant duck.—Notwithstanding all these accidents, we made some
little way, at intervals, under an easy sail, till the 1st of December, when
being attacked by another violent gale, in the latitude of 40d. 1m. North,
and longitude 58d. 37m. West from LONDON, a dreadful sea broke two
of my main chain-plates, and shattered my fore-sail to such a degree, as
rendered it utterly unserviceable.—The only bit of canvass now left, was
the main-sail, which we backed and lay too, having no prospect whatever
before us but what was pregnant with the bitterest distress; for the conflict which our vessel had so long maintained against waves and winds,
had, by this time, occasioned her to leak excessively; and our provisions
were so much exhausted, that we found it absolutely necessary to come
to an immediate allowance of two pounds of bread a week, for each
person, besides a quart of water, and a pint of wine a day.—The alterna-
tive was really deplorable, between the shortness of our provisions, and
the wreck of our ship. If we contrived to keep the latter from sinking, we
were in danger of perishing with hunger, and if we contrived to spin out
the former with a rigid perseverance of oeconomy for any time, there was
but little probability of being able to preserve our ship,—thus, on either
hand, little less than a miracle could save us from inevitable destruction;
if we had an accidental gleam of comfort on one hand, the fate with

which the other so visibly teemed, gave an instant check to our satisfaction, and obscured every rising ray of hope, with an instant cloud of horror and despair.

WE met, indeed, a couple of vessels, one from JAMAICA for LONDON, and another to DUBLIN, from NEW-YORK, who would have probably relieved us, had there been a possibility in so severe a gale, to open any cummunication from ship to ship; all they could do was to speak to us, a circumstance which the reader's own imagination must naturally suppose did not a little add to the misery of our situation.—Disappointed of succour in this quarter, I was under a necessity of contracting the little allowance which had been lately settled for each man; and continued gradually lessening the quantity of provisions, till every morsel was entirely exhausted, and not above two gallons of dirty water remaining in the bottom of a cask. My poor fellows, who from incessant fatigue, and a long want of necessaries, were now reduced to a very weakly condition, began at last to grow impatient, and seized on the cargo, naturally enough observing that the wine and brandy were the only things they had now remaining in the world; and that I must not be surprized if they made very free with both, for their support.—I could neither be sorry nor surprized at this motion.—What gave me concern was, the continual excess to which they drank—and the continual course of execration and blasphemy, which was occasioned by that excess.—For my own part, I abstained, as much as possible, from wine, and very gladly husbanded the dregs of the water cask, which afterwards proved of infinite service to me, and may be not improperly reckoned an essential means of my surviving a complication of the most affecting calamities.

OUR vessel had been for some time tossed about, at the mercy of the winds and waves, when in the midst of our despair, we were suddenly transported with the most extravagant sensations of joy, by the discovery of a sail to the leeward, the 25th of December, in the morning.—Distress generally inspires the human mind with lively sentiments of devotion, and those, who, perhaps, dispute or disregard the existence of a Deity at other times, are ready enough, in the day of adversity, to think every advantageous turn in their affairs a particular exertion of the Divine benignity.—It was, therefore, but natural for some of the people to think that the 25th of December was appointed for their preservation, in a temporal sense, as much as in a spiritual view it was appointed to be the means of their future felicity.—Our thanksgivings, however, to Providence,

though profoundly sincere, were not offered in any great form. We all
crouded upon deck; and hung out, with our utmost expedition, a proper
signal of distress; and, about eleven o'clock, had the unspeakable satisfaction, to come near enough to the ship to engage her in conversation, to
inform her of our distresses; and to obtain from the captain an assurance
of relief.—Indeed the promised relief was but small, nevertheless, the
smallest to people in our circumstances, was inestimable. It was to be
nothing more than a little bread, which was all, as the captain assured
me, that he could spare, as he himself was contracted in every other
article.—This, however, he said we should have, as soon as he had finished
an observation which he was taking, for it was now near twelve o'clock.—
Having no doubt, in nature, but the captain would punctually perform
his promise, I retired to rest myself in the cabbin, being much emaciated
with fasting and fatigue; and labouring, at the same time, not only under
a very dreadful flux, but a severe rheumatism in my right knee; my sight
also was considerably impaired, so that, upon the whole, I exhibited as
striking a picture of misery as could possibly be painted to the eye of
imagination.

I HAD not been many minutes in the cabbin, when my people came
running down, with looks of unutterable despair, and informed me, in
accents scarce intelligible, that the vessel was making from us as fast as
she could, and that there was nothing now left for us but inevitable destruction.—I crawled up to the deck, at this terrible intimation, with all
the expedition I was master of, and found, to my inexpressible affliction,
that their account was but too true.—The captain had taken the reefs
out of his topsails and mainsail, and, in less than five hours, having a fine
breeze in his favour, was entirely out of sight.—As long as my poor fellows
could retain the least trace of him they hung about the shrouds, or ran
in a state of absolute phrenzy from one part of the ship to the other, to
collect still more visible signals of distress,—they pierced the air with their
cries, encreasing in their lamentations as he lessened upon their view, and
straining their very eye-balls to preserve him in sight, through a despairing
hope that some dawning impulse of pity would yet induce him to commiserate our situation, and lead him to stretch out the blessed hand of
relief.—But, alas! to what purpose did we exhaust our little strength in
supplicating for compassion, or aggravate our own misfortunes with a
fruitless expectation of such a change.—The inexorable captain pursued
his course without regarding us, and steel'd, as he undoubtedly must be,

to every sentiment of nature and humanity, possibly, valued himself not
a little upon his dexterity in casting us off.—Notwithstanding I must feel
an everlasting indignation against this barbarous man, for flattering people
in our circumstances, with promises which he never meant to fulfill, I
shall not hang him up to universal detestation or infamy, by communicat-
ing his name to the reader;—if he is capable of reflexion his own conscience
must sufficiently avenge my cause; and God grant that the pungency of
that conscience may be my only avenger.—One instance of his cruelty I
must not forbear to mention.—At our first meeting I told him, neither I
nor any of my men would desire a single morsel of his provisions, provided he only took us out of our own wreck, in which we were every
moment exposed to the mercy of the waves, as our leaks were continually
encreasing, and the men declining in their strength in proportion as the
necessity grew urgent to employ them at the pumps.—This request he
absolutely refused; though the indulgence of it might, in any succeeding
distress, have done him an essential service, and could not possibly expose
him to the least inconvenience.

MY people being thus unhappily cut off from all assistance, where they
were so fully persuaded of meeting with an instant relief, became now as
much dejected with their disappointment as they grew formerly transported with their joy.—A desperate kind of gloom sat upon every face,
which seemed regardless of the horror that was continually expected to
burst upon our heads, at the same time that it indicated a determination
to put off the fatal moment to the utmost verge of possibility: actuated,
therefore, by a resolution of holding out as long as we were able, we
turned our thoughts upon a pair of pigeons and a cat, which we had not
yet destroyed, and which were the only living animals on board besides
ourselves.—The pigeons we killed for our Christmas dinner, and the day
following made away with our cat, casting lots for the several parts of the
poor creature, as there were no less than nine of us to partake of the repast.—The head fell to my share, and, in all my days, I never feasted on
any thing which appeared so delicious to my appetite,—the piercing sharpness of necessity had entirely conquered my aversion to such food; and
the rage of an incredible hunger rendered that an exquisite regale, which,
on any other occasion, I must have loathed with the most insuperable disgust.—After the cat was entirely consumed, my people began to scrape the
barnicles from the ship's bottom; but the relief afforded from this ex-

pedient was extremely trivial, as the waves had beaten off the greatest number that were above water, and the men were infinitely too weak to hang
over the ship's side to gather them; their continued intoxication, however, seemed, in some measure, to keep up their spirits, though it hastened
the destruction of their health, and every dawn of reflexion was carried
off in a storm of blasphemy and execration.

FOR my own part I imbibed the strongest aversion imaginable to wine;
the complicated disorders under which I laboured induced me to abstain
from it at first, and, as the men were perpetually heating it in the steerage
the smell of it became offensive to the last degree; so that I subsisted entirely on the dirty water which they had forsaken, half a pint of which,
together with a few drops of Turlington's balsam[3] being my whole allowance for four and twenty hours.—In this situation I patiently expected
that destiny which I thought it utterly impossible to avoid; and had it
not been for the pangs which I felt on account of my wife and family, I
should have longed for the moment of dissolution, and rejoiced at the
approach of that awful period which was to put an end to all my misfortunes.

WHEN the reader comes to consider our total want of necessaries, that
my vessel had been for some time leaky, that I myself was emaciated with
sickness, and had but one sail in the world to direct her; when he considers that the men were either too weak, or too much intoxicated to pay
a necessary attention to the pump; when he likewise considers the severity
of the season, that it blew "*black December,*"[4] as Shakespeare phrases
it, and is told that we had not an inch of candle, nor a morsel of slush[5]
to make any, having long since eaten up every appearance of either which
could be found; when the reader comes to consider all these things, and
is, moreover, informed, that the general distress had deprived me of all
command on board my own ship, he will scarcely suppose that I could
sustain any new misfortune;—yet, such was the severity of my destiny,
that on the 28th of December (being then driven as far to the northward,
by a series of southerly winds, as 41 or 42 North Latitude) I was overtaken by a most dreadful storm at N.W. by N. and N.W. and had my only
remaining bit of canvas, the mainsail, torn entirely away, so that I was
now become a wreck in the fullest sense of the expression,—and death
became so seemingly unavoidable, that I even gave up hope, that last con-
solation of all the wretched, and prepared for an immediate launch into

the dreadful gulph of eternity. Providence, however, thought proper to dispose of me otherwise; and everlasting thanks to it's infinite mercy, I am still alive to labour for the advancement of my little family.

TO this period of my relation I have been able to proceed circumstantially from a reference to my journal.—The remainder, as I grew from this time utterly unable to hold a pen, must be collected from my memory, and from memorandums which I made at intervals with chalk, of the most remarkable occurences.—The reader will recollect, that the last morsel of meat that we tasted was our cat on the 26th of December.—On the 13th of January following, being still tossed about at the descretion of the sea and wind,—my mate, at the head of all the people, came to me in the cabbin, half drunk indeed, but with looks so full of horror, as partly indicated the nature of their dreadful purpose, and informed me, "that they could hold out no longer,—that their tobacco was entirely exhausted; that they had eaten up all the leather belonging to the pump,—and even the buttons off their jackets, that now they had no chance in nature but to cast lots, and to sacrifice one of themselves for the preservation of the rest, they therefore expected my concurrence to the measure, and desired me to favour them with an immediate determination."

PERCEIVING them in liquor I endeavoured to sooth them from their purpose as well as I could; begged they would retire to rest, and that in case Providence did not interpose in their favour by the next morning we would consult farther on the subject.—Instead of regarding my request, however, they swore, with a determined horror of execration, that what was to be done, must be done immediately; and that it was indifferent to them whether I acquiesed or not; for although they had been so kind as to acquaint me with their resolution, they would oblige me to take my chance as well as another man, since the general misfortune had levelled all distinction of persons.

AS I had long expected some violence to myself, from the excesses of their intoxication, I had, for some time, taken to my arms, to prevent a surprize;—but, alas! this was an idle precaution, as I was by no means able to repel force by force:—finding them, therefore, still deaf to my remonstrances, I told them they might pursue their own course, but that I would on no account either give orders for the death of the person on whom the lot might fall, nor partake, by any means, of so shocking a repast.—To this they answered, that they would not ask my consent to slaughter the victim; and, as to eating or not eating, I might just follow the biass of my own inclination.—So saying they left me, and went into

the steerage,—but in a few minutes came back, informing me, that they
had each taken a chance for their lives, and that the lot had fallen on a
negro, who was part of my cargo.—The little time taken to cast the lot,
and the private manner of conducting the decision, gave me some strong
suspicions that the poor Ethiopian was not altogether treated fairly;—but,
on recollection, I almost wondered that they had given him even the appearance of an equal chance with themselves.—The miserable Black, however, well-knowing his fate was at hand, and seeing one of the fellows load-
ing a pistol to dispatch him, ran to me begging I would endeavour to save
his life.—Unfortunately for him I was totally without power.—They therefore dragged him into the steerage, where, in less than two minutes, they
shot him through the head.—They suffered him to lye but a very little
time before they ripped him open, intending to fry his entrails for supper,
there being a large fire made ready for the purpose;—but one of the fore-
mast-men, whose name was James Campbell, being ravenously impatient
for food, tore the liver from the body, and devoured it raw as it was, notwithstanding the fire at his hand where it could be immediately dressed.—
The unhappy man paid dear for such an extravagant impatience, for in
three days after he died raving mad, and was, the morning of his death,
thrown overboard,—the survivors, greatly as they wished to preserve his
body, being fearful of sharing his fate, if they ventured to make as free
with him, as with the unfortunate negro.—But to return,

THE black affording my people a luxurious banquet, they were busy
the principal part of the night in feasting on him, and did not retire to
rest till two in the morning.—About eight o'clock next day, the mate
came to ask my orders, relative to the pickling the body, an instance of
brutality which shocked me so much, that I grasped a pistol, and mustering all the strength I was master of, I swore unless he instantly quitted
the cabbin, I would send him after the negro.—Seeing me determined,
he withdrew,—but muttered, as he went out, that the provision should
be taken care of without my advice, and that he was sorry he had applied
to me, since I was no longer considered as master of the ship.—Accordingly
he called a council, where it was unanimously agreed, to cut the body into
small pieces, and to pickle it; after chopping off the head and fingers,
which they threw overboard, by common consent.

THREE or four days after, as they were stewing and frying some stakes,
as they called the slices which they cut from the poor negro (for they
stewed these slices first in wine, and afterwards either fryed or broiled
them,) I could hear them say, "Damn him, though he would not consent

to our having any meat, let us give him some;" and immediately one of
them came into the cabbin, and offered me a stake.—I refused the tender
with indignation, and desired the person who brought it, at his peril to
make the offer a second time.—In fact the constant expectation of death,
joined to the miserable state to which I was reduced, through sickness
and fatigue, to say nothing of my horror at the food with which I was
presented, entirely took away my desire of eating.—Add also to this, that
the stench of their stewing and frying, threw me into an absolute fever,
and that this fever was aggravated by a strong scurvy and a violent swell-
[i]ng in my legs.—Sinking under such an accumulated load of afflictions,
and being, moreover, fearful, if I closed my eyes, that they would surprize and murder me for their next supply, it is no wonder that I lost all
relish for sustenance.—In reality, it would have been wonderful, had I preserved the least, and therefore my abstinence is not altogether so merito-
rius a circumstance.

NOTWITHSTANDING the excesses into which my people ran, they
neverthe less husbanded the negro's carcase with the severest oeconomy,
and stinted themselves to an allowance which made it last for many days.—
But when it was nearly expended, I could hear them frequently consulting
among one another, on the most expedient course to provide another
supply.—The result of all these determinations, was to destroy me, before
they ran any risque of destroying themselves.—The reader will naturally
suppose, that if I slept little before I received any positive knowledge of
their intention, I slept still less, when I became acquainted with their
designs.—In proportion as the negro grew less, so in proportion my apprehensions were encreased, and every meal which they sat down to, I considered as a fresh approach to destruction.

IN this manner matters went on, till the 28th or 29th of January,—
when the mate, with more generosity than I could well expect, from the
nature of their late private consultations, came to me again at the head
of the people, saying, that the negro had for some days been entirely
eaten up, and as no vessel had yet appeared, to give us the most distant
glimmer of relief, there was a necessity for casting lots again;—since it was
better to die separately than all at once.—They also told me that they
did not doubt but what I was now hungry, and would of course take my
chance with them, as I had before done, when my situation was infinitly
less desperate.—I again attempted to argue with them, and observed that
the poor negro's death had done them no service, as they were as greedy
and as emaciated as ever.—I therefore adviced them to submit to the dis-

pensations of Providence with temper, and offered to pray with them for
an immediate relief, or an immediate eternity.—The answer which they gave
to this, was, that they were now hungry, and must have something to eat;
and therefore it was no time to pray; and if I did not instantly consent
to cast lots, they would instantly proceed without me.

FINDING them thus inflexible, and having but too much reason to
suspect some foul proceedings unless I became a principal agent in the
affair, I made a shift to rise up in my bed, ordered pen, ink, and paper,
and called them all into the cabbin.—There were seven of us now left;
and the lots were drawn in the same manner as the tickets are drawn for
a lottery at Guildhall.[6]—The lot, indeed, did not fall on me, but it fell
on one David Flatt, a foremastman, the only man in the ship on whom
I could place any certain dependance.—The shock of the decision was
great; and the preparations for execution were dreadful.—The fire already
blazed in the steerage, and every thing was prepared for sacrificing the
wretched victim immediately.—A profound silence for some time took
possession of the whole company, and would possibly have continued
longer had not the unhappy victim himself, who appeared quite re-
signed, delivered himself to the following effect:—"My dear friends,
messmates, and fellow sufferers, all I have to beg of you is to dispatch
me as soon as you did the negro, and to put me to as little torture as you
can:" then turning to one James Doud (the man who shot the negro)
"It is my desire, says he, that you should shoot me."—Doud readily, yet
reluctantly, assented.—The unhappy victim then begged a small time to
prepare himself for death:—to which his companions very chearfully
agreed, and even seemed at first unwilling to insist upon his forfeit life,
as he was greatly respected by the whole ship's company.—A few
draughts of wine, however, soon suppressed these dawnings of humanity;
nevertheless, to shew their regard, they consented to let him live till
eleven the next morning, in hopes that the Divine goodness would, in the
mean time, raise up some other source of relief;—at the same time they
begged of me to read prayers, promising to join me with the utmost
fervency.—I was greatly pleased with this motion,—and though but little
able to go through a task of that kind, I exerted all my strength, and
had the satisfaction to observe, that they behaved with tollerable decency.

FATIGUED with reading so much, I lay down almost ready to faint,
yet could hear the whole ship's company talking to the wretched Flatt;
hoping that the Deity would interpose for his preservation; and assuring
him, though they never yet could catch or even see a fish, they would

at daybreak put out all their hooks again to try if any thing could be
caught to mitigate their distresses, or to avert the severity of his sentence.
—Unhappily, however, the poor fellow, unable to stand the shock of his
destiny, grew astonishingly deaf by midnight, and was quite delirious by
four in the morning.—His messmates discovering this alteration, debated
whether it would not be an act of humanity to dispatch him immediately:
—but the first resolution to spare him till eleven, visibly preponderating,
they all retired to rest, except the person who was to take care of the fire.
In all their excesses they were sensible of what importance it was to preserve the fire, and therefore never went to bed without leaving a centinel
to keep it up.

ABOUT eight o'clock the next morning, as I was ruminating in my
cabbin on the approaching fate of the poor fellow, who had now but
three hours to live, two of my people came hastily down, with looks full
of the strongest expectation, and seizing my hands, without saying a
syllable, gave me no little apprehension that they intended to postpone
his fate for some time, and to sacrifice me in his stead:—I was the more
confirmed in this opinion, as the unhappy man still continued out of his
senses, and on that account might be judged improper sustenance;
especially as notwithstanding all their necessities, they threw Campbell
overboard through a fear of catching his infection.—Fraught with a notion
of this nature, I disengaged myself as well as I was able, and snatching up
one of my pistols, resolved to sell my life as dearly as I could.—The poor
men, guessing at my mistake, with some difficulty told me, that their
behaviour was not the effect of any ill intention, but the actual consequence of their joy,—that they had descried a sail to the leeward, which
appeared to be a large vessel, and that she seemed to stand for us in as
fair a direction as we could possibly wish.—The rest of the crew came
down immediately after their companions, and confirmed the report of a
sail, but with this material difference, that she seemed to bear off upon
quite a contrary course.

IT is impossible to describe the excess of my transport upon hearing
that there was a sail at any rate in sight—my joy, in a manner, over-
powered me; and it was not without the utmost exertion of my strength
that I desired them to use every expedition in making a signal of distress.—
Our vessel, indeed, itself was a most striking signal; but as there was a
possibility for the ship in view to suppose that there was not a living creature on board, I judged it absolutely expedient to prevent the likelihood
of so dreadful a mistake.—My poor men found my orders now so essential

to their own preservation, that I was obeyed with all imaginable alacrity, and had frequently the inexpressible happiness to hear them jumping on the deck, and crying out, "she nighs us; she nighs us; she is standing this way."—The ship coming visibly nearer and nearer, my people now began to think of their unfortunate messmate Flatt, who was, however, utterly unable to receive any account of the deliverance which was so happily at hand:—nevertheless, in the midst of all their sympathy for his situation, they proposed a can of joy;—and it was with the greatest difficulty that I could prevail on them to acknowledge the strong impropriety of such a motion in their present circumstances.—I observed that if they appeared any way disguised with liquor the ship might probably decline to take us on board; and endeavoured to convince them that their deliverance in a very great measure depended upon the regularity of this moment's behaviour.—My remonstrances had some effect,—and all but my mate, who had for a considerable time abandoned himself to a brutality of intoxication, very prudently postponed so untimely an instance of indulgence.

AFTER continuing for a considerable time, eagerly observing the progress of the vessel, and undergoing the most tumultuous agitation that could be created by so trying a suspence, we had at last, the happiness to see a boat drop astern, and row towards us full manned, with a very vigorous dispatch.—It was now quite calm, yet, the impatience with which we expected the arrival of the boat was incredible; the numberless disappointments we had met in the course of our unfortunate voyage, filled us with an apprehension of some new accident that might frustrate all our hopes, and plunge us again into an aggravated distress.—Life and death seemed, in short, to sit upon every stroke of the oar; and as we still considered ourselves tottering on the very verge of eternity, the conflict between our wishes and our fears may be easily supposed by a reader of imagination.—The boat, at length, came along-side: but our appearance was so ghastly that the men rested upon their oars, and, with looks of inconveivable astonishment, demanded what we were.—Having satisfied them in this point, they immediately came on board, and begged we would use the utmost expedition in quitting our miserable wreck, lest they should be overtaken by any gale before they were able to recover their ship; at the same time seeing me totally incapable of getting into the boat without assistance, they provided ropes, by which I was quickly let down, and my people followed me, I need not, I believe, observe, with all the alacrity they possessed.

WE were now just preparing to set off, when one of my people cried out that the mate was still on board.—In the general hurry every man's attention was engaged by the thought of his own preservation, and it was almost a matter of wonder that any body remembered the absence of the mate.—He was, however, immediately called to, and, after some time, came to the gunnel, in a seeming astonishment, at such a number of people, the can of joy, with which he had been busy, having completely erased every idea of the preceding occurrences from his recollection.— Having got him into the boat, we instantly put off, and in about an hour came up to the ship, which was rather better than two miles from our wreck, and we were received with a humanity on board, that did the highest honour imaginable to the character of the captain.—When we came along side, he, together with his passengers and people, were upon deck, from an equal mixture of compassion and curiosity,—but our hollow eyes, shrivelled cheeks, long beards, and squallid complexions, had such an effect upon them, that the captain himself absolutely shook with horror, as he was politely leading me to his cabbin, and generously thanking God for being made the instrument of my deliverance.

BEFORE I proceed farther, it is necessary to inform the reader of the person to whose benignity my people and I were indebted for our preservation.—His name is THOMAS EVERS,—he commands the ship Susanna, in the Virginia trade, and was now returning from VIRGINIA to LONDON; to the latter of which places his vessel belongs.

I HAD no sooner got on board the Susanna, than dropping on my knees against a hencoop on the deck, I poured out my soul in a strain of the sincerest gratitude to the great Author of all things for the abundance of his mercy, and in the fulness of my heart began also to express my sensibility to the captain for his readiness to assist the distressed; but it was much easier for the generous EVERS to perform fifty good actions, than to hear the just applause of one.—He begged I would be silent on the subject, at least for that time,—advised me to take a little rest, and promised, if the weather proved any way moderate, he would lye by my wreck the whole night, and try if there was not a possibility to save some of my cloaths, assuring me at the same time, that my people should be treated with every necessary attention.

I WAS not on board for three or four days when I found some little inclination to eat:—the rest which I had taken during that interval giving me some distant dawnings of an appetite, I therefore hinted my desire to the captain, who had repeatedly applied to me from my first arrival to take a little food, and he immediately ordered some sego[7] to be dressed, of which I ate, without finding any relish whatever, my taste being rendered insensible, as I apprehend, from so long a discontinuance of sustenance.—Next day I had a little chicken broth, which agreed tolerably well with the weakness of my stomach;—but having an occasion for a particular indulgence of nature, I thought I should have expired in performing it,—the pain it gave me was excruciating to the last degree, and the parts were so contracted having never been once employed for a space of thirty-six or thirty seven days, that I almost began to despair restoring them to their necessary operations.—I was, however, at last relieved by the discharge of a callous lump about the size of a hen's egg, and enjoyed a tranquility of body, notwithstanding all my disorders, with which I was utterly unacquainted for some preceding weeks.

THE undeviating tenderness which my worthy friend, the captain, shewed to every thing which concerned my case, or tended to the recovery of my health, in a short time made me able to crawl upon deck by myself, though at first I could by no means face the wind:—the air, however, did me incredible service, and I continued daily increasing in my strength when a fresh calamity seemed ready to involve us, and threatened not only to fall upon my people and myself, but, in some measure, through our means, upon the worthy captain EVERS, his passengers, and ship's company.—The Susanna, it seems, a few days before she took me up, had been attacked by a hard gale of wind, in which, shipping a heavy sea, they lost four hogs, four or five hogshead of fresh water, forty or fifty head of fowls, and twenty or thirty geese and turkies:—she had also lost her caboose and copper, and, in short, had suffered not a little, although, to the infinite credit of her commander, these misfortunes did not occasion the least diminution of his humanity, when he was called to by the voice of distress.—These losses, together with the unexpected addition of seven persons, and a long series of very bad weather, obliged the captain to set all hands to an allowance, which was established at two pounds and a half of bread per week, a quart of water, and half a pound of salt provisions, a day for each man on board.—In this situation, with a head wind, and the pumps continually at work, his ship being very leakey, we began to keep as good a look out as possible in hopes of meeting with some vessel which might oblige us with a salutary supply of provisions.—No vessel, however, encountered us, but a Frenchman from Cape FRANCOIS,[8] who stood as much in want of necessaries as ourselves.—Nevertheless, about the first or second of March we happily reached the LAND'S END,[9] and took in a pilot, who hailed us off DARTMOUTH,[10] came on board, and carried the ship into that harbour:—there the captain and the passengers went on shore, and gave me a most cordial congratulation on my arrival. Once circumstance I had almost forgot; though it was to me a very material one.—After I had gained a little strength on board the Susanna, I thought I might mess in common with the captain and passengers, but indulging myself rather too freely on a roasted turkey, it threw me into a fever; at which the good-natured captain was so much affected, that he took upon himself the office both of physician and nurse, and kept me under a proper restraint in my food during the remainder of our voyage.

THE next day my inconsiderate mate, Mr. Archibald Nicolson, who had so long wallowed, as I may say, in every mire of excess, having reduced himself, by a continued intoxication, to such a state, that no proper sustenance would stay on his stomach, fell a martyr to his inebriety; having a watch and some trinkets about him, which defrayed the expense of his funeral, he was decently interred.—As to the rest of my people, the unhappy Flatt still continued out of his senses, and there were but two of the whole six in a condition to do any duty from the time of our being taken up by captain EVERS till our arrival at DARTMOUTH.

WHILE we lay here the governor, Mr. ARTHUR HOLDSWORTH, treated me with remarkable civility, sending Mr. Stapleton, his secretary, on board with a desire of seeing me.—I immediately accepted of his polite invitation, and, after dinner, he generously offered to furnish me with money, or any thing I might want for my journey to LONDON.—The worthy captain EVERS had rendered every assistance of this nature unnecessary, so that I declined his offer with a proper acknowledgment.—Captain EVERS having by this time sent in a proper supply of provisions, we set sail for the DOWNS[11] that evening.—On our arrival here the captain, who was a RAMSGATE[12] man, and had several near relations at that place, took me ashore with him, on a visit to his friends, who received me with every mark of good-nature and cordiality.—We staid at RAMSGATE two days, and then took a post-chaise[13] to MARGATE ROADS,[14] with an intent of meeting the ship; but the pilot, having a fresh wind, had taken her by; on which we proceeded to CANTERBURY,[15] where we lay that night, and the next morning set out in the machine for LONDON.

As I had insured at NEW-YORK I thought it necessary, for the interest of my owners, to lodge a Protest[16] for their indemnity.—Accordingly, on my arrival at LONDON I had recourse to a Notary Public for that purpose, and have here inserted the papers and attestations which were consequently drawn up, as a proof of the principal circumstances which I have mentioned in the foregoing narrative.—I am now returning to NEW-YORK, in the ship Hope, captain BENJAMIN DAVIS; where I shortly hope the goodness which I have already experienced at the hand of Providence will be crowned by a joyful meeting of my wife and family.

NOTES

1. Fyal. Faial or Fayal, westernmost island of the center group of the Azores.

2. SANDY HOOK. A six-mile peninsula in northeast New Jersey, fifteen miles south of Manhattan.

3. Turlington's balsam. A medicinal syrup composed largely of alcohol and various balsam oils. Also called Friar's Balsam.

4. *"Black December." Cymbeline* III, iii, 36-39: "When we shall hear / The rain and wind beat dark December, how / In this pinching cave shall we discourse / The freezing hours away?"

5. Slush. Refuse grease and animal fat from cooking.

6. Lottery at Guildhall. In this instance, slips of paper appear to have been drawn out of a hat or drum, one of the slips being marked with the "lot." At Guildhall in London, tickets would have been sold prior to the drawing, each bearing a number corresponding to that on a slip drawn from a wheel.

7. A flowering plant, *Calochortus Nuttallii,* with an edible bulb.

8. Cape FRANCOIS. Northwest point of Avalon Peninsula, Newfoundland, twenty miles west of St. John's.

9. LAND'S END. Cape, southwest coast of Cornwall, southwest England, the westernmost land of England.

10. DARTMOUTH. Borough in Devonshire, southwest England, on the English Channel at the mouth of the Dart River.

11. DOWNS. Roadstead in the English Channel, along the east coast of Kent, about nine miles long and six miles wide; affords excellent anchorage, protected by a natural breakwater, the Goodwin Sands.

12. RAMSGATE. Borough in Kent, southeast England, on North Sea, seventeen miles north of Dover.

13. Post-chaise. A travelling carriage, with closed coach seating from two to four persons, usually rented for a specific journey.

14. MARGATE ROADS. Borough, in Kent, on the Isle of Thanet, sixty-five miles east of London.

15. CANTERBURY. City in Kent, on the Stour River, fifty-three miles east southeast of London.

16. Protest. A written document drawn up by a ship's captain and attested to before a justice of the peace (or consul or vice-consul in foreign parts), describing the damages incurred by the vessel on the voyage and intending to show that such loss did not occur as the result of negligence or misconduct.

GLOSSARY

Abaft. Behind a thing, towards the stern of a ship.

Aft. Towards the stern; opposite of *fore.*

Ballanced Main-Sail (Ballanced Reefed Main-Sail). Balanced. To balance is to contract a sail into a narrower compass, by retrenching or folding up a part of it at one corner. The *main-sail* is balanced, after all its *reefs* are taken in, by rolling up a portion of the *clew,* or lower aftmost corner, and fastening it strongly to the *boom.*

Ballest. Ballast. That stone, iron, gravel, or like material deposited in the hold, generally under the *cargo,* used to counterbalance the wind upon the masts and give the ship stability.

Banker. A vessel employed in the cod-fishery, on the banks of Newfoundland.

Bare-Poles. The situation of a ship without any sail set in a gale of wind. A ship said to be "under bare-poles" is one having no sail set when out at sea.

Barke of Aviso. A general name for a small ship intended to relay information, messages, or a limited number of passengers.

Barricado (Barracado). A strong wooden rail, supported by *stanchions* (upright pieces of wood), extending across the foremost part of the *quarter-deck.*

Batacke (Bittakle). Binnacle. A wooden case or box that contains the compass.

Beams. Strong, thick pieces of timber, stretching across the ship from side to side to support the decks and to maintain the sides at their proper distance.

Before the Wind. In front of the wind; a ship before the wind is pushed or driven by the force of the wind.

Bilg. Bilge. The floor of a ship, on either side of the *keel.*

Bitts. A frame composed of two strong pieces of timber, fixed perpendicularly in the forepart of a ship, whereon the *cables* are fastened as she rides at anchor.

Blown up. Sprung, broken by the action of the sea; applied to decks.

Boatswain. The officer who has the boats, sails, *rigging, colors,* anchors, *cables,* and *cordage* in his charge.

Boltsprit (Bowsprit). A large boom or mast, which projects over the *stem* of the *bow,* to carry sail forward.

Boom. A long pole run out from the mast or other part of the ship to extend the bottom of a sail.

Borolins. See *Bowlin.*

Bow. The rounding part of a ship's side forward, beginning where the planks arch inward; commonly the front end of a ship.

Bower. The anchor(s) carried on the bow(s) of a ship.

Bowlin. Bowline. A rope fastened near the middle of the "leech," or perpendicular edge of the sail, by three or four subordinate ropes, called "bridles." The bowline is used when the wind is so unfavorable that the sails must be all braced sideways, or *close-hauled* to the wind; in this situation the bowlines are employed to keep the *windward* edges of the sails tight forward and steady.

Breaches. Breakers. Waves that break over rocks or landforms lying close under the surface of the sea.

Brig (Brigantine). A small merchant vessel with two masts; in a later period, *brig* denoted square sails on both masts, *brigantine* square sails on the *fore-mast,* fore-and-aft sail on the *main-mast;* in colonial times, however, the terms were often used interchangeably, without respect to rig.

Bring About. Turn the ship around.

Broach'd too. Broach-to. The situation of a ship in which her side is suddenly brought into the wind; a ship carrying much sail in this situation is in considerable danger, for as the sails suddenly fill and pull upon the masts, the masts act like levers applied against the ship, acting to upset her.

Broad off the Wind. Sailing with the wind coming well abaft the beam (middle), but not yet over the *quarter* (sternmost one-fifth).

Bulk-Heads. The inner walls of a ship.

Cable. A large, thick, strong rope, generally formed of three ropes twisted together, called "strands." The anchor is fastened to a cable.

Caboose. A sort of box or house, resembling a sentry-box, used to cover the chimney of some merchant ships. It generally stands against the barricade on the forepart of the *quarter-deck.*

Cap. A strong, thick block of wood having two large holes, one square and the other round; the former is fixed upon the upper end of the lower mast, and the latter holds the *top-mast*, hence joining the two masts securely.

Capstone (Capstern). Capstan. A strong column of wood, into which horizontal bars are placed, so the column may be turned to act as a winch to raise and lower the anchor or other weights.

Careen'd. The operation of heaving the ship down on one side, thus elevating the opposite side for cleaning.

Cargo. The "lading," or whole quantity of whatever merchandise with which a ship is freighted; usually, but not always, distinct from *ballest.*

Cat-Head. A beam of timber projected horizontally from the ship's bows, used to suspend the anchor clear of the ship.

Cedge Anchor. Kedge. Commonly the smallest anchor on a ship.

Chocks. Wedges used to confine a boat or other object in a certain place to prevent it from moving about when the ship is in motion.

Clew. The lower corners of square sails, the aftmost only of *stay-sails.*

Close-Hauled. The arrangement, or "trim," of a ship's sails, when she attempts to sail into or nearly into the wind. In this disposition, the sails are all extended sideways on the ship, so the wind fills them as it crosses obliquely towards the *stern* from forward.

Cock-Swayne. Cockswain. The officer who has charge of the ship's boat, steers it, and has charge of the boat's crew.

Colors (Colours). The flags or banners that distinguish the ships of different nations.

Companion. A sort of wooden porch placed over the entrance or staircase of the master's cabin in a ship.

Copper. Copper sheathing on the bottom of a ship.

Cordage. A general term for the ropes used in the rigging of a ship; also for the rope on board kept in reserve.

Crotch. Crotches are crooked timbers that are placed upon the *keel* in the fore and aft parts of a ship, upon which the frame of her hull grows narrower below, as it approaches the stem afore and the stern-post aft.

Crutch. A support for the *main-boom* of a sloop, brig, cutter, and so on when their sails are *furled.*

Cuddies. Cuddy. A sort of cabin or cook-room in the forepart, or near the *stern,* of a small ship.

Cutlash (Cutlass). A short, heavy, curved sword.

Dead Light. A strong wooden port, made to fit the cabin windows, the glass being removed, used during rough weather.

Deep-Sea Lead (Dipsing Lead). An instrument for measuring the depth of water, composed of a large piece of lead (twenty-five to thirty pounds) and a long line called the lead line, which is marked in increments of *fathomes.*

Deep-Wasted. Deep waisted. The arrangement of a ship's decks, when the *quarter-deck* and *fore-castle* are elevated from four to six feet above the level of the *main-deck,* to leave a vacant space, called the *waist,* on the middle of the upper plane of decks.

Double Reefed. (Reeft). A sail shortened, or its area diminished, two increments. See *Reef'd.*

Drove a Stern. To drive is to be impelled along the surface of the sea at random by the wind or current; in this instance the boat was driven backwards.

Easy Sail. A sail or combination of sails set to minimize the sail area; for rough weather.

Fashion-Piece. Fashion-pieces are the aftmost or hindmost timbers of a ship that terminate the breadth and form the shape of the *stern.*

Fathome (Fatham, Fadome). Fathom. A measure of six feet.

Feeling the Helm. The pressure the *rudor* transmits to the *helm* can be felt by the "helmsman," or one who steers the ship; by feeling the helm he calculates the reverse pressure he must apply to the rudder through the helm to keep the ship on course.

Flat. A flat-bottomed boat of one mast and a single square sail.

Flewks & Stock. "Flukes," or palms, of an anchor are the triangular plates at the extremity of each arm of the anchor; the stock consists of two oak (or later, iron) pieces that cross the top of the "shank," or vertical piece, of the anchor and are bound together by bolts.

Flying-Jib. A sail sometimes set upon a *boom,* rigged out beyond the jib-boom, a continuation of the *bowsprit* forward.

Fore. The front part of a ship; towards the front.

Fore-Castle. A short deck placed in the forepart of a ship, above the upper deck; the compartment below is traditionally the living quarters of the crew.

Fore-Courses. The courses are the principal forward sails of a ship; the fore-courses are on the *fore-sail.*

Fore-Main-Shrouds. The forwardmost shrouds (large ropes extended from the top of the mast to the sides of the ship to support the mast) of the *main-mast.*

Fore-mast. That mast which stands nearest the front, next in size to the *main-mast.*

Fore-Mast Head. The top of the *fore-mast.*

Fore-Mast-Men. Sailors assigned to take in the *Top-sails,* sling the *yards, furl* the sails, handle lines and rigging, and take their turns at the *helm.*

Fore-Mast Yard. A long piece of timber suspended upon the *fore-mast,* to extend the *fore-sail.*

Fore-Sail. The principal sail, that is, the lowest on the mast, the course, on the *fore-mast.*

Fore-Scuttle. A small hatchway or hole cut in the ship's side, to facilitate removing water from the deck; in this instance, the forwardmost scuttle.

Fore-Sheets. Sheets are ropes fastened to the lower corners of a sail to extend it or hold it in position; in this instance the sheets of the *fore-sail.*

Fore-Shrouds. Large ropes extended from the top of the *fore-mast* to the sides of the ship to support the mast.

Fore-Stay. A large, strong rope employed to support the *fore-mast* on the forward part, as the *fore-shrouds* do on either side.

Fore-Stay-Sails. Triangular sails extended from the *fore-stay.*

Fore-Top-Mast. A mast added to the *fore-mast* to extend its heighth; connected to the fore-mast by a *cap.*

Fore-Top-Sail. The sail employed on the *fore-top-mast.*

Fore-Yard. See *Fore-Mast Yard.*

Founder. A ship is said to founder when, as a result of a leak or of seas breaking in on her, she is so filled with water that she can neither veer nor steer and will eventually sink.

Four Points on the Quarter. The quarter is the sternmost one-fifth of a ship's side; in this instance it refers as well to an arc of the horizon formed by a line from the stern to any distant object; points are the thirty-two points of the compass.

Frigate. Implies the disposition of decks in merchant ships that have a descent of four or five steps from the *quarter-deck* and *fore-castle* into the *waist,* as opposed to ships whose decks are continued on a line throughout their entire length; also a general name for small, swift vessels.

Furl. To wrap or roll a sail close up to the *yard, stay,* or mast to which it belongs and wind a cord about it to fasten it thereto.

Gage. The "weather," or windward, gage is the situation of one ship being to the windward of another.

Galley. As a type of ship, it refers to the disposition of the upper deck, being continuous in a line throughout the vessel's length, without *fore-castle* or *quarter-deck* above. Also the cook-room of a ship.

Goose-Neck. A sort of iron hook fitted on the inner end of a *boom* and
introduced into a clamp of iron, or "eye-bolt," which encircles the
mast, so the boom may be connected to the mast at will.

Great Guns. Cannon, as distinguished from muskets or pistols.

Gunel (Gunwalls). Gunwale. The upper edge of a ship's side.

Gunner Roome. Gun-room. An apartment on the after-end of the "gun,"
or lower, deck.

Half-Deck. Also called the *steerage.* The forward portion of all that compartment contained under the *quarter-deck;* the cabin occupies the
aft portion and is separated from the half-deck by a *bulk-head.*

Hand. To hand sails is to *furl* them.

Hard a Starboard. The act of directing a vessel sharply to the right.

Hass. Hawse. The anchor cable.

Hatch (Hatchway). A square or oblong opening in the deck of a ship,
forming passages from one deck to another and to the *hold.*

Heave to. To bring the ship to a standstill by setting the sails to counter-
act one another.

Heel. In this instance, the lower end of the *bowsprit.*

Helm. The appartus by which a vessel is steered. The helm is usually composed of the wheel, the *tiller,* and the *rudor.*

Hogshead. A large cask, commonly of sixty-three gallons; the hogshead
for molasses was fixed at one hundred gallons in 1749.

Hold (Hould). That cavity of a ship between the floor and the lowest
deck, throughout her whole length; used to store the *cargo.*

Holland Duck. A superior type of sail-cloth.

Hollocke. A small part of a sail (the other parts being *reef'd*) employed
when the wind is very strong or in a storm; in most cases the hollocke
is the single sail remaining before a vessel goes to *bare-poles.*

Horse Piece. A thick rope extended down the fore or after side of a mast,
to hoist or extend a sail thereon.

Hove Down. See *Careen'd.*

Jears. An assemblage of tackles, by which the lower *yards* of a vessel are
hoisted or lowered along the mast to or from their usual position.

Jib. The foremost sail of a ship, being a large *stay-sail* extended from the
outer end of the *bowsprit* by the jib-boom.

Junk. Any remnant or piece of old cable.

Keel. The principal piece of timber in a ship; the lowermost timber, laid
first in building.

Knees. Crooked pieces of timber, having two branches or arms and generally
used to connect the *beams* of a ship to her sides.

Lading. The *cargo.*

Laid Her Head. To position the ship in a certain direction (into the wind, for example).

Lanch. Launch. A ship's boat, similar to the *long boat.*

Lanyards. Short pieces of rope employed to extend the *shrouds* and *stays* of the masts.

Larboard. The left side of a ship when looking forward.

Laying by (Lying to). The positioning of one ship to await another.

Lead. See *Deep-Sea Lead.*

League. Three nautical miles, about 3.5 land miles.

Lee (Leeward). That direction or side of the ship away from the wind; opposite of *windward,* the direction from which the wind comes.

Long Boat. The principal boat of a ship, generally furnished with a mast and sails.

Loose. The broadest part of the *bow.*

Lying a Hull (Lies a Hull). Situation of a ship when all her sails are *furled* and her *helm* is lashed on the lee side; she then lies nearly with her side to the wind and sea.

Main-Boom. The *boom* of the *main-mast.*

Main-Chain-Plates (Main Chains). Chain plates are iron plates bolted to the ship's side, to which iron chains are fastened, to which in turn the *shrouds* are connected.

Main-Deck. The deck of a ship lying between the *quarter-deck* and the *fore-castle.*

Main-Hall-Yards. Halyards are ropes or tackles employed to hoist or lower a sail upon its respective mast (in this case, *main-mast*) or *stay.*

Main-Hatches. The principal *hatch,* or opening, in the deck of a ship.

Main-Mast (Maine-Mast). The largest mast of a ship, standing nearly in midships.

Main-Sail(e). The largest, lowermost sail on the *main-mast.*

Main-Sheet. A rope fastened to one or both corners of the *main-sail.*

Main-Shrouds. A range of ropes extending from the top of the *main-mast* to each side of the ship to support the mast.

Main-Top-Gallant Yard. The horizontal timber suspended upon the *main-mast* that extends the main *top-gallant sail,* the third sail on the main-mast.

Main-Top-Mast. An extension of the *main-mast.*

Main-Top-Sail (Mayne Top-Sayle). The second sail on the *main-mast;* above the *main-sail* (or course), below the top-gallant.

Main-Yard. The principal *yard* on the main-mast.

Man of War. A term generally applied to a ship carrying from twenty to one hundred and twenty guns.

Mizzen (Mison, Mizen). The hindmost of the fixed sails on a ship.

Mizzen-Ballast. In this instance it appears to mean to *scud* before the wind under *bare-poles.*

Netting Rail. A fence of rope-netting supported by upright posts and stretched along the upper part of a ship's *quarter.*

Oakum (Okam, Ocam). The substance into which old ropes are reduced when untwisted and pulled into small pieces; used to caulk the gaps or seams between planks or timbers.

Observation. Measuring the altitude of the sun or a star to determine the latitude.

Oznabrigs (Ozenbrigs). Osnaburg. A coarse linen, originally made in Osnaburg, Germany.

Painter. A rope employed to fasten a boat either alongside a ship or to a wharf, dock, and so on.

Periagua. A sort of large canoe.

Pink (Pinck). A name generally given to a ship with a very narrow *stern;* hence, pink-sterned vessels.

Pinnace. A small vessel, navigated with oars and sails, having generally two masts, which are rigged like those of a *schooner.*

Plied to the Windward. Plying is the act of making, or attempting to make, progress against the general direction of the wind.

Points. Short, flat pieces of braided rope used to *reef* the sails of a ship.

Points of the Wind. There are thirty-two equal points into which the horizon is divided according to the compass. Wind direction is then identified according to the given number of points from zero degrees from which the wind blows.

Poop. The highest and hindmost deck of a ship.

Poop'd (Poopt). Situation of a vessel in which the following seas are of such height as to break over the *stern* of the ship.

Ports. The openings in the side of a vessel, wherein the cannon are ranged.

Pump. The typical pump of the colonial period was composed of a wooden tube whose lower end extended into the ship's bottom; in the middle of the tube was a chamber with pistons, which when operated by a lever drew up and discharged the water.

Pump Hook. A device for drawing up the pump for examination or repair.

Quadrants. An instrument used to take the altitude of the sun or a star to determine latitude; forerunner of the sextant.

Quarter. That part of a vessel's side that lies nearest the *stern;* roughly the hindmost one-fifth of a vessel's side.

Quarter-Deck. A short deck placed in the *aft* section of a ship, above the upper deck.

Quarter-Master. A minor officer assigned to assist the mates.

Rake. That portion of a vessel, front and back, that extends beyond a line extended vertically from the end of the *keel.*

Reef Plat. A braided rope, also called a "reef-line" or "kittle," used to *reef* the sails.

Reef'd (Reeft, Reefs, Double Reeft). A reef is that portion of a sail contained between the top or bottom, and a row of eye-holes parallel thereto. There are several rows of such holes in larger sails. Tying off one or more reefs reduces the amount of sail exposed to the wind.

Rigging. A general name given to all the ropes employed to support the masts and to extend or shorten the sails.

Ring-Bolts. Iron bolts connected to the deck, with an eye at the other end, through which an iron ring is passed. Used to fasten *tackle,* lines, or cannon in place.

Robins. Small lines used to fasten the bottom of a sail to the *yard.*

Rope-Yard. The smallest and simplest part of any rope, being one of the threads of which a strand is formed.

Round-House. A cabin or apartment built in the afterpart of the *quarter-deck,* and having the *poop* deck for its roof.

Rudor. Rudder. The flat timber(s) that form the lower part of the *helm* and whose action in the water steers the ship.

Run on Soundings. The operation of navigating a vessel by determining at regular intervals the depth of water; done near landfall when changes in depth cannot be discerned by the color of the water.

Runner. A thick rope used with a *tackle.*

Sciffe. Skiff. A ship's boat, similiar to, although usually smaller than, the *long boat.*

Schooner. A two-masted vessel whose *main-sail* and *fore-sail* are suspended from gaffs reaching from the mast towards the *stern* and stretched out below by *booms.*

Scud. The movement by which a vessel is driven rapidly across the surface of the water by strong winds. Usually only the *fore-sail* is set in this situation.

Scud a Hull. To scud with no sails set.

Sculler. An oarsman; one who rows.

Scuttle. A small *hatchway,* often within a hatch-cover.

Seizing. The operation of fastening two ropes together with a small line or cord.

Settled. Lowered.

Shallop. A large boat with two masts, usually rigged like a schooner.

Shank. The shaft of an anchor.

Sheathing. A protective casing or covering laid on the outside of a vessel's bottom; frequently of lead or copper.

Sheet Anchor. The largest of a ship's anchors, usually retained for emergencies; the *bower* is used principally.

Sheet Lead. The material used for *sheathing.*

Shift Anchor. A spare anchor, smaller than the *bower.*

Shipp'd. Took in, as in shipped water during a storm.

Shrowd (Shroud). The shrouds are a range of large ropes extended from the top of the masts to either side of the ship to support the masts.

Sloop. A single-masted vessel, the sail of which is attached to a gaff above and a *boom* below.

Slop'd. Took an oblique course, close to the direction of the wind.

Snow. A two-masted vessel, rather like a *brig,* except for the addition of a small mast set directly behind the *main-sail* and equipped with a triangular sail.

Soundings (Sounded) (Sound). The action of discovering the depth of the water. See also *Deep-Sea Lead.*

Sparre Decke. Spar deck. In this instance, the uppermost deck.

Spritsail. A sail attached to a *yard* that hangs under the *bowsprit.*

Square Sail Head. The square sail forward, on the *fore-mast.*

Stand(ing) (for). The movement by which a ship advances towards a certain object (for); or away from (off).

Standing Jib. A fixed, or permanently placed, *jib.*

Stantion (Stanchion) (Staunchings). Stanchions. Small pillars of wood used to support decks, rails, netting, and awnings on a ship.

Starboard. The right side of the ship when looking toward the *bow.*

Stays. Large ropes employed to support the masts on the forepart, extended from the top of the mast towards the front of the vessel.

Stay-Sail. A triangular sail extended upon a *stay.*

Steerage. An apartment connected to the great, or main-cabin, and separated from it by a partition. Sometimes used as the living quarters of the minor officers.

Steer'd Before the Wind. Directing the vessel in the same direction that the wind blows; with the wind.

Stem (Stemme). A circular piece of timber, into which the two sides of a ship are joined at the fore end; the lower end is fastened to the *keel,* the upper to the *bowsprit.*

Stern (Stearne). The posterior face of a ship.

Stern Lights. The *dead lights* in the *stern.*

Stoppers. Certain short pieces of rope, commonly knotted at one or both ends, used to suspend any weight or retain a *cable, shroud,* and so on in a fixed position.

Swivel Gun. A small cannon mounted on a rotating block.

Tack'd (Tack). The operation of making an oblique progress on a course, necessitated because of the course's being into the wind. A tack is also the distance a vessel sails on this oblique to her true course.

Tackle (Tackling). A pulley.

Taffril. Taffrail. The upper part of a ship's *stern,* being a curved piece of wood, typically ornamented or sculptured.

Tarpaulin. A broad piece of canvas well daubed with tar ("tar-pawling") used to cover *hatchways.*

Tiller. The bar or lever used to turn the *rudor* in steering. See also *Helm.*

Toping-Lift. Topping-lift. A large and strong tackle used to suspend the outer end of a gaff or of a *boom* of a *main-sail* or *fore-sail.*

Top-Gallant Duck. The cloth used for the *top-gallant sails.*

Top-Gallant Gailes. A breeze sufficient to employ the *top-gallant sails.*

Top-Gallant Sails. The sails immediately above the *top-sails,* set on a yard across the top-gallant mast.

Top-Masts. Those masts fastened to and immediately above the *main, fore,* or *mizen* masts.

Top-Sail. The sail extended from a *yard* on a *top-mast.*

Top-Sail Gale. A breeze sufficient to fill the *top-sails.*

Top-Sail-Sheet Bitts. Wooden frames used to fasten the top-sail-sheets, the ropes by which the lower corners of the top-sails are extended.

Trade-Winds. Certain regular winds blowing within or near the tropics and being either periodical or perpetual. In the Indian Ocean they blow alternately from different points of the compass during a limited season; in the Atlantic they continue almost without interruption in the same direction.

Trausam. Transom. A certain beam(s) or timber(s) extended across the inside of the *stern* of a vessel to strengthen her afterparts.

Trim. A term denoting that general arrangement of the sails best calculated to accelerate the vessel's course.

Trough of the Sea. The hollow or interval between two high waves that resembles a broad and deep trench constantly fluctuating; the trough is at right angles to the direction of the wind.

Tunne. Tun. A large cask or barrel; a measure of capacity for liquids; the equivalent of four *hogsheads.*

Under the Fore-Sail. Using only the *fore-sail* to catch the wind. See also *scud.*

Waist (Waste). That part of the ship contained between the *quarter-deck* and the *fore-castle,* being usually a hollow space with steps to either of these two places.

Ware. Wear. The operation by which a ship in changing her course from one tack to another, turns her *stern* to *windward.* Also called veering.

Warp. To change the situation of a ship, by pulling her from one part of a harbor to another, by means of "warps"—ropes or hawsers attached to buoys, other ships, or anchors sunk in the bottom; the vessel is drawn forward by pulling on the warps by hand or drawing them up by a *windless* or *capstone.*

Watch. The space of time wherein one division of the ship's crew remains on deck to perform their duties while the other division is relieved of duty; commonly four hours in length; the name is also applied to the divisions of the crew as well.

Water-Way Plank. A long piece of timber serving to connect the sides of a ship to her decks and form a sort of channel to carry off water from the decks through the "scuppers," a series of drains at the edge of the deck.

Weather-Bow. That side of the *bow* toward the wind.

Weather-Cloth. A large piece of canvas hung or extended across a *companion* to keep out spray or rain.

Weather-Gunnel. That side of the ship closest to the wind.

Weather-Main [Shroud]. Those *shrouds* running from the top of the *main-mast* to that side of the vessel closest to the wind.

Weather-Most. Closest to the wind.

Weather-Side. The side closest to the wind.

Wherry. A light boat, used when a ship is in harbor to ferry passengers from ship to shore.

Whipstaffe. Whipstaff. A long pole, attached to the *helm,* extended upward through a hole in the deck to the *steerage,* where the helmsman uses it to guide the helm.

Winded. To wind a ship is to change her position 180 degrees to bring her head to the former position of the stern.

Windlass. A large cylindrical piece of timber employed like a winch to raise and lower the anchors.

Windward. The direction from which the wind blows.

Wore Ship. See *Ware.*

Work About. To manuever the ship around to a new direction; to reverse direction. To work is to do this when the wind is contrary.

Wronged. Outdistanced.

Yard. A long piece of timber suspended upon the masts to extend the sails.

Yard-Arms. The extremities of the *yard.*

BIBLIOGRAPHY

Bercovitch, Sacvan, ed. *Typology and Early American Literature.* Amherst: University of Massachusetts Press, 1972.

Carroll, Peter N. *Puritanism and the Wilderness: The Intellectual Significance of the New England Frontier, 1629-1700.* New York: Columbia University Press, 1969.

Cawley, Robert R. *Unpathed Waters: Studies in the Influence of the Voyagers on Elizabethan Literature.* Princeton: Princeton University Press, 1940.

Donahue, Jane. "Colonial Shipwreck Narratives: A Theological Study." *Books at Brown* 23 (1969): 101-34.

Huntress, Keith. "Another Source for Poe's *Narrative of Arthur Gordon Pym.*" *American Literature* 16 (1944): 19-25.

———. *Narratives of Shipwrecks and Disasters, 1586-1860.* Ames: Iowa State University Press, 1974.

Jantz, Harold S. *The First Century of New England Verse.* Worcester: American Antiquarian Society, 1944; rpt. New York: Russell, 1962.

Lewis, Charles Lee. *Books of the Sea: An Introduction to Nautical Literature.* Annapolis: United States Naval Institute, 1943.

Lowance, Mason I., Jr. *Increase Mather.* New York: Twayne, 1974.

Meserole, Harrison T. *Seventeenth-Century American Poetry.* New York: New York University Press, 1968; rpt. New York: Norton, 1972.

Minter, David L. "By Dens of Lions: Notes on Stylization in Early Puritan Captivity Narratives." *American Literature* 45 (1973): 335-47.

O'Gorman, Edmundo. *The Invention of America: An Inquiry into the Historical Nature of the New World and the Meaning of its History.* Bloomington: Indiana University Press, 1961.

Pearce, Roy Harvey. "The Significances of the Captivity Narrative." *American Literature* 19 (1947): 1-20.

Philbrick, Thomas. *James Fenimore Cooper and the Development of American Sea Fiction.* Cambridge: Harvard University Press, 1961.

Santraud, Jeanne-Marie. *La Mer et le Roman Americain dans la Premiere Moitie du Dix-Neuvieme Siecle.* Paris: Didier, 1972.

Stein, Roger B. "Copley's *Watson and the Shark* and Aesthetics in the 1770s." In *Discoveries and Considerations: Essays on Early American Literature and Aesthetics Presented to Harold Jantz,* ed. Calvin Israel, pp. 85-130. Albany: State University of New York Press, 1976.

_____. "Pulled Out of the Bay: American Fiction in the Eighteenth Century." *Studies in American Fiction* 2 (1974): 13-36.

_____. *Seascape and the American Imagination.* New York: Clarkson Potter/Whitney Museum of American Art, 1975.

_____. "Seascape and the American Imagination: The Puritan Seventeenth Century." *Early American Literature* 7 (1972): 17-37.

Tichi, Cecelia. "Spiritual Biography and the 'Lords Remembrancers.' " *William and Mary Quarterly* 28 (1971): 64-85.

VanDerBeets, Richard. "The Indian Captivity Narrative as Ritual." *American Literature* 43 (1972): 548-62.

Watson, Harold F. *The Sailor in English Fiction and Drama.* New York: Columbia University Press, 1931.

Wharton, Donald P. *Richard Steere, Colonial Merchant Poet.* University Park: Pennsylvania State University Press, 1978.

Wilmerding, John. *A History of American Marine Painting.* Salem and Boston: Peabody Museum/ Little, Brown, 1968.

Wright, Louis B. *Religion and Empire: The Alliance between Piety and Commerce in English Expansion 1558-1625.* Chapel Hill: University of North Carolina Press, 1943; rpt. New York: Octagon, 1965.

INDEX

About the Editor

Donald P. Wharton is Assistant Professor of English and of American Studies at Pennsylvania State University of Altoona. He is the author of *Richard Steere: Colonial American Poet.*